NORTHERN LIGHT

Northern Light

THE ARCTIC AND SUBARCTIC PHOTOGRAPHY OF

Dave Brosha

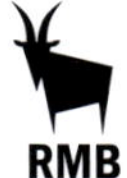

RMB

Contents

Foreword

BY PAUL ZIZKA

"I think it's busted, Paul," Dave said as he stood by the snowmobile. It was a bone-chilling April evening and we were somewhere well north of the Arctic Circle, in a remote corner of Nunavut's Baffin Island. With our vehicle out of order, we had lost not only our means of transportation but also our safety net. Prior to heading out, we had discussed the dangers of roaming through polar bear country, and decided we were fine as long as we stayed close to the Ski-Doo. Now we found ourselves looking at a smouldering, motionless snowmobile several hours' walk from the community of Arctic Bay. We were expected in town first thing in the morning to lead a photography workshop -- the main reason we had made this journey to the North in the first place – and we still had work to do to get organized for the next day's events. Now that we were on foot, time definitely wasn't on our side. Dave put his head down, casually picked up his camera gear and headed south, in the general direction of the hamlet. I followed into the everlasting Arctic sidelight.

After a few kilometres of walking through some of the most desolate, yet beautiful, scenery I had ever come across, we finally stumbled into the Tangmaarvik Inn at around one a.m. A short sleep later, and thanks to Dave's organizational and people skills, we were introducing local photographers to the concepts of aperture and composition. Later in the day, we learned that three polar bears had been seen on the edge of town – awfully close to where we had been walking on our way back from our abandoned snowmobile. Yet here were were, gathered in a tiny building in Arctic Bay, getting creative in the middle of nowhere, like nothing had ever happened. The day went flawlessly.

Through this experience, I realized that this was just another day for Dave Brosha. It was simply my first time witnessing how his drive and passion – combined with his social skills, resourcefulness and familiarity with the high latitudes – would allow not only for the show to go on, but rather seamlessly. No matter any drama going on in the background, in the end he left a dozen folks feeling inspired, and a fellow photographer feeling very much humbled. I'd soon find out this was the standard with Dave.

+++

As is usually the case in this age of social media, I first met Dave online, years before our brush with Arctic predators. Immediately, I was struck by two things. For one, Dave, who was at that point living in Yellowknife, seemed to "own" the North. Arctic Canada is a big place, yet this one guy seemed to do every portrait and commercial shoot between Kluane and Baffin Island – from Gordie Howe to the Royal Family and everything in between. His omnipresence across the North hinted at a level of dedication and client care that I would eventually witness in person years later.

The second attribute that leaped out at me was how versatile a photographer Dave was and continues to be. In the photography industry, one thing you continually hear is the importance of finding your niche and sticking to it. Part of the reason is that, typically, photographers who spread themselves too thin take the risk of creating mediocre work across several genres, as opposed to excelling in one branch of the medium. Yet Dave dabbles like no one else and is somehow making it work. He effortlessly juggles various genres, from underground mining shots in the Northwest Territories to creative portrait shoots with off-camera lighting at Lake Louise, from aurora shots in Greenland to macro diamond images and studio work back home. There is no way to do this unless you are very talented, a master at problem-solving and truly passionate about all aspects of photography. Dave often mentions in workshops that he simply loves photography, and it shows. His passion transcends genres, and so does his approach to the craft.

Dave's versatility spans many genres, but is also very much at work within a specific genre. Take a look at his landscape work, and you'll see how many different ways he goes about creating his images. His choice of lenses is all over the place. His compositional techniques vary wildly. No two images are created using the same recipe. And the same thing is true for his portrait work. The images you'll find in this book demonstrate his tremendous adaptability in terms of subject, composition, lighting and environment. I think this is due to Dave's freestyling, his experimental approach in the field and the fact that he does not pigeonhole himself as a photographer. He simply follows his curiosity wherever it leads him.

It is therefore not surprising to see that Dave's work has been recognized accordingly: he is now well-known in Canada and beyond for his portrait work, his astrophotography, his landscape imaging, his impactful black-and-whites and his commercial photography. There is proof of this in the publications and awards that his images, from a variety of genres, have garnered over the years.

+ + +

Dave's success over the years can also be attributed to another unique aspect of his personality that isn't particularly photography-related. He possesses a remarkable ability to gather and elevate others. I have experienced this side of him first-hand, countless times, including the first time we finally met in person. On that first meeting, in early 2014, Dave reached out to me on Facebook to see if we could get together, and drove through a snowstorm from Calgary to the mountains just to meet up for a pizza. By the end of the meal, we had our first photography workshops planned. Since then, we have collaborated on dozens of events and brought keen photographers to the wildest of locations, including Greenland, Iceland, Namibia, the Faroe Islands, the Torngat Mountains and Banff National Park. He also put an incredible amount of faith in me in partnering up to launch a new online photography community and workshop company that we (aptly) called OFFBEAT.

Since that first slice of pizza, I've seen Dave's power to gather and elevate others play out over and over again. I have watched participants crowd around Dave during portrait workshop demos and have their "aha" moments. I've experienced his contagious enthusiasm despite days of virtually no sleep while co-leading demanding events. I have seen him showcase the work of fellow photographers – photographers many would consider to be his competition. Online, I have seen how Dave's ever-uplifting and encouraging voice inspires people to go out and create, no matter the genre or the level of experience or ability. Being his supportive, engaging self, he has gathered 4,000 like-minded people in his Dave Brosha Workshops Facebook community.

More recently, I sat in the Brosha family barn on Prince Edward Island with dozens of wide-eyed photographers at a five-day conference created by Dave called Land & See – an annual gathering that truly culminates his contribution to the photo community. This casual, retreat-like event encourages creativity, connection and making progress through the photographic journey, but in the most laid-back environment you can think of. Dave's family are wonderful hosts, and a 100-year-old barn on his property, converted into a studio/meeting space, does the trick. As we gathered in that barn this past summer, living and breathing photography, it felt like Arctic Bay all over again. No matter the logistics and troubleshooting likely going on in the background, Dave was cool as a cucumber, watching his vision – the fruits of his passion – unfold, a smile plastered on his face.

Although the red sands and seascapes of PEI are now home to the Broshas, no one but Dave is better equipped to create a book of this magnitude about the North. I've spent enough time "North of 60" with Dave to see that he truly thrives in the high latitudes and knows the Arctic like few others. Dave's photography journey started in Resolute Bay, and it shows. The challenges of life in an isolated northerly town shape people into resourceful and resilient folks and can really sharpen one's sense of community. Years later, those traits are very much still present in the way Dave photographs and spreads his passion for the craft. This thoughtful and powerful collection of images is a testament to Dave's versatility as one of Canada's foremost photographers and to his uncanny ability to reach people and adapt to any subject.

Enjoy this compelling photographic journey through the North!

Foreword

BY MARTIN HARTLEY

I first met Dave in the winter of 2002, in a remote Inuit hamlet in the Far North of Canada: a wild place called Resolute Bay. The circumstances were unusual. It was my first visit to the Canadian High Arctic; I was on an assignment for the London *Times*, covering a story on Pen Hadow, a polar explorer preparing for an unsupported North Pole solo expedition. I had been out on the sea ice, photographing Pen with Dave and Dave's then-boss, the late, great Gary Guy, the John Wayne of Nunavut if there was ever such a person.

We had gotten lost in a storm with Gary on our way back to Resolute. Only with a huge slice of luck were we able to find our way back. We arrived back to Resolute after dark, shaken and stirred. Dave immediately invited Pen and I – along with Pen's "wing man," Ian Wesley – over to his apartment for a (much needed) drink. Without realizing it, by inviting three total strangers he had only met earlier that day into his home, he single-handedly restored my faith in the High Arctic, with his warm, welcoming nature and generosity of spirit. Dave was then based in Resolute Bay with his lovely wife, Erin, working as an assistant operator for Nunavut Power. We talked a lot about photography that night, and Dave asked if the next day I would look at some of his images. I popped over to Dave and Erin's warm home the next day and looked at some of Dave's photography. Thankfully Dave was shooting on transparency film back then. I say thankfully as it's easier to see straight away how a person sees the world on film – all the mistakes, or experiments, are right there unedited. Also, any photographer who has shot on film understands the creative process far better than a photographer who has gone straight to digital. Shooting on film is a craft bordering on a "dark art."

After looking at Dave's rolls of film, I could see there was some "magic" in the mix, in between the less successful frames on the rolls. Dave wanted to know if he could make it as a photographer. I recall being fairly harsh with my critique, and to Dave's credit he took it well. I finished by suggested to Dave that he put his screwdrivers down and pick his camera up more often, if he wanted to be a photographer. We all know the answer to that question now!

Dave has returned from his travels across the globe to Egypt, Namibia, Antarctica, Australia, Baffin Island, the Faroe Islands… the list goes on, with a wealth of photographic riches. But for me it is in portrait work and his dedication to this difficult genre that Dave truly shines.

His portraits are all robust documents. Dave's portrait photography is pure photographic alchemy. These are real portraits, not just photographs of faces. Dave really does grab a hold of his subject's personality and shows us in a single frame who they are. Dave is not just a creative photographer; he is the master of the very technical outdoor lighting, which, truth be told, leaves me a little envious, as I have a few things I can learn from Dave here. I make no apologies for all this gushing; great photographers deserve to be celebrated.

A great photographer is not simply a creative force or a master technician. Great photographers are the most important of communicators. The global language of photography is the most important currency of our modern era. In this Anthropocene period we are living in, photography surrounds our daily lives more than it ever has. Photography is our modern cave painting, and these "paintings" are a huge part of our daily lives. Photography is the primary way we learn about the world around us. Lucky for us, we have Dave to help guide us through this world. Not only is Dave a great communicator, his gesture back in 2002 taught me that he is a great human being too – both of the qualities that are the making of a great photographer.

Introduction

I was born a Northern boy and a Northern boy I'll die.

My childhood was spent exploring the forests, riverbanks, fields and creeks of Fort Vermilion, a tiny little hamlet in northern Alberta that we – my brothers and sisters and I – thought was as far north as north can be. Winters were harsh, but home. Cold dripped into our veins and crisp, crunchy snow was frequently our soundtrack.

We were not far from the Northwest Territories-Alberta border, and during spring breakup we would often drive north of High Level – where the pavement turned to gravel and dust and dirt – towards Enterprise, Northwest Territories, and then, finally, the Mackenzie River. There, my father and I would fish for northern pike, tell stories and make campfires. The expanse of land seemed endless and the rivers and waterfalls impossibly grand. I never thought these lands would someday be *south* for me, but years later – after I completed high school and university on the east coast of Canada – I would find out that *North* is an incredibly large concept.

In 2002, my wife, Erin, and I moved to an even tinier place called Resolute Bay, Nunavut. Two hundred twenty or so souls living far north of the Arctic Circle. We were living outside Antigonish, Nova Scotia, when the call came for Erin to interview for a job that she quickly secured; we had to take out the atlas to see where it was that we had agreed to move. Our eyes widened when we realized that Resolute was the second-most northerly community in Canada – in a country known for its northern communities.

I credit Resolute and our time there for making me a photographer. I was in my early 20s and just content to see where life would take me; I moved north without any specific knowledge of photography other than the fact that I had a little point-and-shoot camera with a promise to our families back home to "send pictures."

How quickly that changed.

In Resolute I rediscovered a love of the North that had been buried in my soul since childhood. Snow and ice and fresh air and wildlife and, well, a sense of *perseverance*. My camera quickly became my creative outlet, and a little hobby soon became an obsession. My peace and joy outside my "real" job was exploring – either by foot or by snow machine – the environment around me, and I found excitement in climbing up snow canyons, in crawling on my stomach into holes in small icebergs, and in watching the symphony of changing Arctic colours as the seasons turned into one another.

One fortuitous day I met Martin Hartley, a British photographer. He was in Resolute as expedition photographer for fellow Brit Pen Hadow's attempt on the North Pole. Luckily for me, I was also helping out on the expedition, and when Martin discovered that I had an interest in photography, he invited me to head out shooting with him. Martin was, and still is, my photographic hero, and when I saw what he did for a living, and the magic he captured with his camera and lenses, I could only dream of someday doing what he did. The notion to me of ever being a professional seemed so far-off as to be impossible, but Martin encouraged and inspired. Creatively, I felt like I finally had a purpose in life; the Arctic was my launch pad.

Once I discovered photography and the joy it gave me, there was no turning back; it became all-encompassing. I wanted to learn as much as I could about the craft – I pored over photography books and magazines and blogs – while at the same time always trying to remember, while in the field, to not get so caught up in the technical nuts and bolts that I failed to just observe and enjoy the moments spent outside. The world outside was simply too beautiful to *not* appreciate.

Photography was the perfect hobby, starting out – a hobby that grew into so much more. I've always been a creator: I love going through each and every week knowing that I've outputted, in some shape or fashion, *something*. I'm not one for sitting around and letting life go by. Photography allowed me, in a sense, to accumulate creations: in the early days, this was the thrill of receiving in the mail a batch of processed slides; later, it would be the instant thrill of seeing a moment come alive on the back of my digital viewfinder that might become a print or a memory shared with others via social media.

Since those earliest hobbyist days, I've learned and come to appreciate the immense power of photography. Photographs have the power to record time, to educate, to promote, to allow appreciation and to inspire. One of the encounters in my own journey that has stuck with me is the time I ran into an Inuk woman, Anna, at the local grocery store in Resolute. She stopped me in an aisle and said she had been looking at some of my photos online. "I've lived here (in

Resolute) pretty much my whole life," she said. "I always thought it was sort of ugly… but seeing your photos has made me realize we really do live in a beautiful place. Thank you so much for that!"

Those are the moments I live for in photography. I try to make photographs that resonate with me, sure, but when the rare image resonates with *someone else*: that's the connection that many photographers strive for. It is why we're outside in poor conditions, in the dark and in the cold, and why we spent countless moments simply *waiting*. And watching. It's the thrill of the chase, and the high you receive when those countless moments pay off. When you feel that you've captured something special – something different; something *unique*.

The North, I feel, is my own unique world. It's a place where I go to feel alone, and out of that aloneness I gain so much community: a contradiction I feel many who have ventured north will understand, agree with and share in. These, here, are some of my favourite images from approximately 15 years spent documenting various parts of the North. No matter where I end up living in this world, the North will always be part of me. It's my community.

Acknowledgements

The North is a vast place, geographically, and when you cover its thousands of kilometres of territory, you can't help but meet countless people whose hospitality, kindness and inspiration help make your own journey possible. It's an impossible task to give thanks to each person individually, but there are a few individuals I would be remiss in not personally thanking.

First and foremost, I want to thank my wife, Erin, for all her encouragement and endless support in my photographic journey these past 17 years. It was Erin who was by my side when I first picked up a camera, and it was Erin who gave me the nudge (a swift kick in the butt) to be brave enough to walk away from the security of a normal job and take a chance on a passion – and I couldn't have more gratitude and love for her support.

Our three children – Luke, Liam and Lily – are my world and give me the fuel I need to work hard and do better. Their love is the greatest gift I have ever received, and I do what I do for them.

Martin Hartley was the first "hero" I ever really had. He came into my world when I was a complete newbie, and instead of laying down discouragement and judgement as a pro, offered nothing but encouragement. I'll forever thank him, and forever aspire to be the photographer he is.

Eleanor, a.k.a. Mom, gave me her beloved Pentax when I first caught the travel bug. The photos from those early days were the first creative thing I did that felt like *mine*. She ignited a spark that I know will never die. Mom, I love you.

Lou, a.k.a. Dad, you gave me my love of the outdoors. Thank you – and I miss you.

Paul Zizka is my business partner in a wonderful company called OFFBEAT, but more importantly is a friend and constant source of inspiration and encouragement. One of the most selfless people I know, Paul is a light of kindness and creativity, and this book wouldn't be possible without the journeys and explorations we have taken together.

To the people who have worked for me over the years as photographic assistants, or with me as studio or business partners, including Anne, Amy, Susan, Chris, Tara, Meghan and Shannon – your help, patience and hard work have played a huge part in my journey. A special shout-out to Cathie Archbould for all her assistance in my trips to the Yukon, and to Clare Kines for his Nunavut support.

I'm fortunate to have some great sponsors in this photographic journey. The gear never makes the images, but having great companies supporting you has made a definite impact. Sigma Canada and Strobepro, thank you for supporting Canadian photographers, but more importantly, thank you for being great organizations to work with.

Finally, to the guys in #thewaynelife and all my wonderful mentees who I've shared countless conversations with – you know who you are.

Northern Soul

THE PORTRAITS

When I first moved to the North, I was, photographically, afraid of people. I loved interacting socially, but my solace with my camera was being outside. Breathing fresh air. Climbing on top of small icebergs that had frozen into the sea ice of Resolute Bay and peeking down into their souls, looking for their secrets. Going for walks out on the vast tundra, appreciating the tiniest of its plants in the summer and losing myself in its hypnotic dry-snow crunch in the winter. Taking my Polaris snowmobile into small canyons, seeking out light and peace and moments of beauty. I would find a place, off on my own, where I could sit on a rock and simply take in the Arctic and think and feel. Sometimes I would make images, but most important to me, at that time, was to simply *be*. My camera was my tool to take me outside. The photos were the excuse (not that I needed much of an excuse) to appreciate the outdoors.

I became a portrait artist begrudgingly.

Rocks and tundra and ice and trees and snow don't talk back. They speak a language, of course, but they don't judge. Nature didn't give me the pressure of people. So when people – knowing that I was into photography – asked me about potentially taking their portrait, I would always have an polite excuse. *Sorry, but I don't photograph people. I'm a landscape photographer. There are other photographers I can recommend.*

Somewhere along the line, I broke. I believe it was a co-worker, in my pre-professional days. She was relentless, and insisted that I photograph her and her husband. *I don't care what the photos look like… I just want you to take them.* I relented. I caved. And I'm so, so happy I did.

The floodgates opened. I realized in that hour-long session that I actually enjoyed the process. Trying to find the magic in a personality. In personalities. To crack their code and find the angle and the expression and the moment where it all came together and the photograph crossed from a simple snapshot to something meaningful.

There was no turning back.

Journeying into the world of Northern portraiture, I learned something that shouldn't have been a surprise: the North is home to some of the most incredible faces and personalities our world has to offer. It takes a strong personality to weather the Arctic and Subarctic environments, and I discovered strength, love, vulnerability, perseverance and even creativity in the people I encountered with my lens and camera.

I've always said that I don't consider my portraits my own. And they aren't. It takes a collaboration to make a portrait: the photographer and the subject. It's a dance. A coming together – sometimes for a brief moment and other times for extended periods – where there's a back and forth, a rhythm, a connection, all in the hopes of finding the quintessential moment where the subject gives you the perfect moment… and you can only hope as the photographer that you're prepared to receive it.

Here is a collection of 30 portraits from a collection of tens of thousands of images of hundreds and hundreds of subjects. These are people I feel blessed to have met throughout the North, and having the opportunity to photograph each and every one of these subjects is something that will stay with me my entire life.

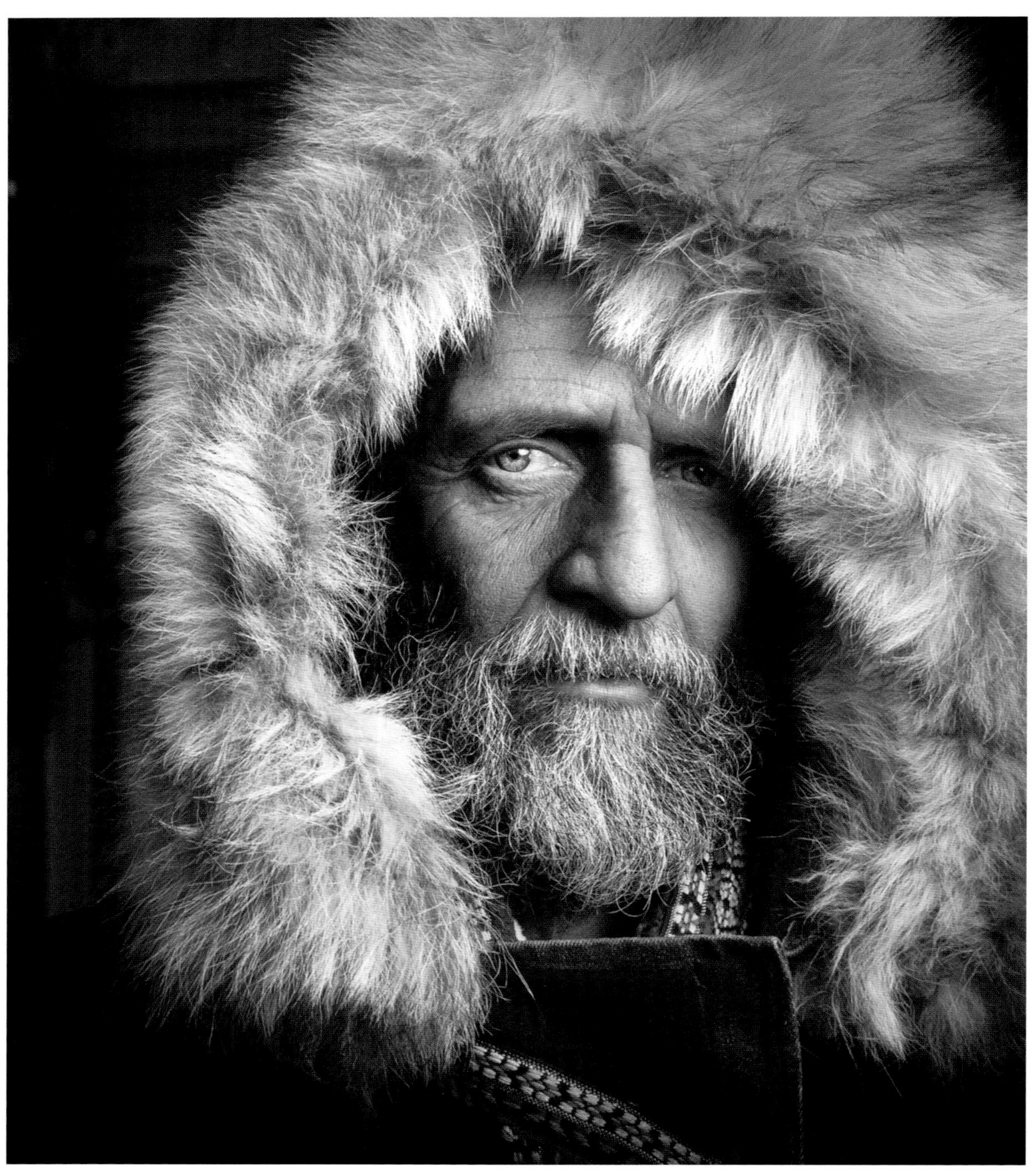

8 Roch Boivin at Fish Lake area, Yukon

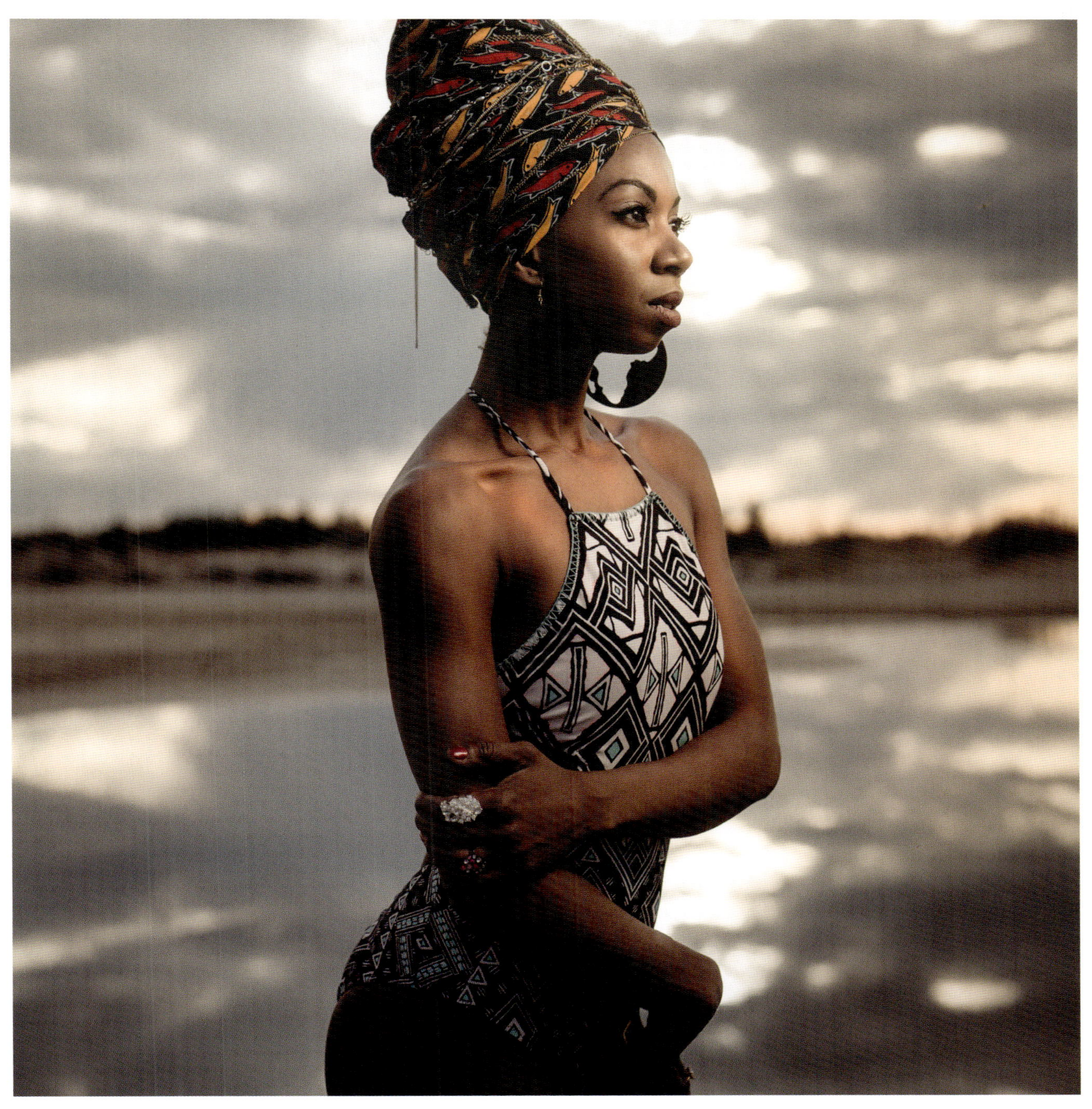

Inemesit Graham in Yellowknife, Northwest Territories

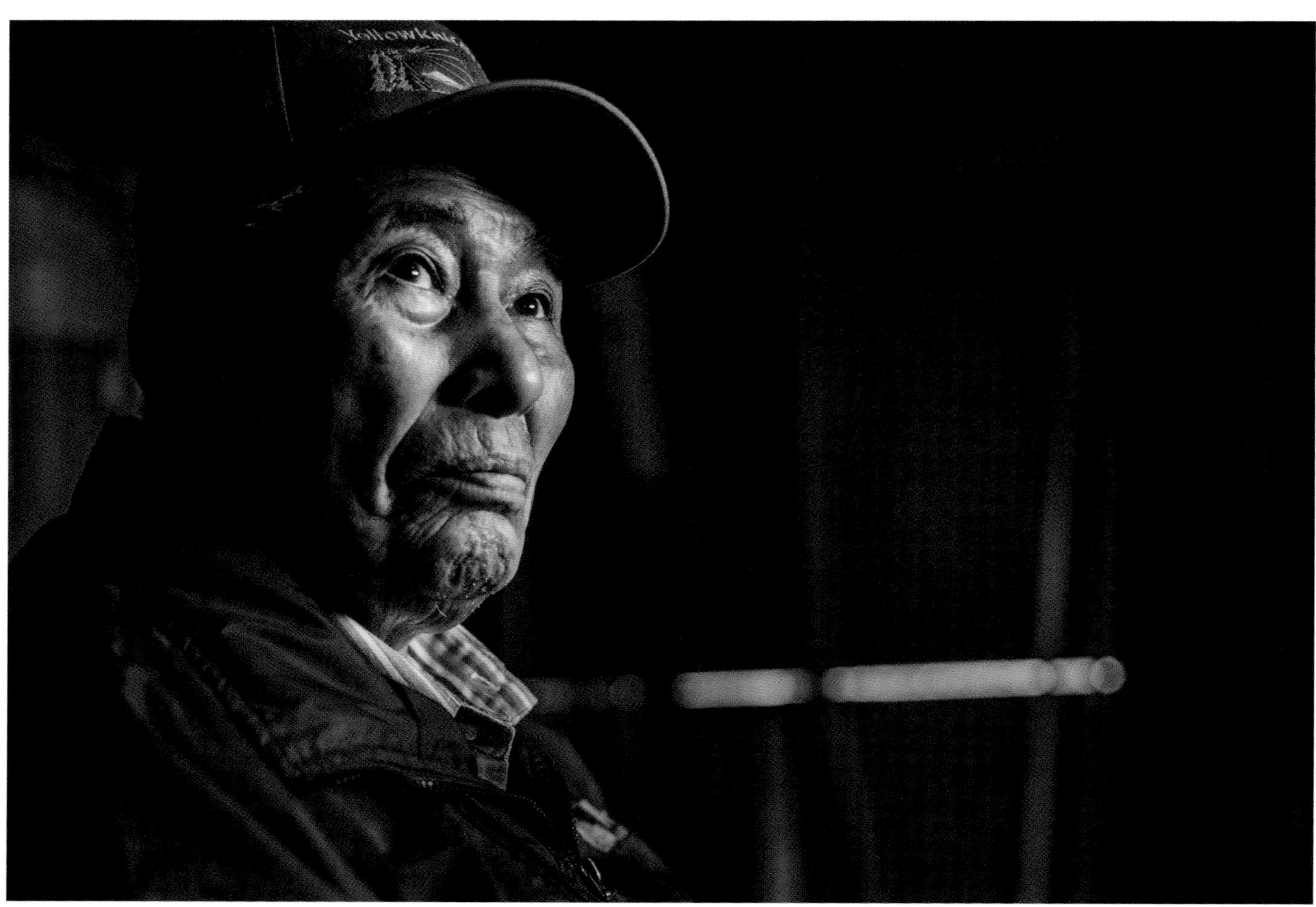

 Philip Huskey in Behchokǫ̀, Northwest Territories

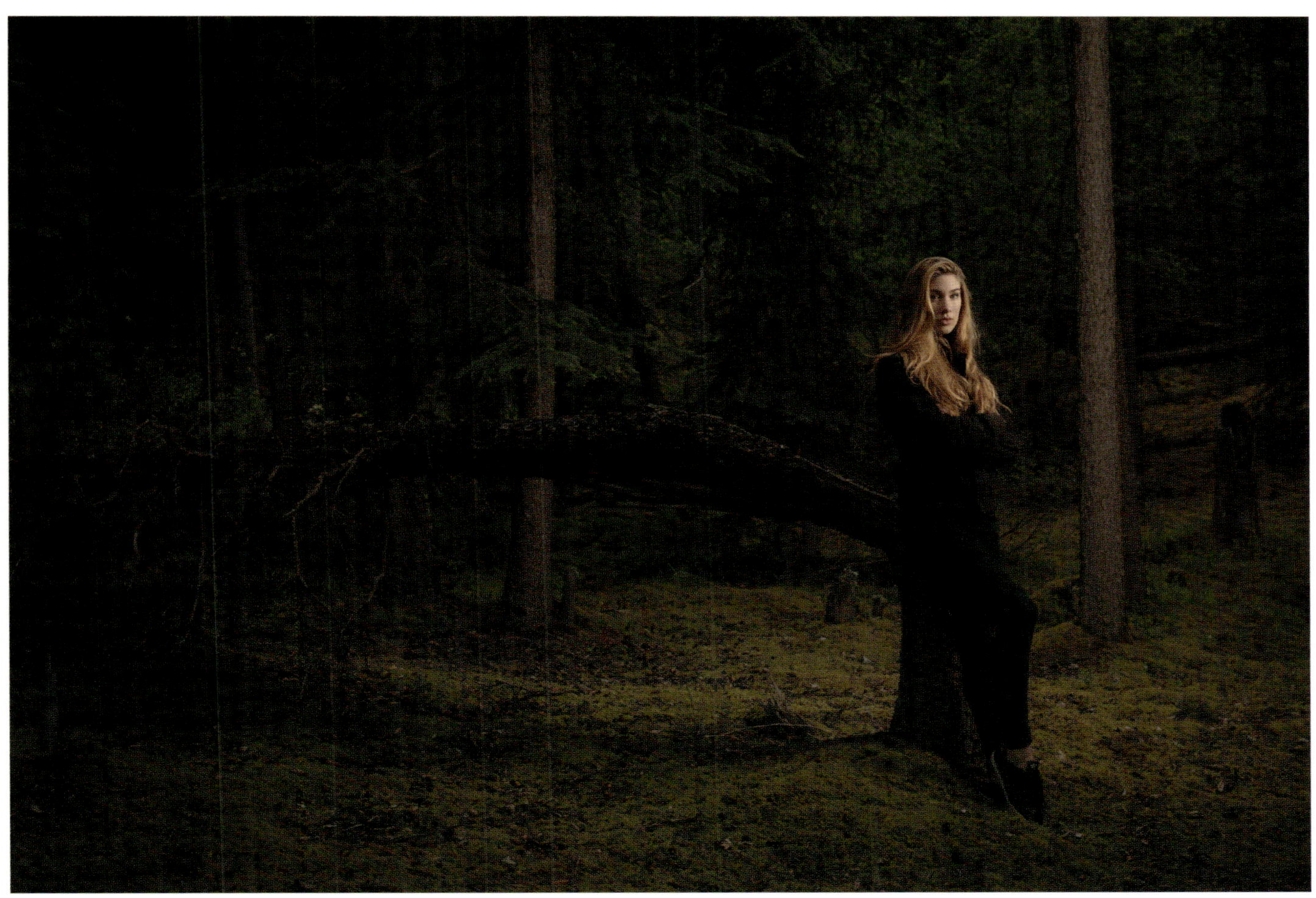

Odessa Beatty in Whitehorse, Yukon

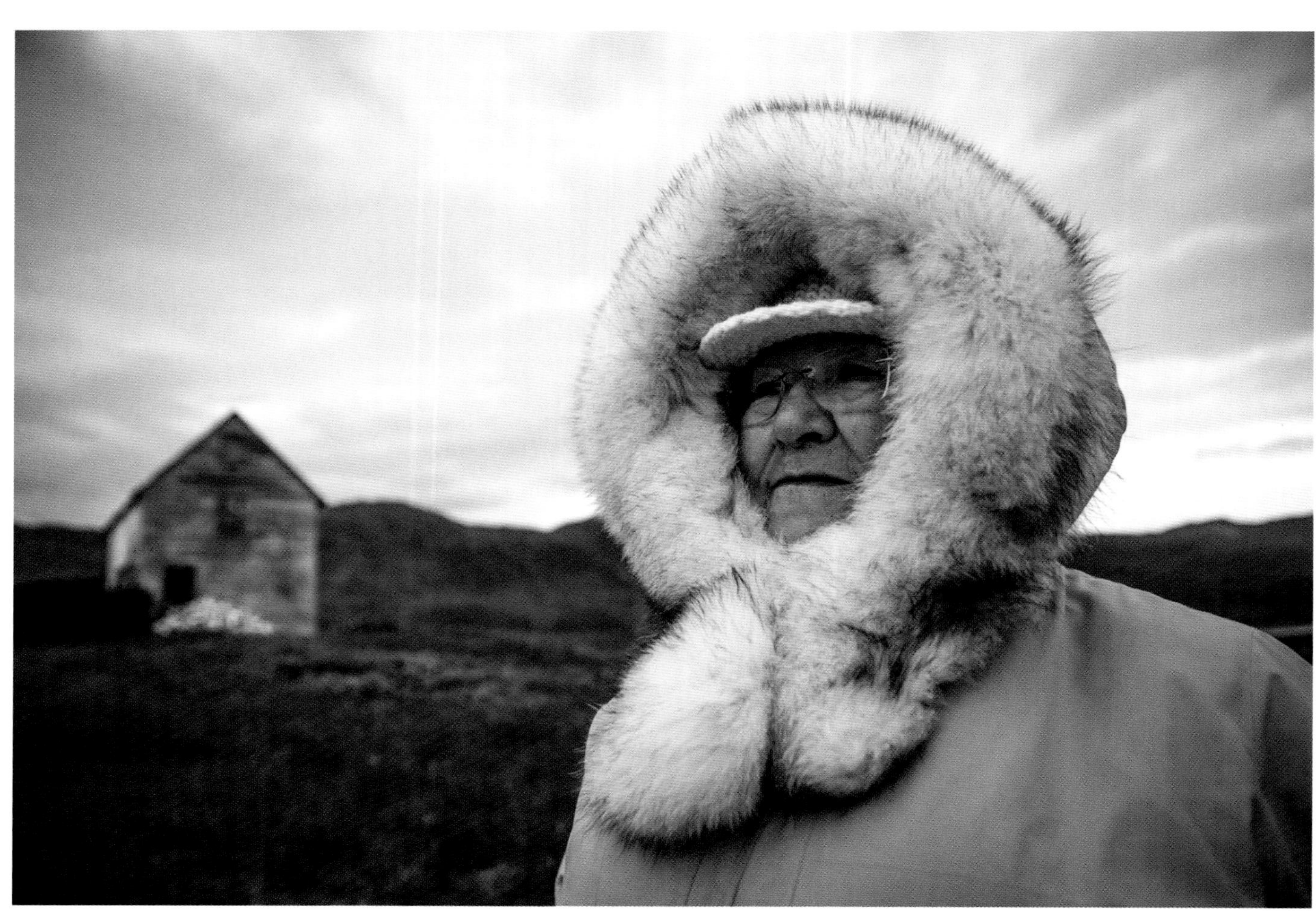

 Sophie Keelan in Hebron, Labrador

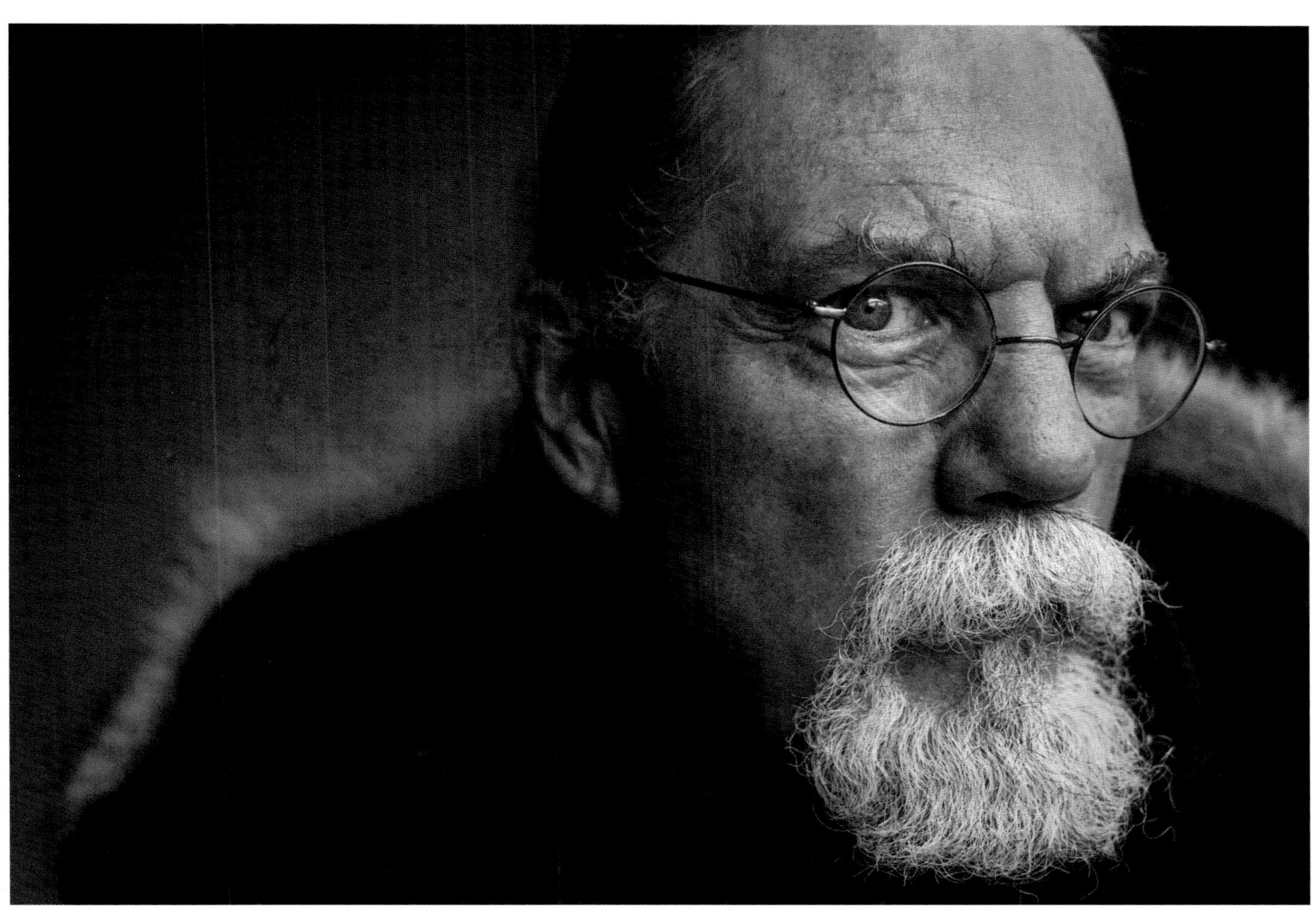

Donald C. Watt in Whitehorse, Yukon

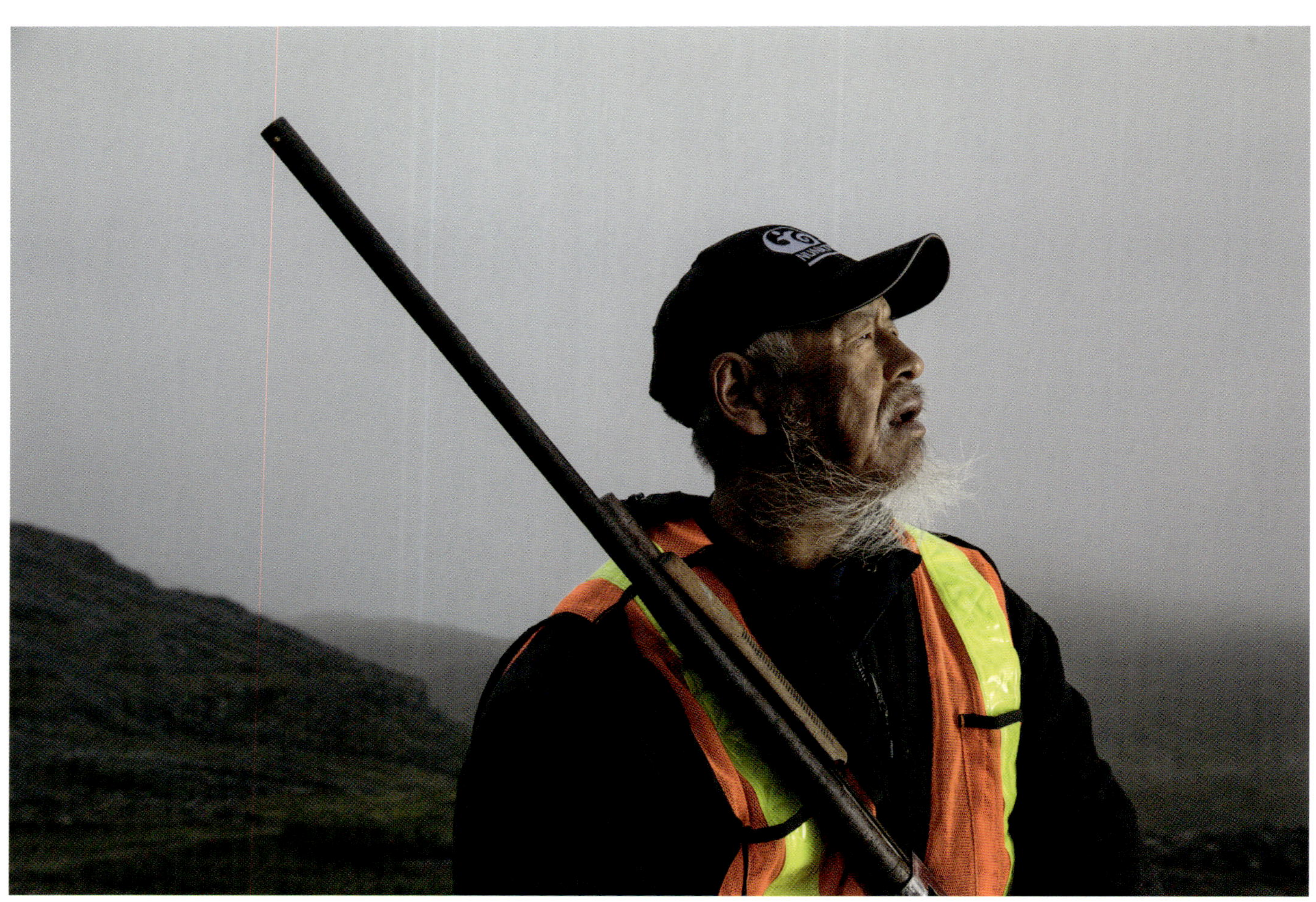

 Abia Zarpa in Hebron, Labrador

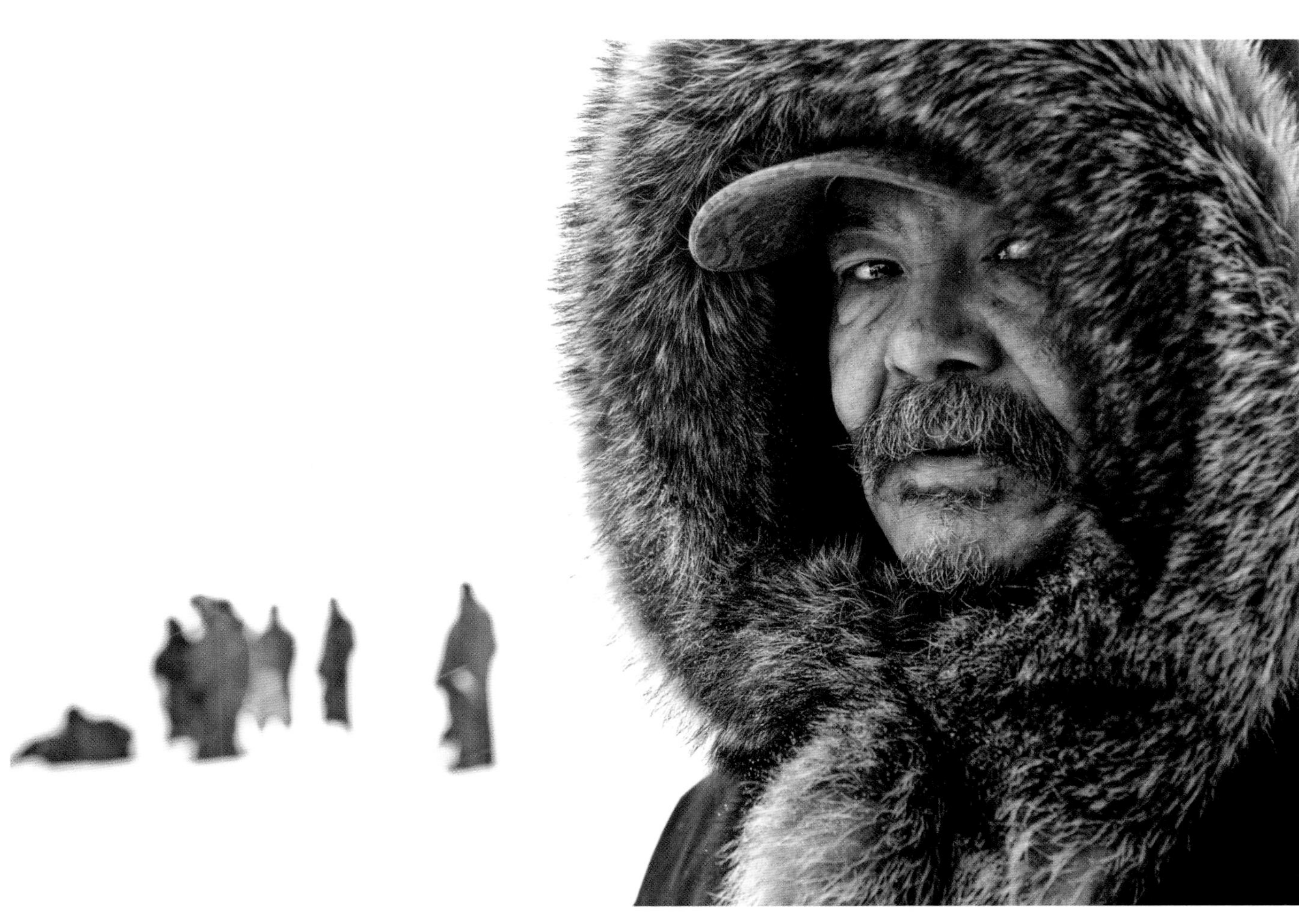

Mark Amarok on Ward Hunt Island, Nunavut

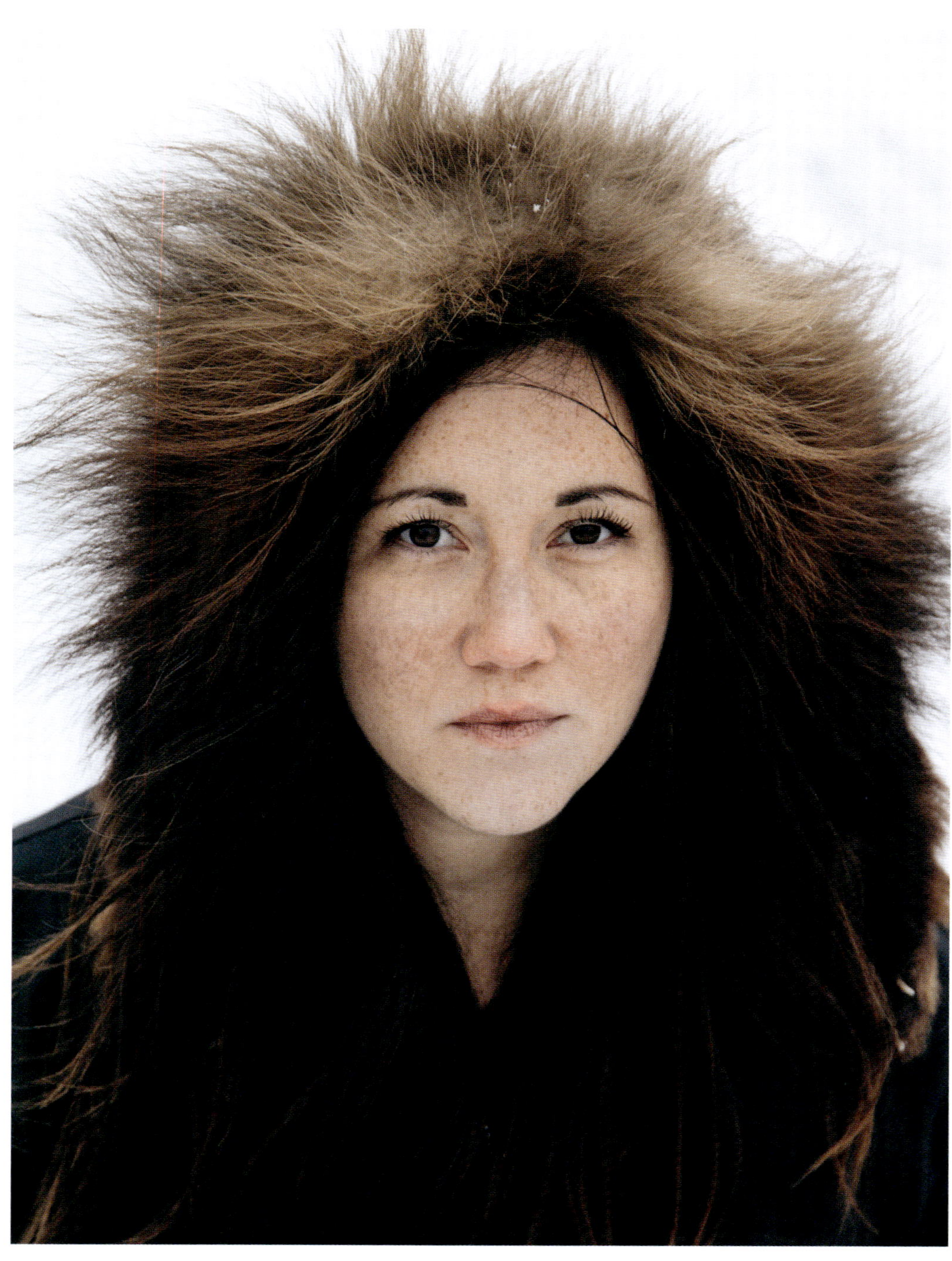

Danielle Mager in Yellowknife, Northwest Territories

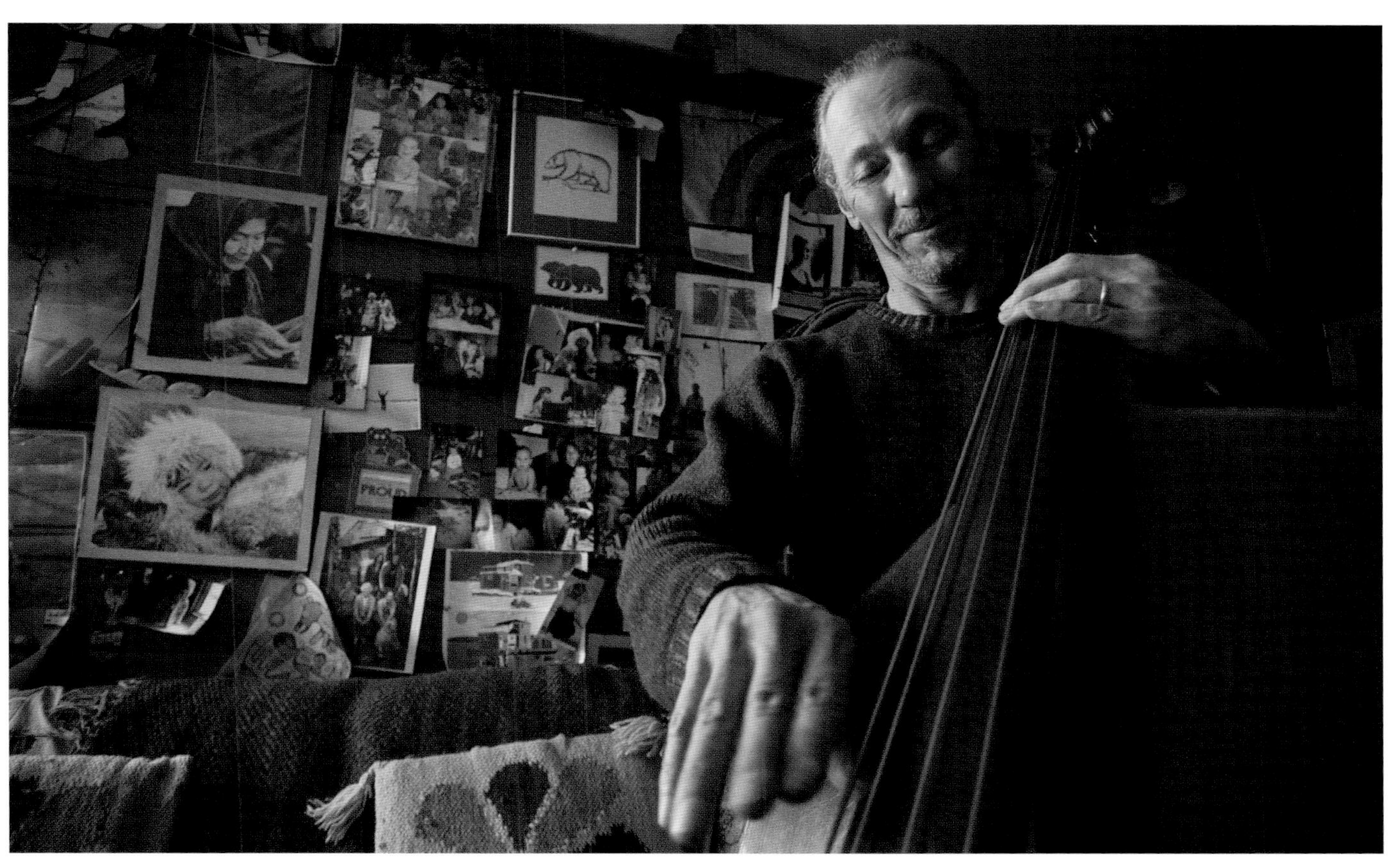

Pat Braden in Yellowknife, Northwest Territories

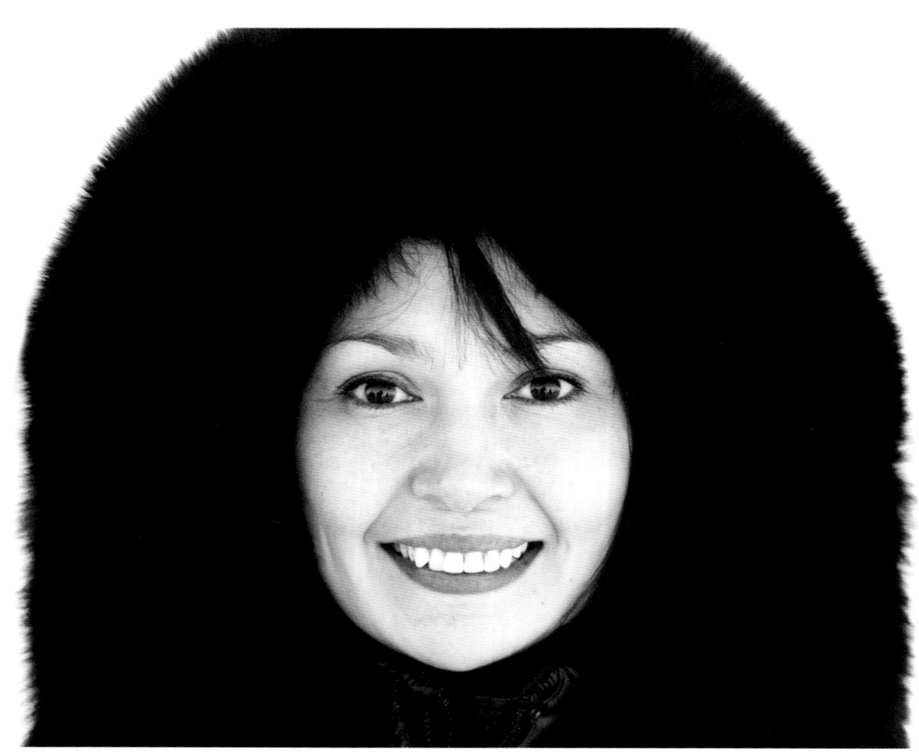

 Darlene Willie in Arctic Bay, Nunavut

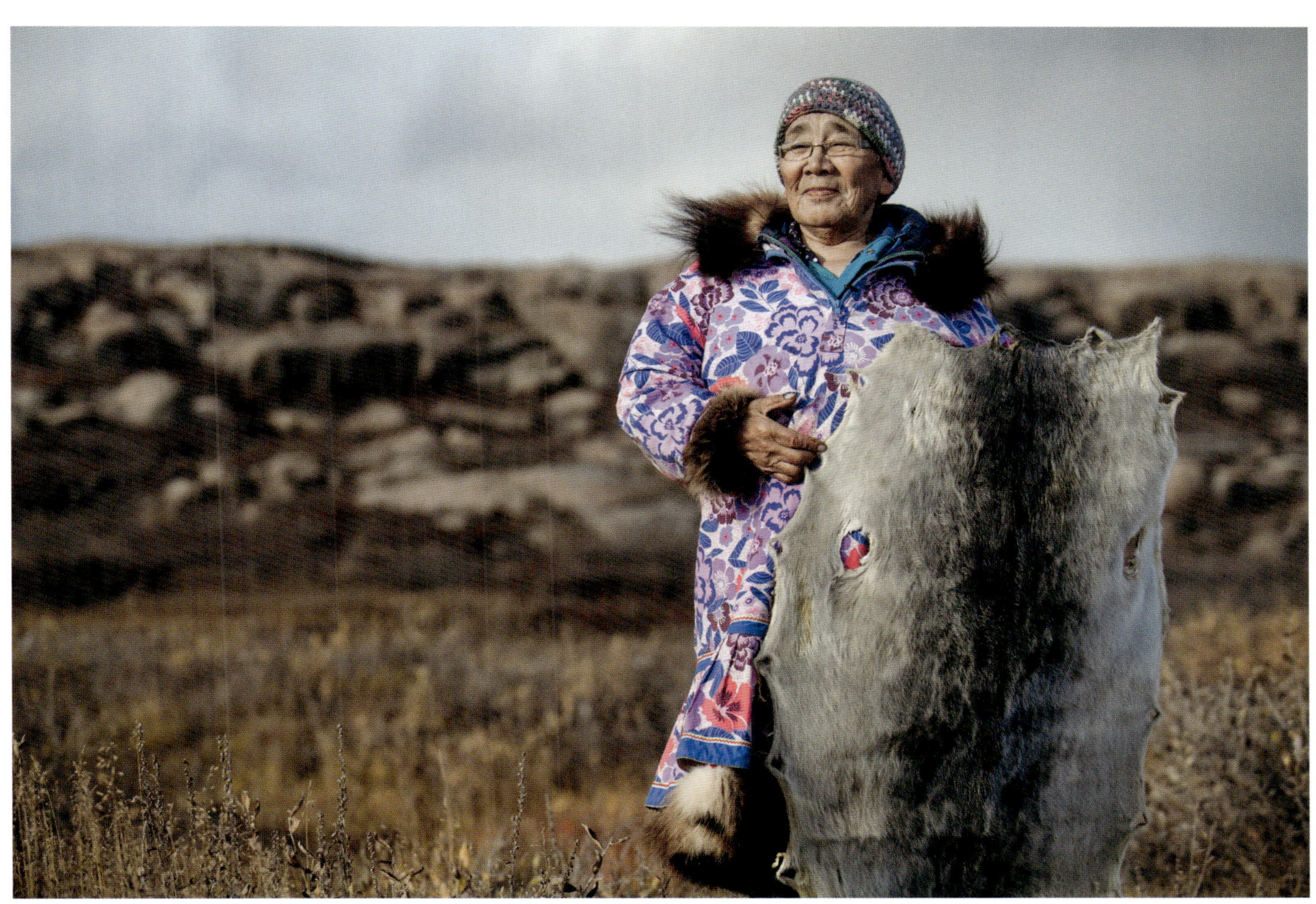

Alice Ayalik in Kugluktuk, Nunavut

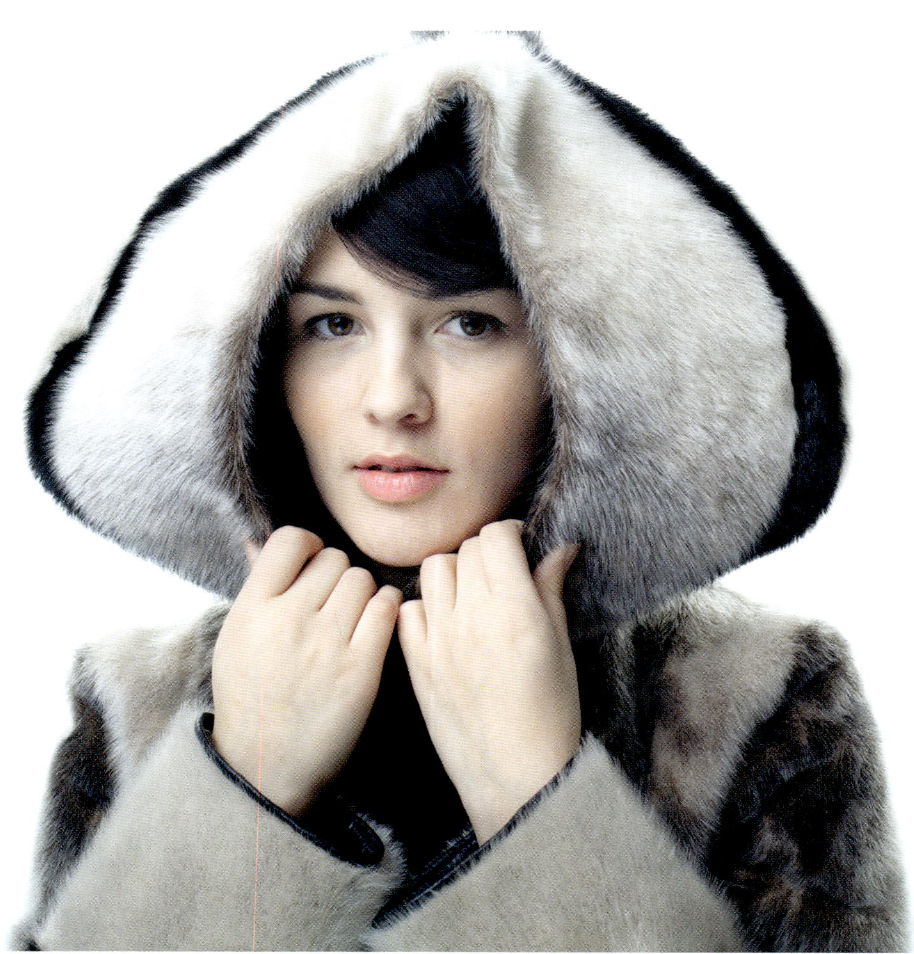

 Ruthanne Klengenberg in Yellowknife, Northwest Territories

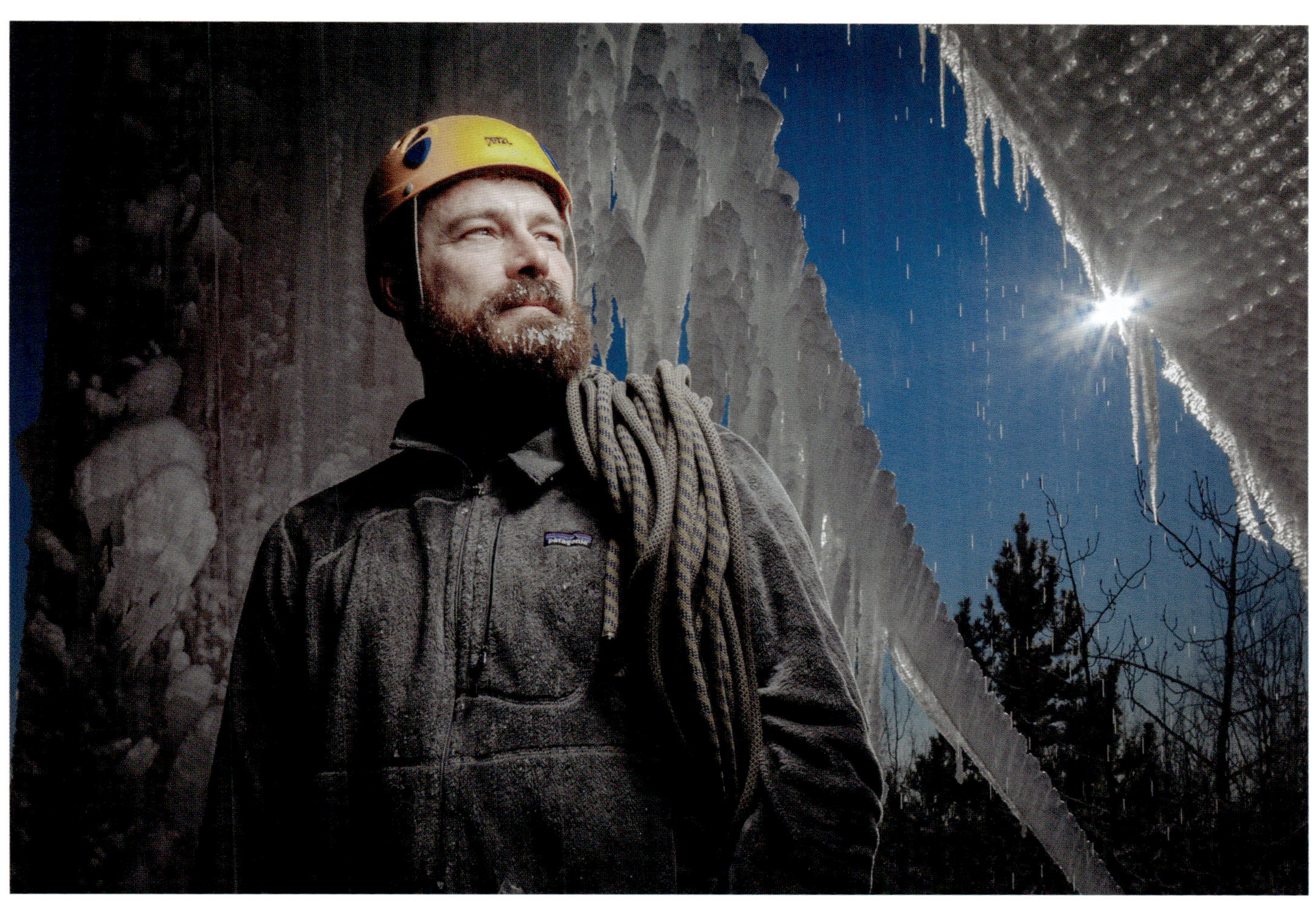

Christopher Gishler at Takhini Hotsprings, Yukon

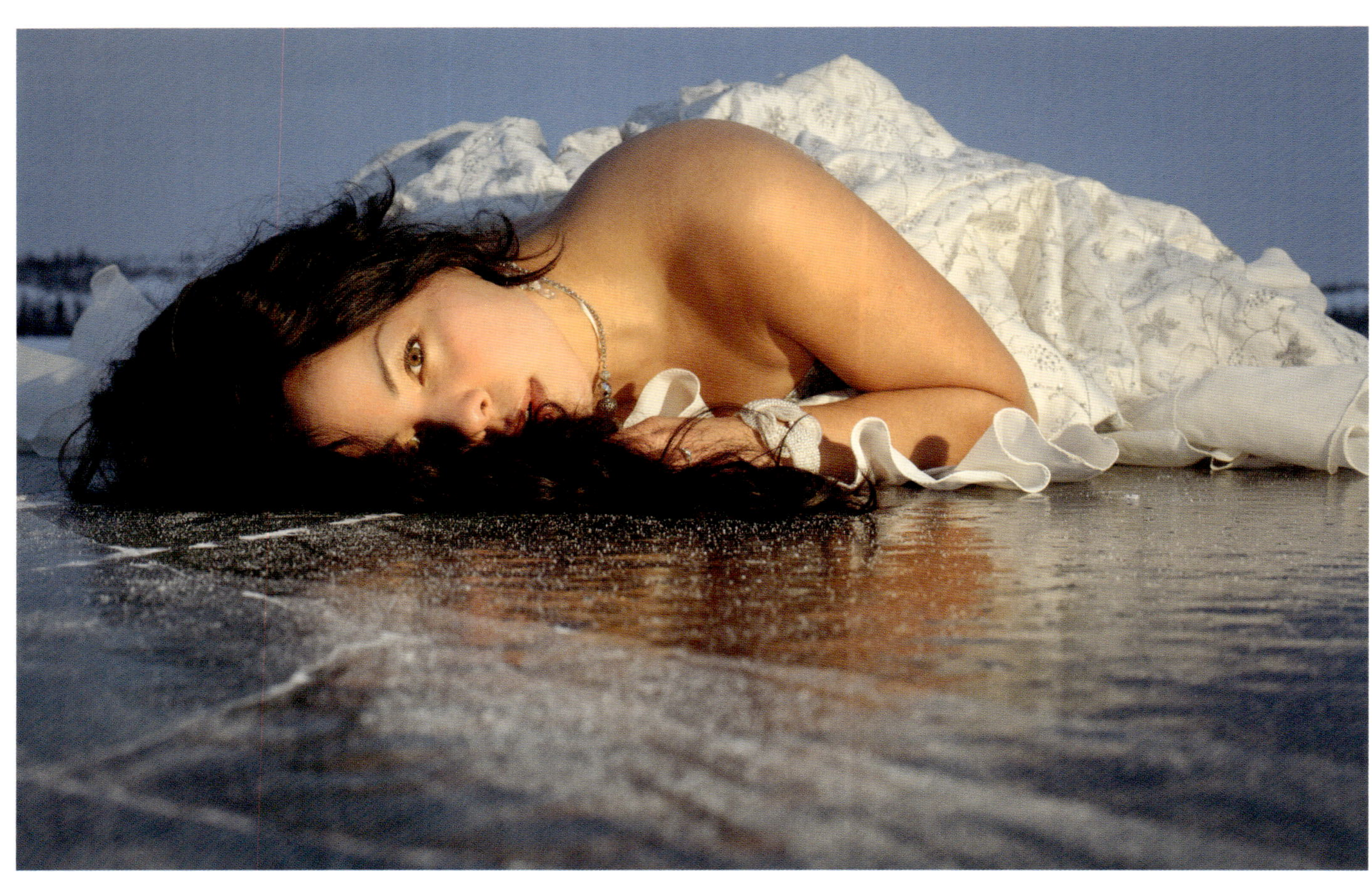

 Tiffany Ayalik in Yellowknife, Northwest Territories

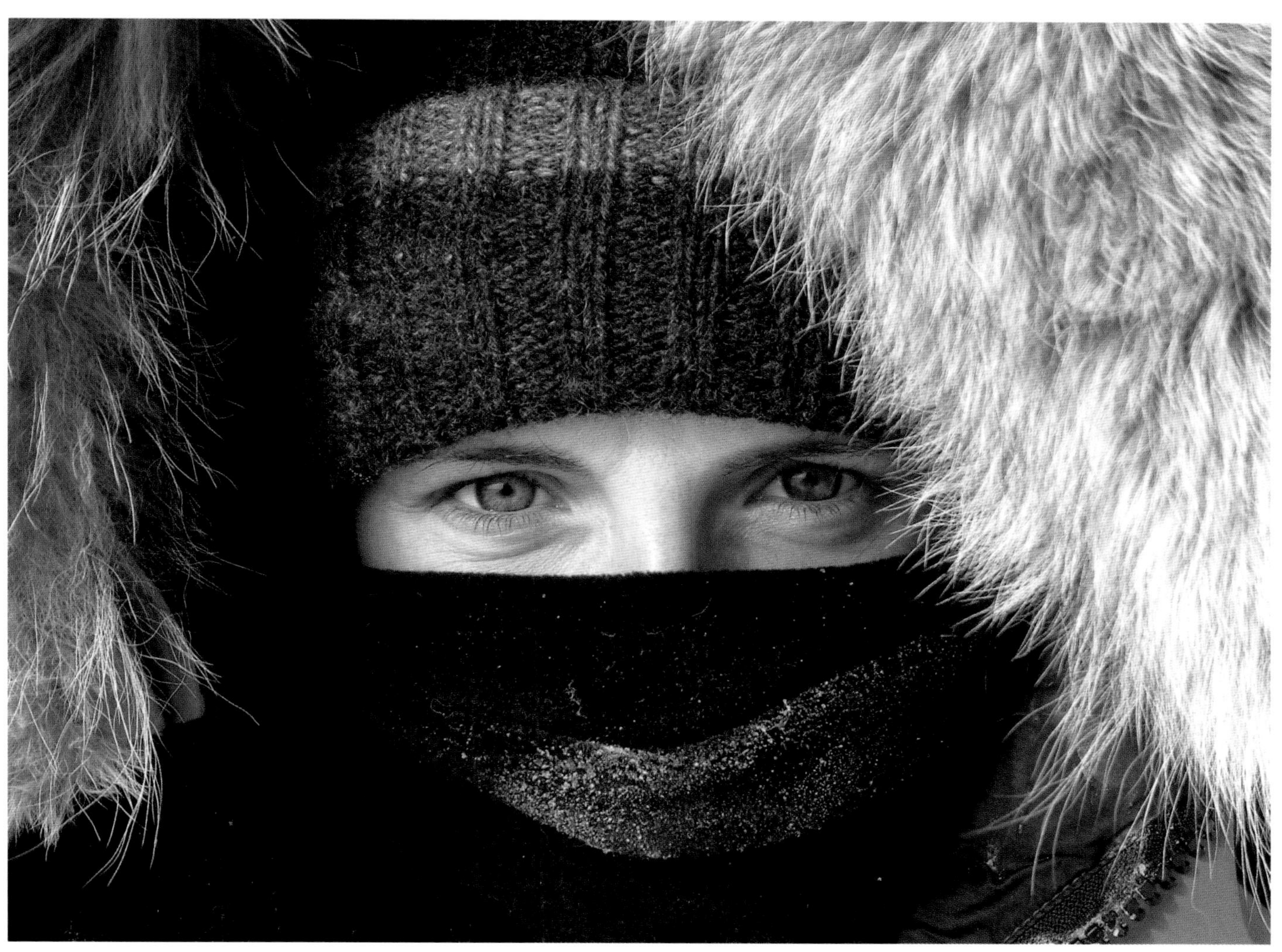

Erin Brosha in Resolute Bay, Nunavut

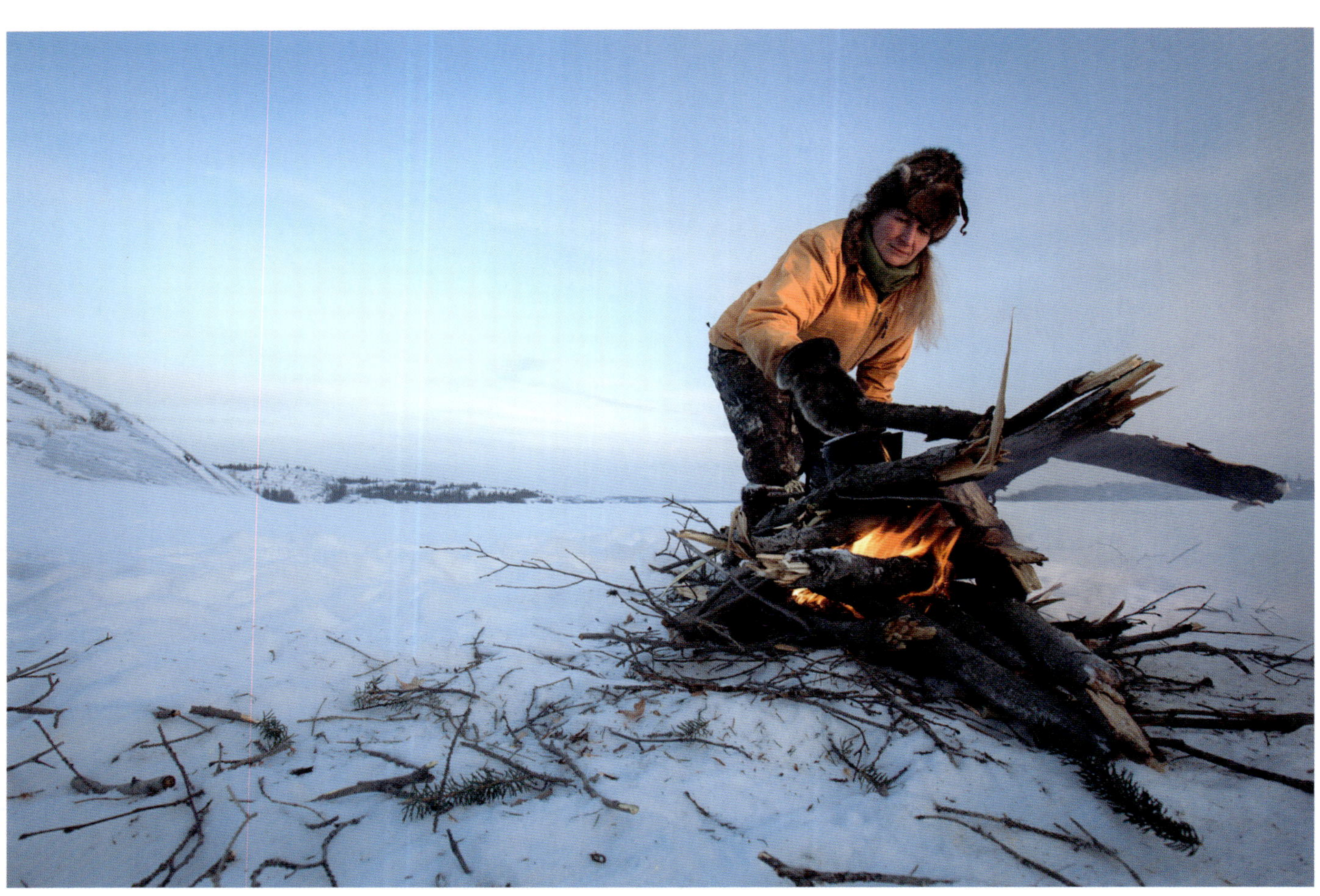

 Catharine Allooloo at Back Bay, Yellowknife, Northwest Territories

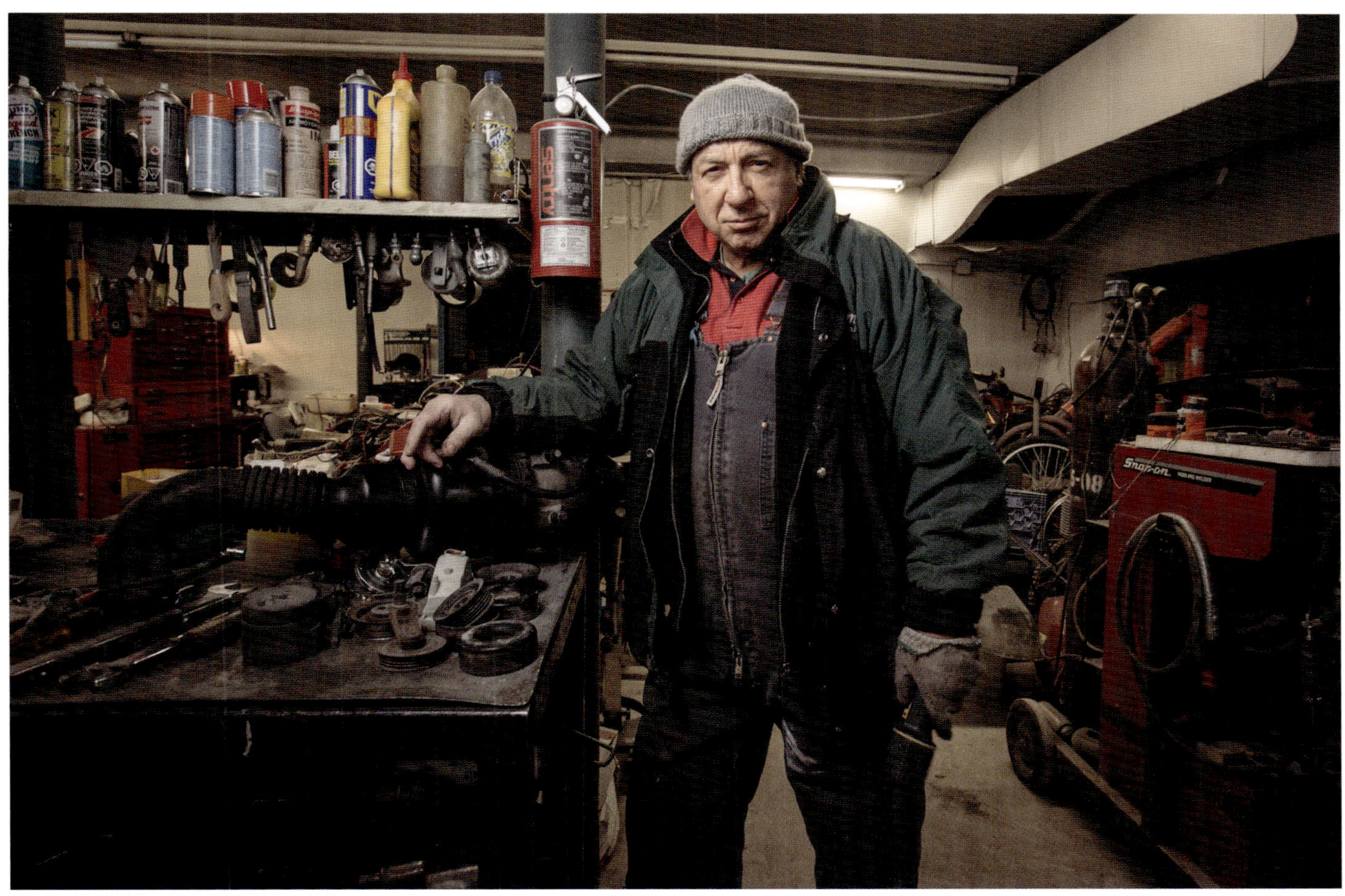

Elias Saravanja in Old Town, Yellowknife, Northwest Territories

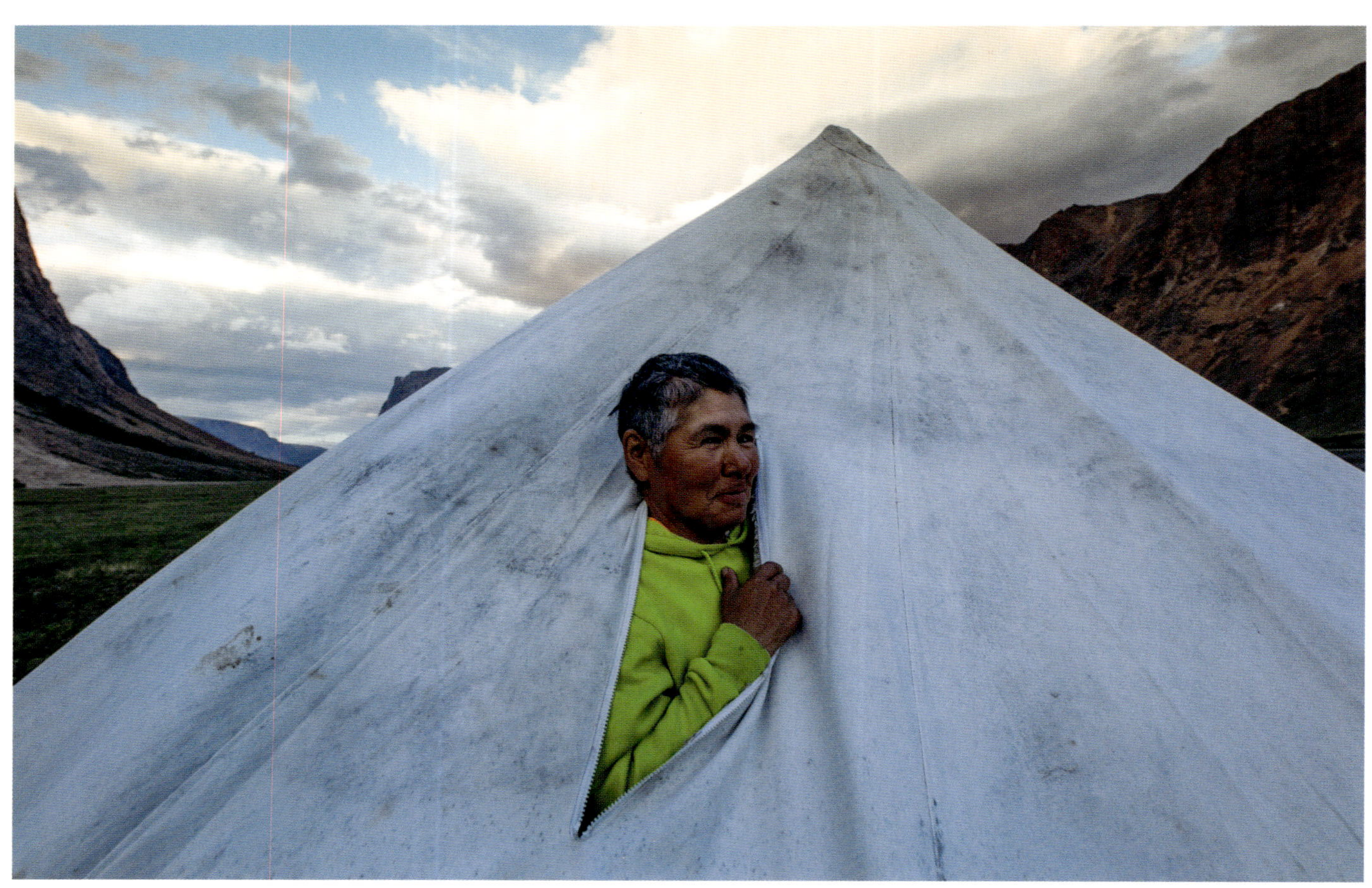

 Boonie Merkuratsuk in the Torngat Mountains, Labrador

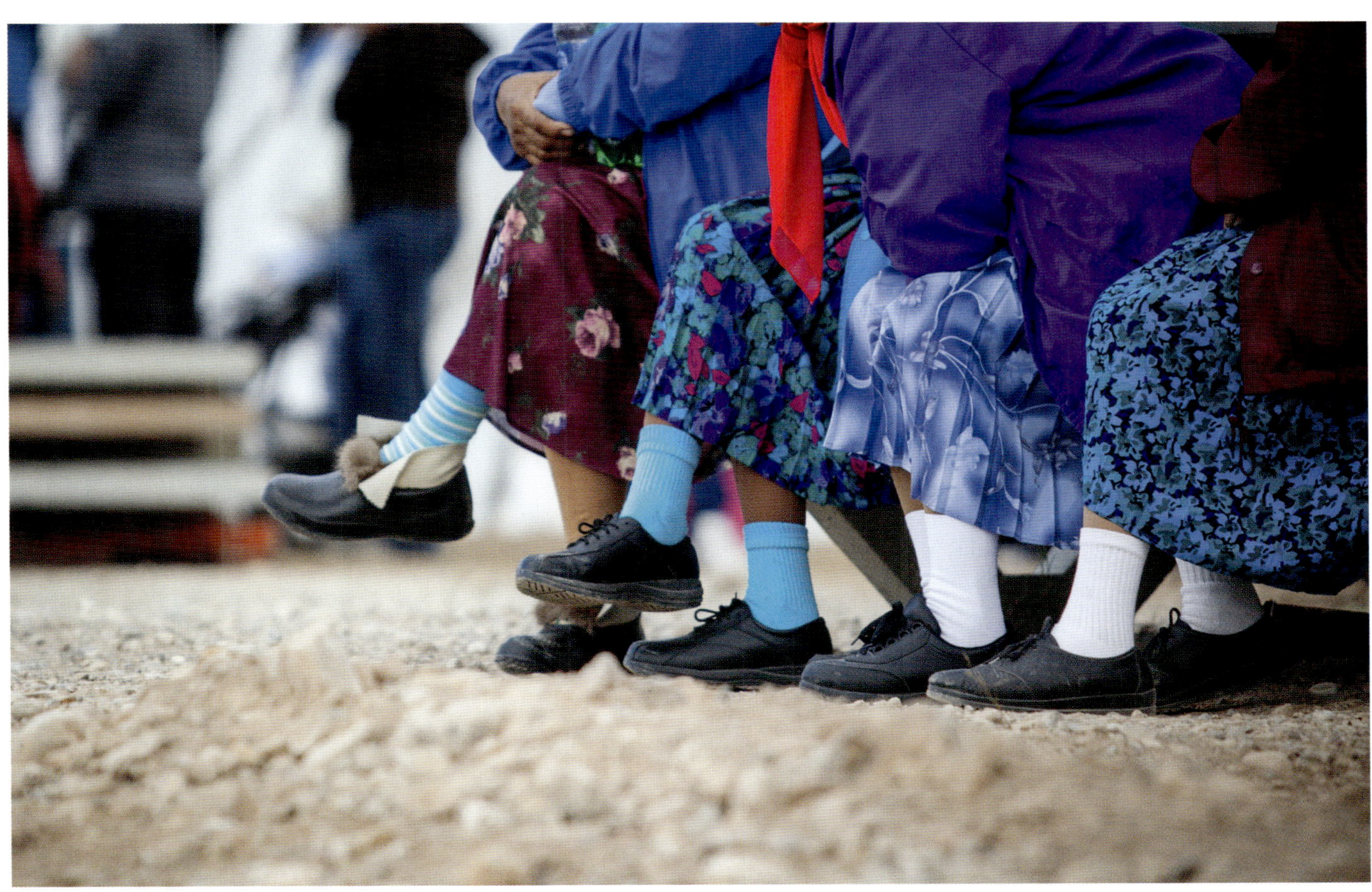

The Ladies of Rae in Behchokǫ̀, Northwest Territories

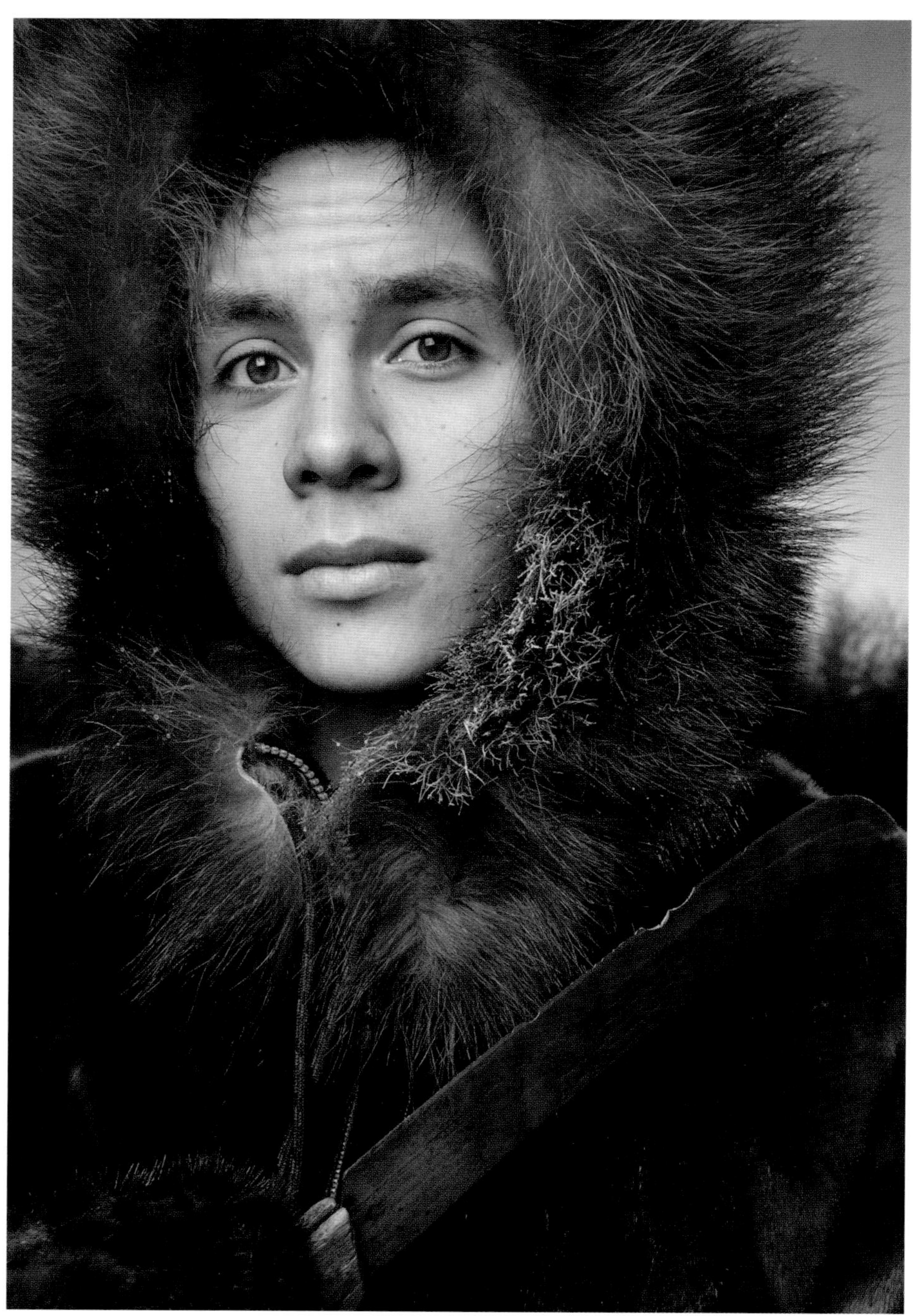

Devon Allooloo in Yellowknife, Northwest Territories

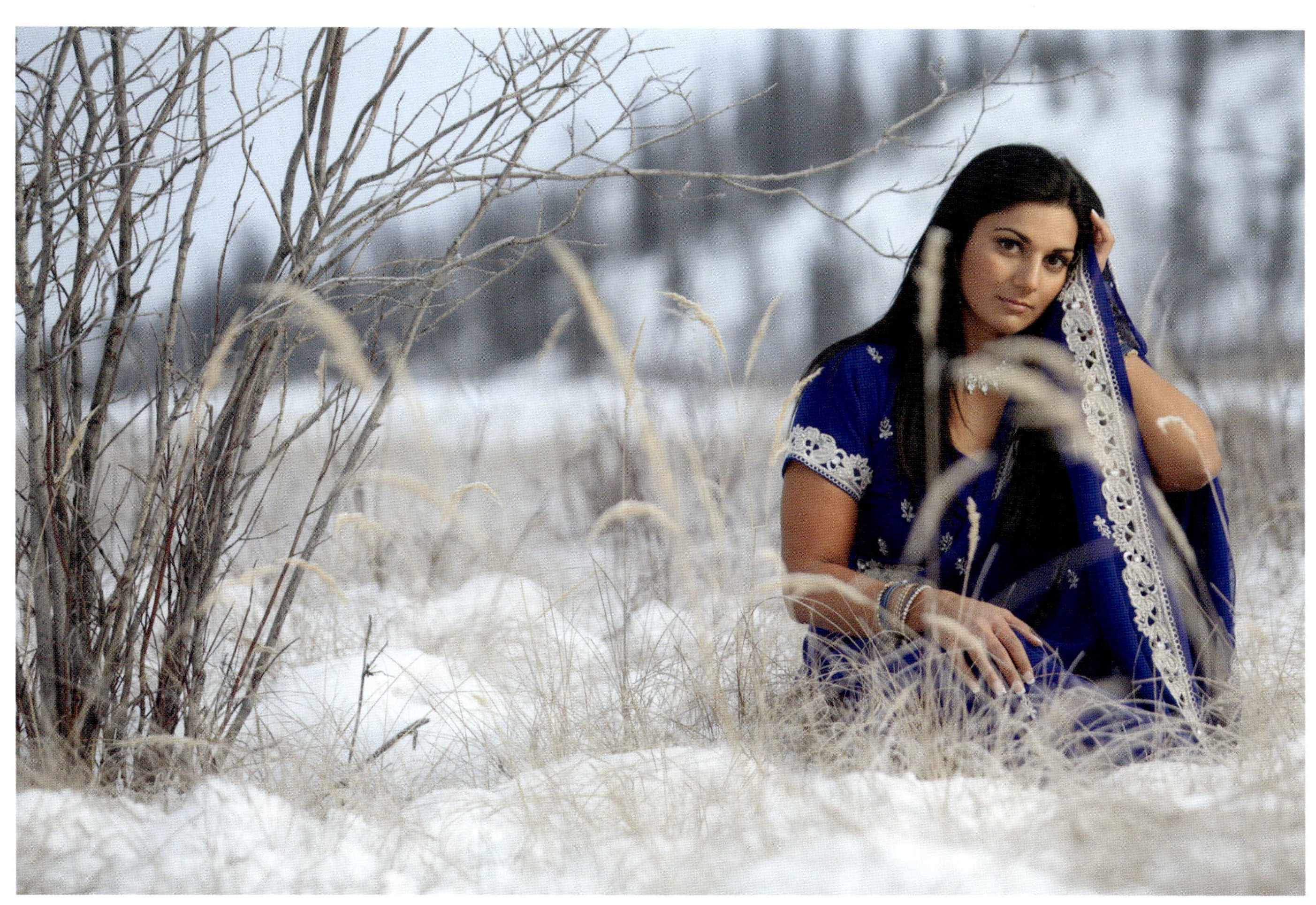

Kam Hogan in Yellowknife, Northwest Territories

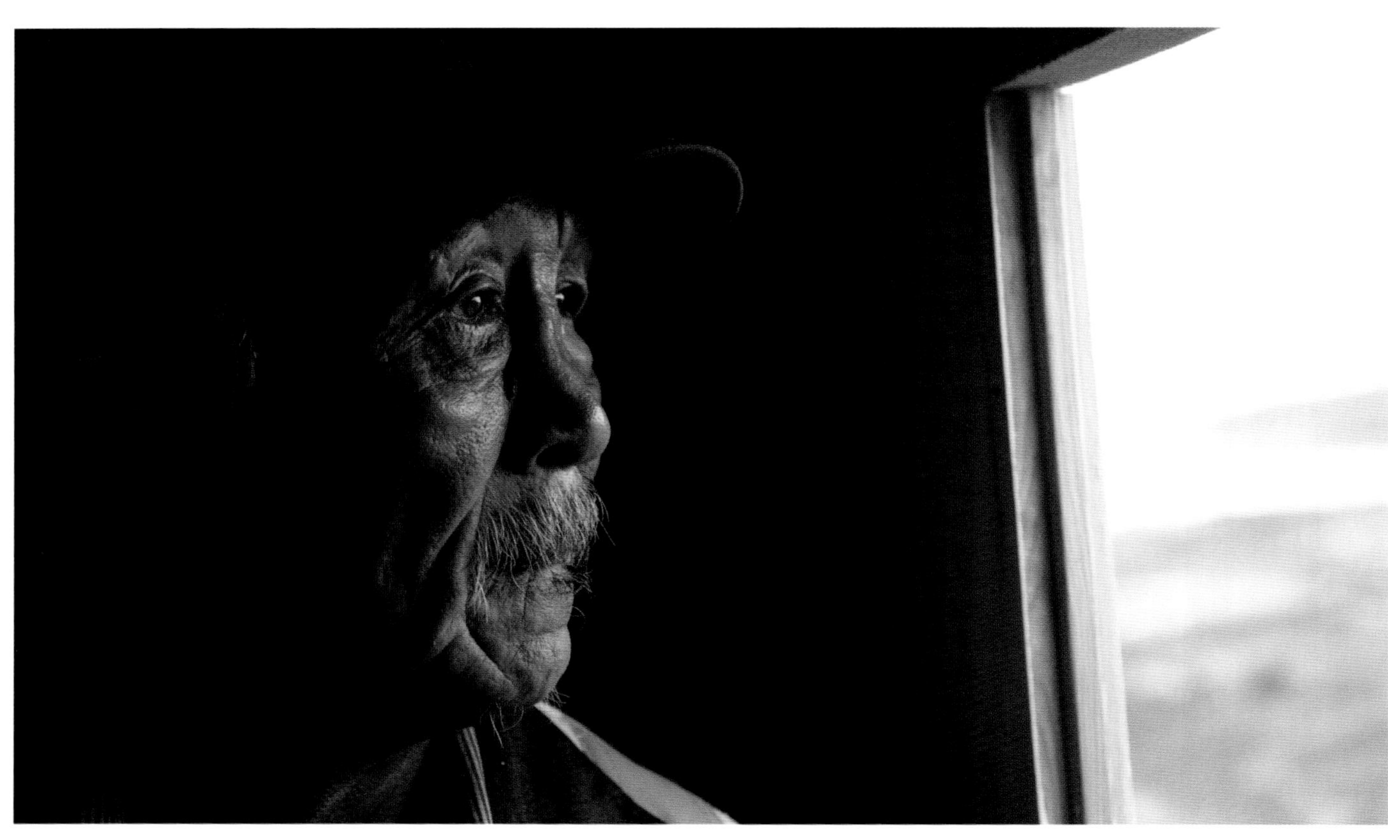

 Gus Semigak in Hebron, Labrador

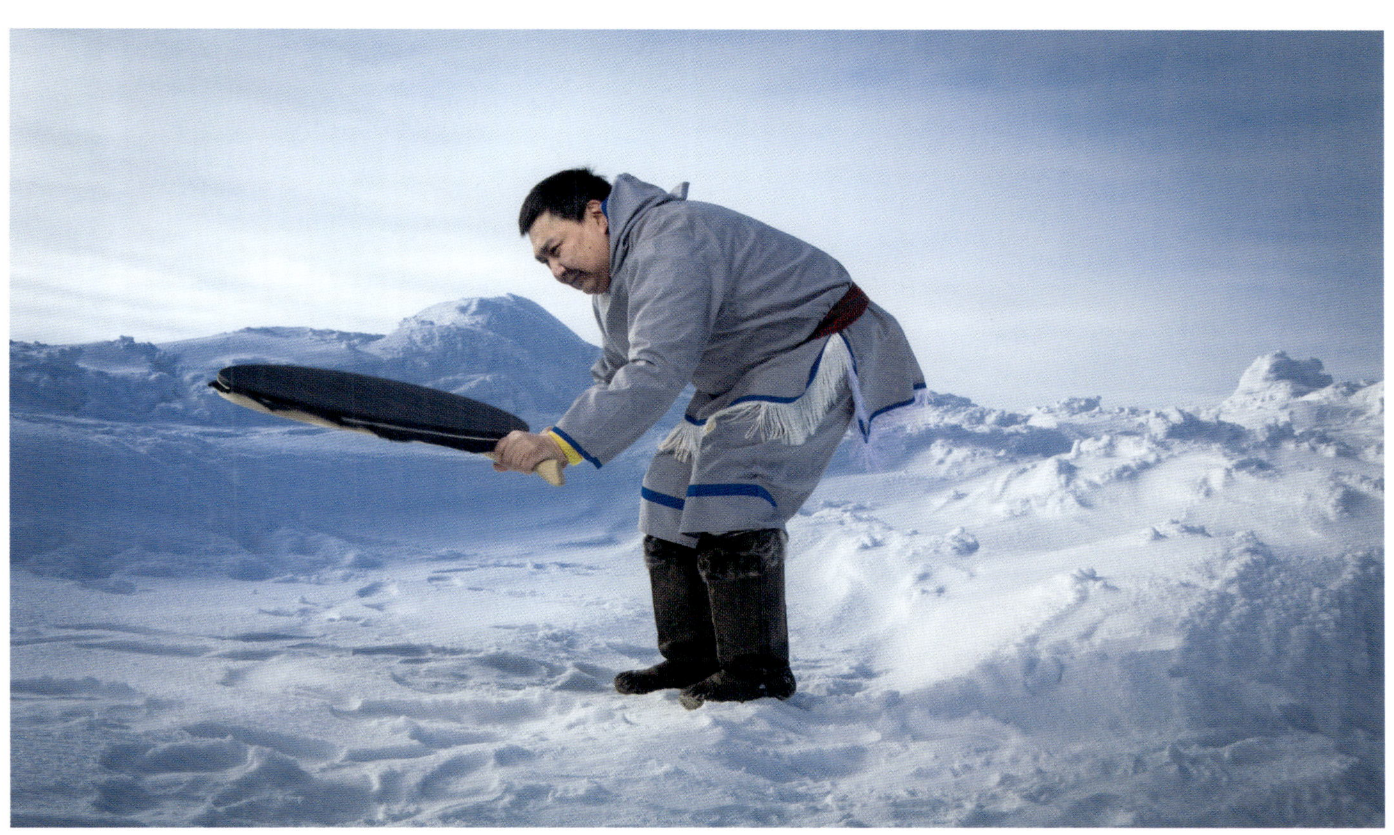

Noah Tiktak in Rankin Inlet, Nunavut

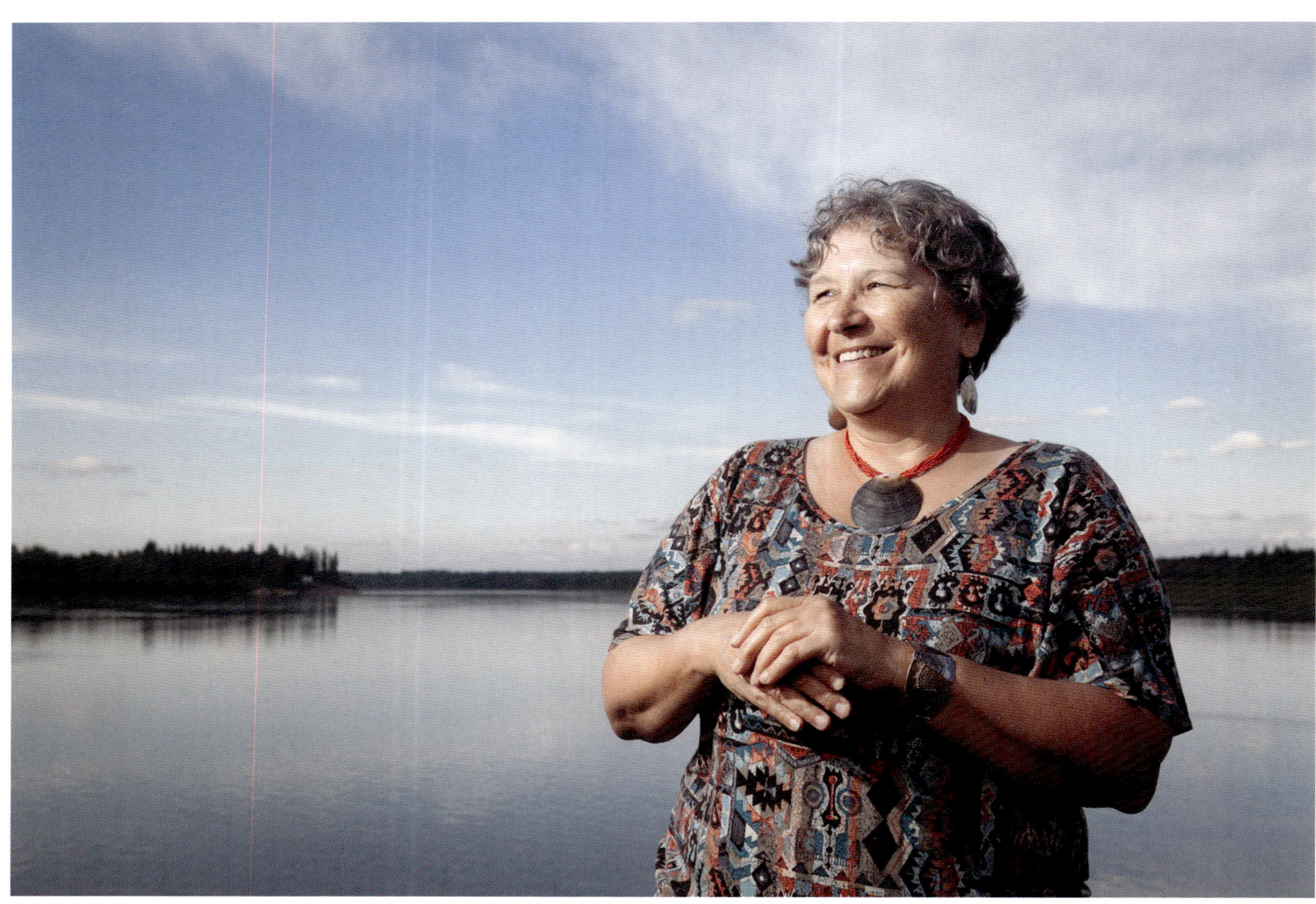

Priscilla Lepine in Fort Smith, Northwest Territories

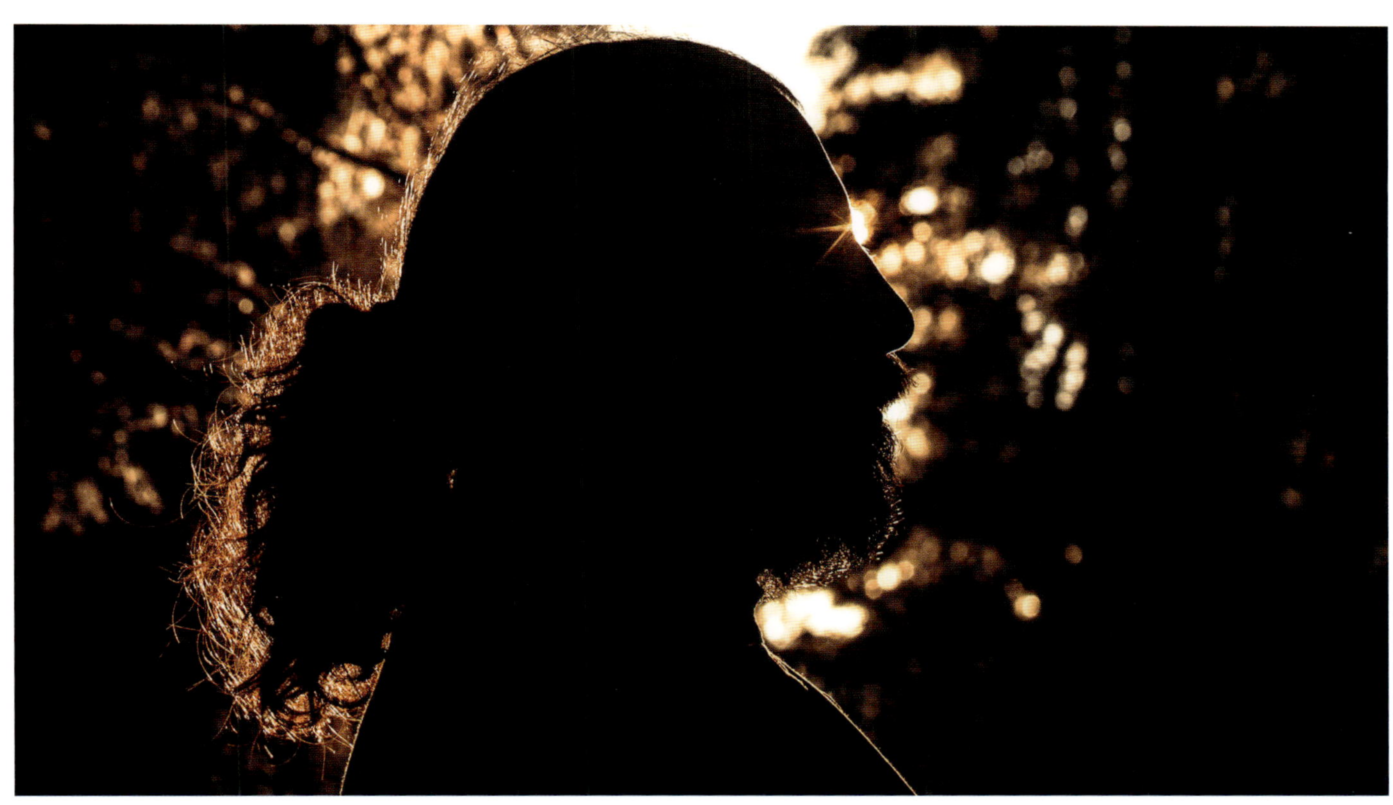

Pablo Saravanja in Fort Smith, Northwest Territories

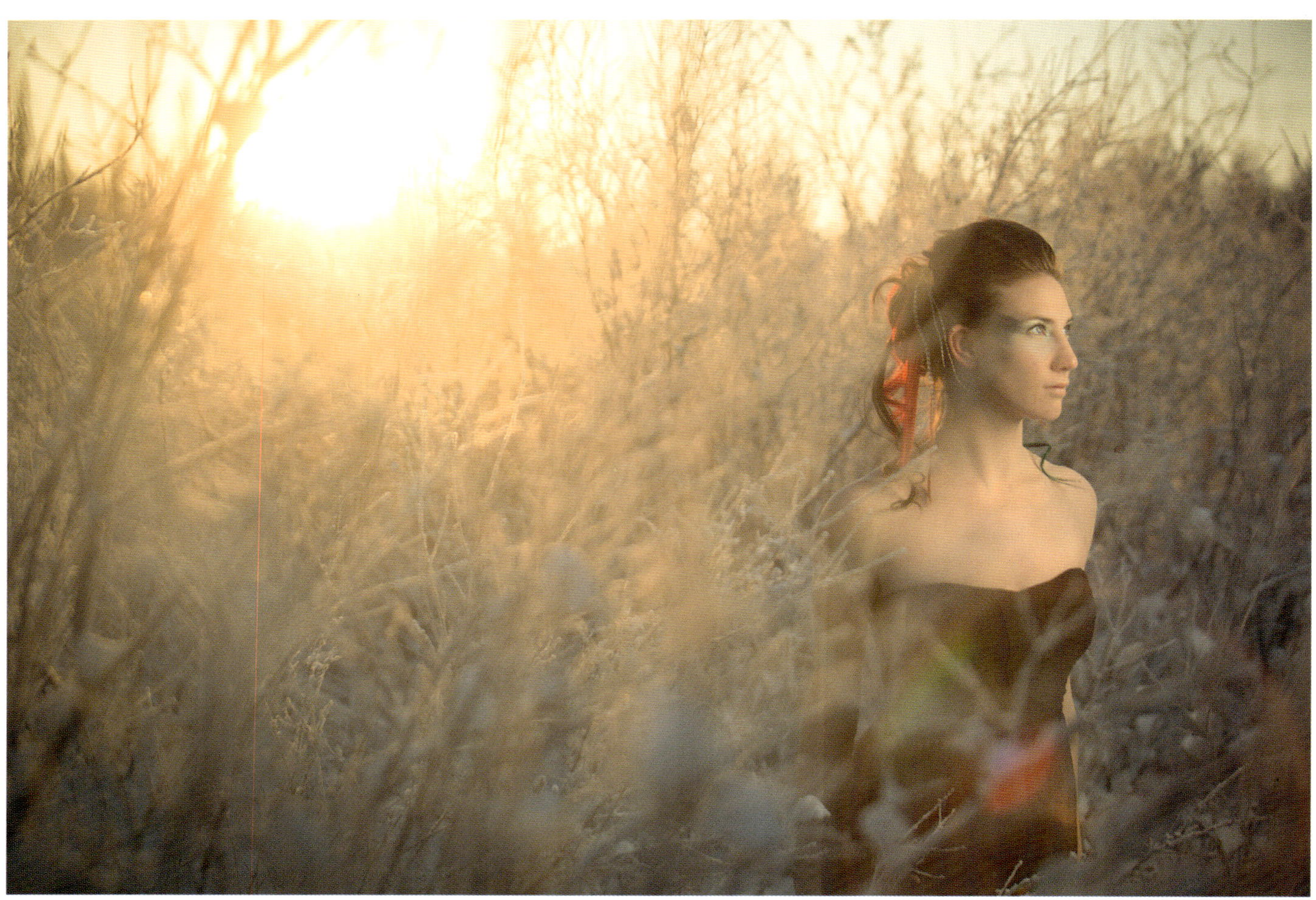

 Elora Braden in Yellowknife, Northwest Territories

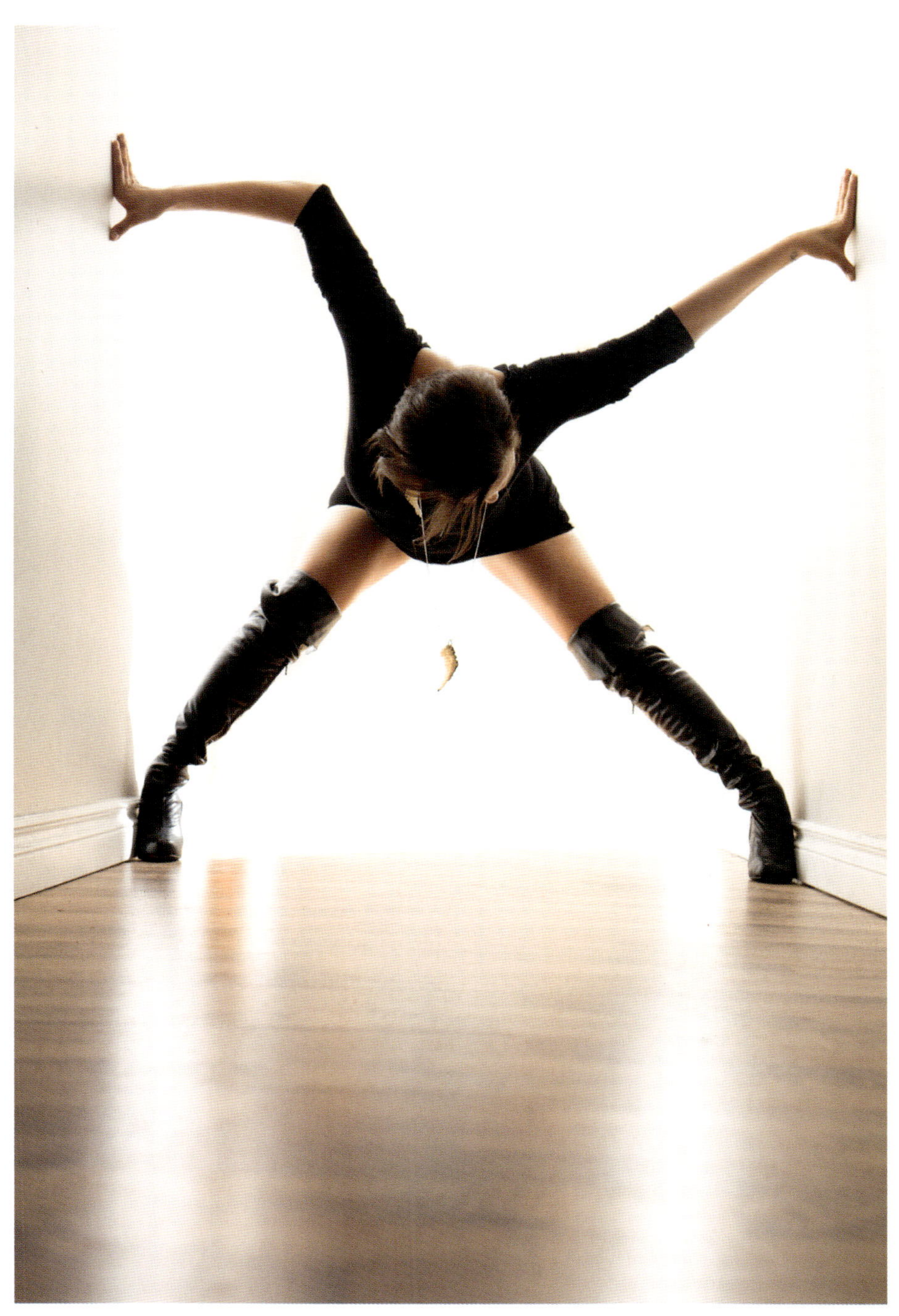

Tanya Tagaq Gillis in Yellowknife, Northwest Territories

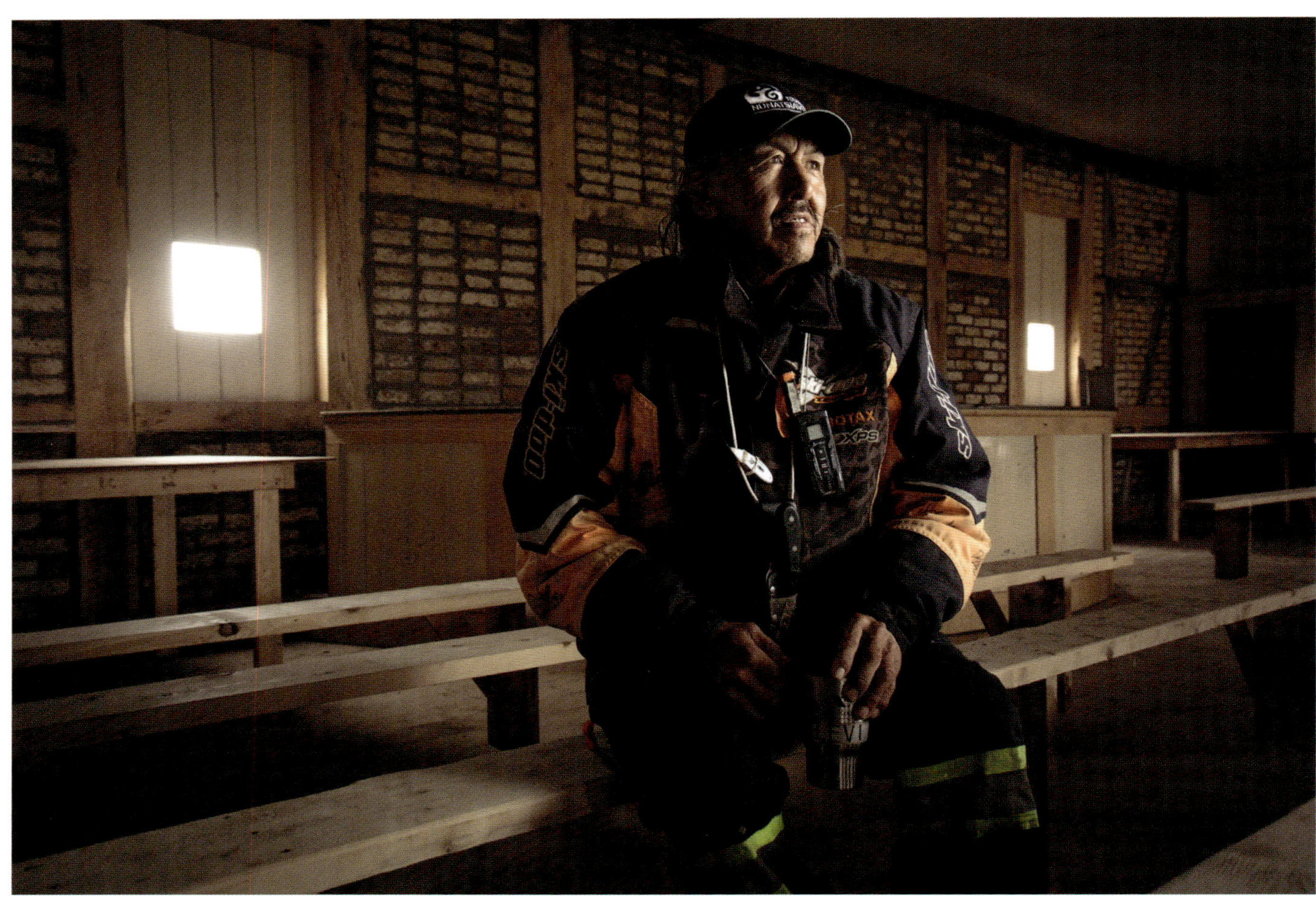

Levi Nochasak in Hebron, Labrador

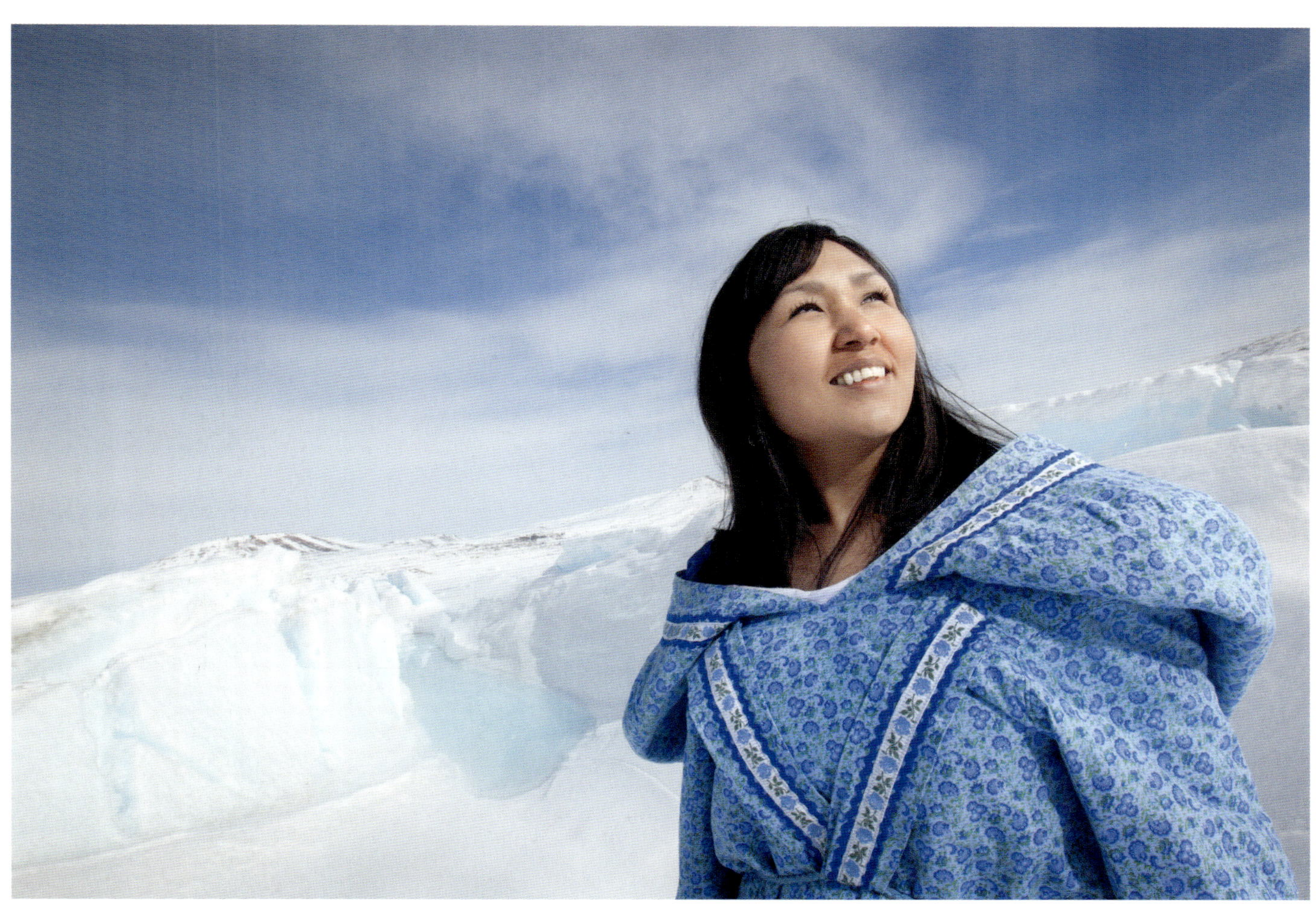

Hershie Enoogoo in Arctic Bay, Nunavut

Greenland Grandeur

I can remember, clearly, the first time I laid eyes on Greenland. I was a university student taking a midwinter trip with a buddy to historic Scotland – the home of my mother's ancestors. Somewhere into the flight, I opened my window shade to look down upon one of the greatest scenes I've witnessed: pink-hued magic light spilling across a seemingly endless ice cap. Seeing this beauty woke me out of my daze, and when I checked, the in-flight screens said we were somewhere over Greenland. *I have to get there, someday*, I thought. But this was before I was a photographer – before I really discovered my love of the outdoors. It was just a dream.

Little did I know, then, that I would eventually return to Greenland many times, and it would become one of my most-loved places to explore in the entire world.

My first trip to Greenland happened sort of by accident: I was in Alert, in the Canadian Arctic, on a story assignment for *Above&Beyond* magazine, and I was at the complete mercy of the Canadian military for my travel in and out. Although my "in" to Alert was straightforward – Trenton to Iqaluit to Resolute to Alert – on the way out they decided to route me through the US Thule Air Base in Greenland, where I would spend a few days waiting for the next flight (eventually to Winnipeg). I was in Greenland! I was so excited, yet photographically it was still out of my grasp: I was confined to the dorms and mess halls of the air force base. I could see rugged hills and tundra in the distance, and I knew there was so much beauty just outside the base perimeter, but it was, unfortunately, off limits. *Next time*.

Next time didn't happen for about another five or six years, when I would begin a pretty much yearly pilgrimage to the Ilulissat and Disko Island areas of Greenland both for my own personal shooting and for the photo workshop trips I co-lead with Paul Zizka and others.

Through these trips I discovered a world of beauty containing some of the most incredible sights I have yet seen in this world. Greenland definitely has similarities to other Arctic places I have been, but I feel the *rugged* factor is amplified. Some of the world's largest icebergs break off from the Ilulissat Icefjord, and these giants line many of the bays and shores of southwestern Greenland; its coastline sports some of the unique natural formations I've had the chance to photograph. From incredible basalt columns to hulking hills and mountains to epic sea cliffs to incredibly picturesque waterfalls to the spirit and hospitality of the Greenlandic people, Greenland is a country and a landmass that really has it all from the photographer's perspective.

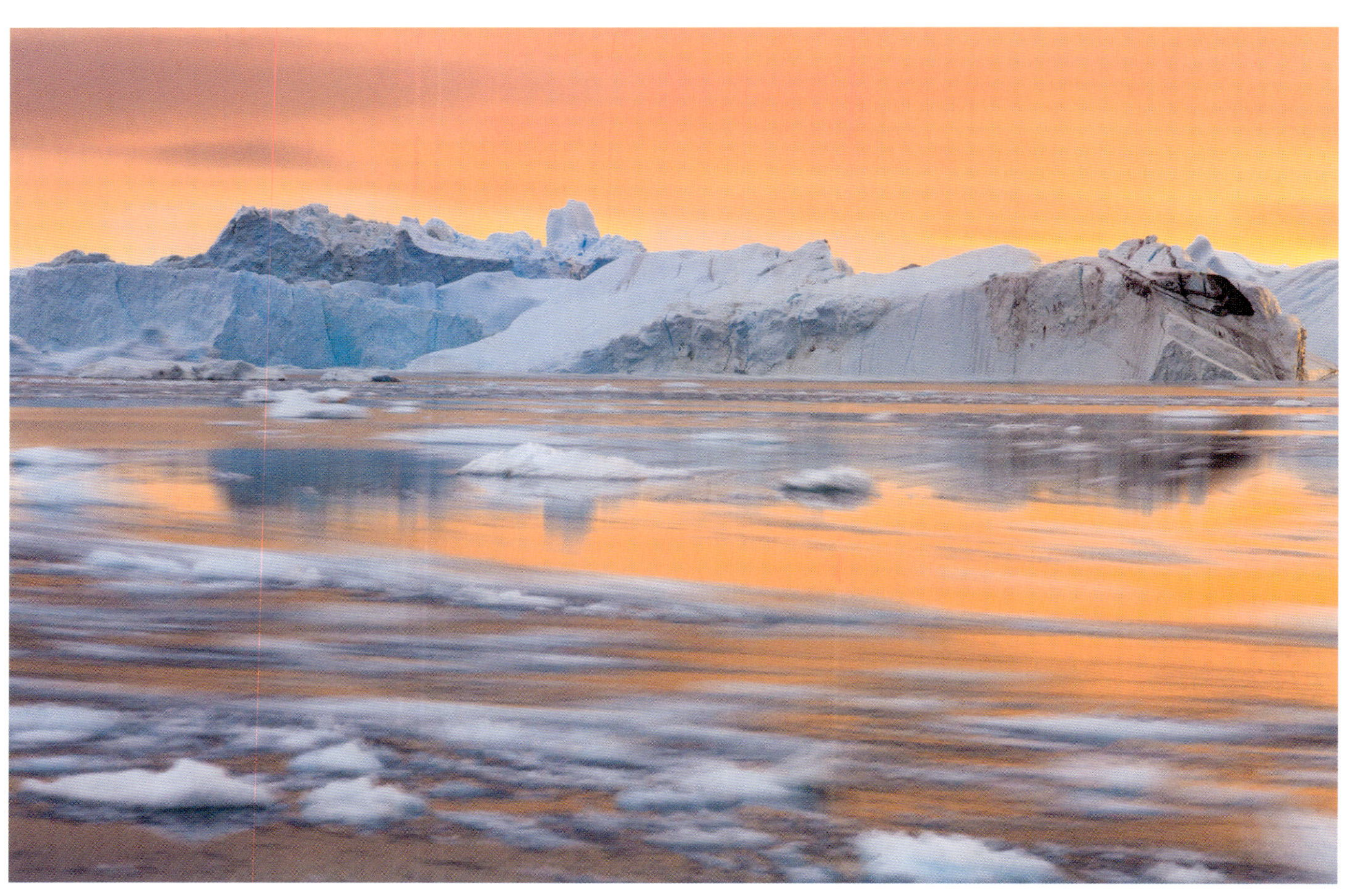

Fantasia
Ilulissat, Greenland

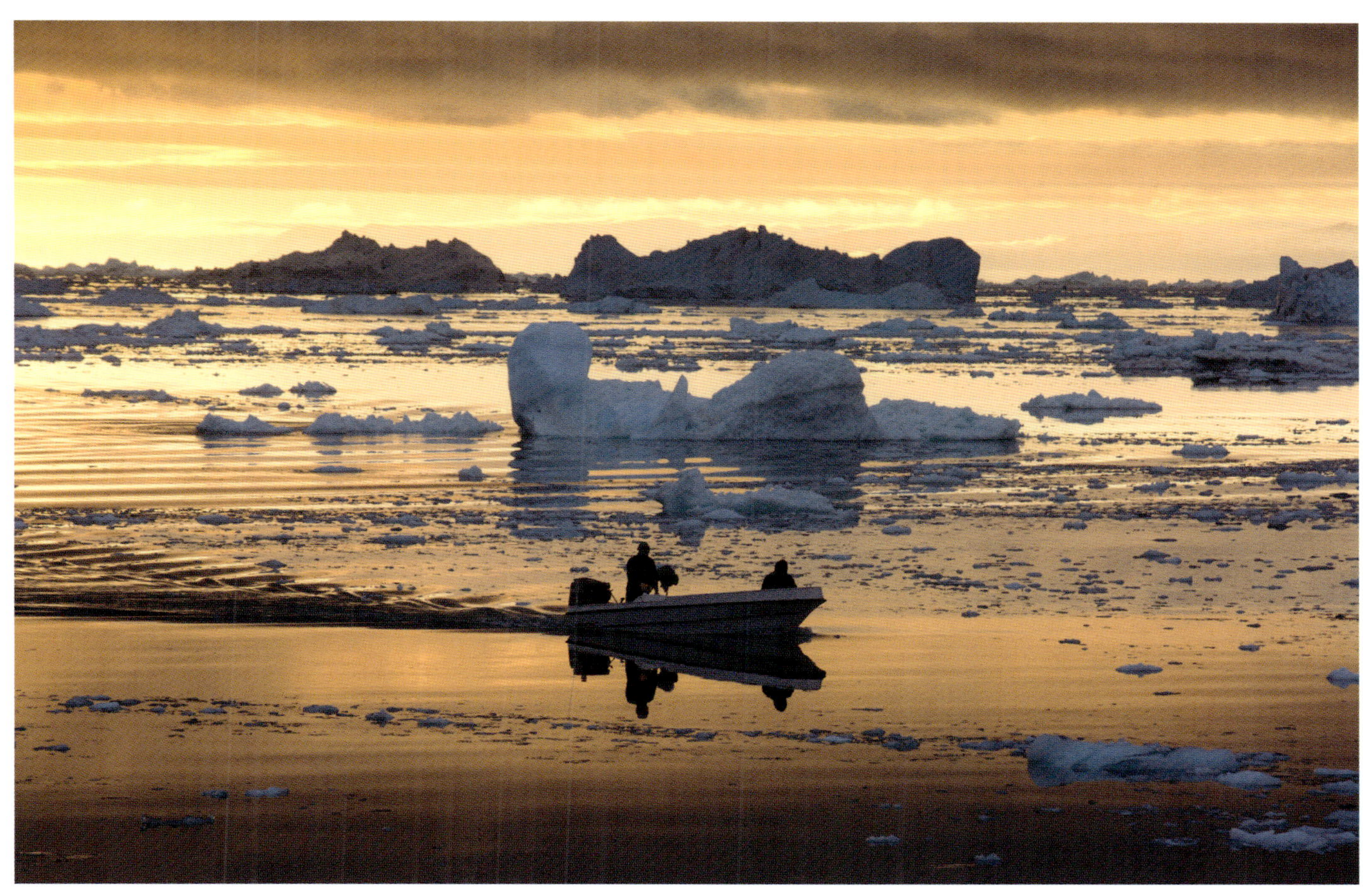

The Golden Highway
Ilulissat, Greenland

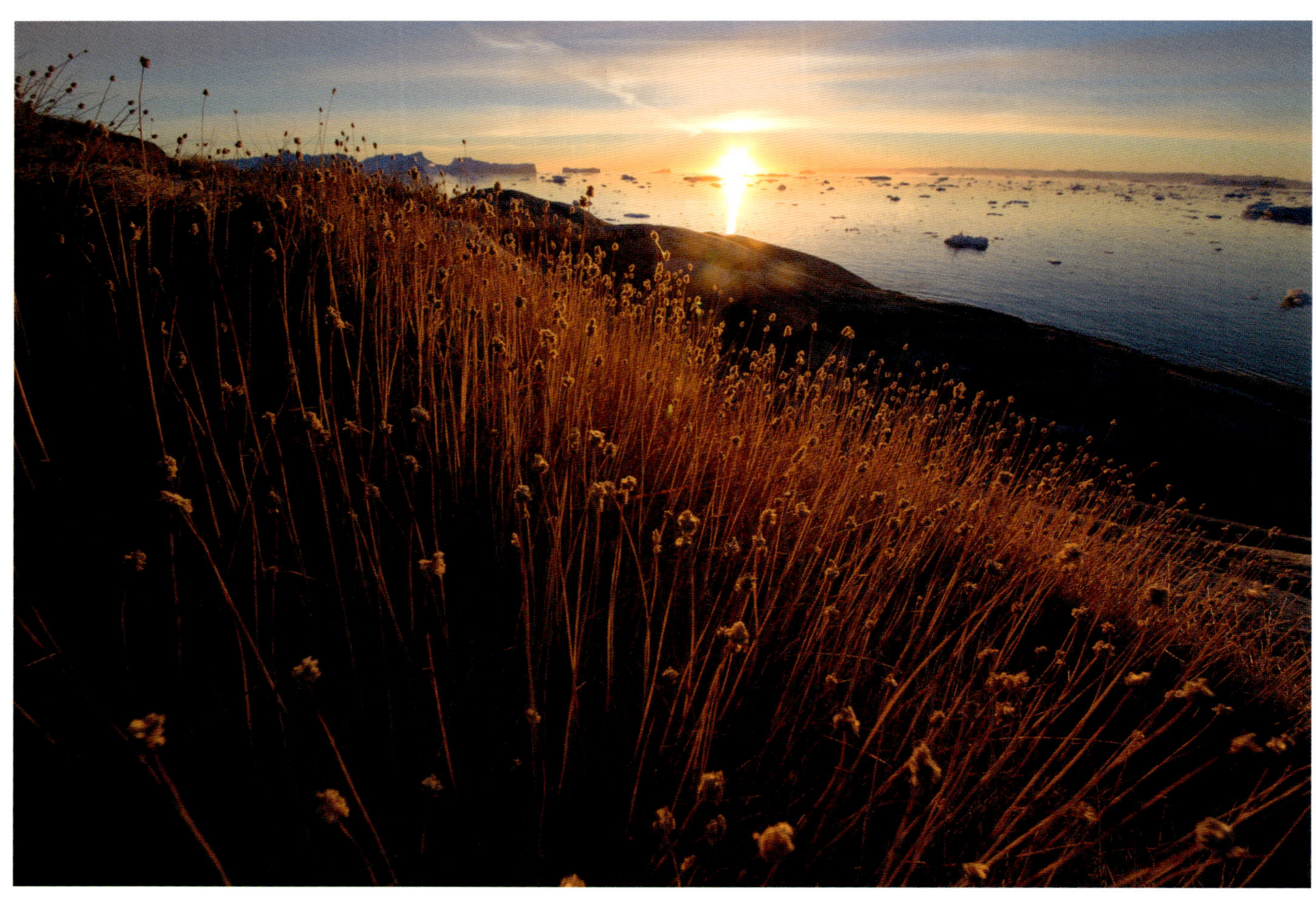

Greenland Golden Light

Ilulissat, Greenland

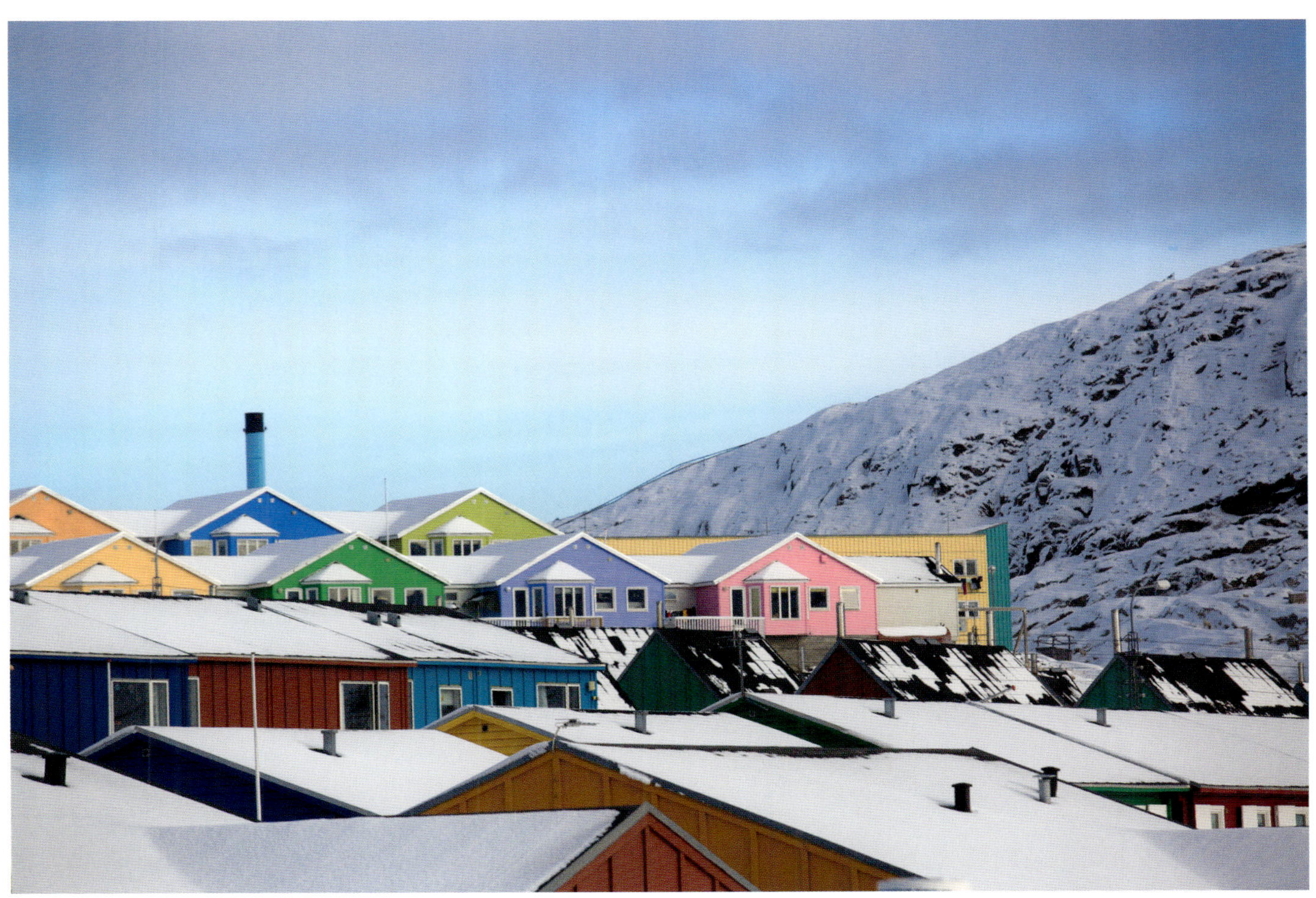

Little Boxes
Ilulissat, Greenland

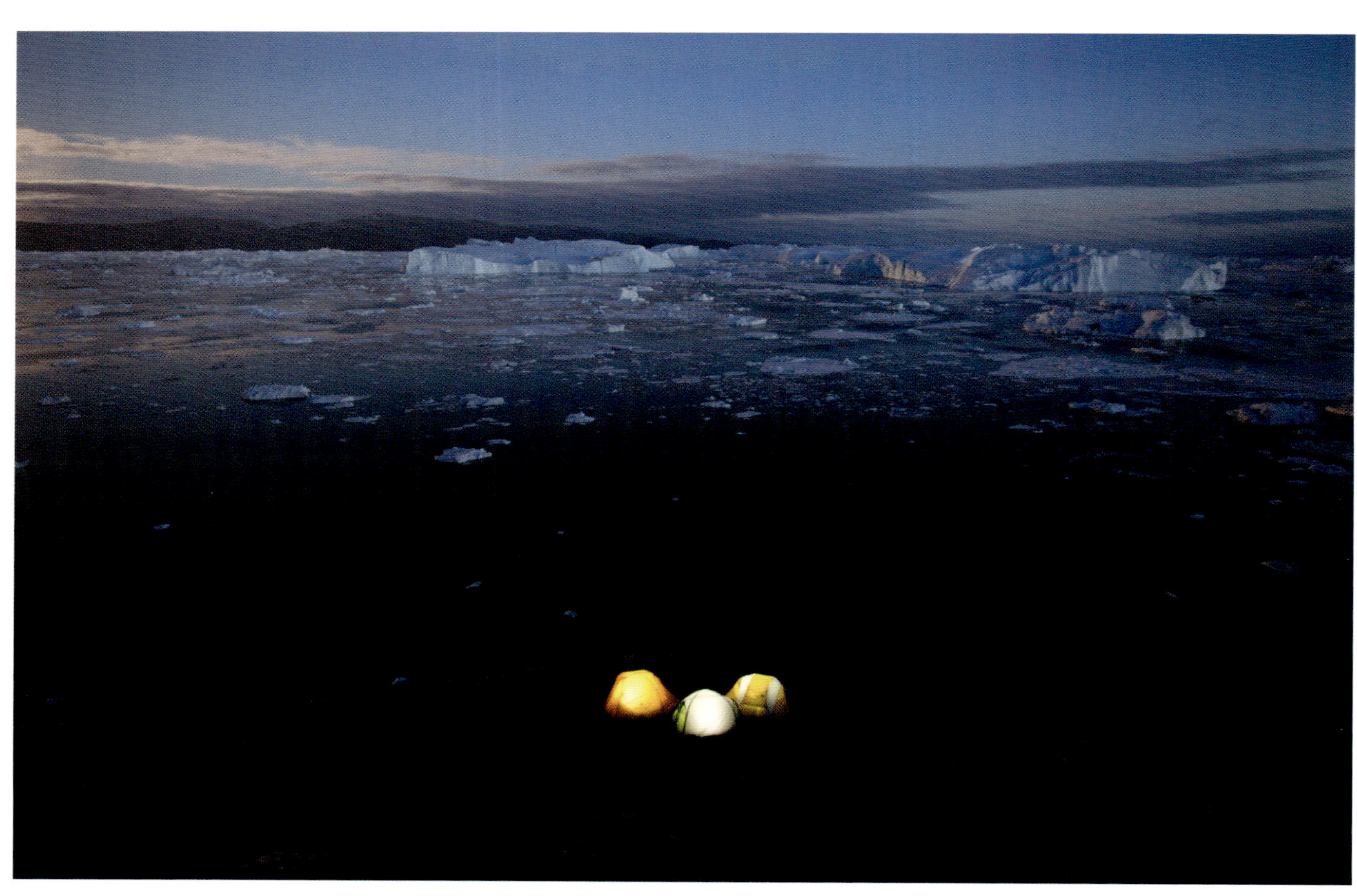

Silence of the Night
Ilulissat, Greenland

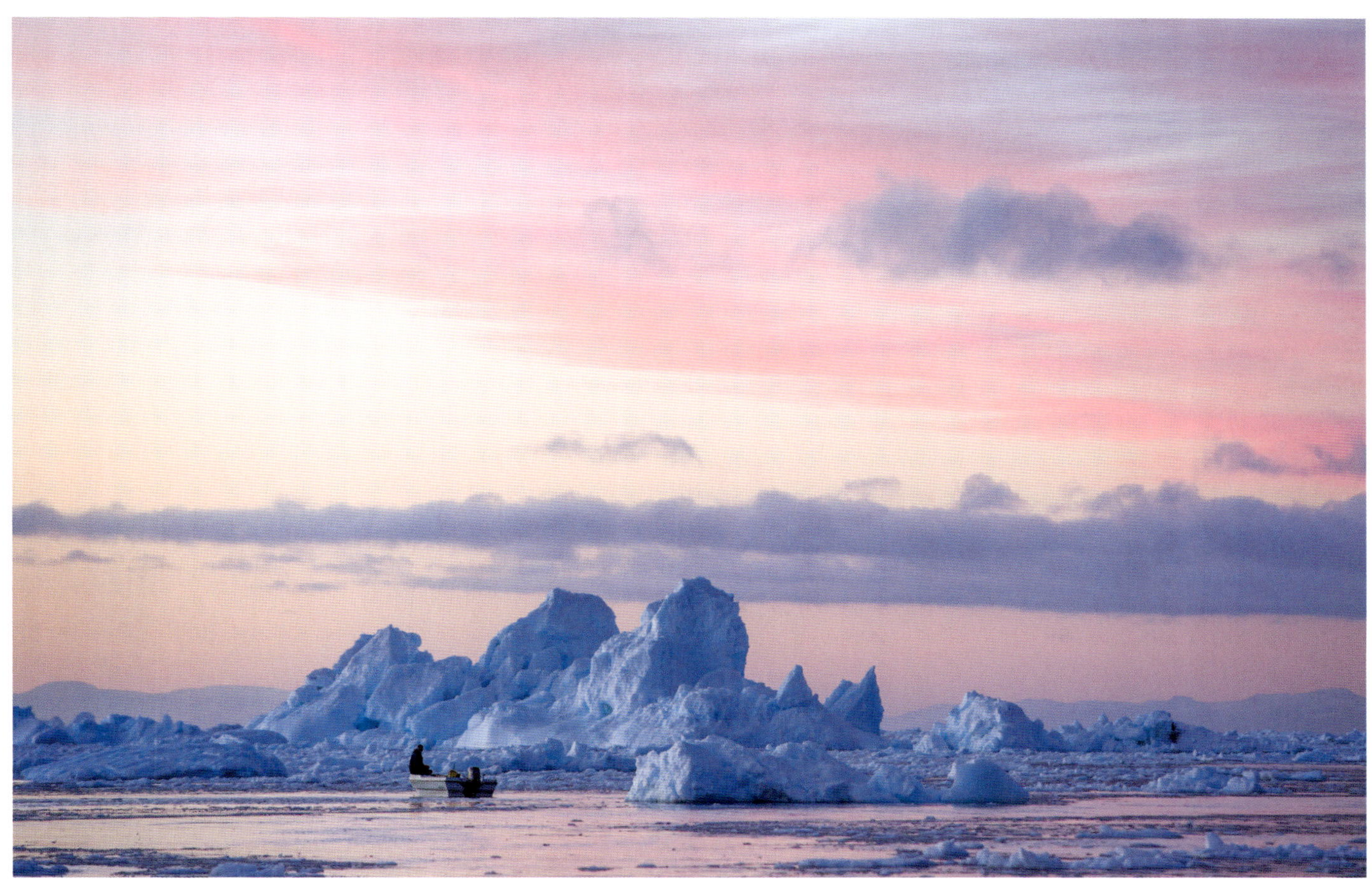

Go Gently into That Good Night
Ilulissat, Greenland

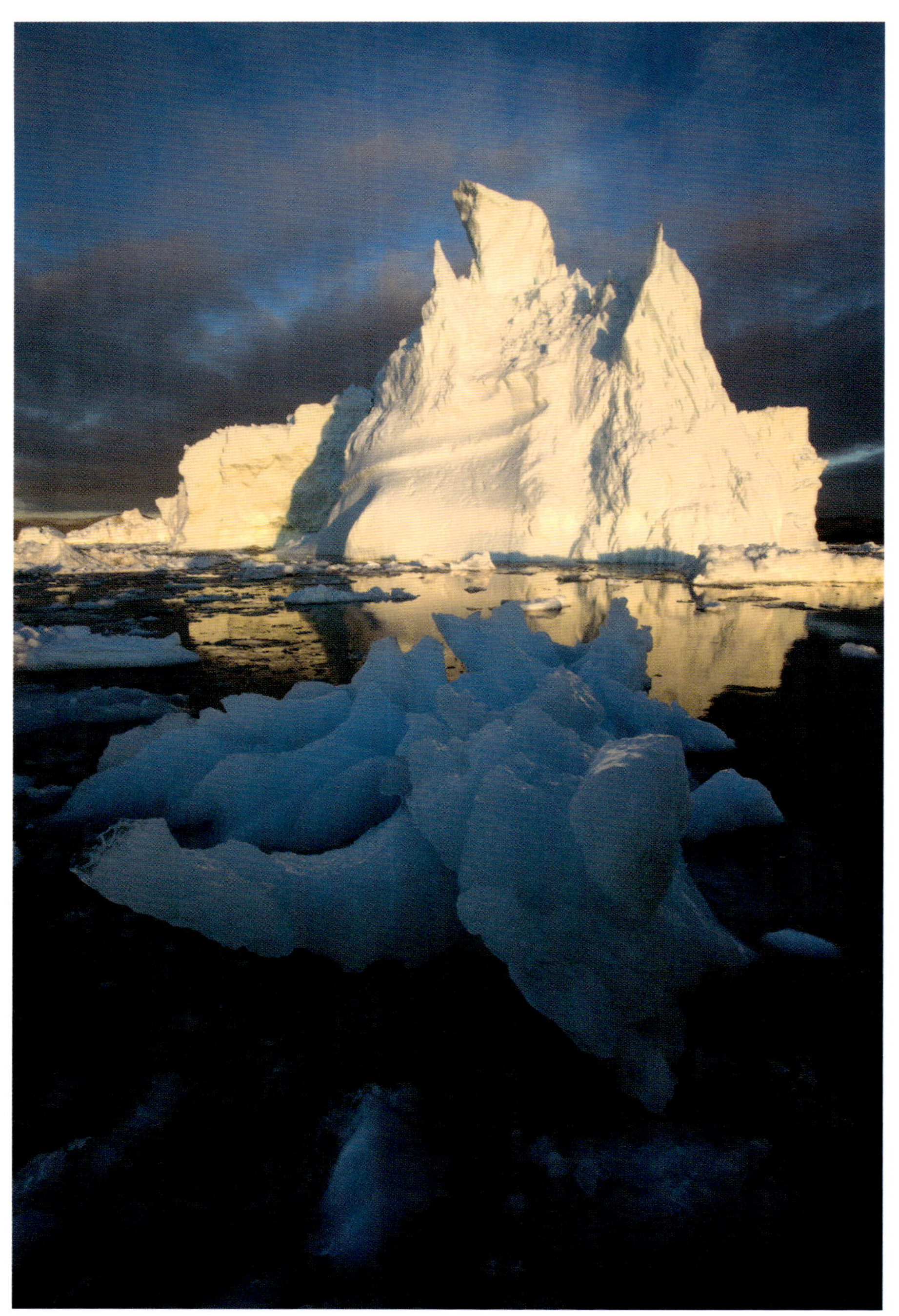

The Fortress

Ilulissat Icefjord, Greenland

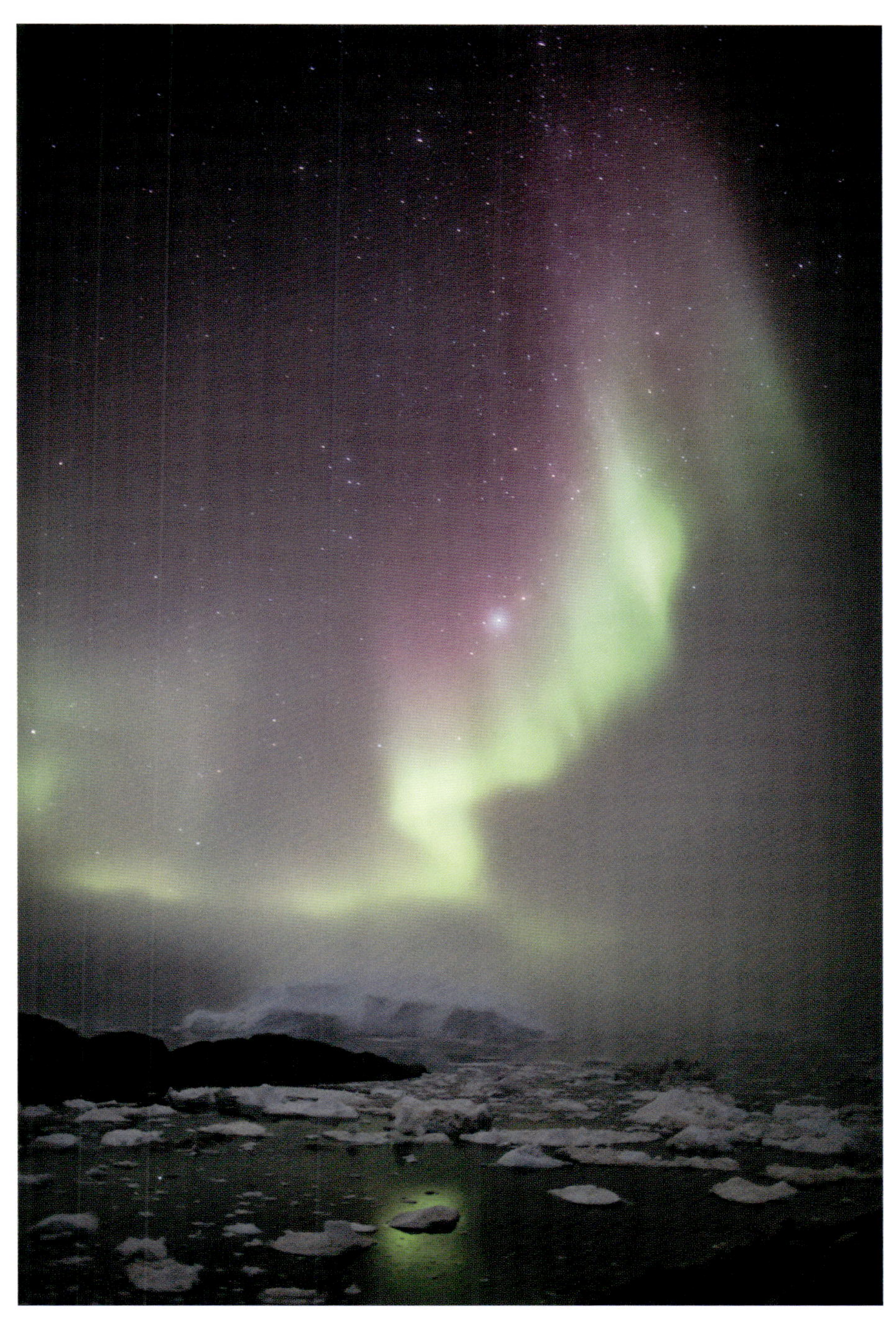

One Berg to Rule Them All
Ilulissat Icefjord, Greenland

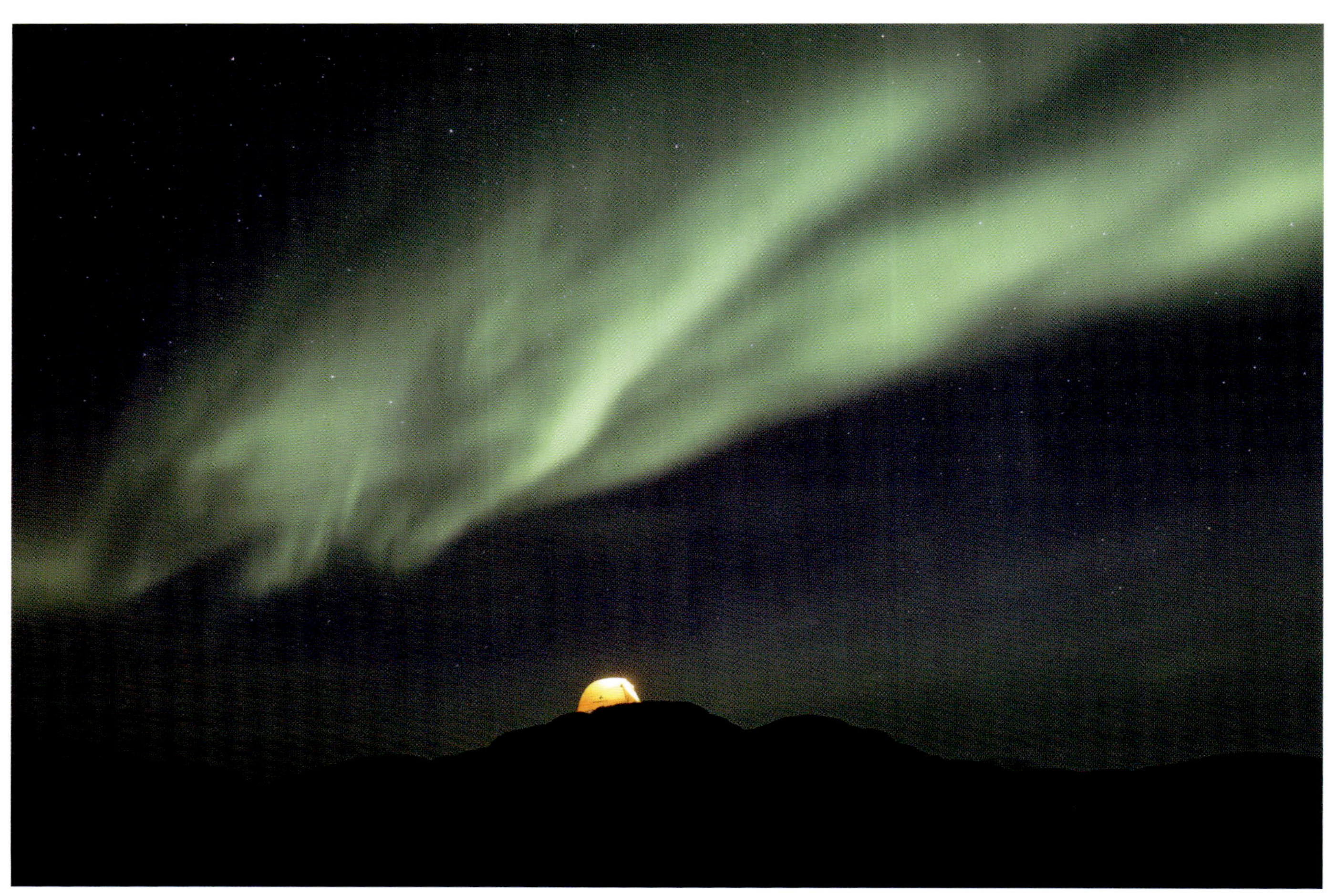

Holy Night
Ilulissat, Greenland

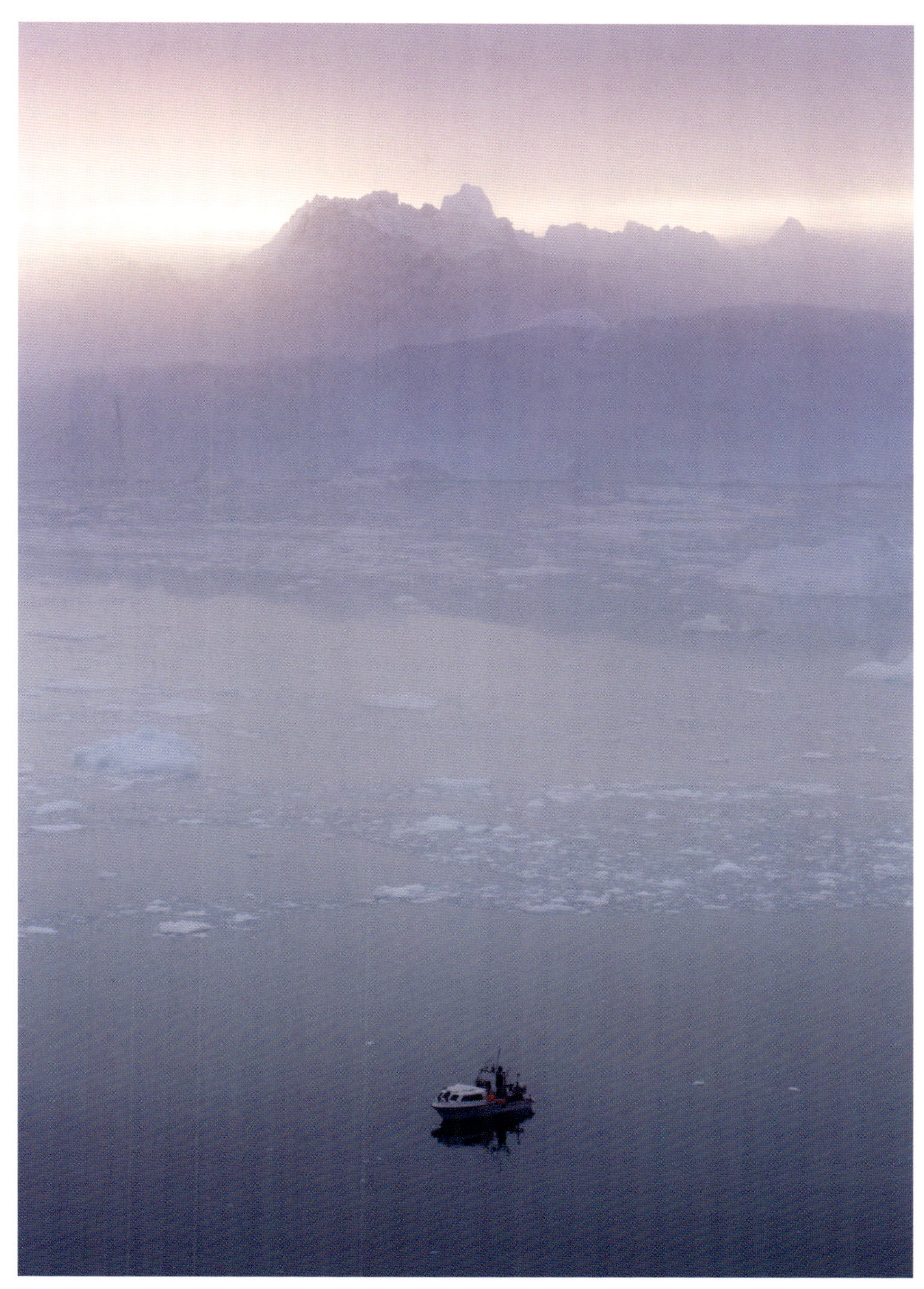

Foggy Dawn
Ilulissat, Greenland

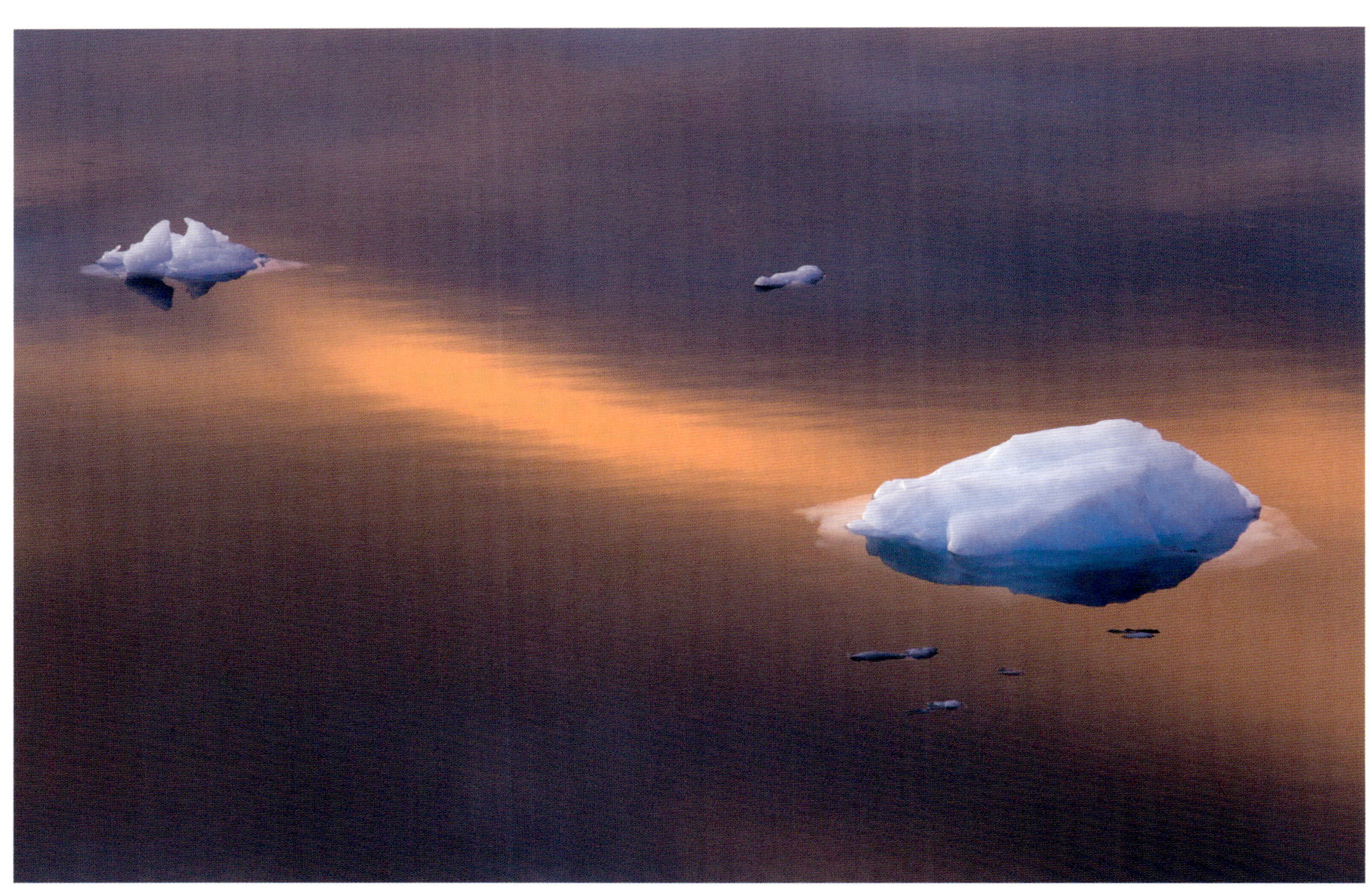

We're All in This Together
Ilulissat Icefjord, Greenland

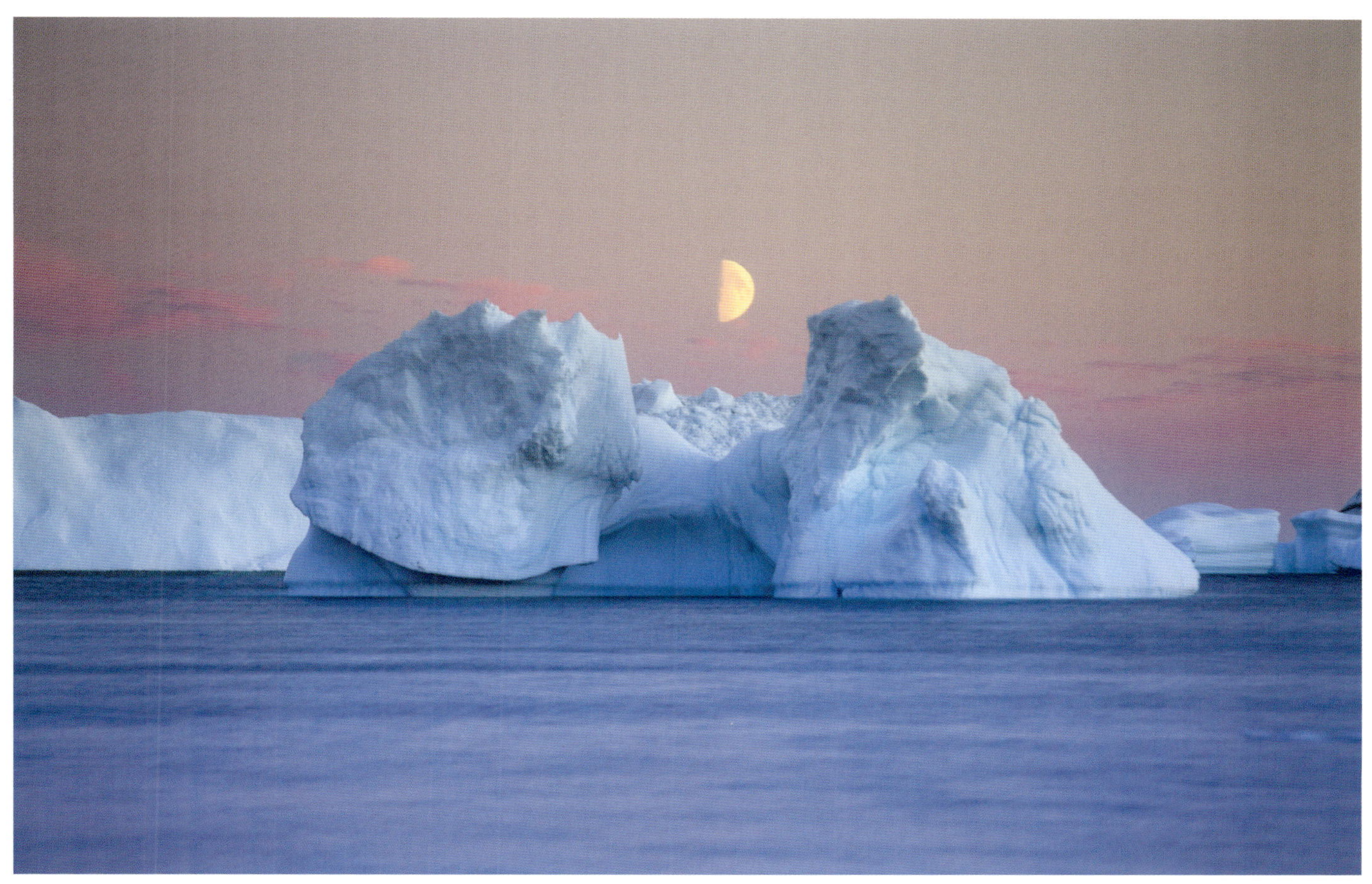

The Good Night
Qeqertarsuaq, Disko Island, Greenland

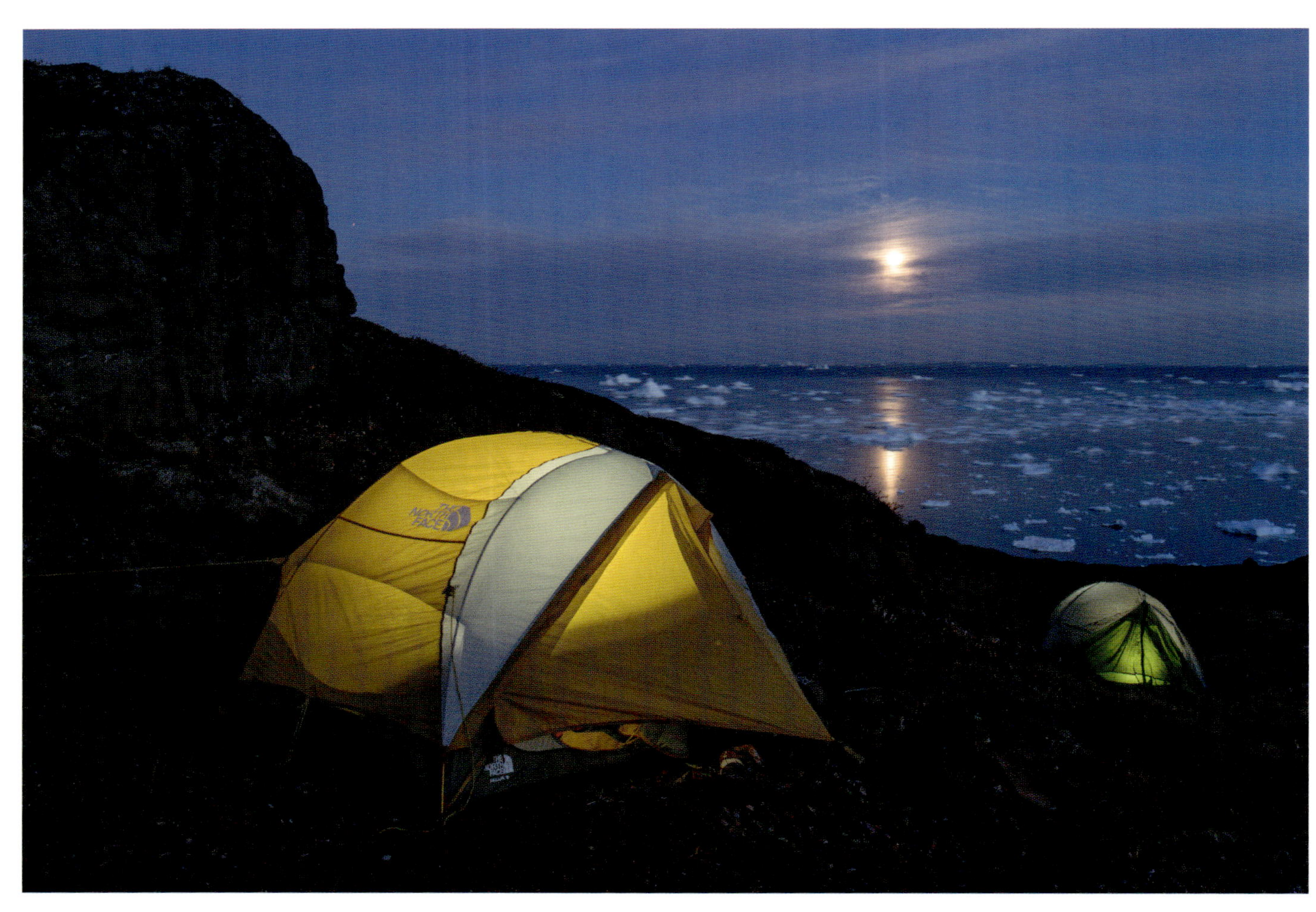

Side by Side
Disko Island, Greenland

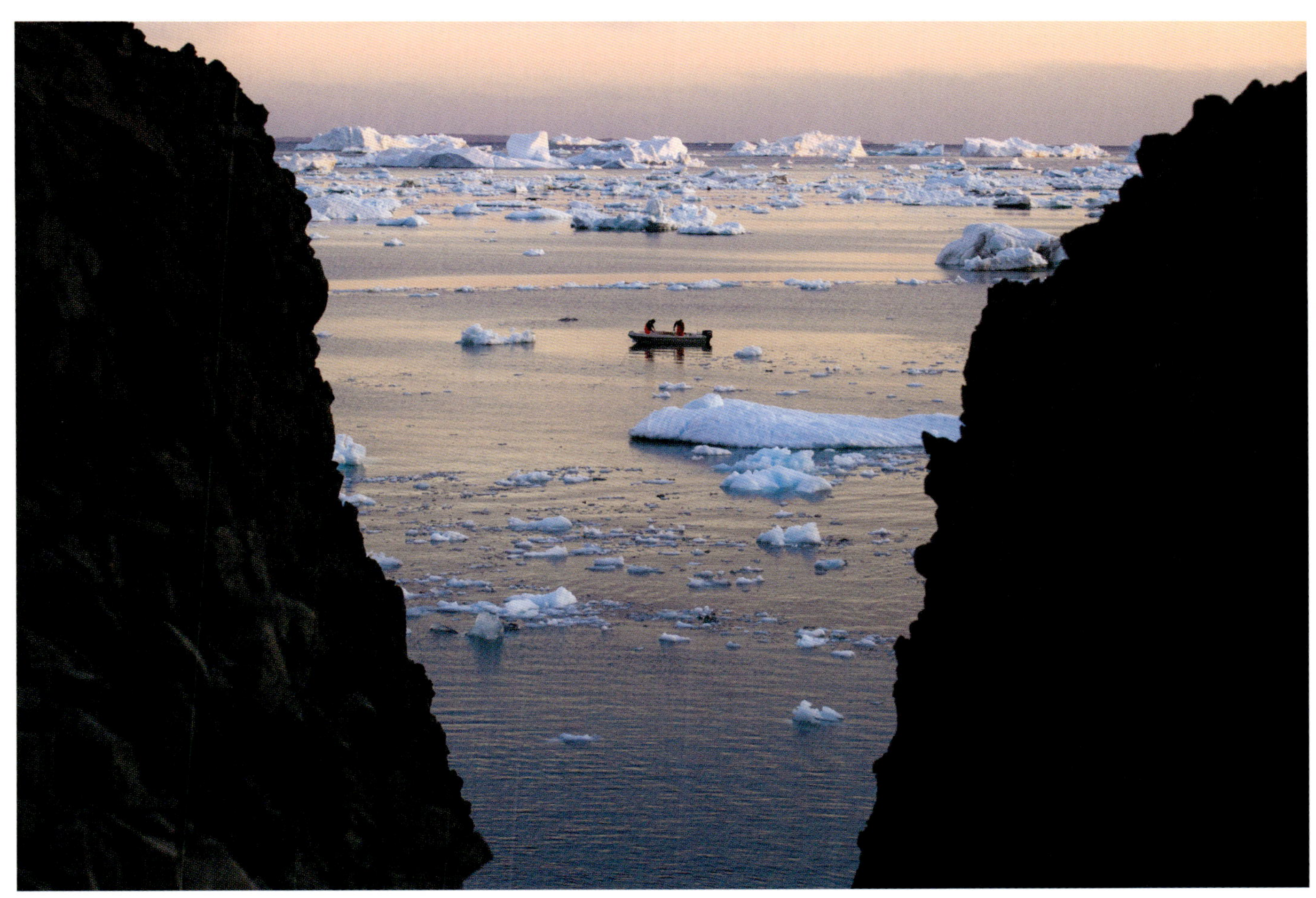

Two by Two

Disko Island, Greenland

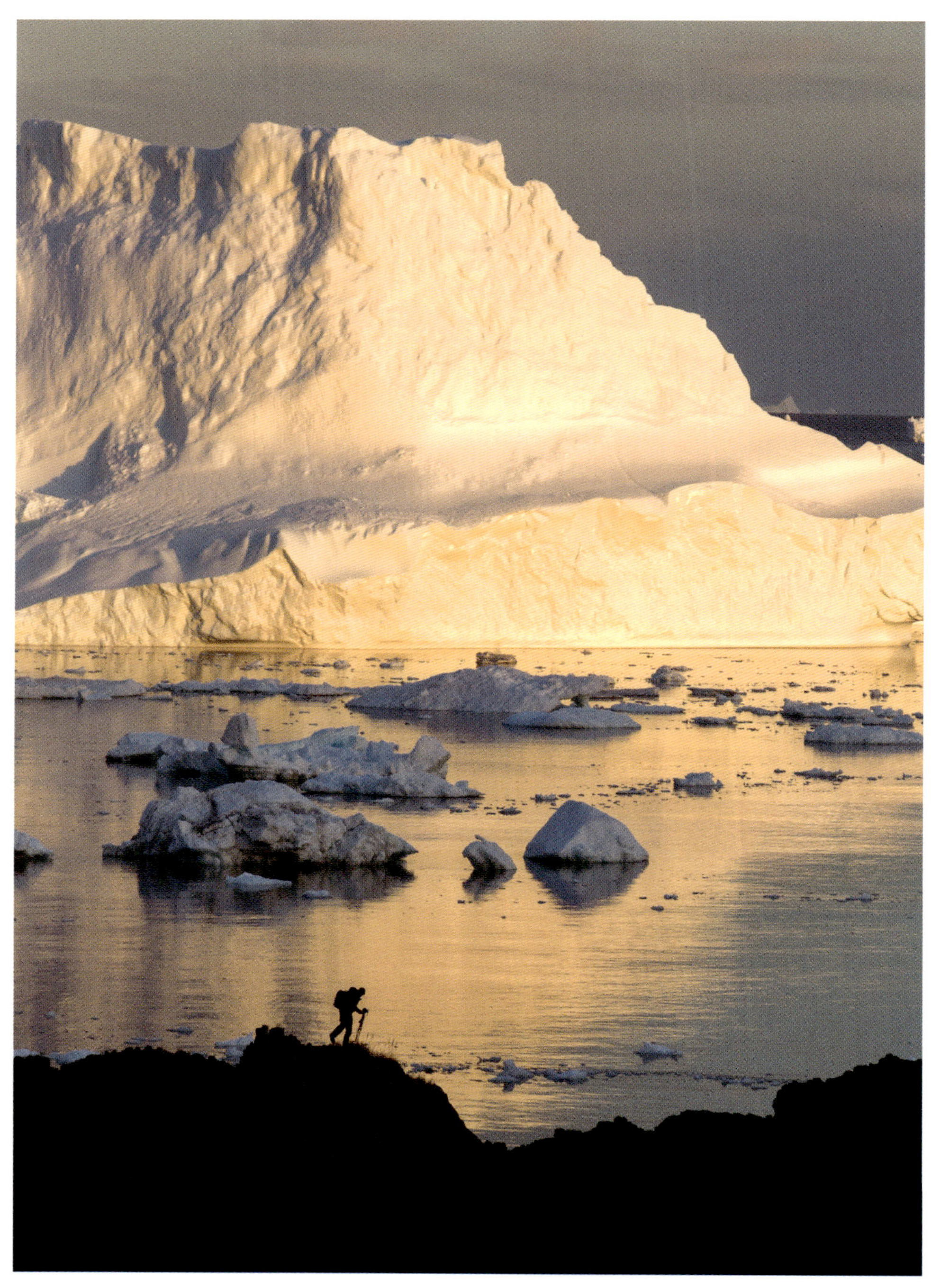

Go Your Own Way

Paul Zizka on Disko Island, Greenland

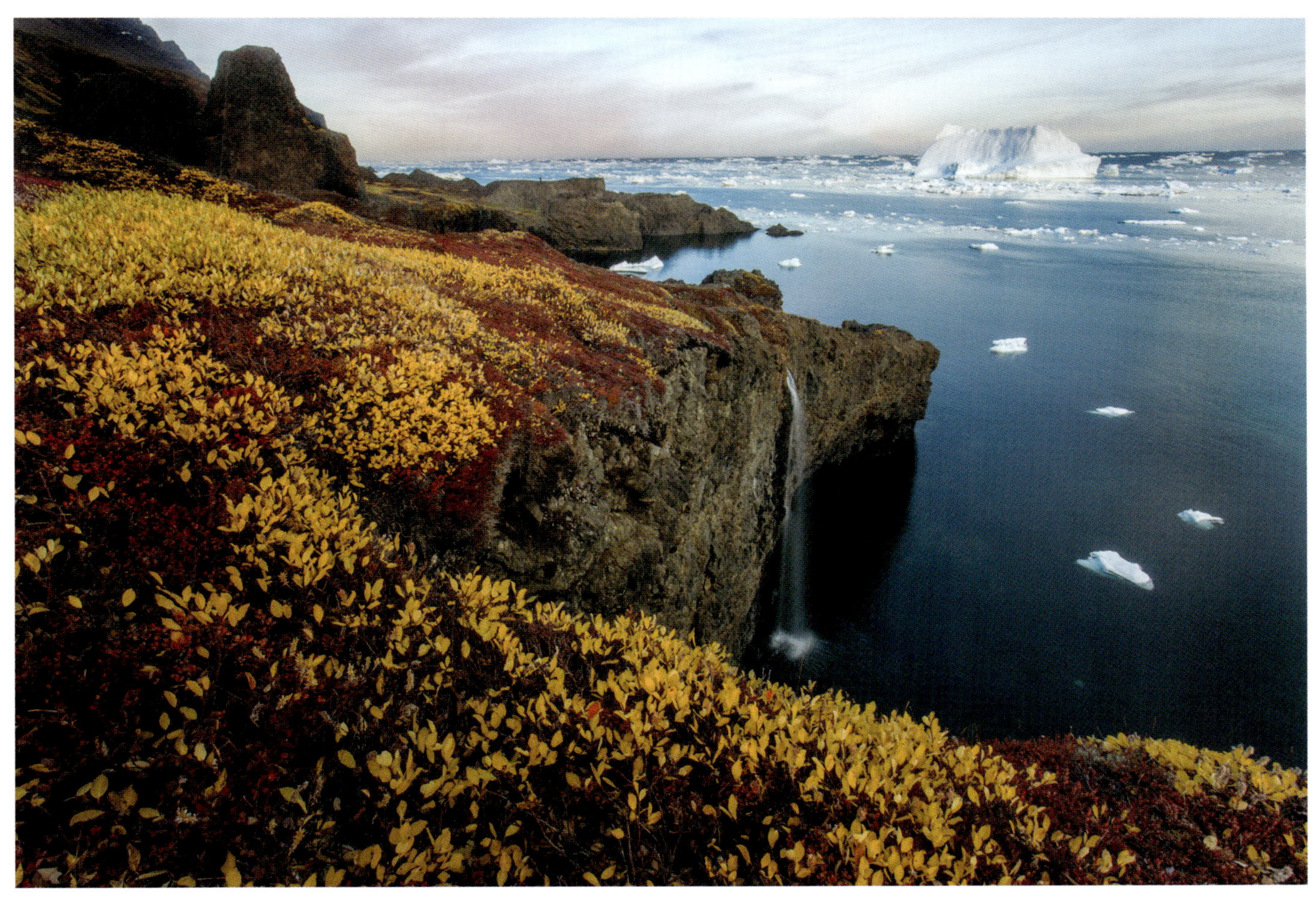

Arctic Eden
Disko Island, Greenland

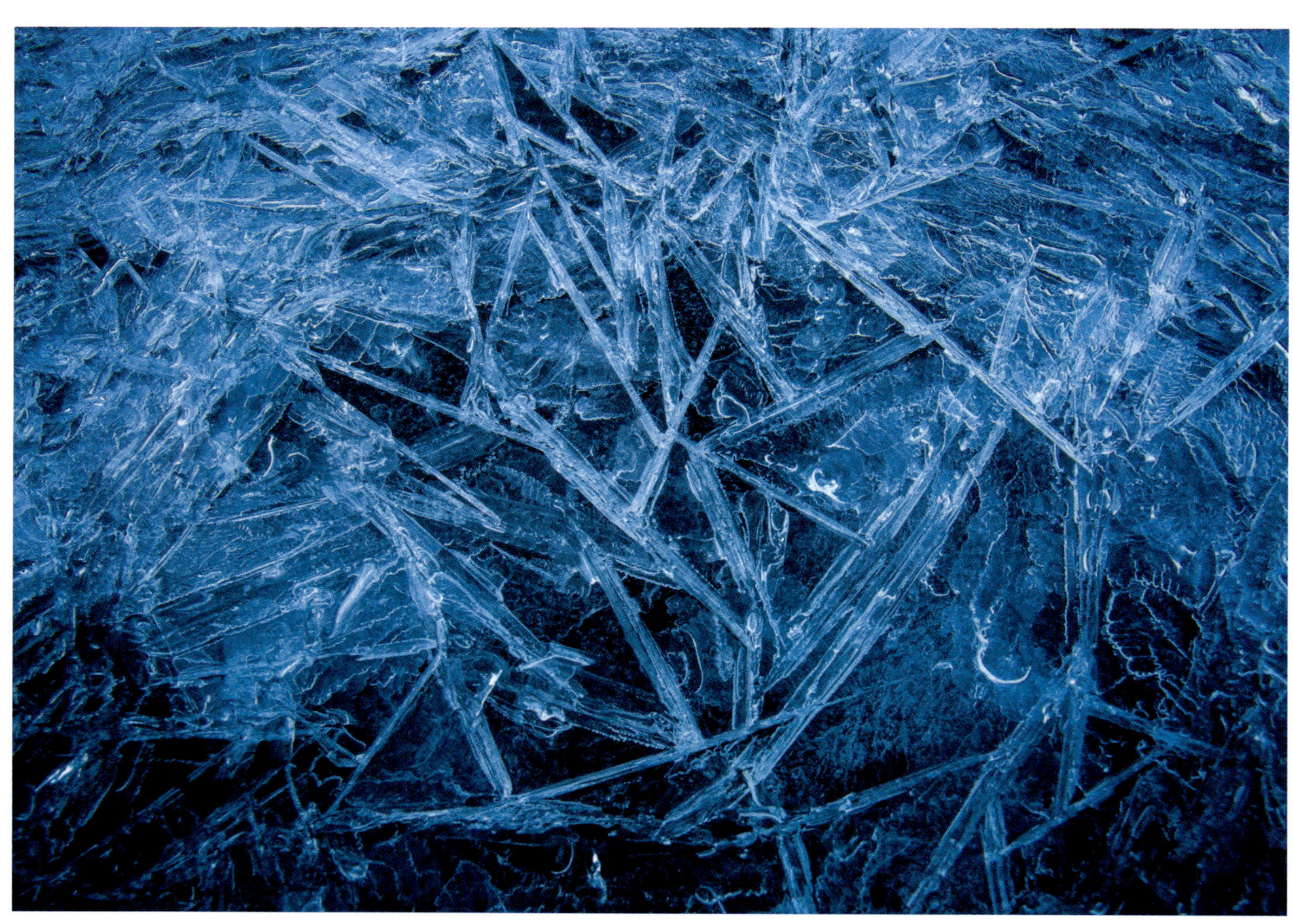

Abstractions

Disko Island, Greenland

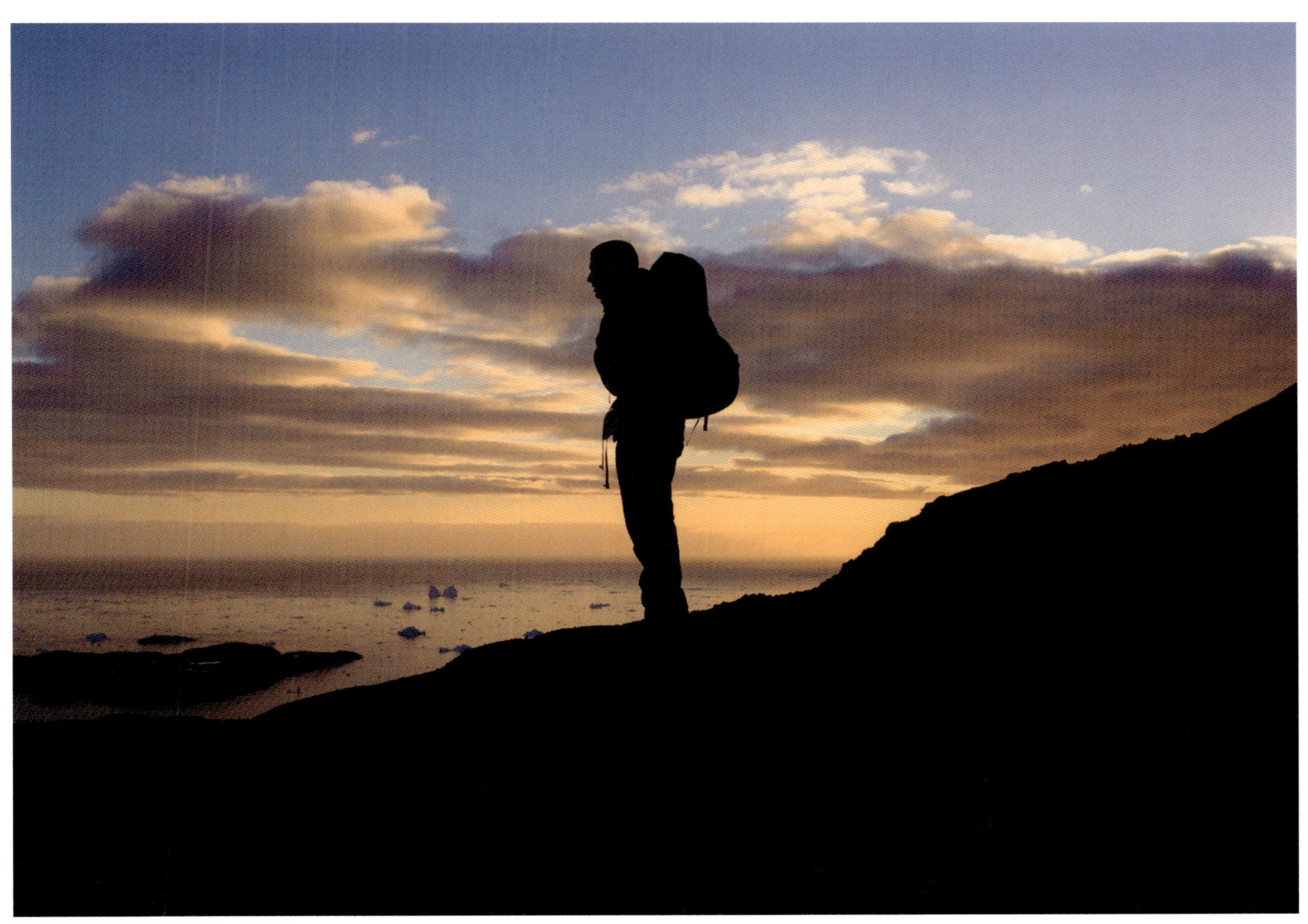

Evening Glory

Stephen DesRoches on Disko Island, Greenland

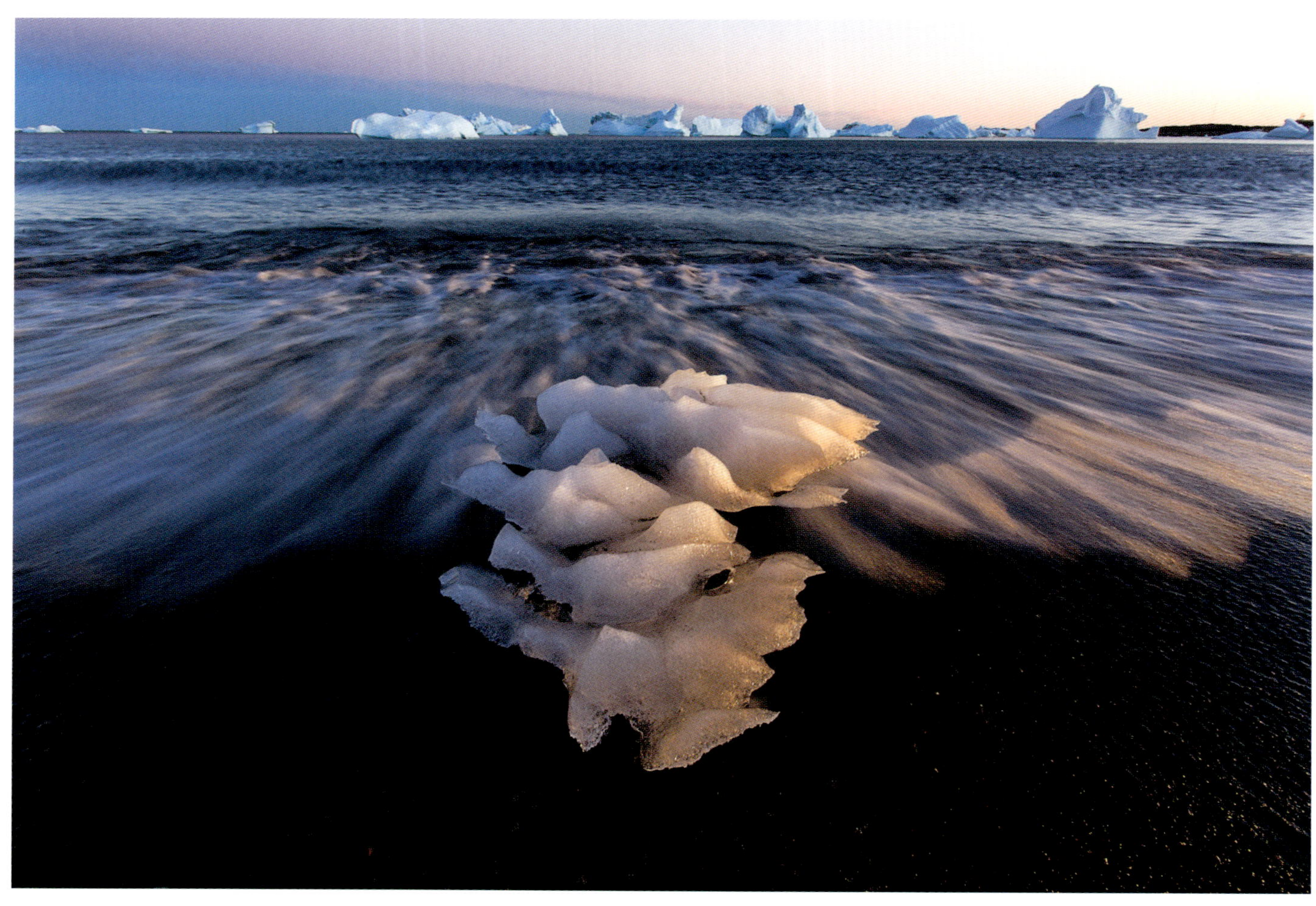

Taking Flight

Qeqertarsuaq, Disko Island, Greenland

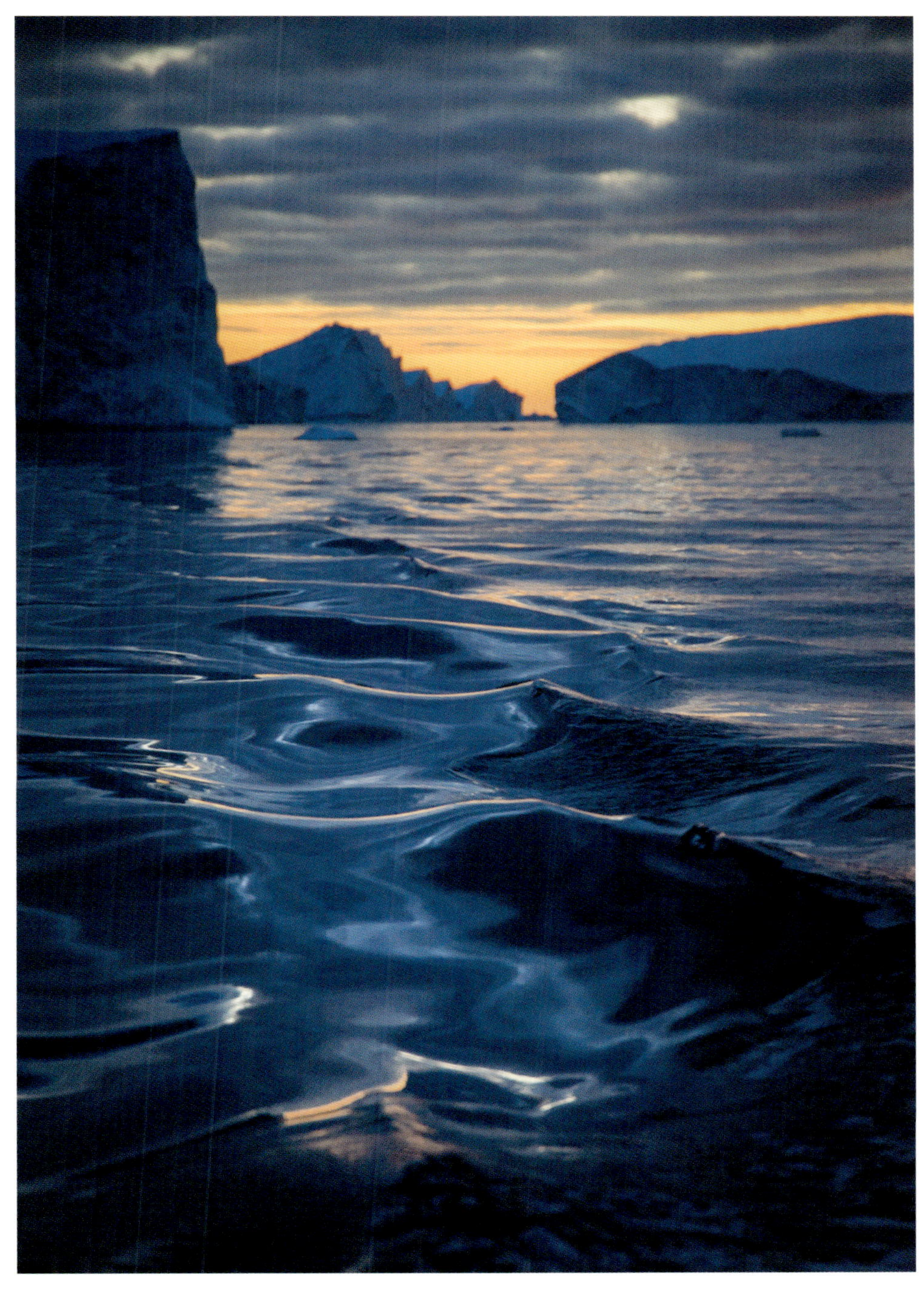

Nightswimming
Ilulissat, Greenland

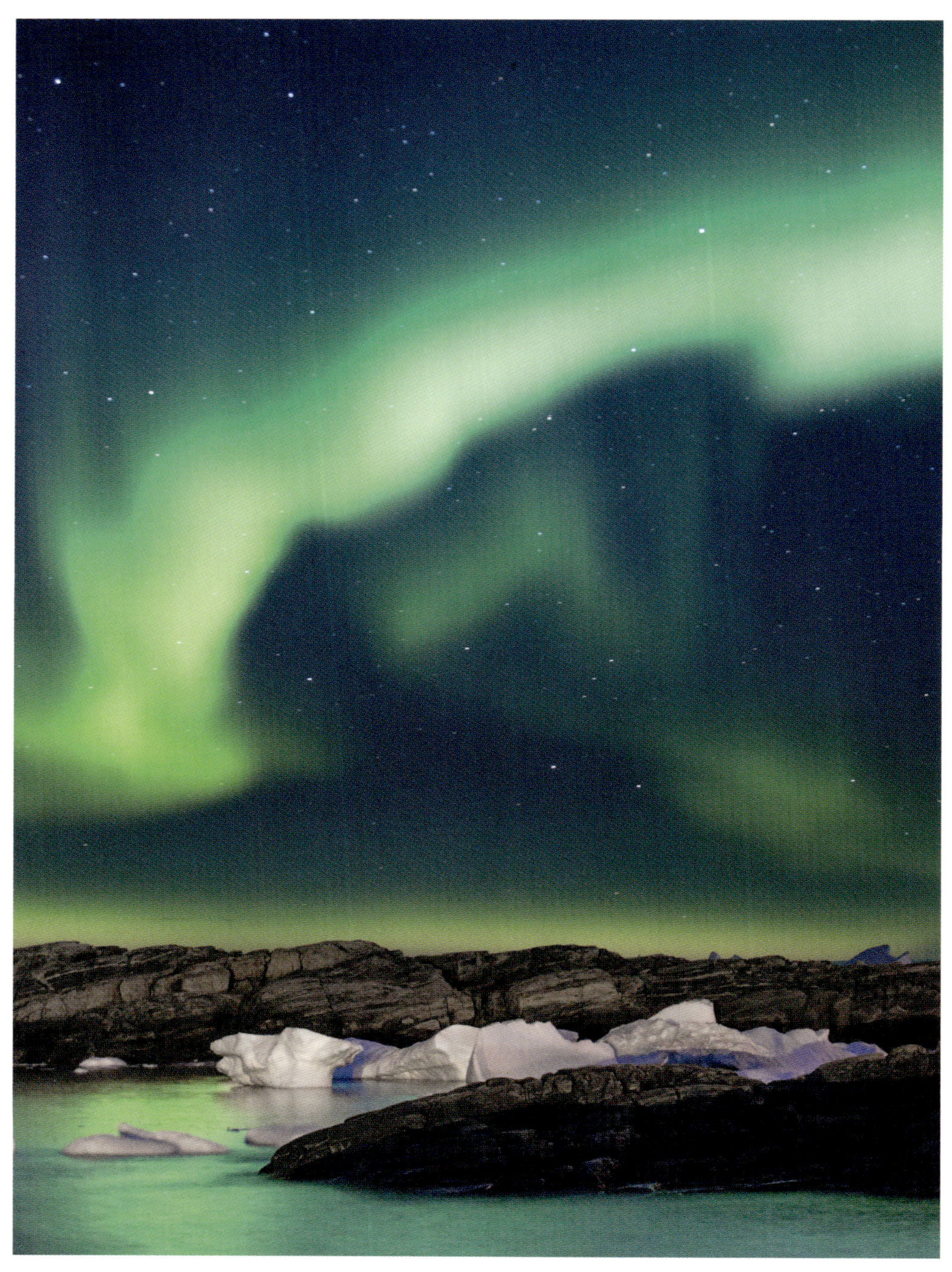

The Diskoball

Qeqertarsuaq, Disko Island, Greenland

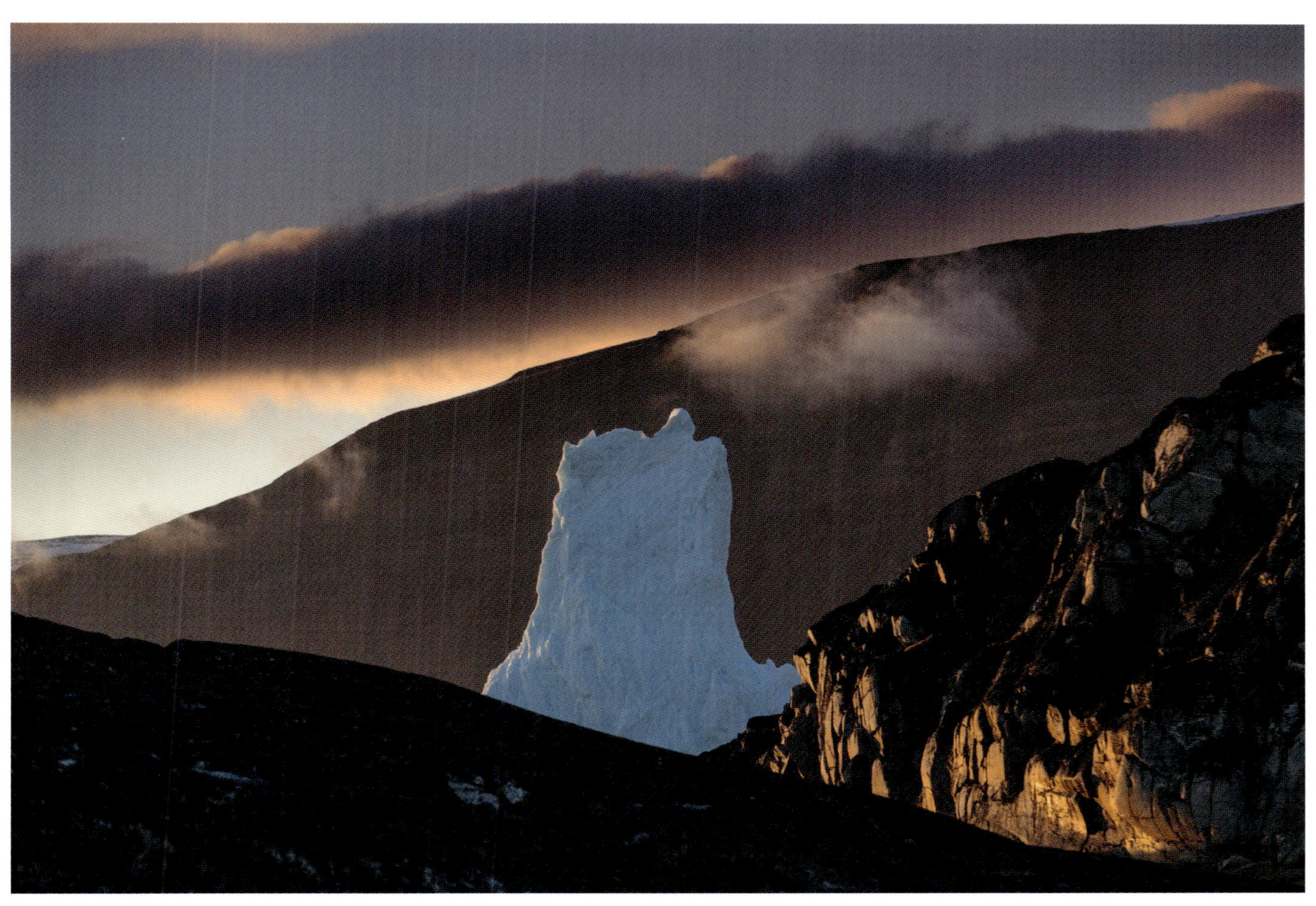

Stuck in the Middle
Qeqertarsuaq, Disko Island, Greenland

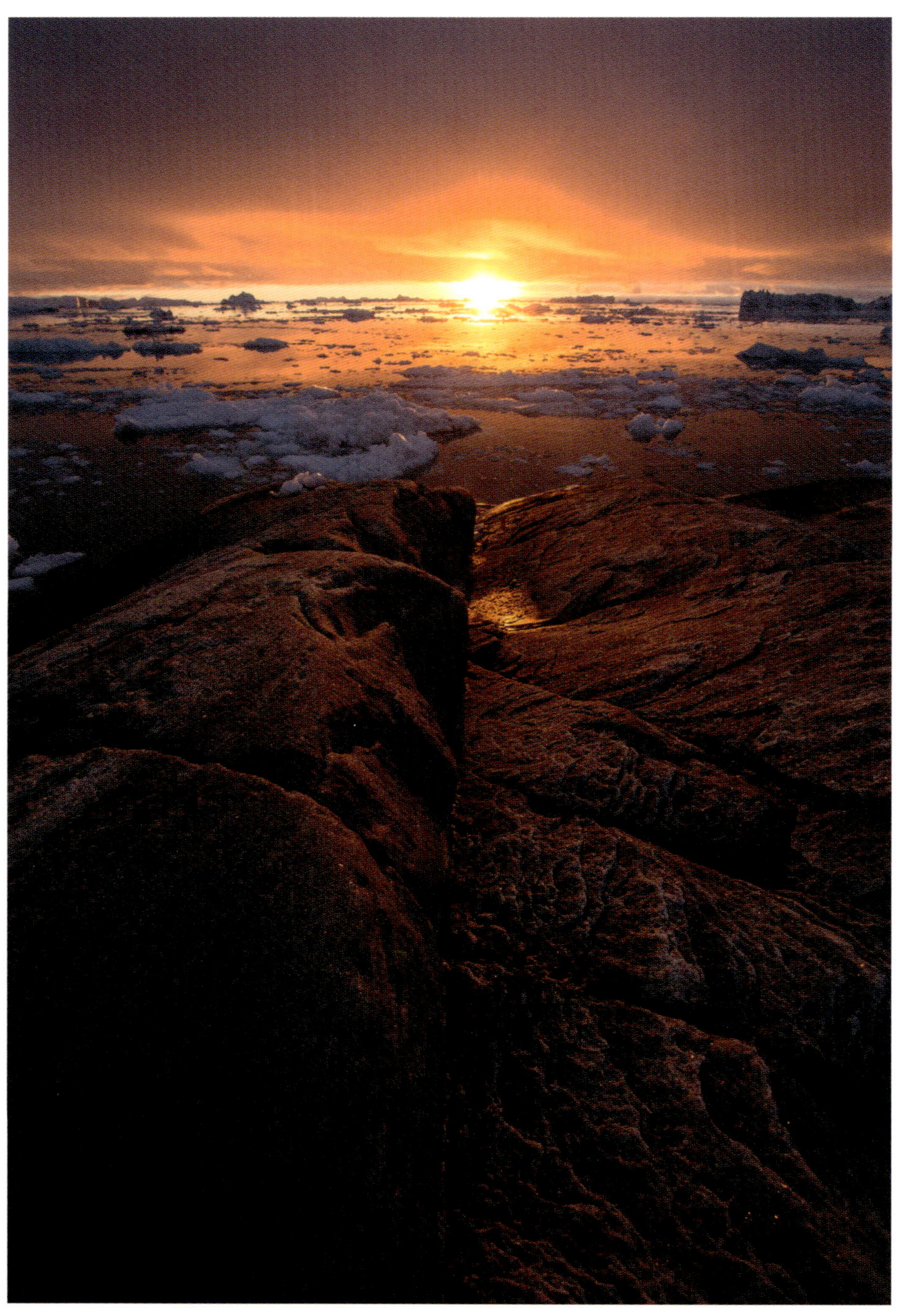

Last Light before an Arctic Night
Ilulissat, Greenland

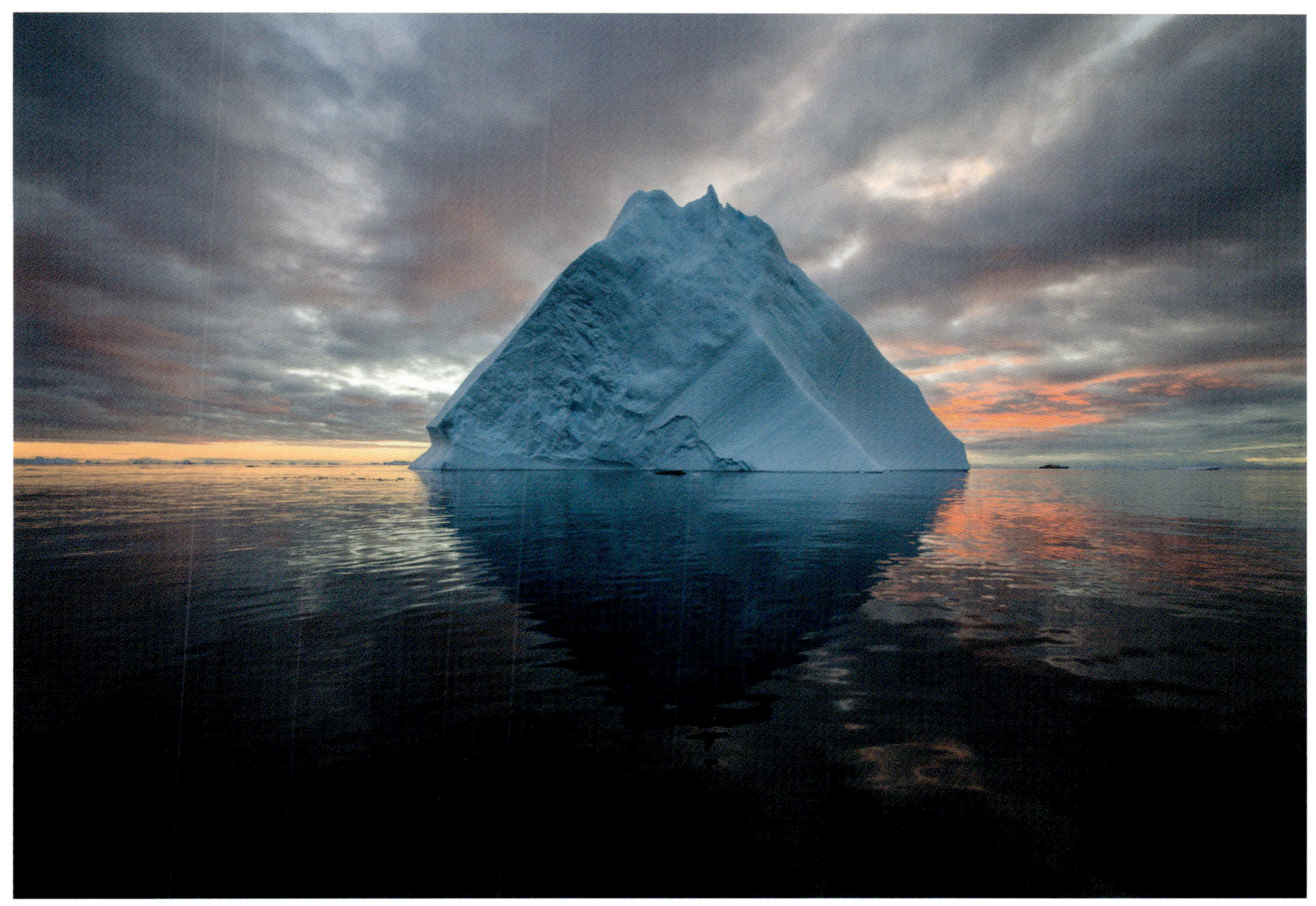

(In the Sky) With Diamonds
Ilulissat, Greenland

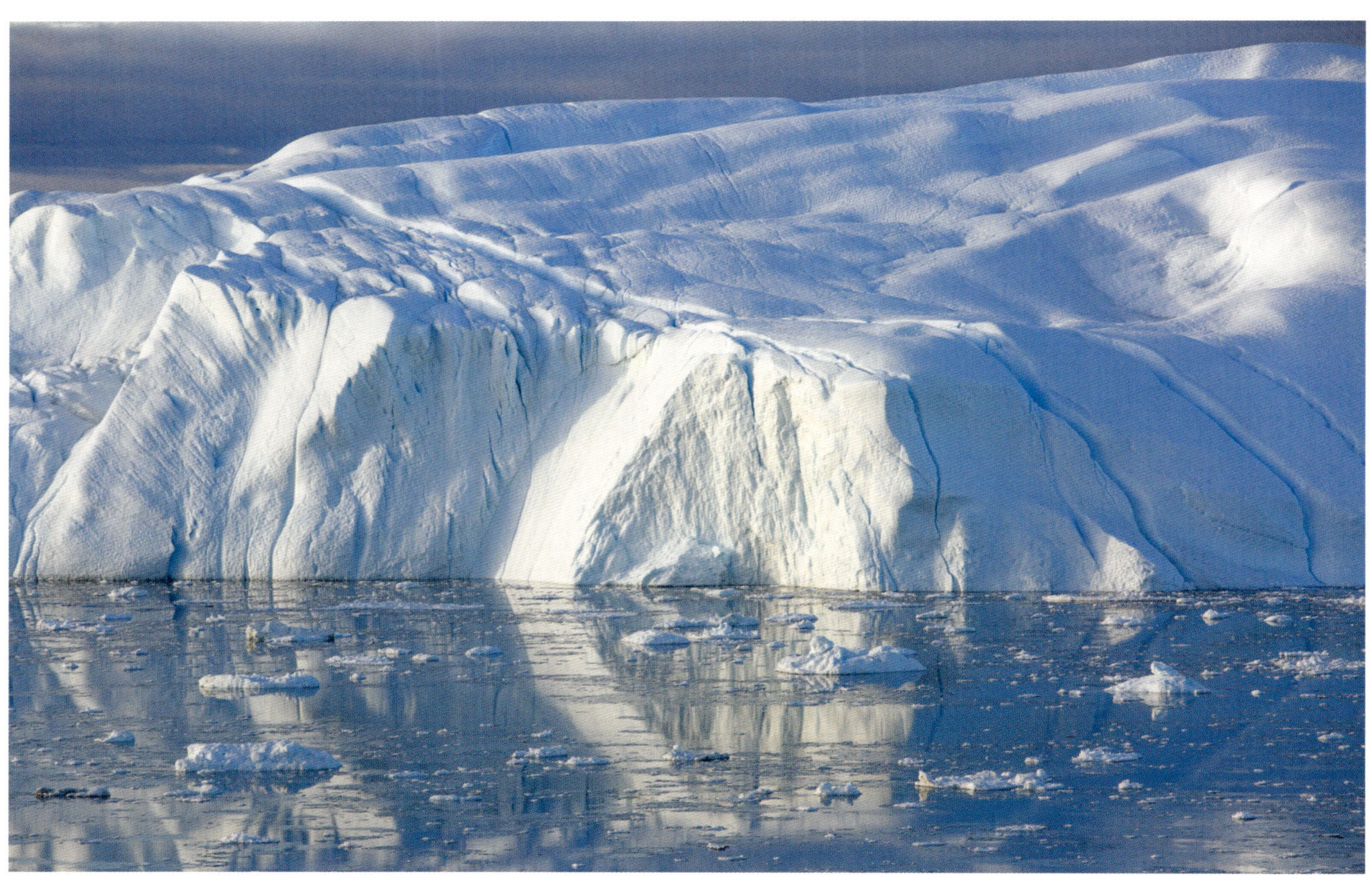

 Silent Giants
Ilulissat, Greenland

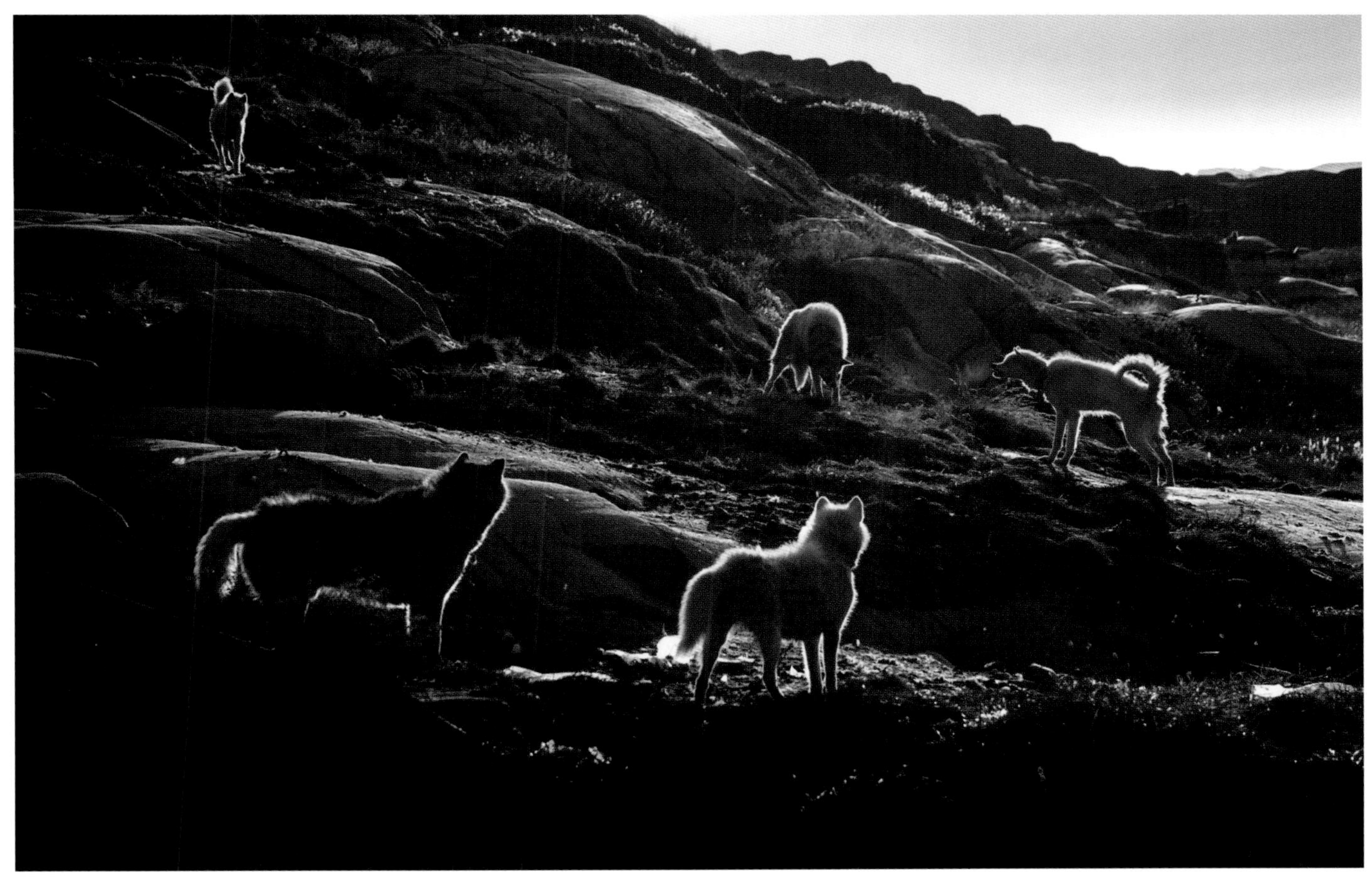

The Gathering
Ilulissat, Greenland

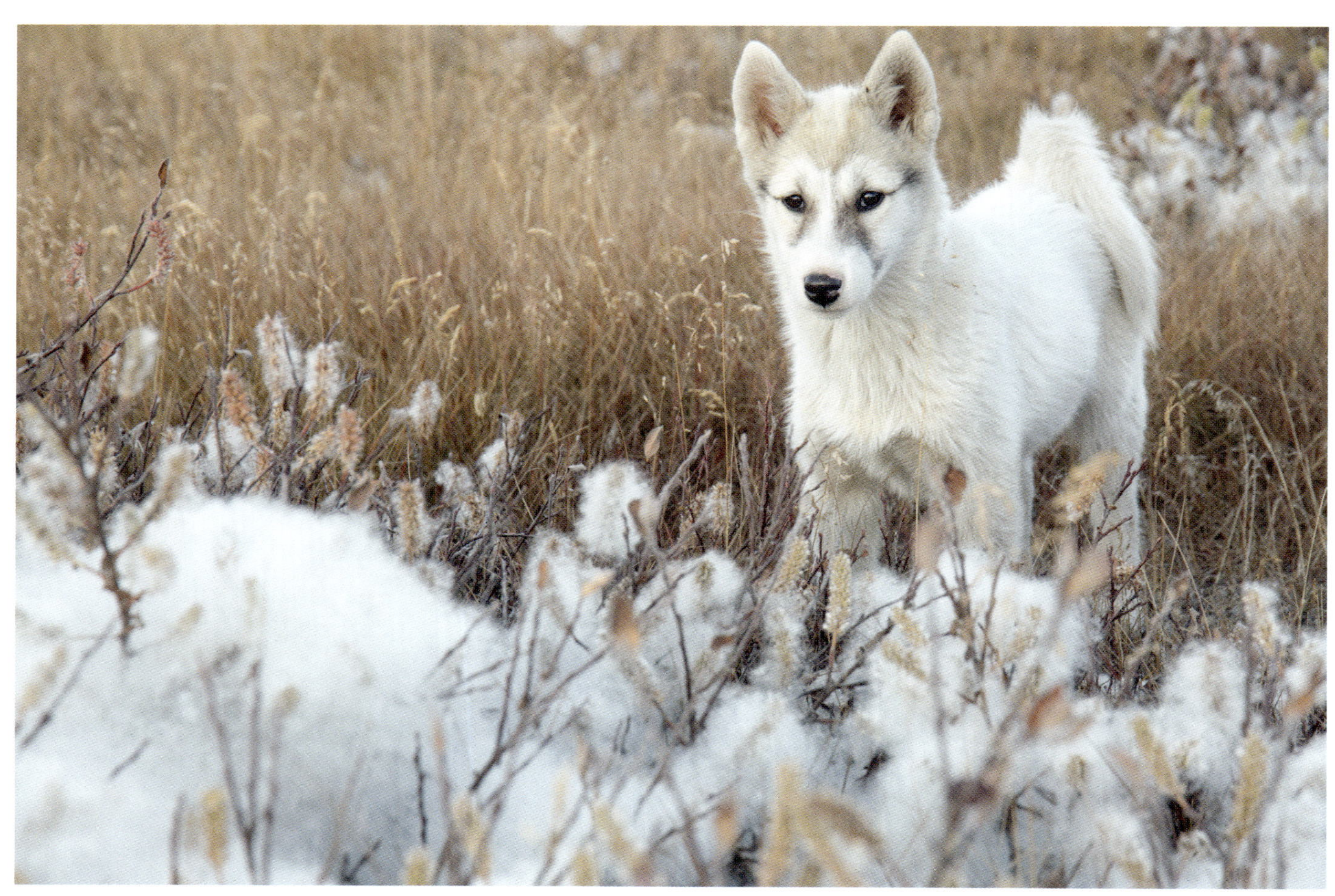

Cotton
Ilulissat, Greenland

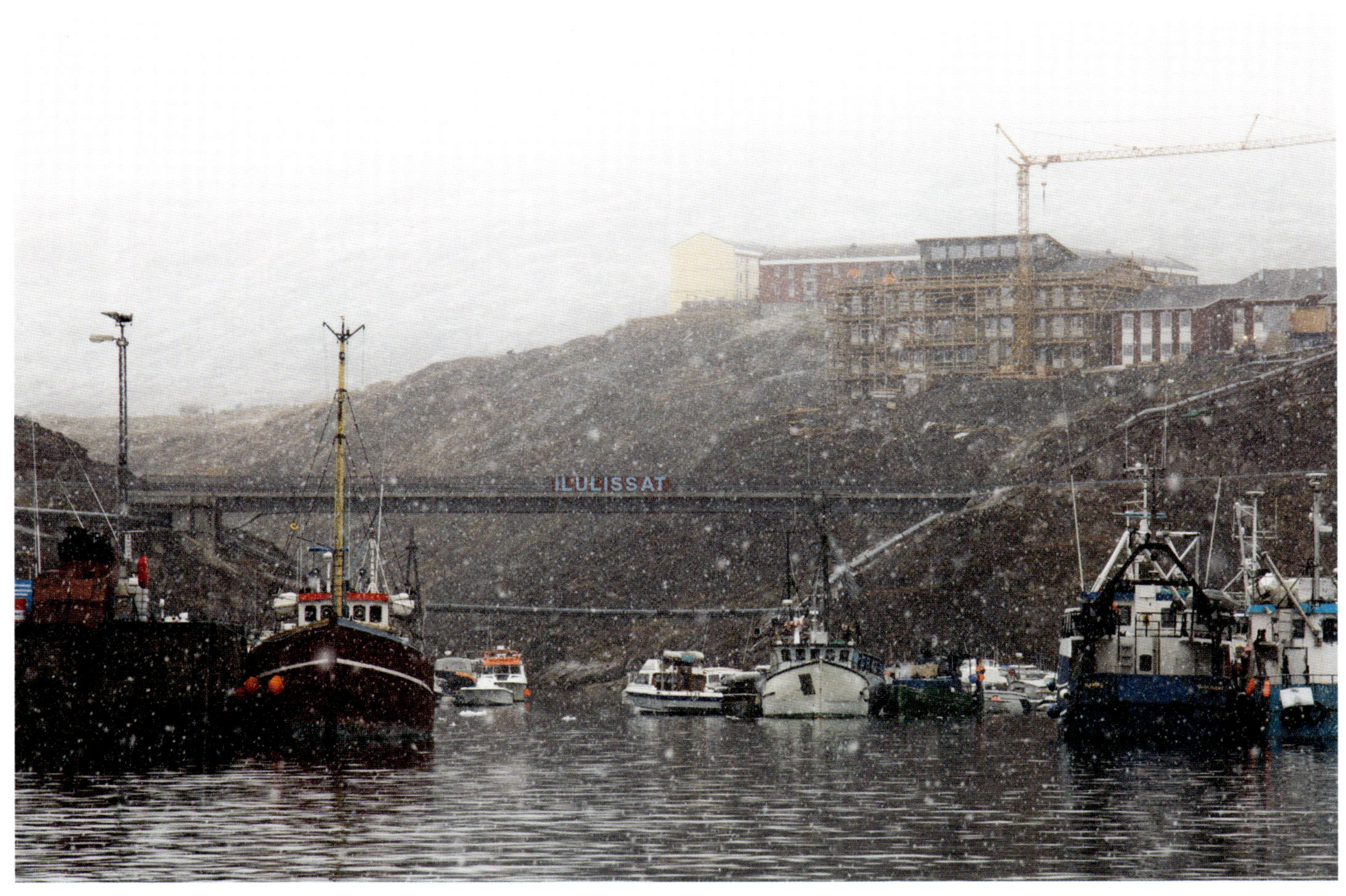

The Harbour
Ilulissat, Greenland

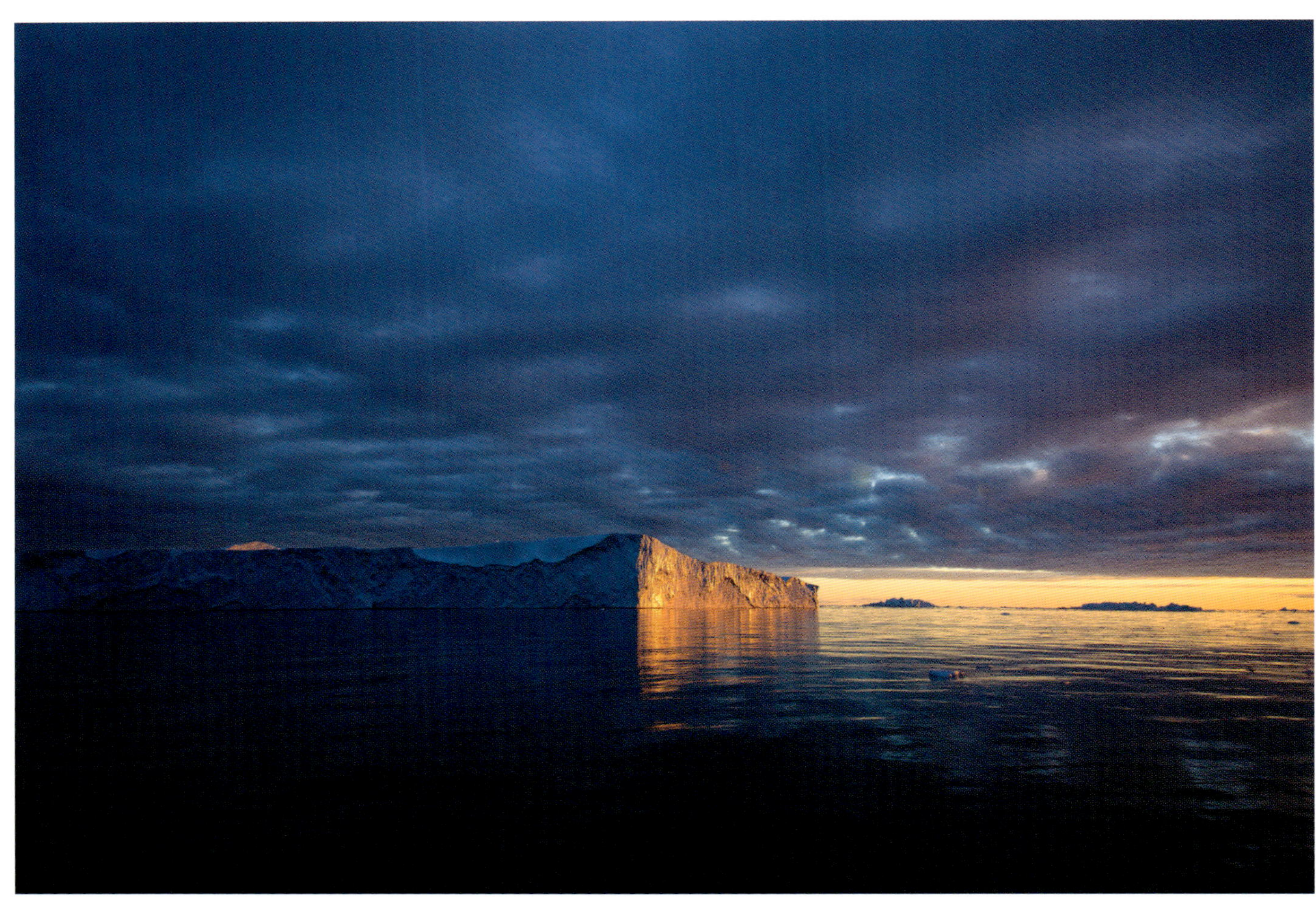

Last Kiss

Ilulissat, Greenland

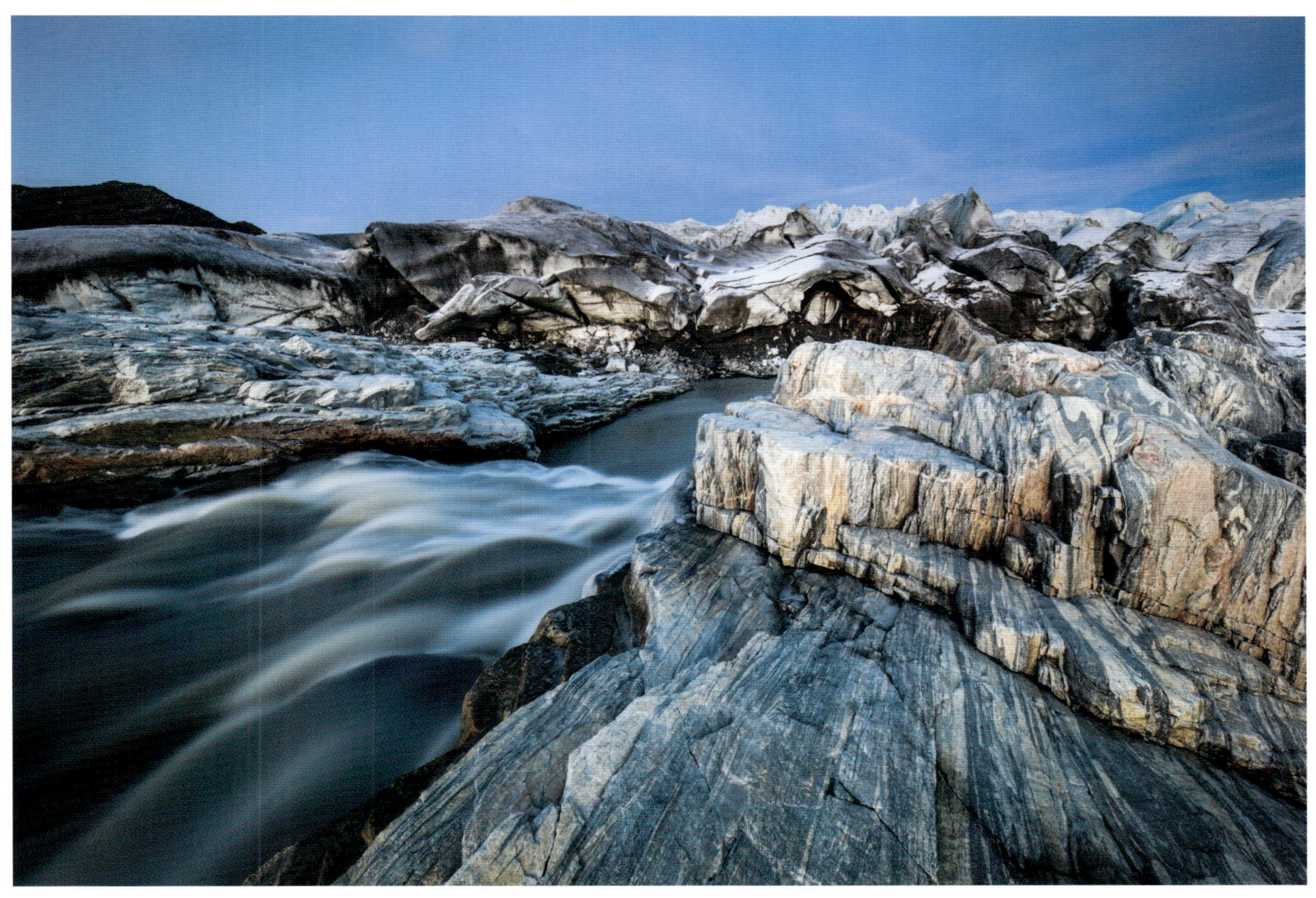

Beyond the Wall
Russell Glacier, Greenland

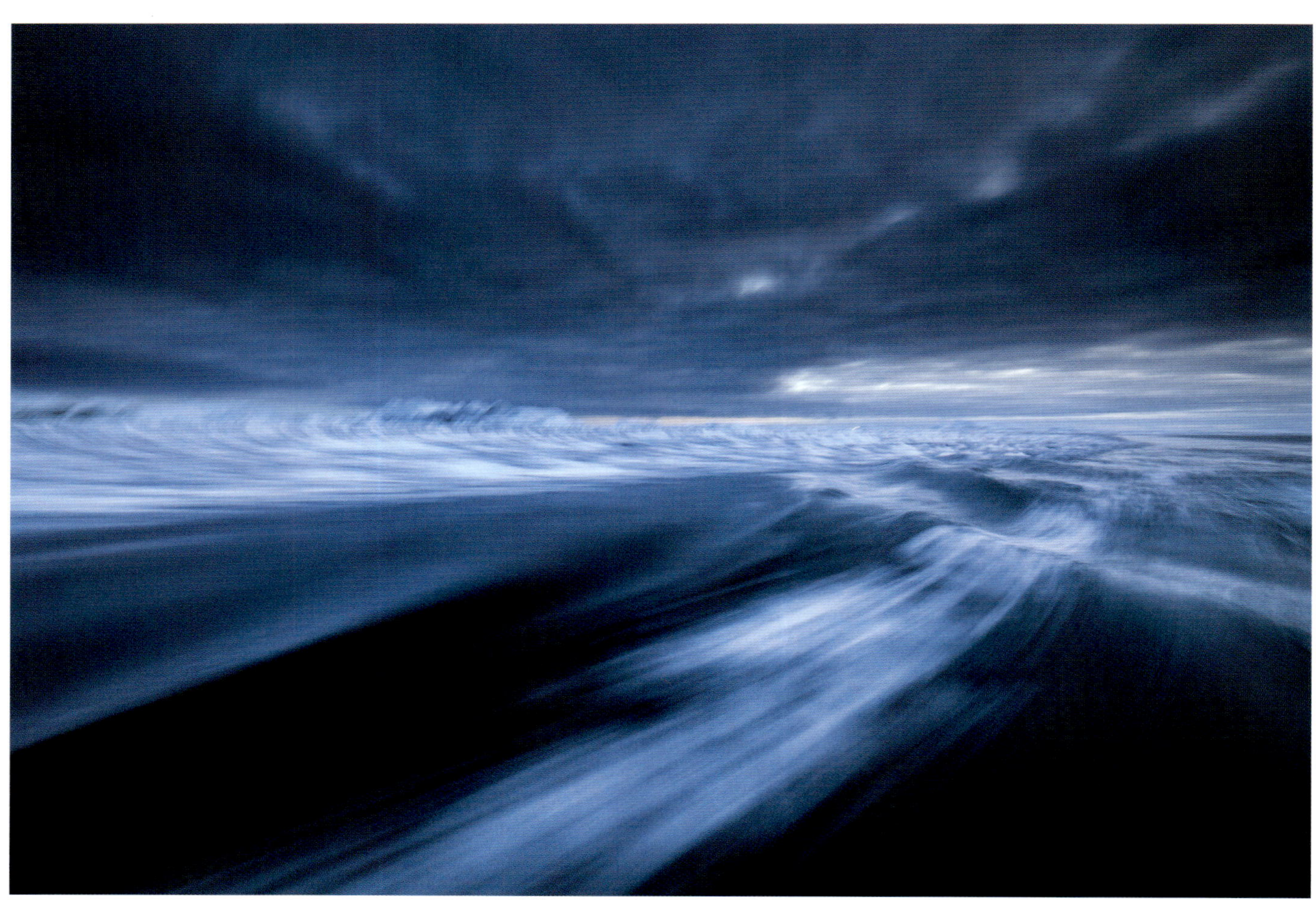

Order in the Chaos
Ilulissat, Greenland

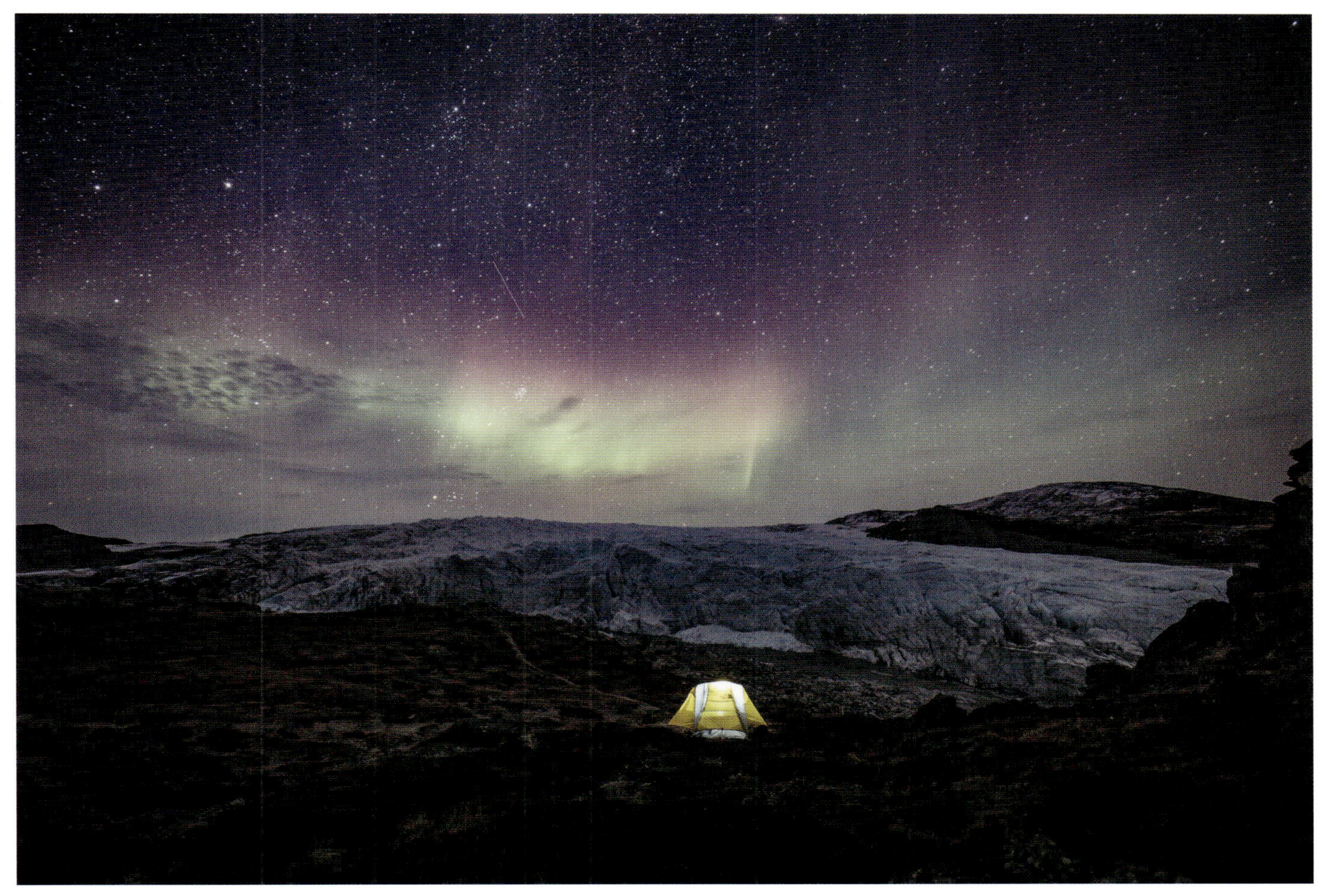

The Grande Finale

Russell Glacier, Greenland

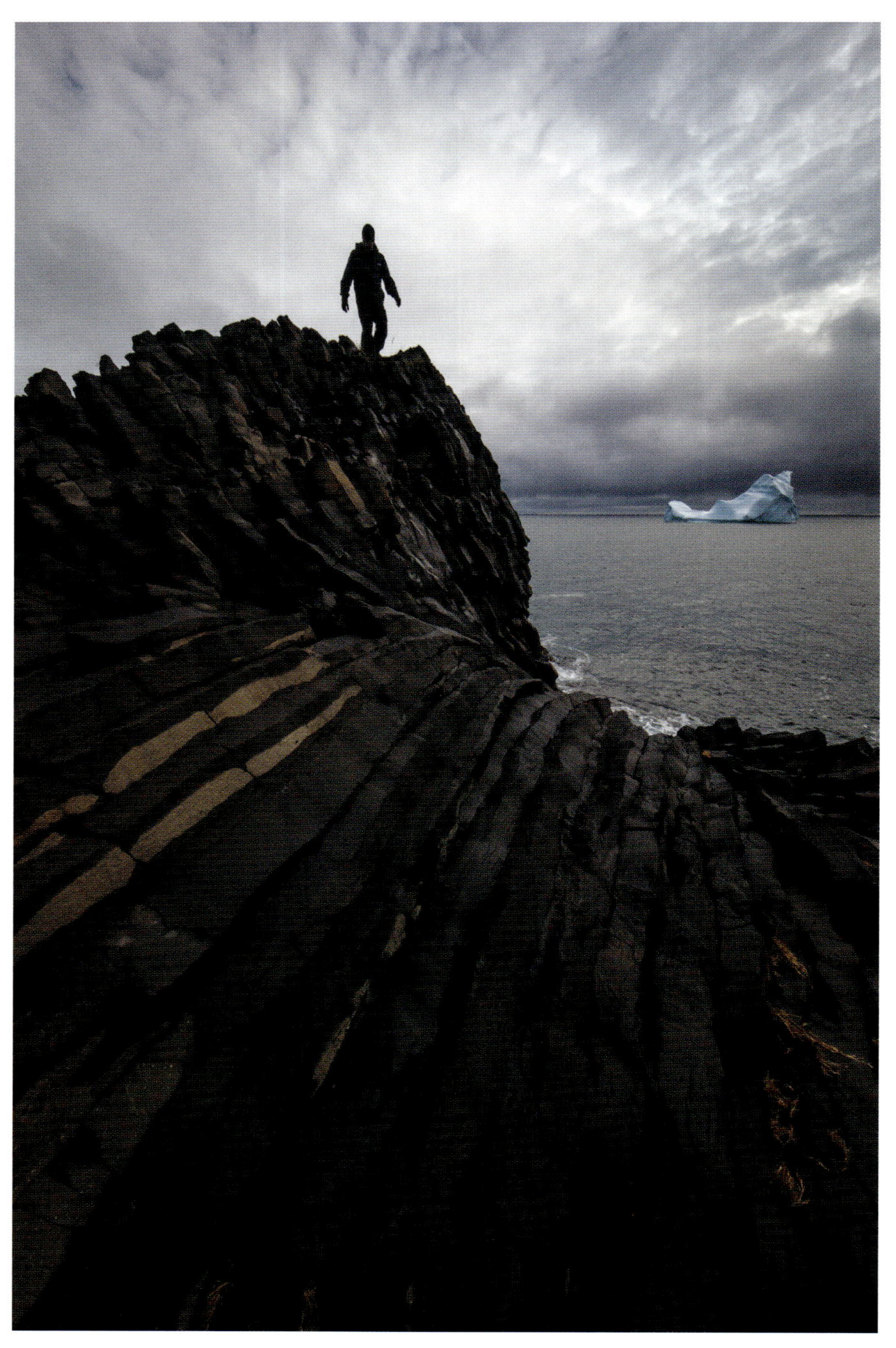

Disko Fever
Disko Island, Greenland

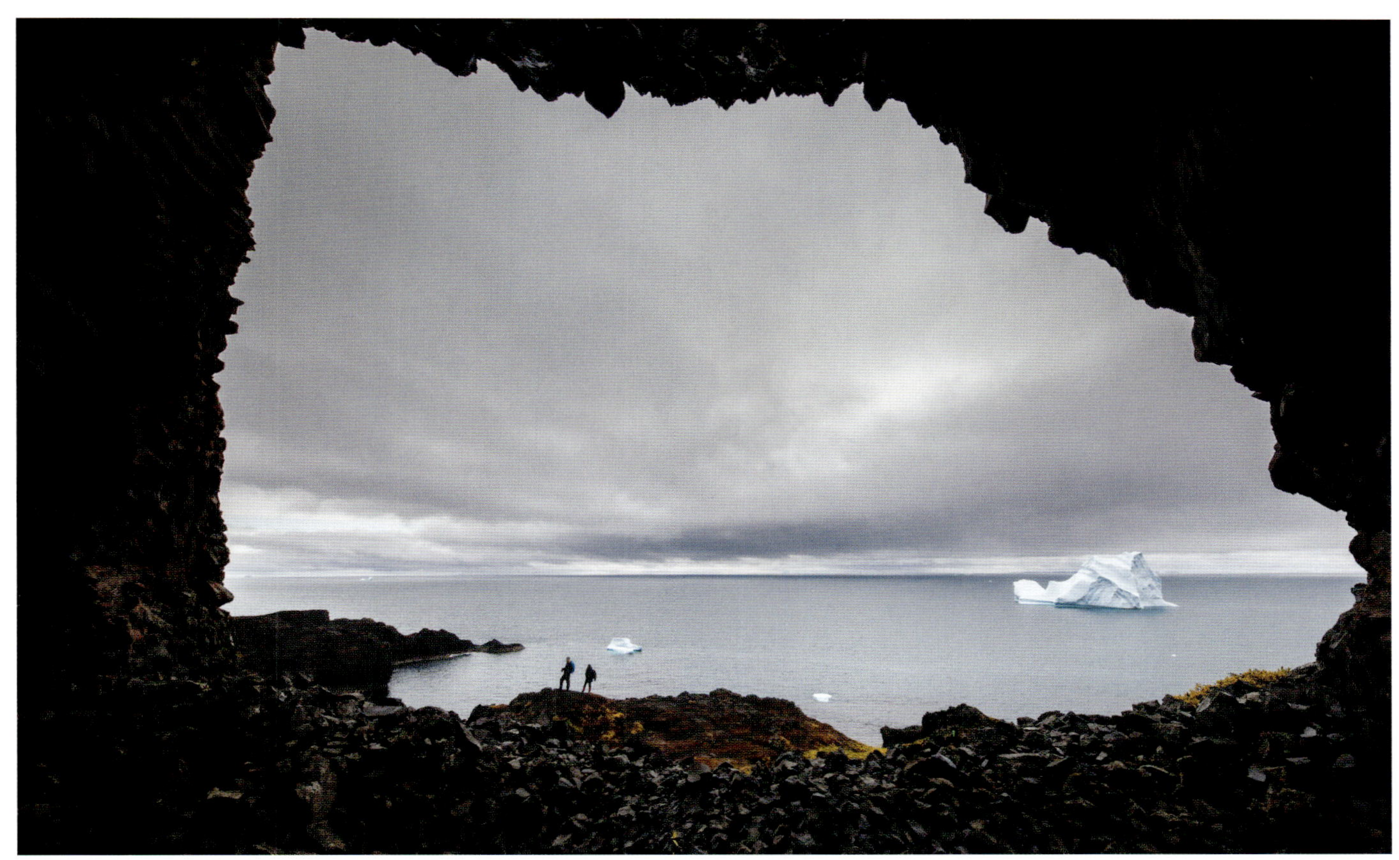

The Disko Frame
Disko Island, Greenland

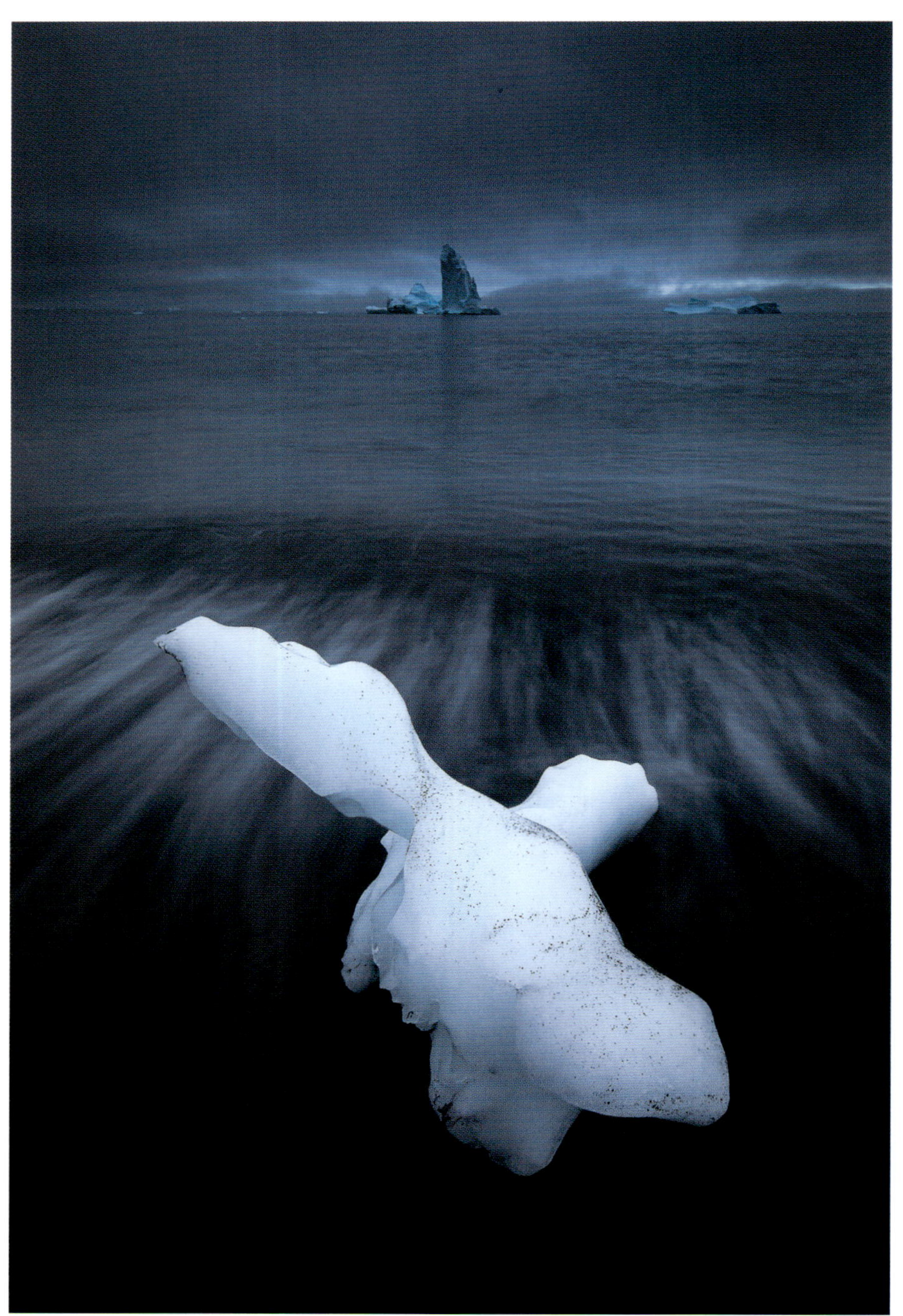

Ice Flight

Qeqertarsuaq, Disko Island, Greenland

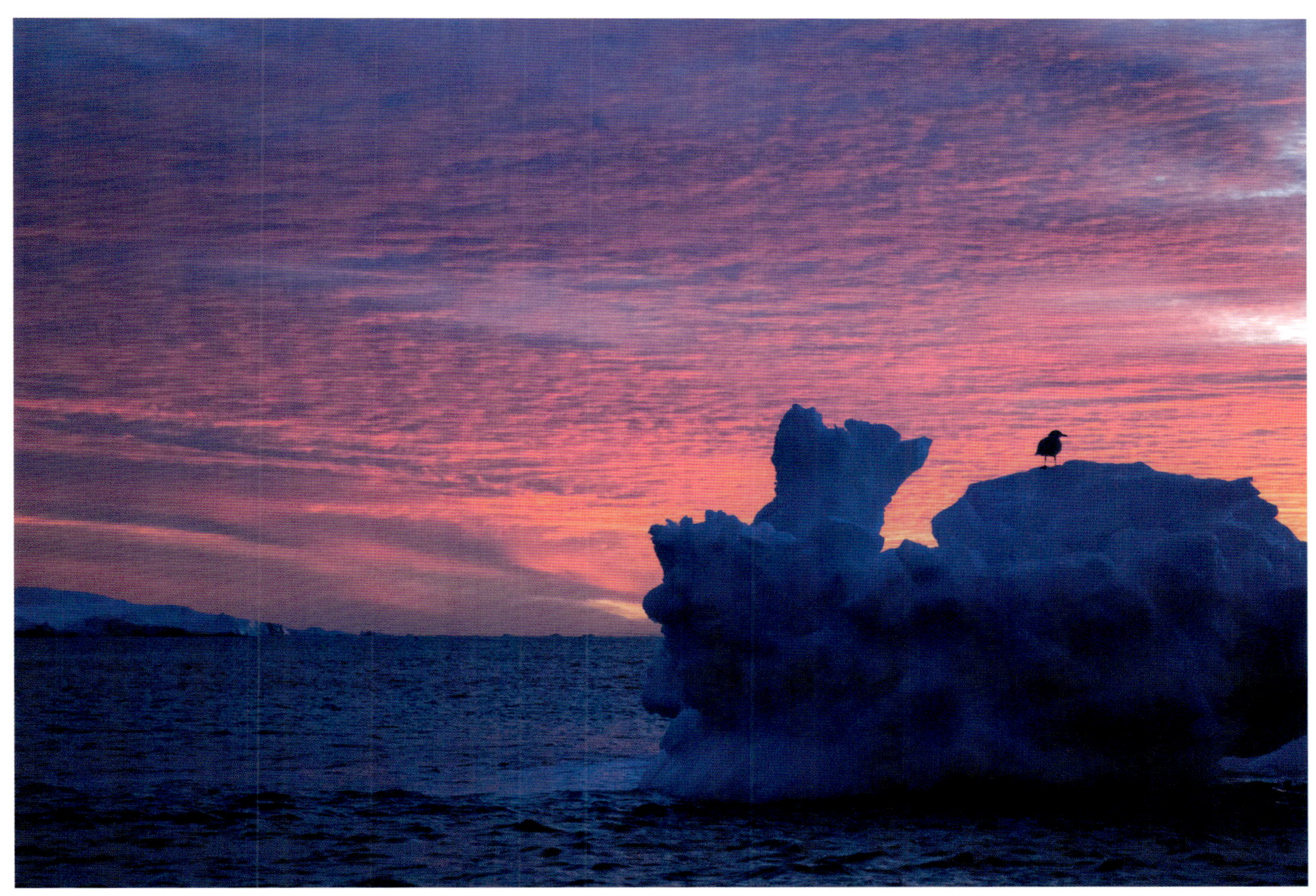

The Show
Ilulissat, Greenland

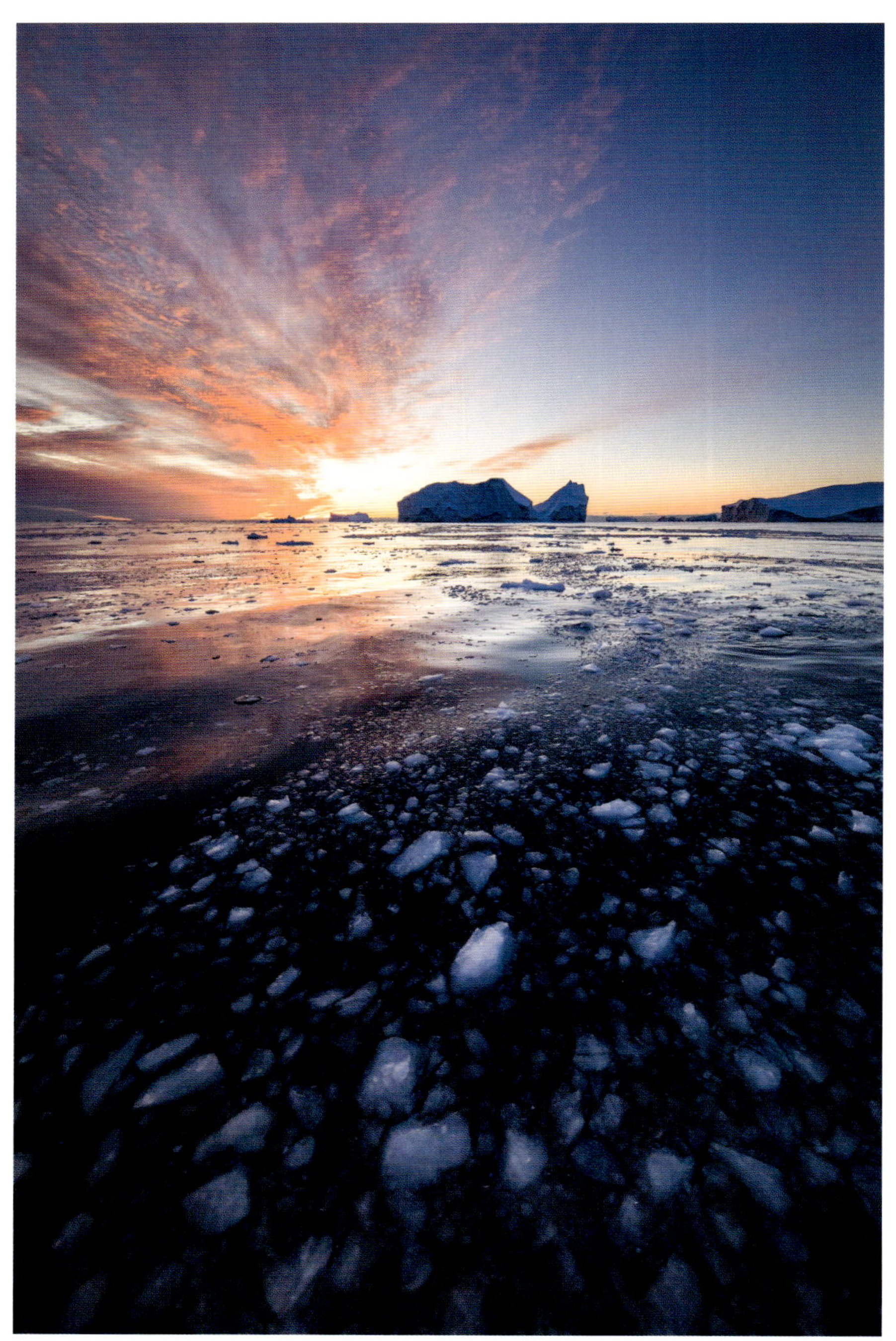

I've Seen Fire, and I've Seen Ice...
Ilulissat, Greenland

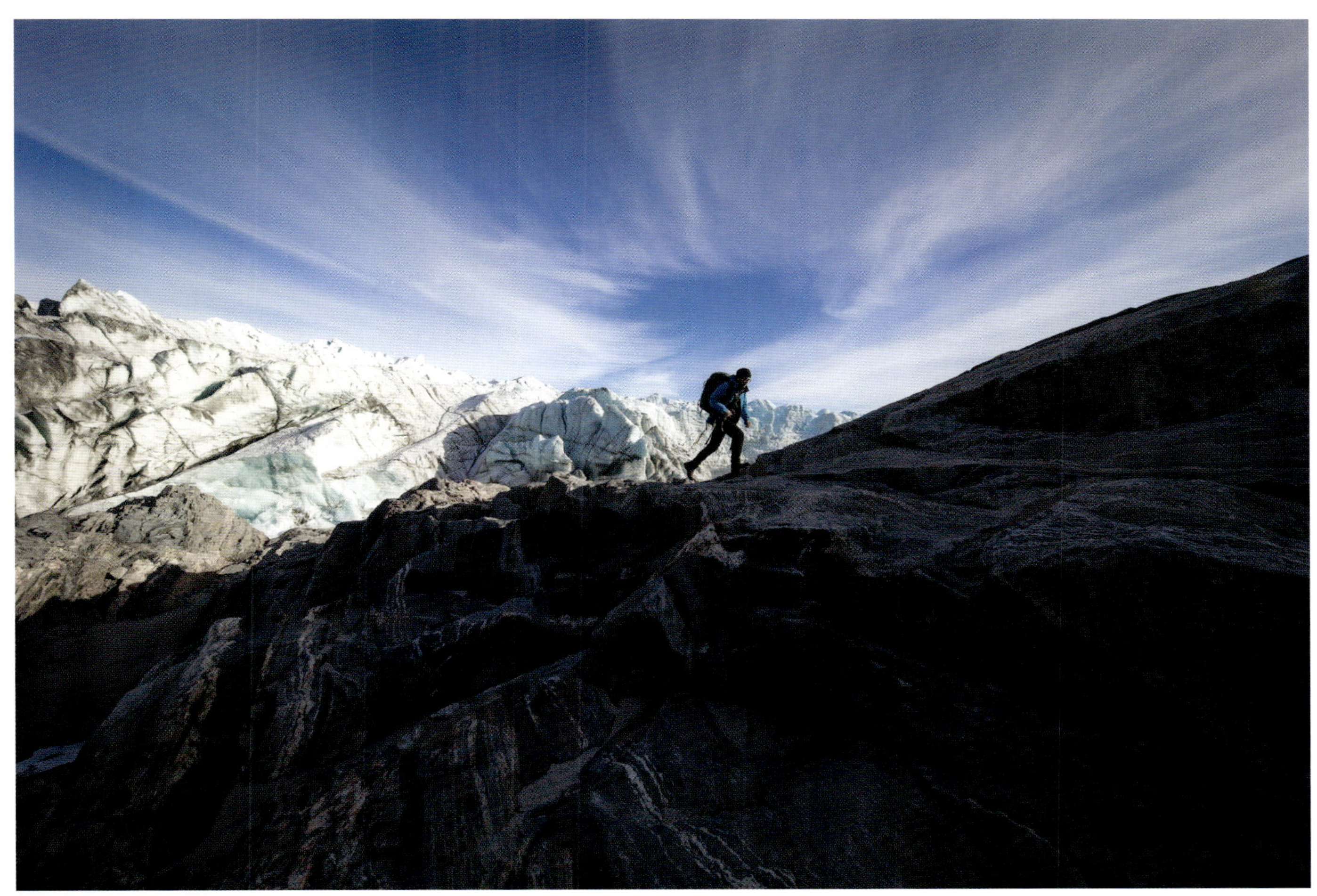

Arctic Air
Curtis Jones at Russell Glacier, Greenland

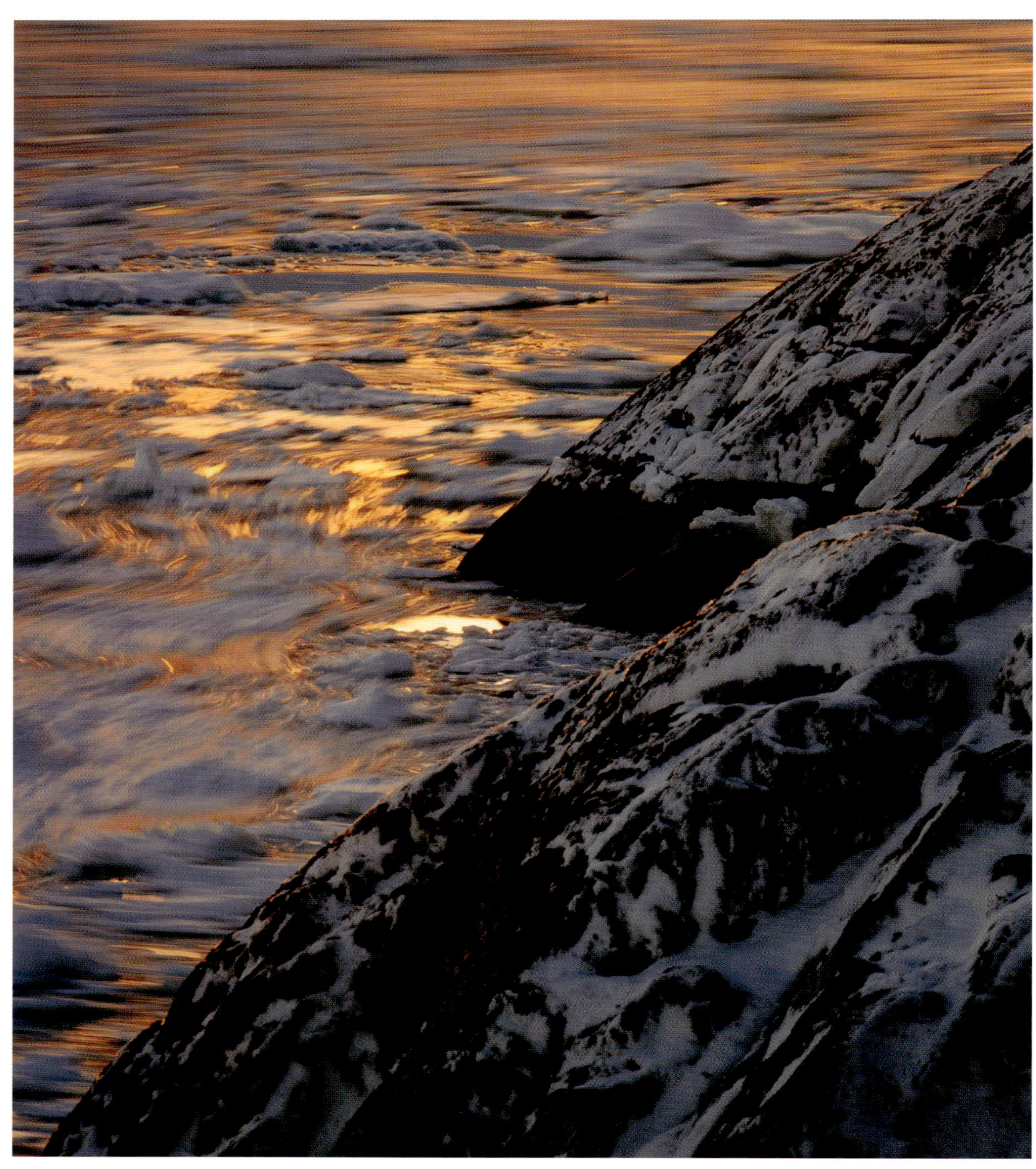

Collide

Ilulissat, Greenland

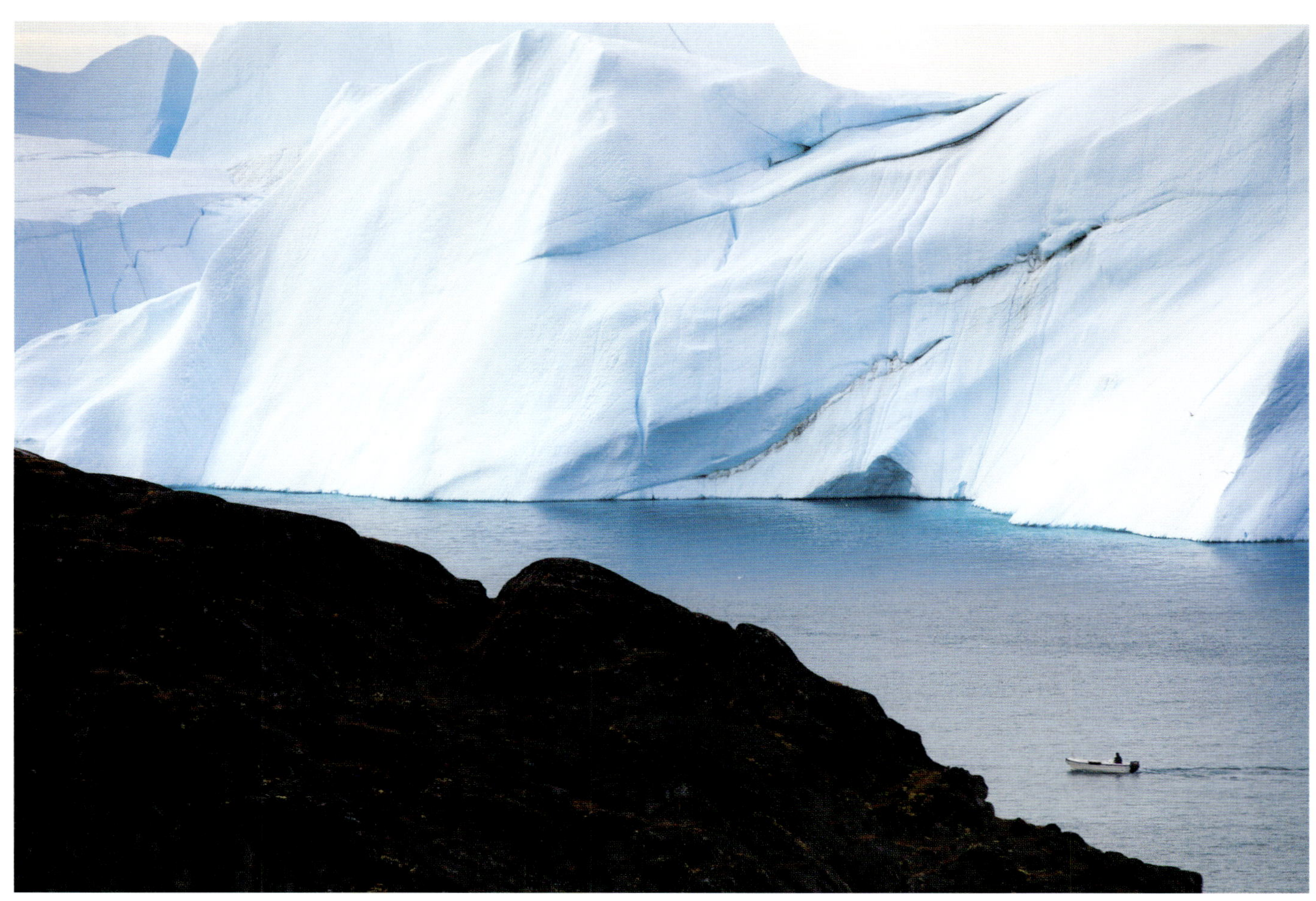

Threading Needles
Ilulissat, Greenland

The Iceland Sagas

Iceland has become, in the past decade, one of the most sought-out locations in the world for photographers, and for good reason. It stocks a large inventory of many of the things landscape photographers hold dear – interesting scenery, uncluttered scenes and an abundance of unique light. Rare is the place that you can see such a grand diversity not only in landscape but in weather conditions as well, all from the comfort of your vehicle – something not common in my explorations in the North, where much of the "good" stuff is often away from roads and requires a big effort to get to. Much of the Arctic, for example, is devoid of roads. Your feet, skis, snowshoes, snow machines, ATVs, boats and planes become your primary "access" to your photographic scenes.

Yes, Iceland is one of those countries where you can indeed drive to many of its most spectacular locales; it's a country where you find yourself saying, "Oh, wow," every five minutes, as each bend in the road brings new visual delight. On my first visit to Iceland, I was floored even by the first 50 kilometres leaving the capital of Reykjavik. I only learned, later, that this was the "boring" section of the country… but I impress easily. If you're brave enough to venture away from the highway, though, these delights amplify. Mountains, basalt, glaciers, ice caves, lava formations, endless waterfalls, moss, plains, fields, rivers, cascades, sheep and beauty. Oh, and the weather – I've never seen such weather diversity as in Iceland.

The weather blasts you, but rather than being put off by it, as a photographer you're excited, because on the edges of bad weather often come great photographic conditions. Rain gives way to rainbows. Dark skies gives way to blasts of truly magical light. Wind and snow and rain have a tendency to push away the tourist hordes, and when they stop, you magically have a location to yourself.

Iceland mesmerizes me. Truly. It's a place where I can stand out in its wilds, breathe deeply and just wonder how it's all possible. That Earth can offer up such stunning beauty. That we, as humans, were given the gift of being able to recognize and comprehend the aesthetics of nature (even if we don't always appreciate this fact).

Photographers seek subjects of interest. We seek beauty. We seek stories that resonate within, and we seek to do these stories justice. Iceland speaks to my "Northern soul," but at the same time feels like a world onto itself. It is a story I want to tell, again and again. I want to speak to its ruggedness – but also to its elegance. Here are some of the Icelandic stories I've felt compelled to tell; I have a feeling I've only just begun, that I'll have many more to tell from this incredible land in the years to come.

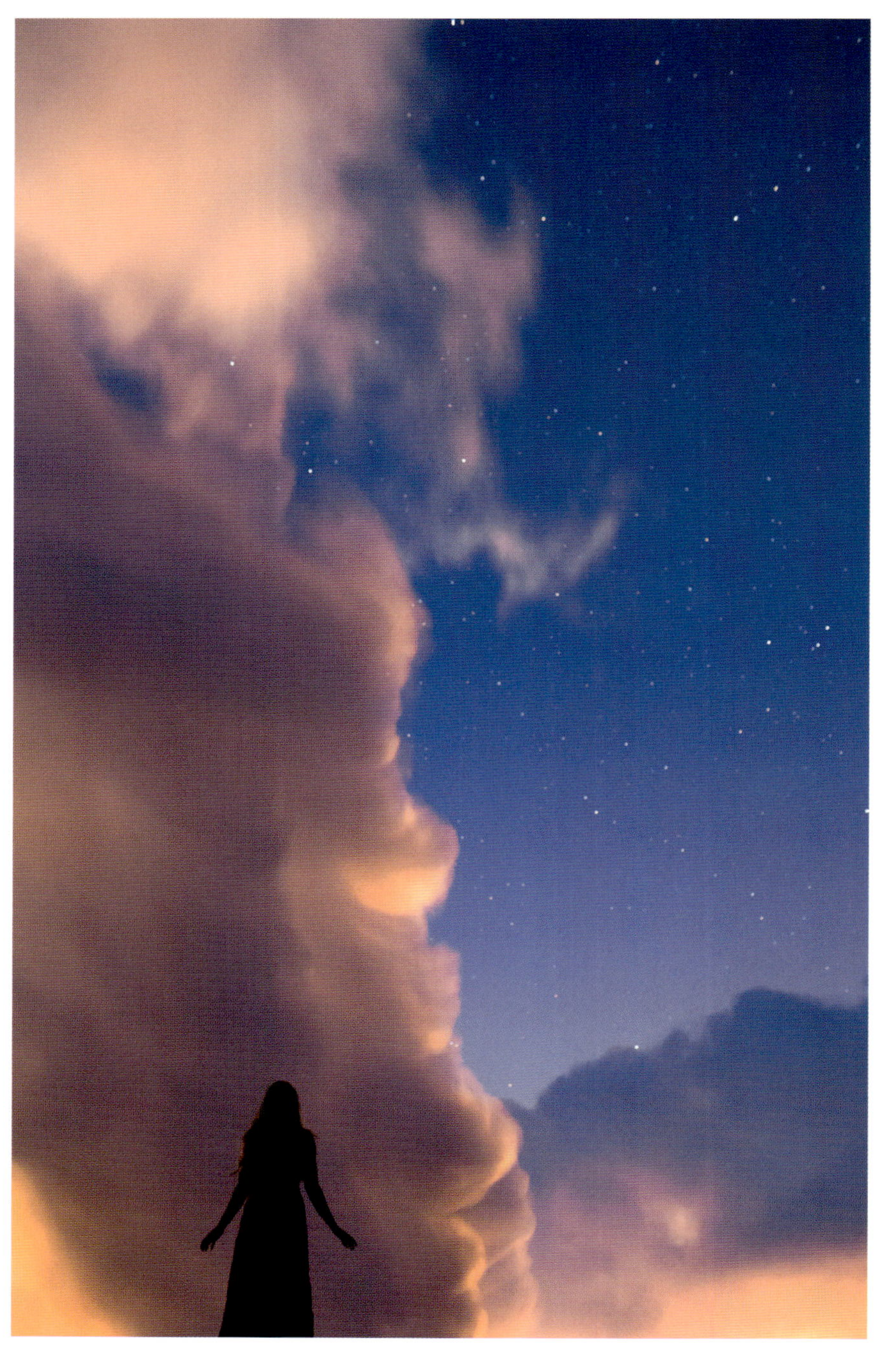

Rise

Lizzy Gadd at Gunnuhver, Iceland

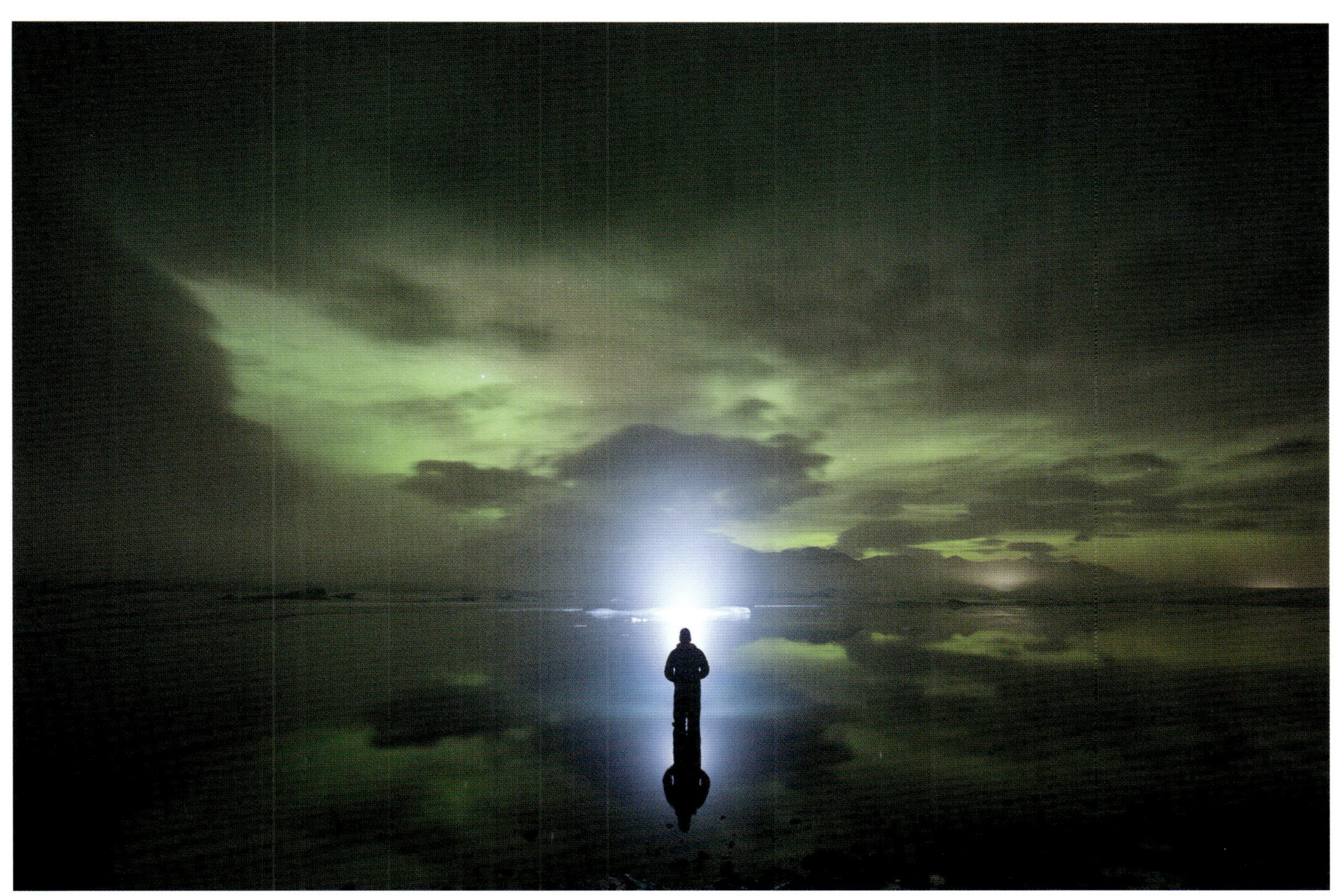

Force Field

Paul Zizka at Jökulsárlón Glacier Lagoon, Iceland

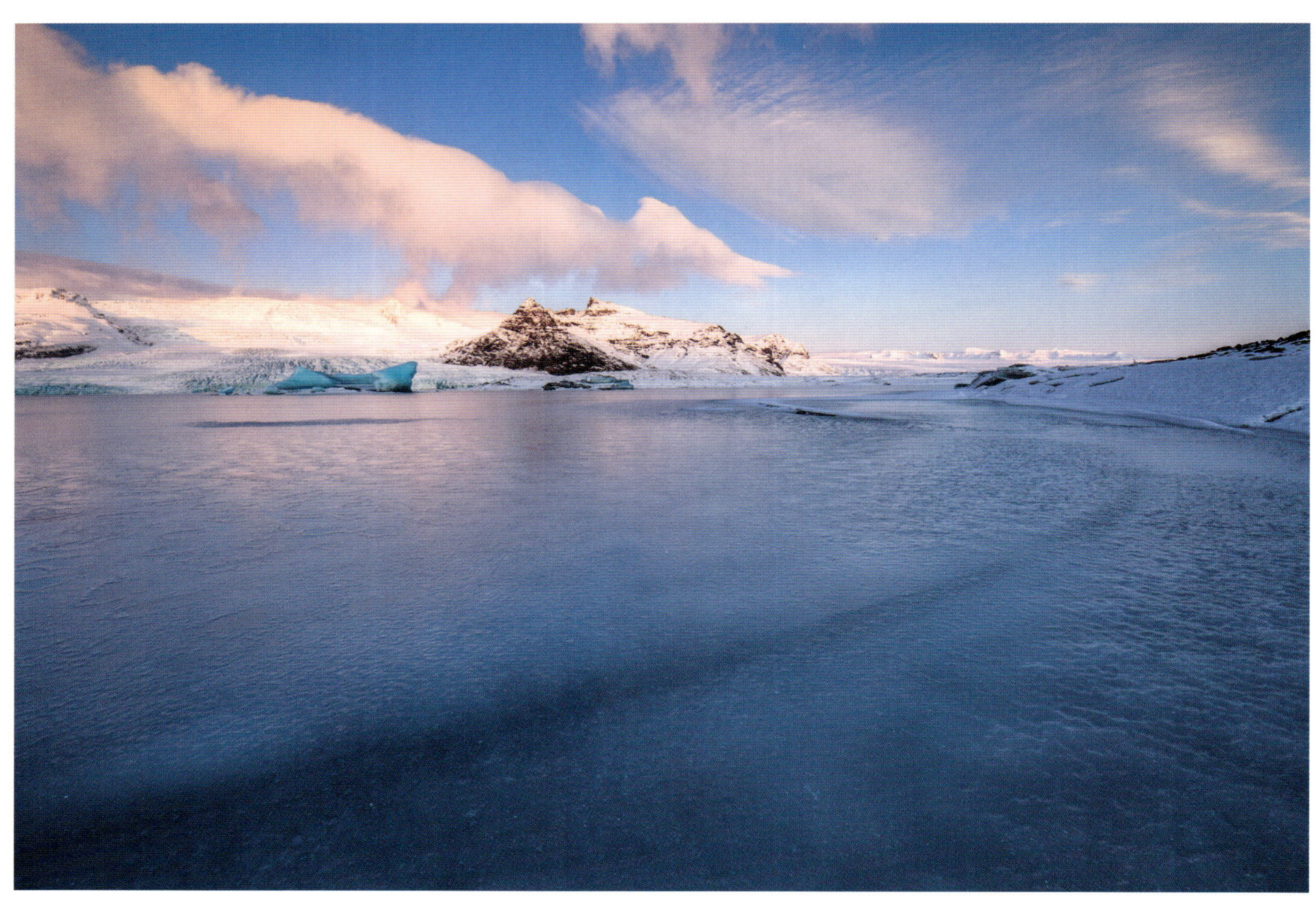

The Beauty Curve

Fjallsárlón Glacier Lagoon, Iceland

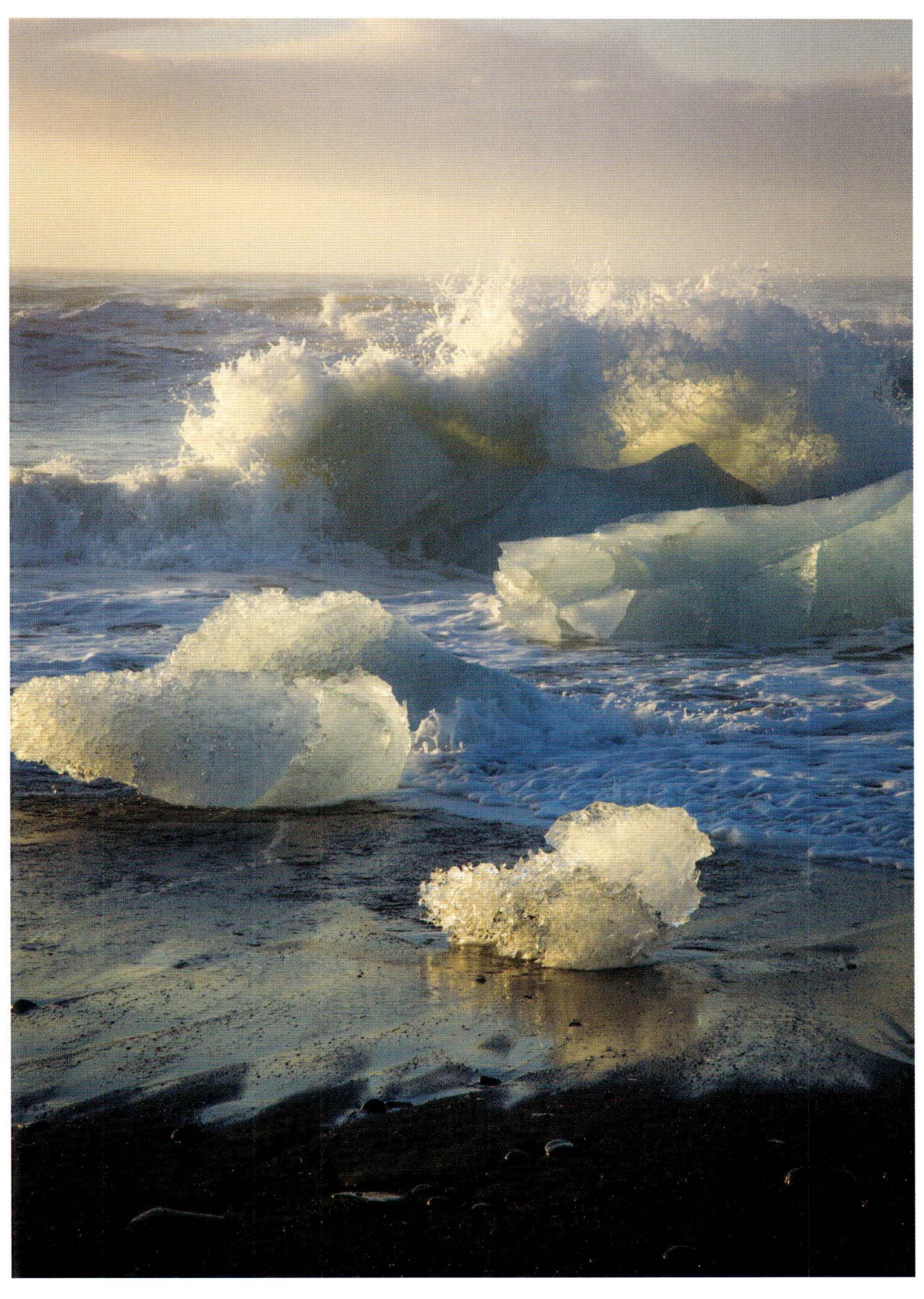

The Morning Dance

Diamond Beach, Jökulsárlón Glacier Lagoon, Iceland

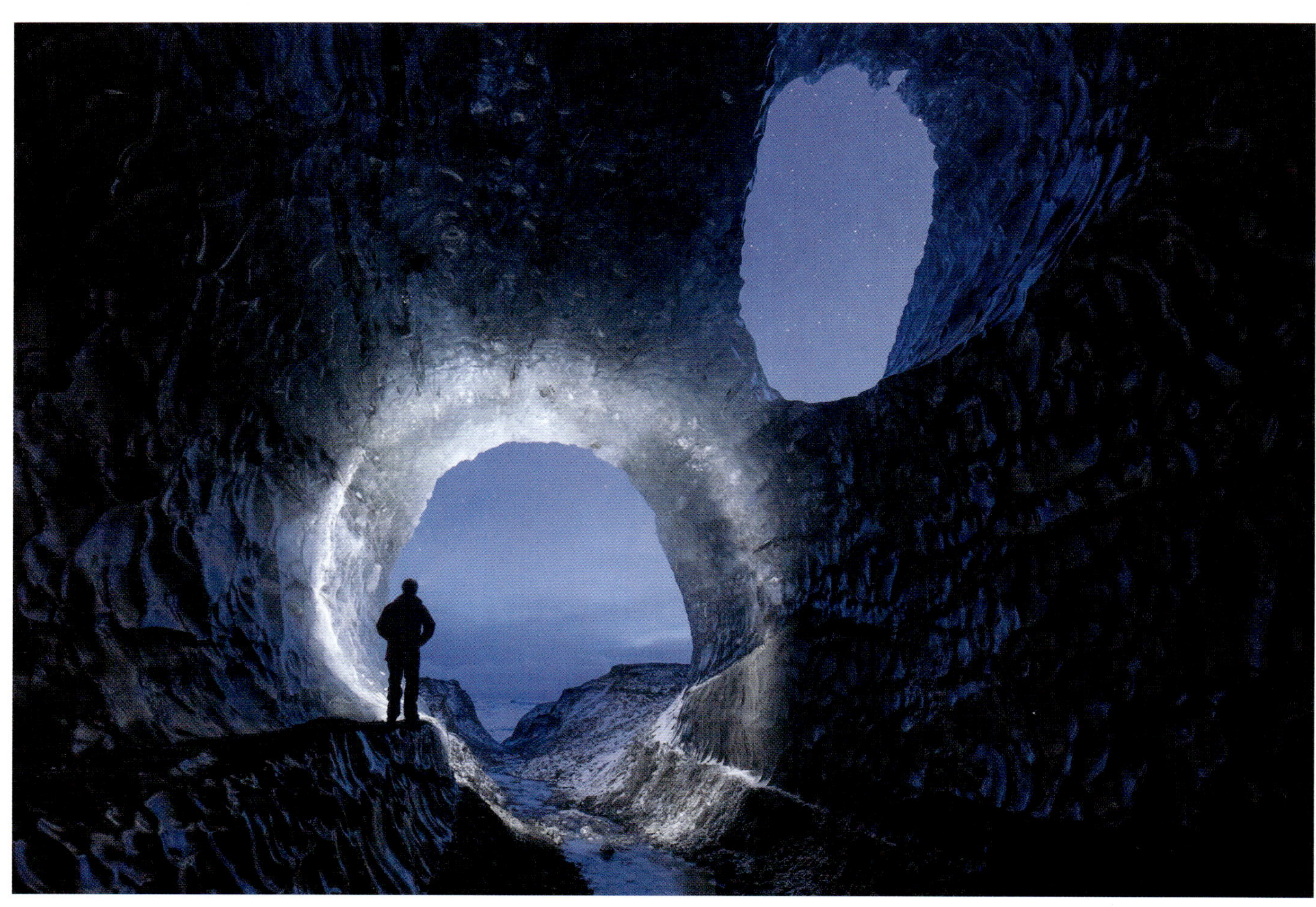

 Window on the World

Self-Portrait in Skaftafell – Vatnajökull National Park, Iceland

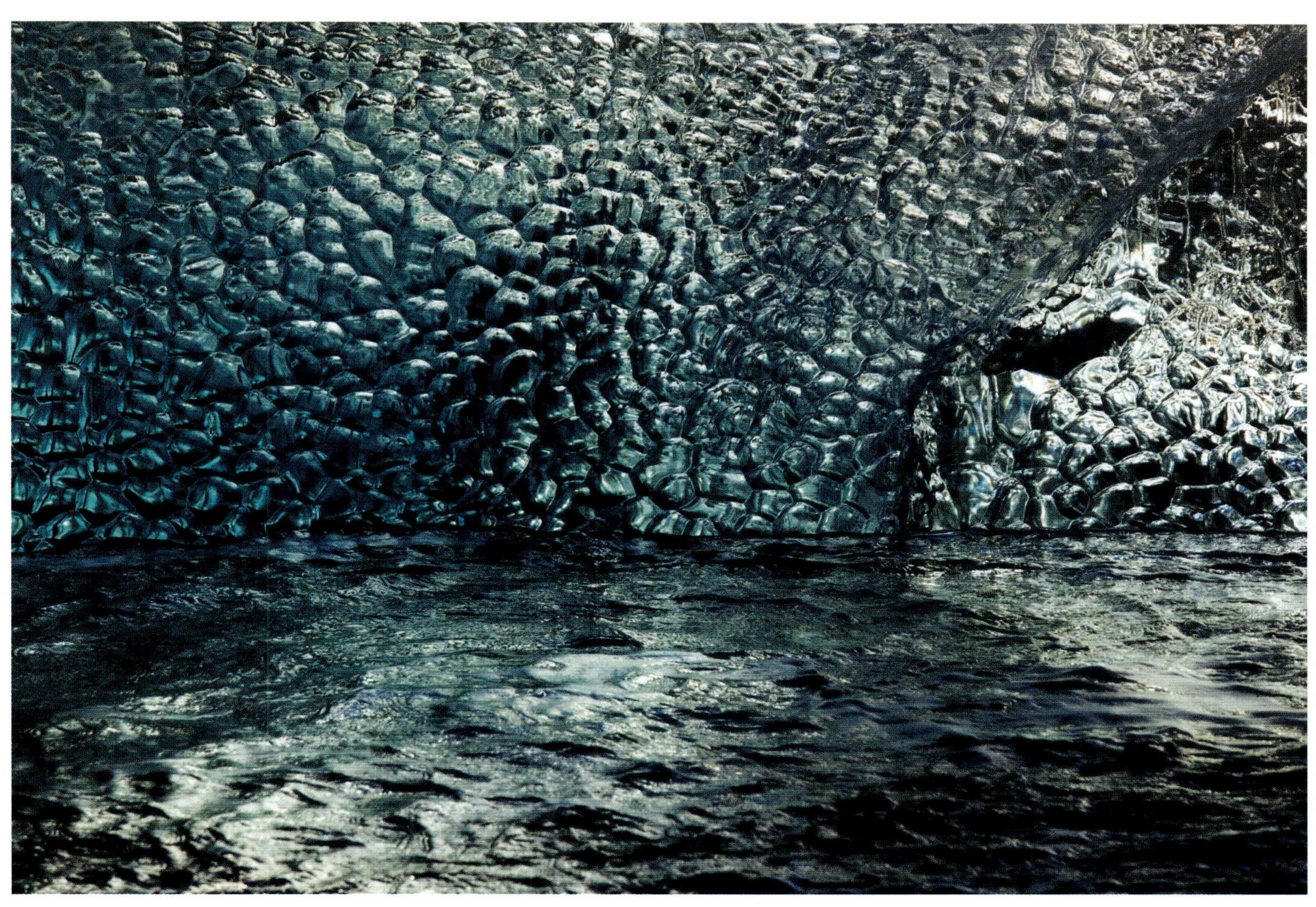

Diamond Wall

Diamond Beach, Jökulsárlón Glacier Lagoon, Iceland

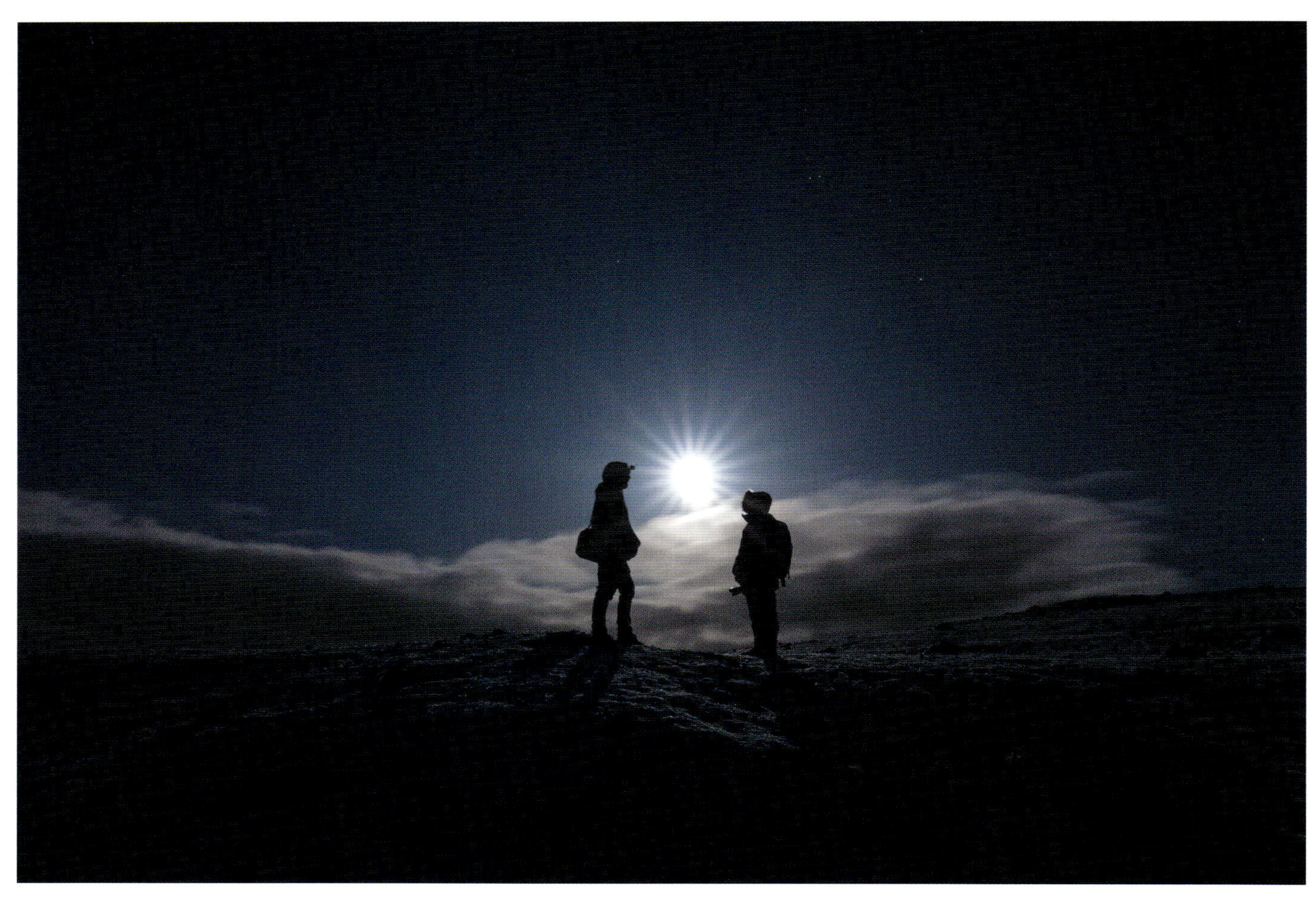

Night Talks

Mike Last and Will Johnson at Fjallsárlón Glacier Lagoon, Iceland

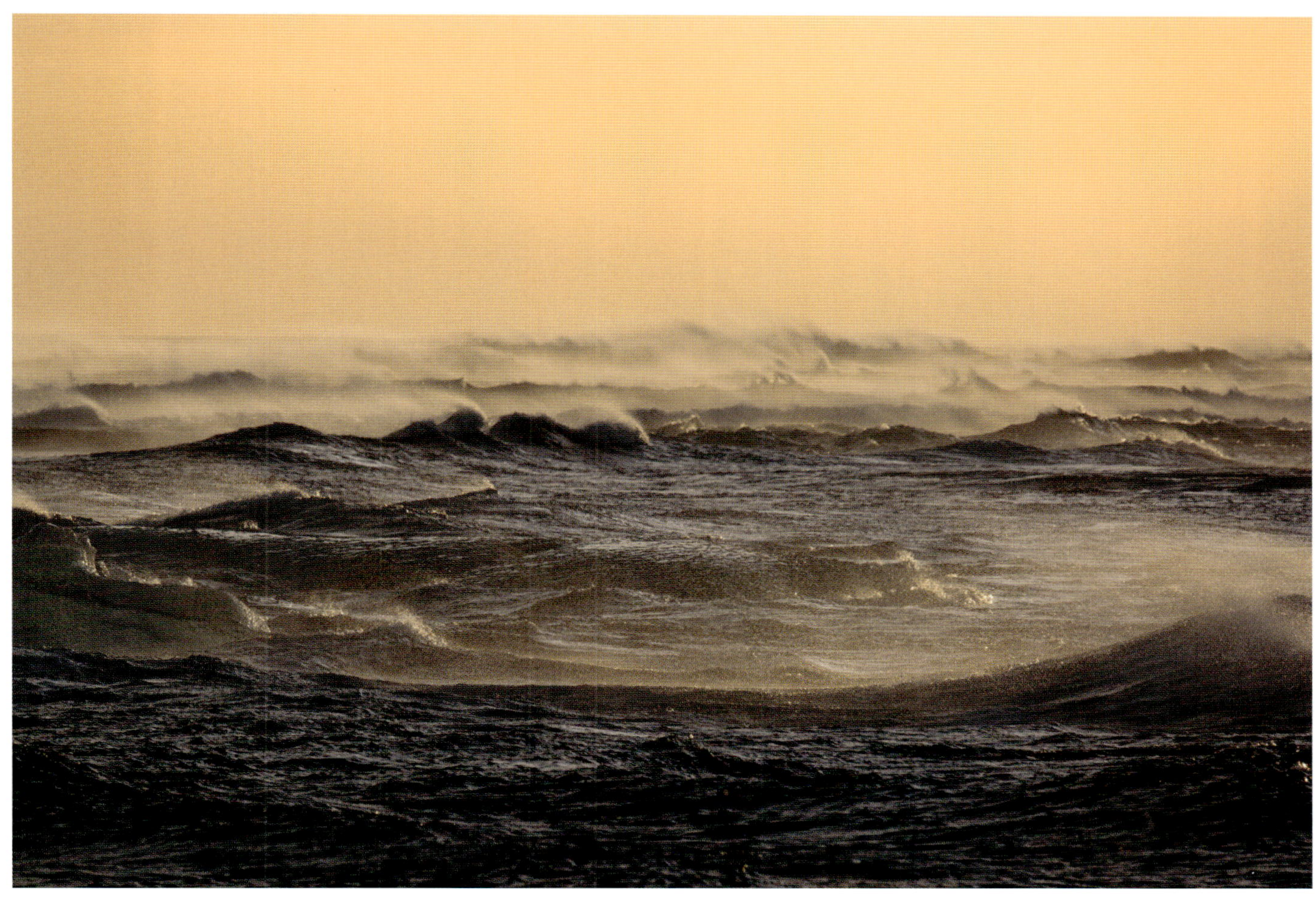

Wild Winds Blow

Diamond Beach, Jökulsárlón Glacier Lagoon, Iceland

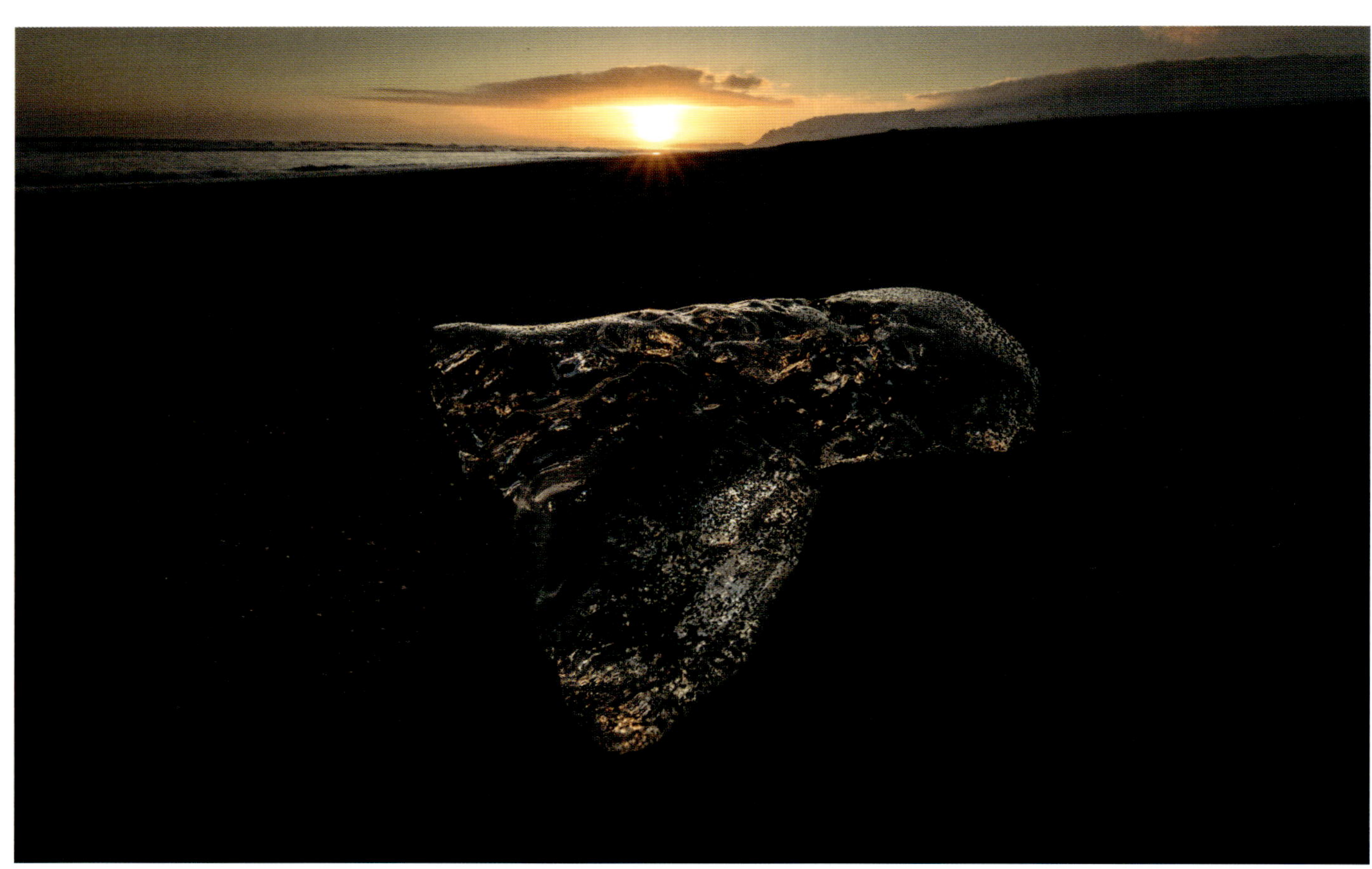

Diamonds and Gold

Diamond Beach, Jökulsárlón Glacier Lagoon, Iceland

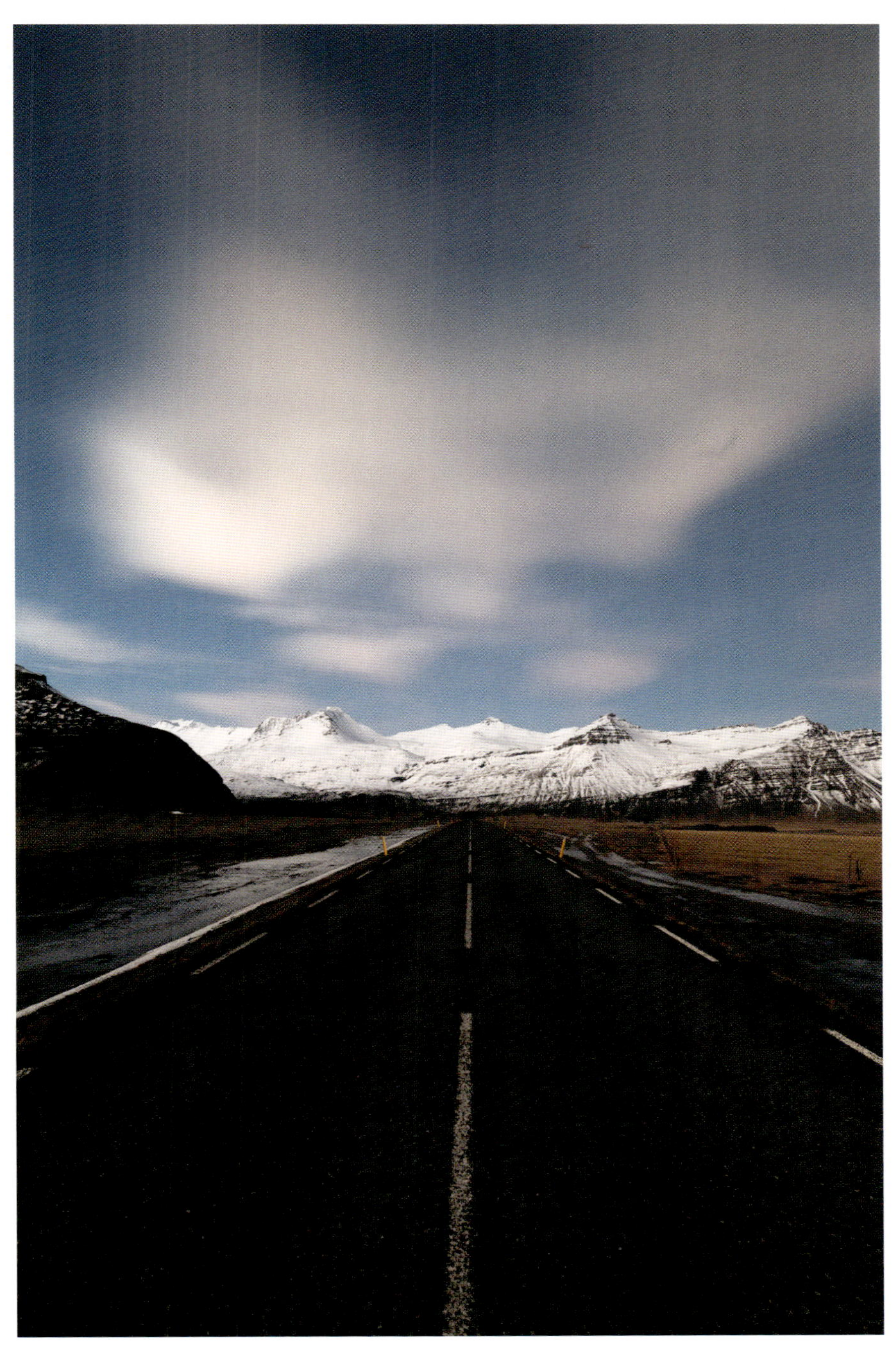

The Ice Way
Southeast Iceland

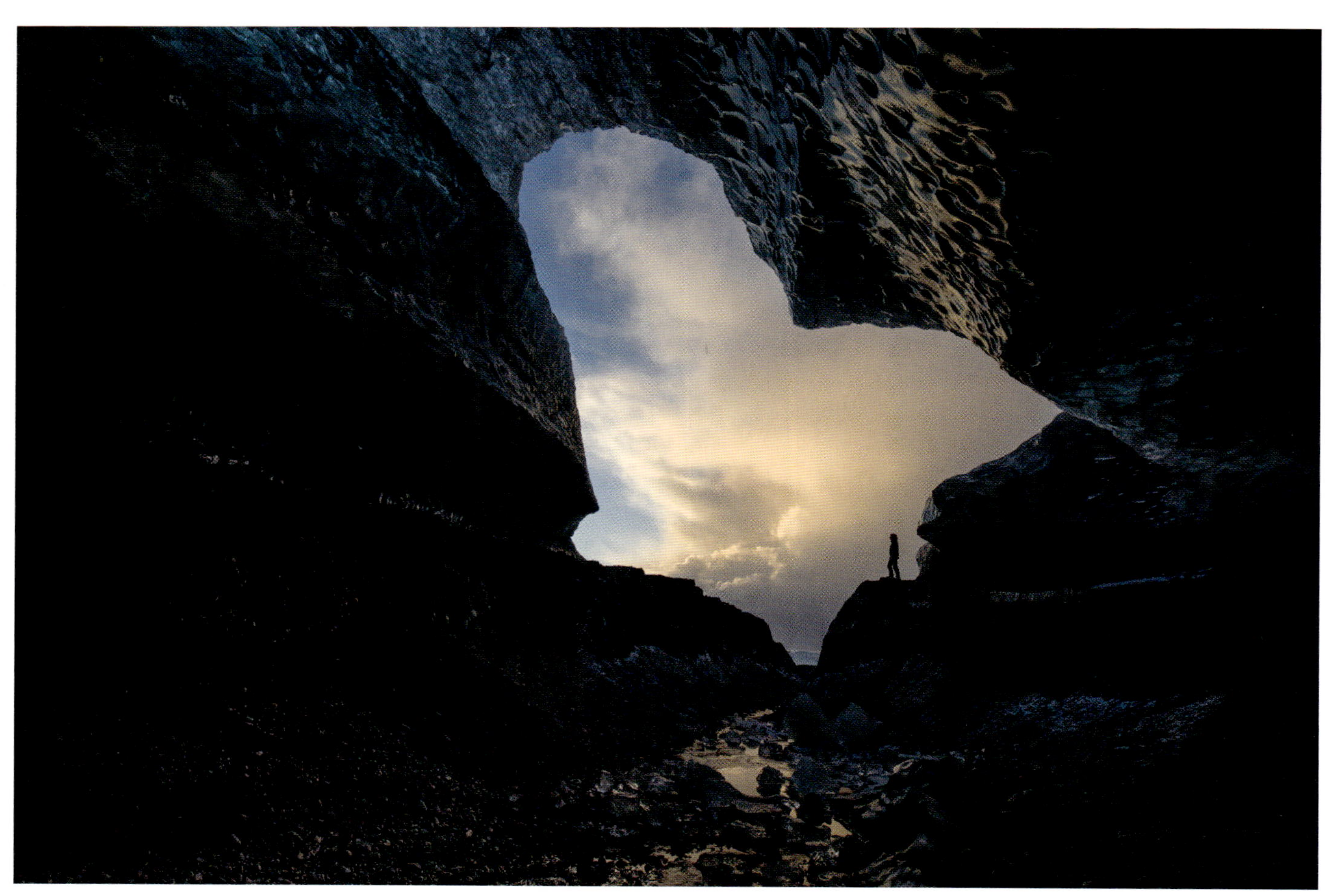

Discovery

David Sinclair in Skaftafell – Vatnajökull National Park, Iceland

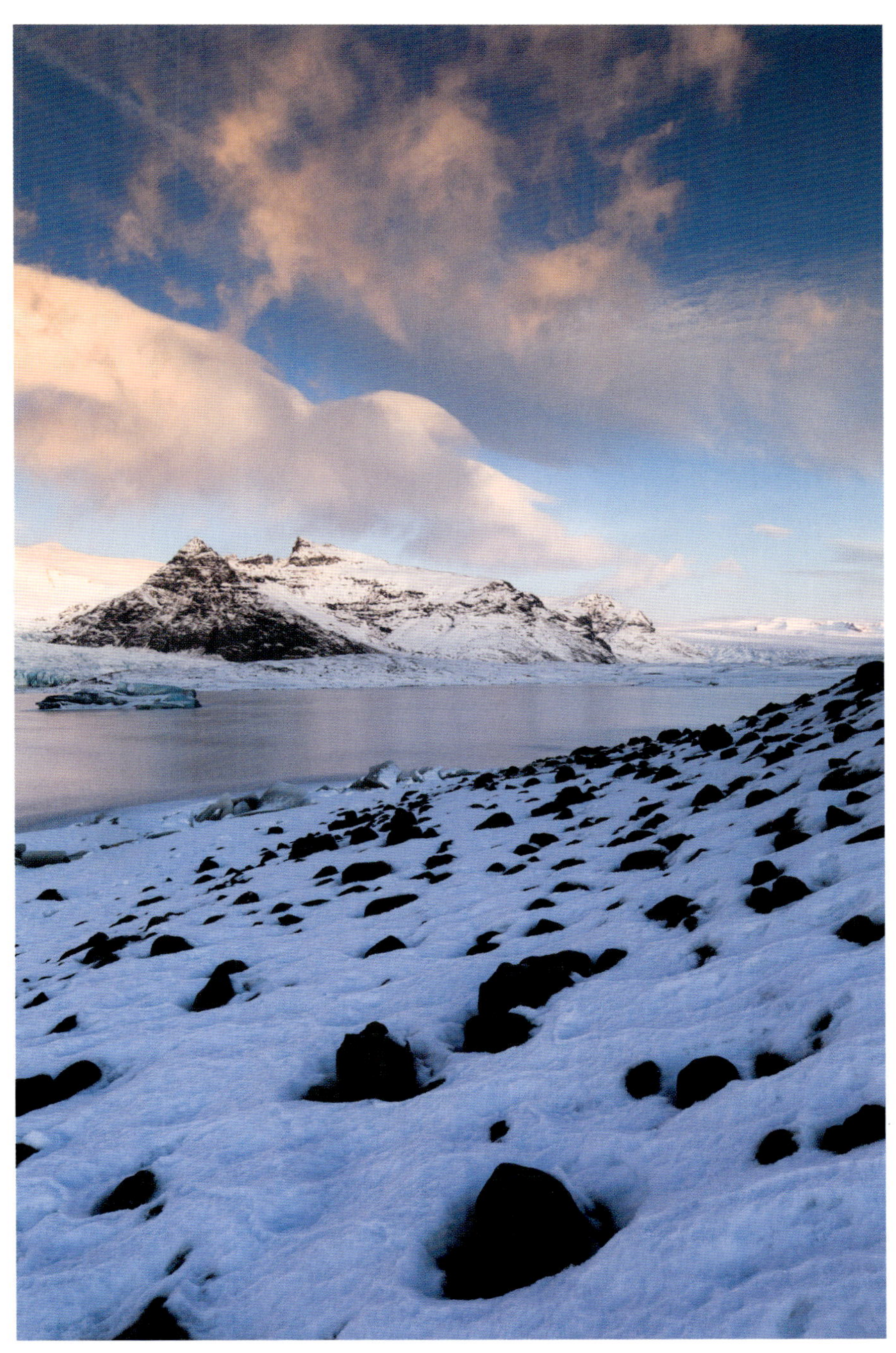

Elements

Fjallsárlón Glacier Lagoon, Iceland

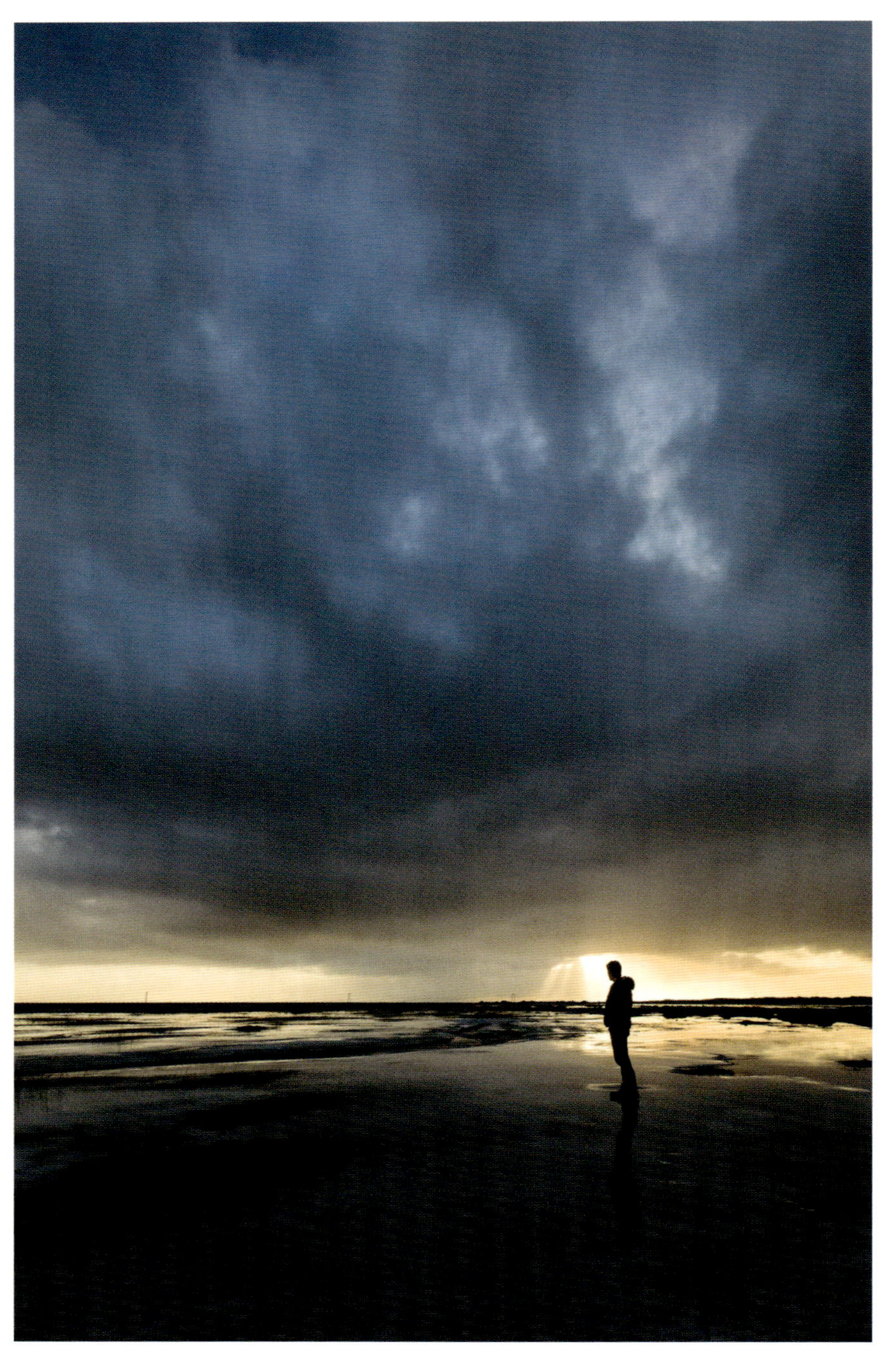

Weathered

Paul Zizka in Southern Iceland

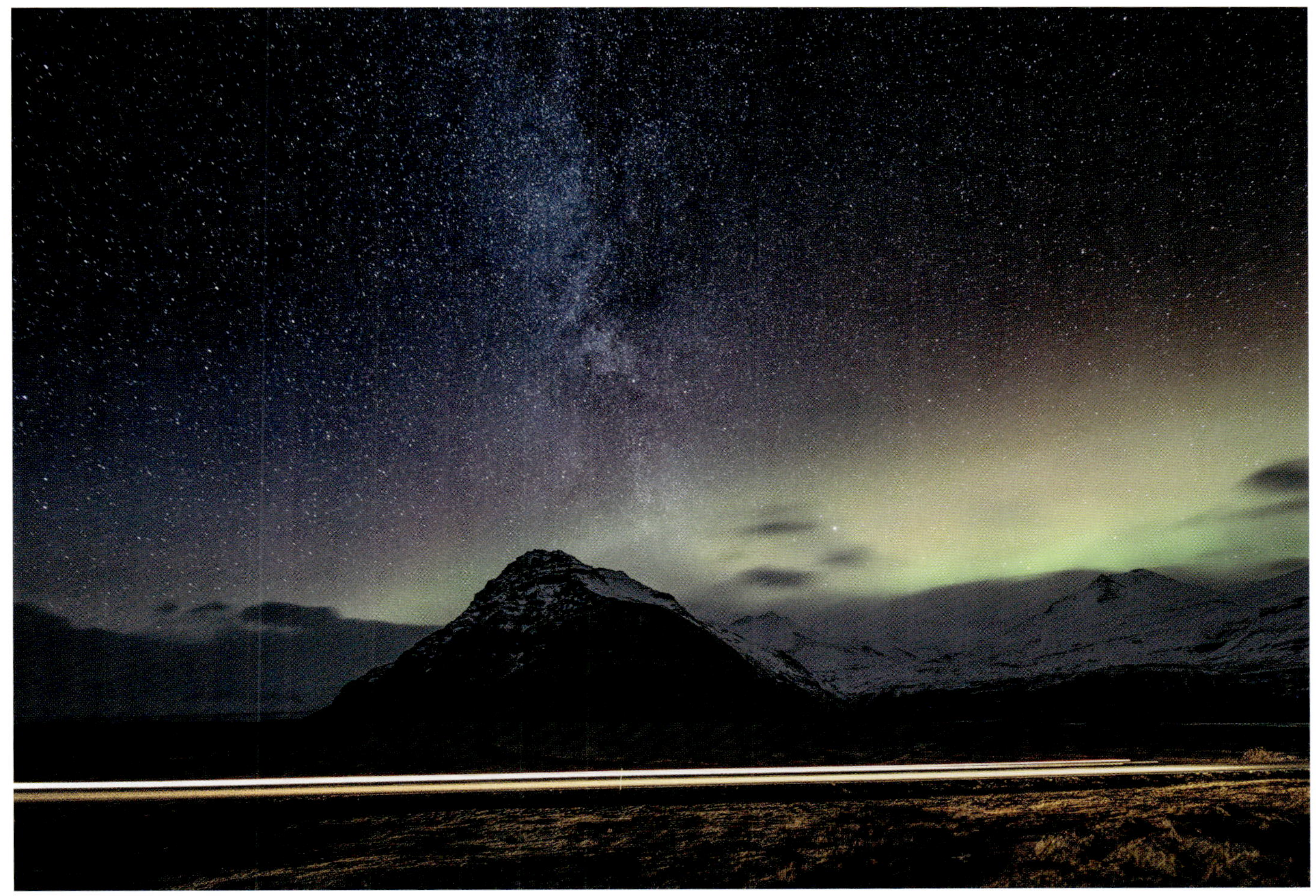

Time/Space Continuum
Southeast Iceland

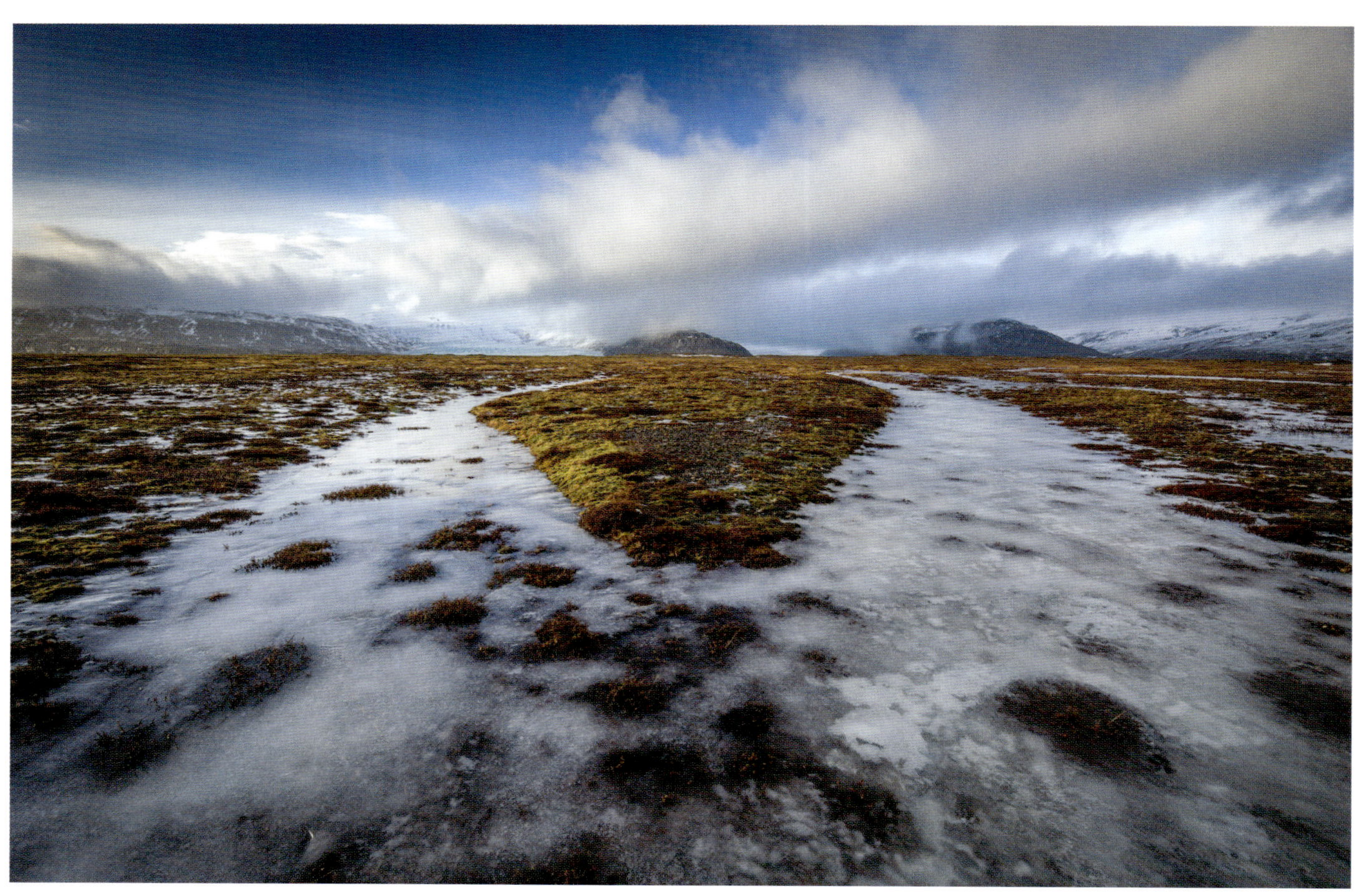

Ice/Land

Vatnajökull National Park, Iceland

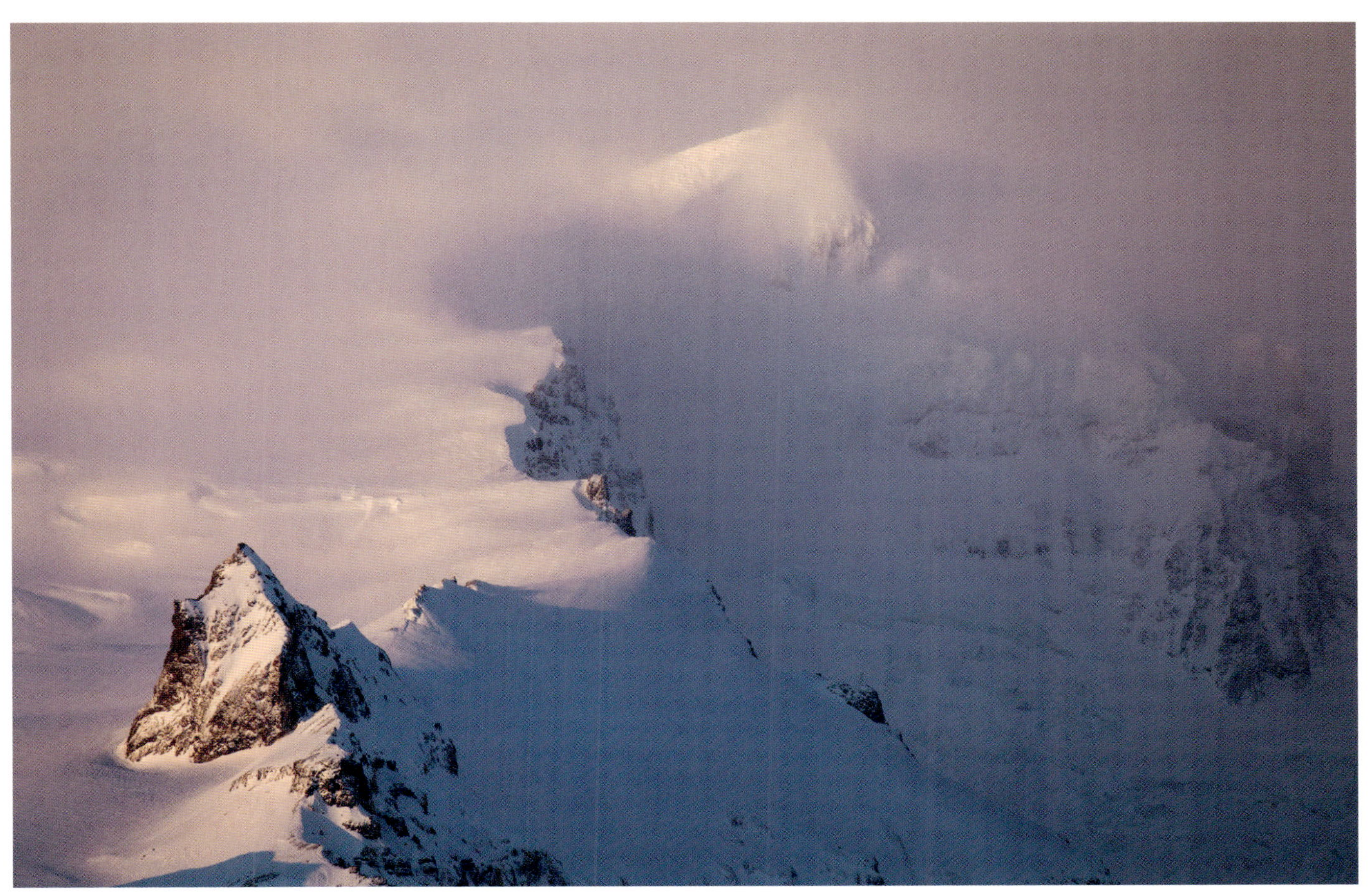

Emergence
Fjallsárlón Glacier Lagoon, Iceland

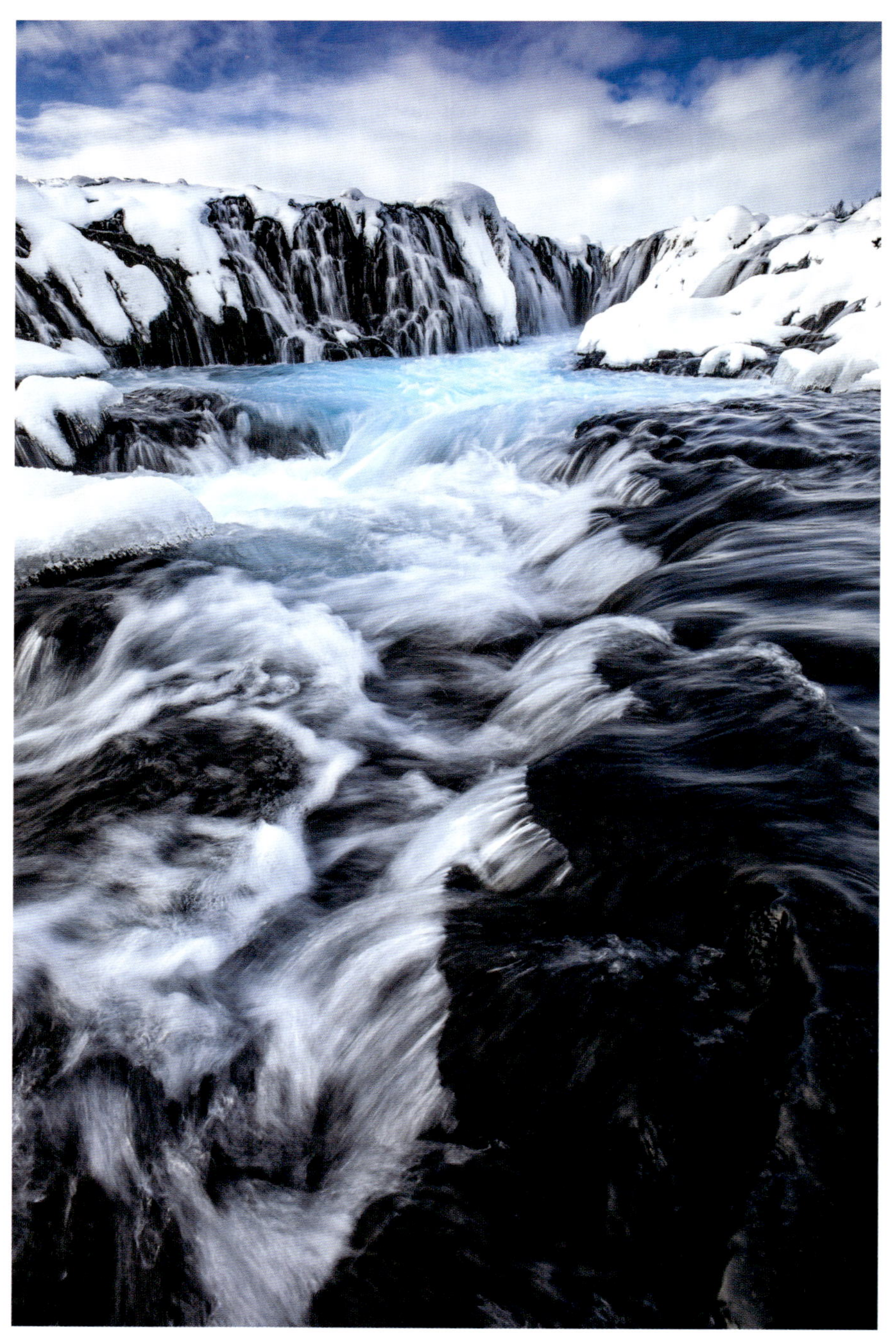

Ice Birth

Brúarfoss, Iceland

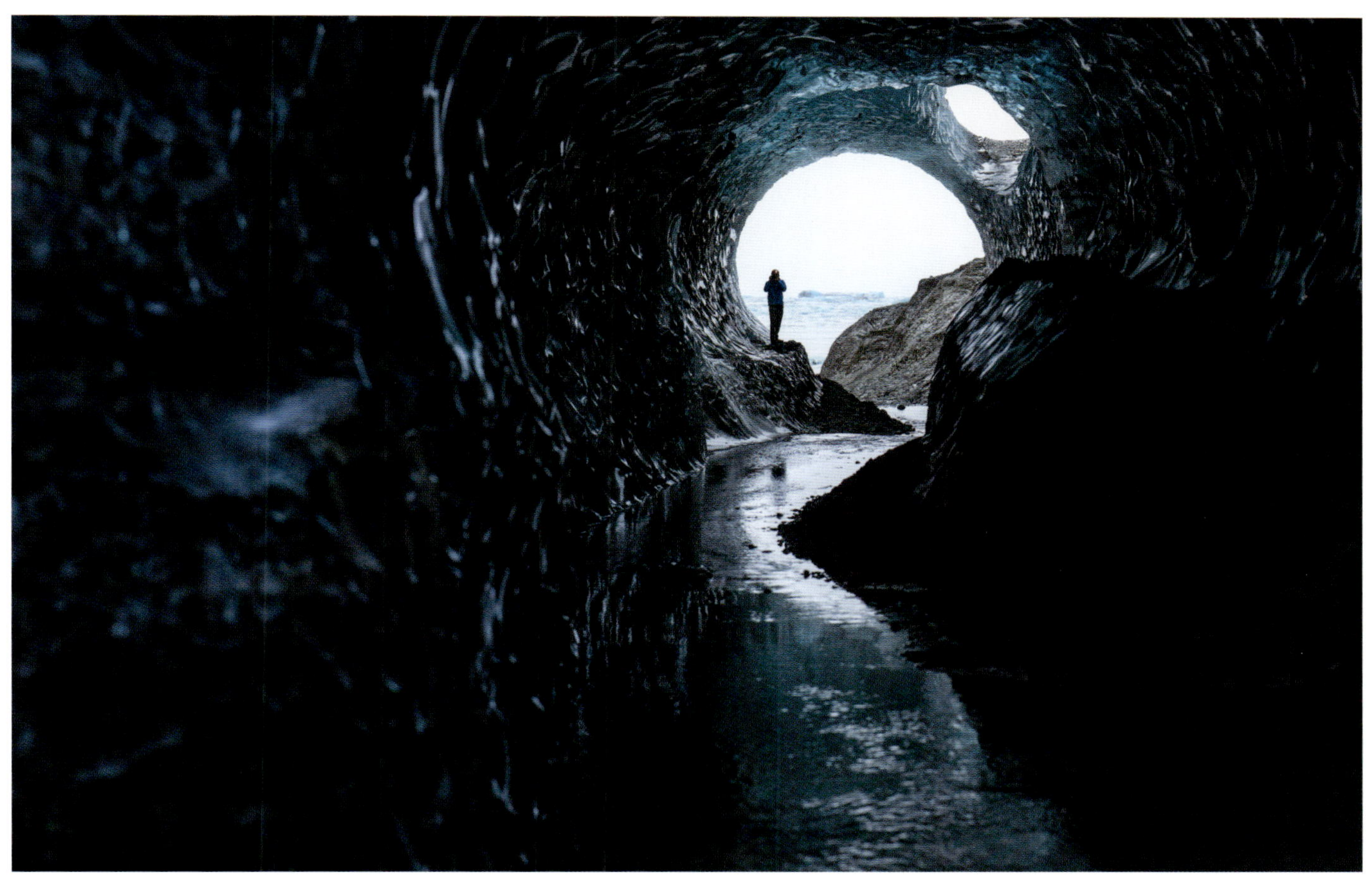

Inner Depths

David Sinclair in Skaftafell – Vatnajökull National Park, Iceland

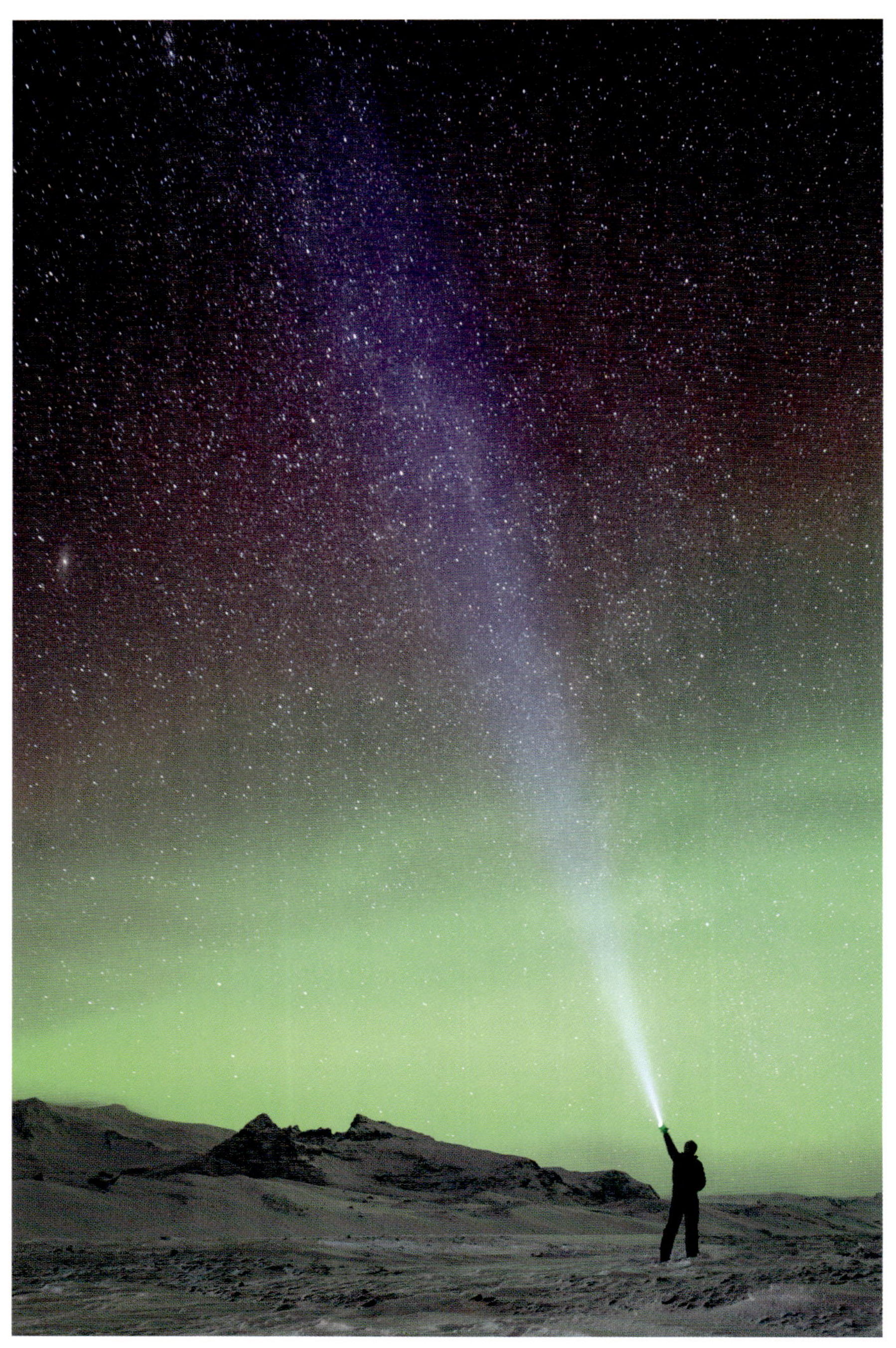

Darkness, My Old Friend
Paul Zizka in Southeast Iceland

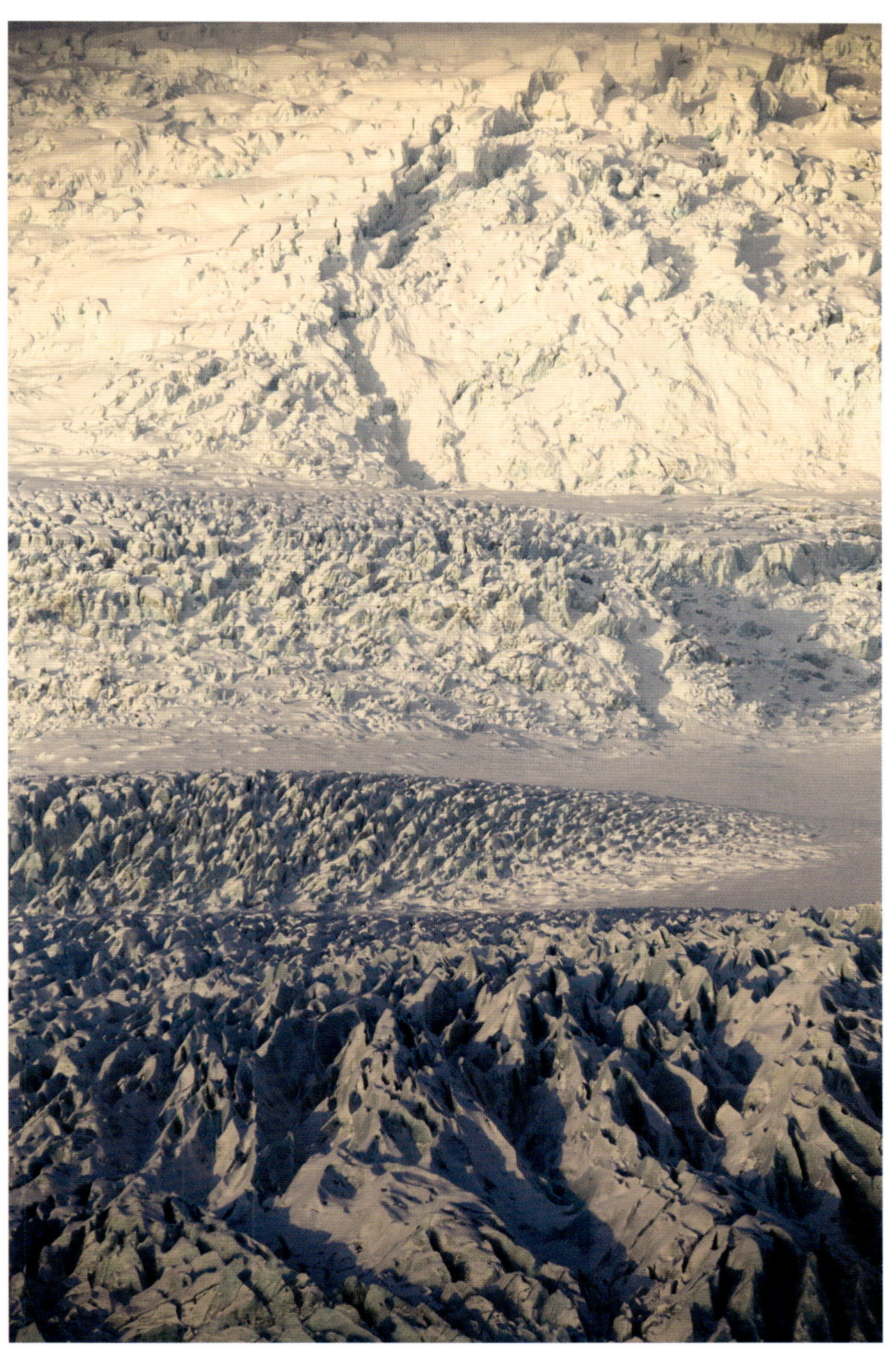

Cascade

Fjallsárlón Glacier Lagoon, Iceland

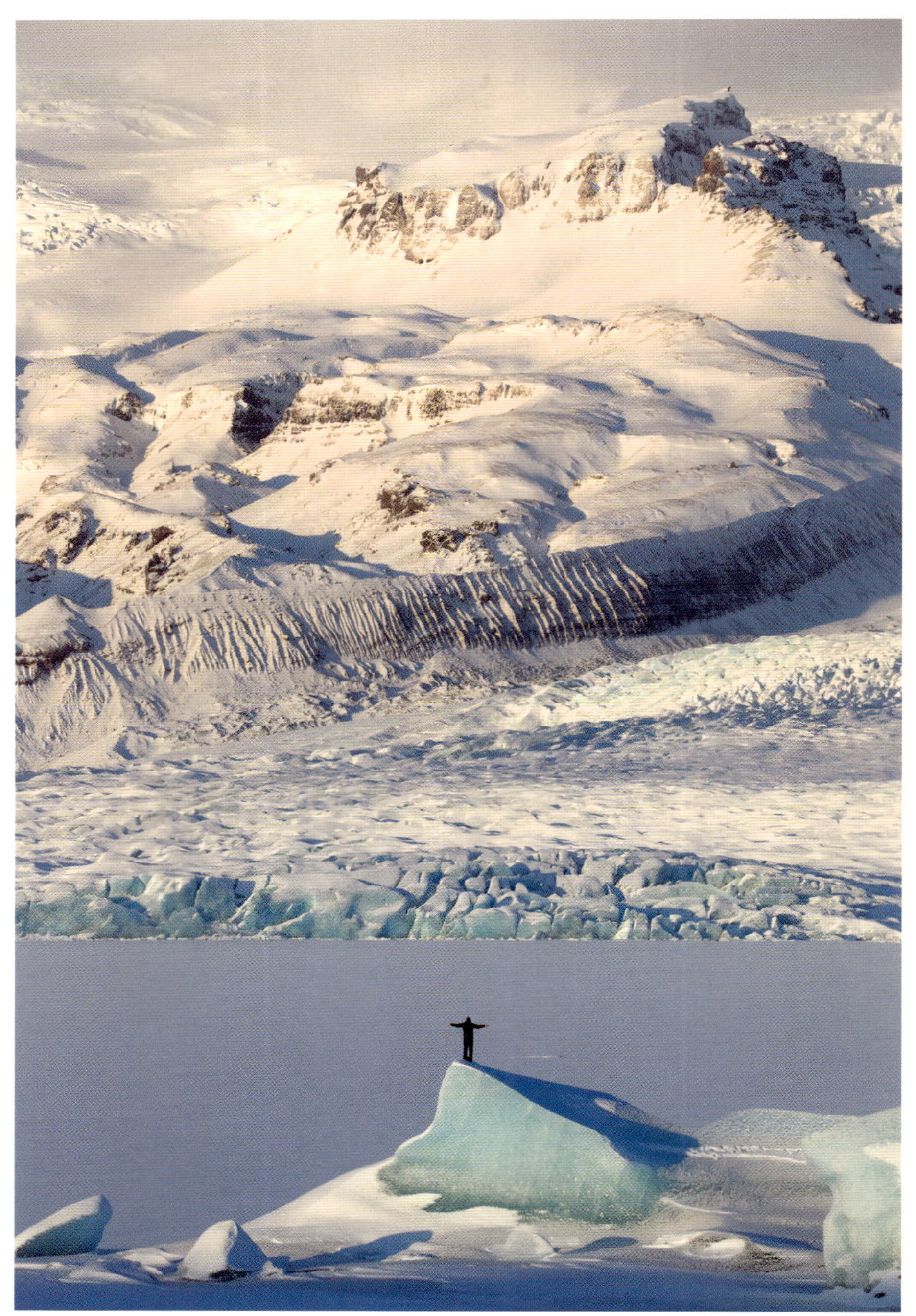

Freedom

Jesse Milner at Fjallsárlón Glacier Lagoon, Iceland

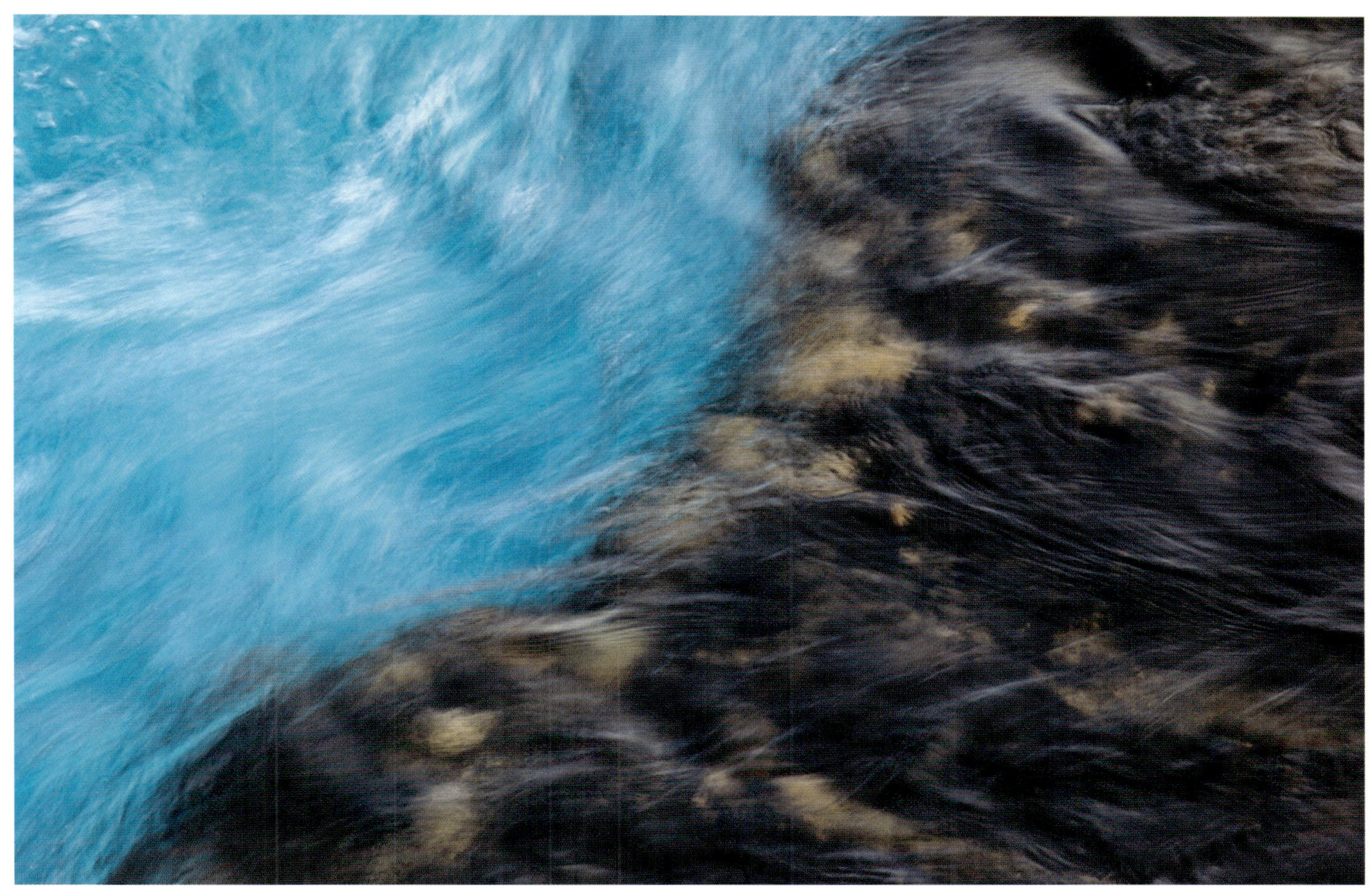

Convergence
Brúarfoss, Iceland

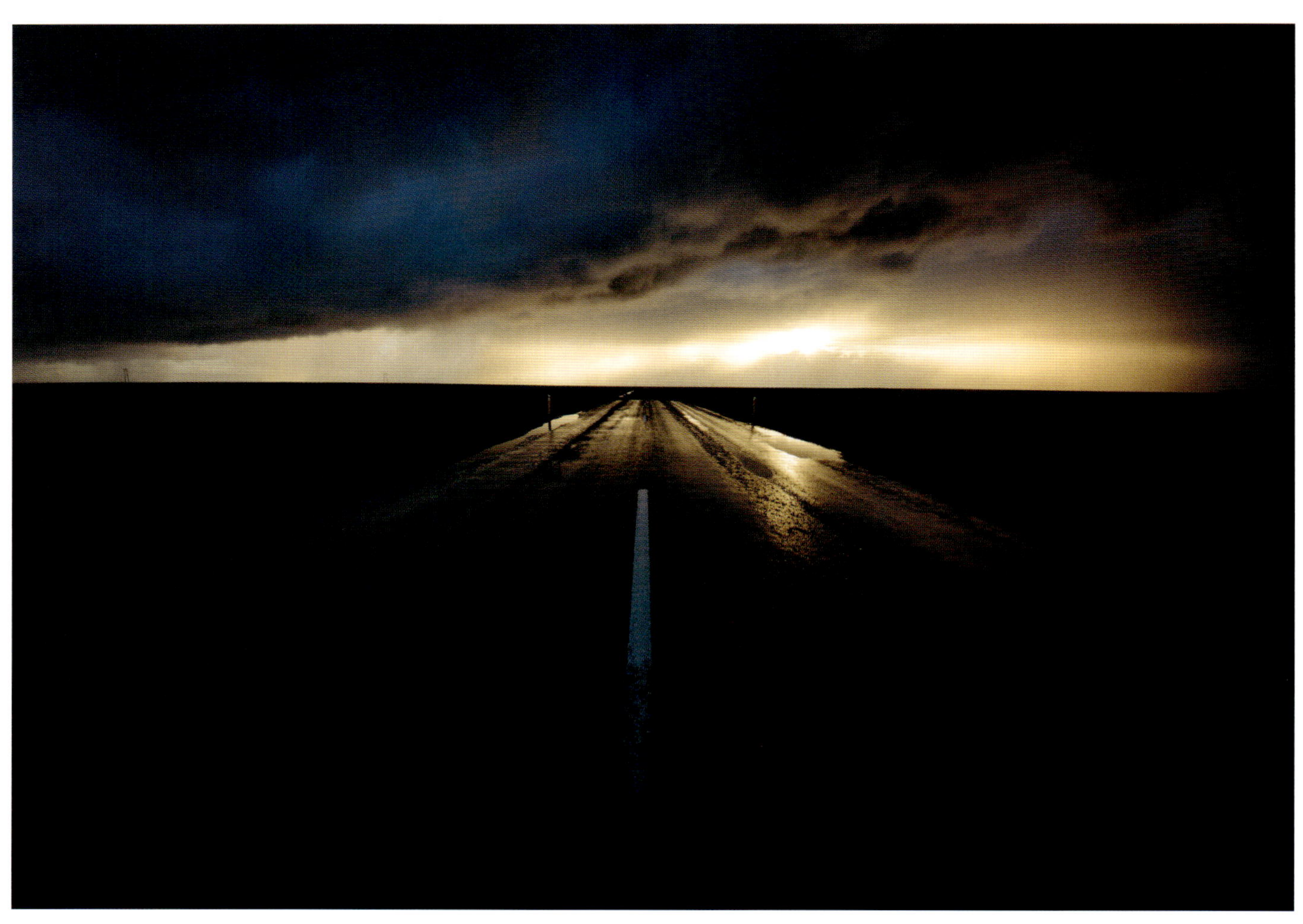

Light My Way

Southeast Iceland

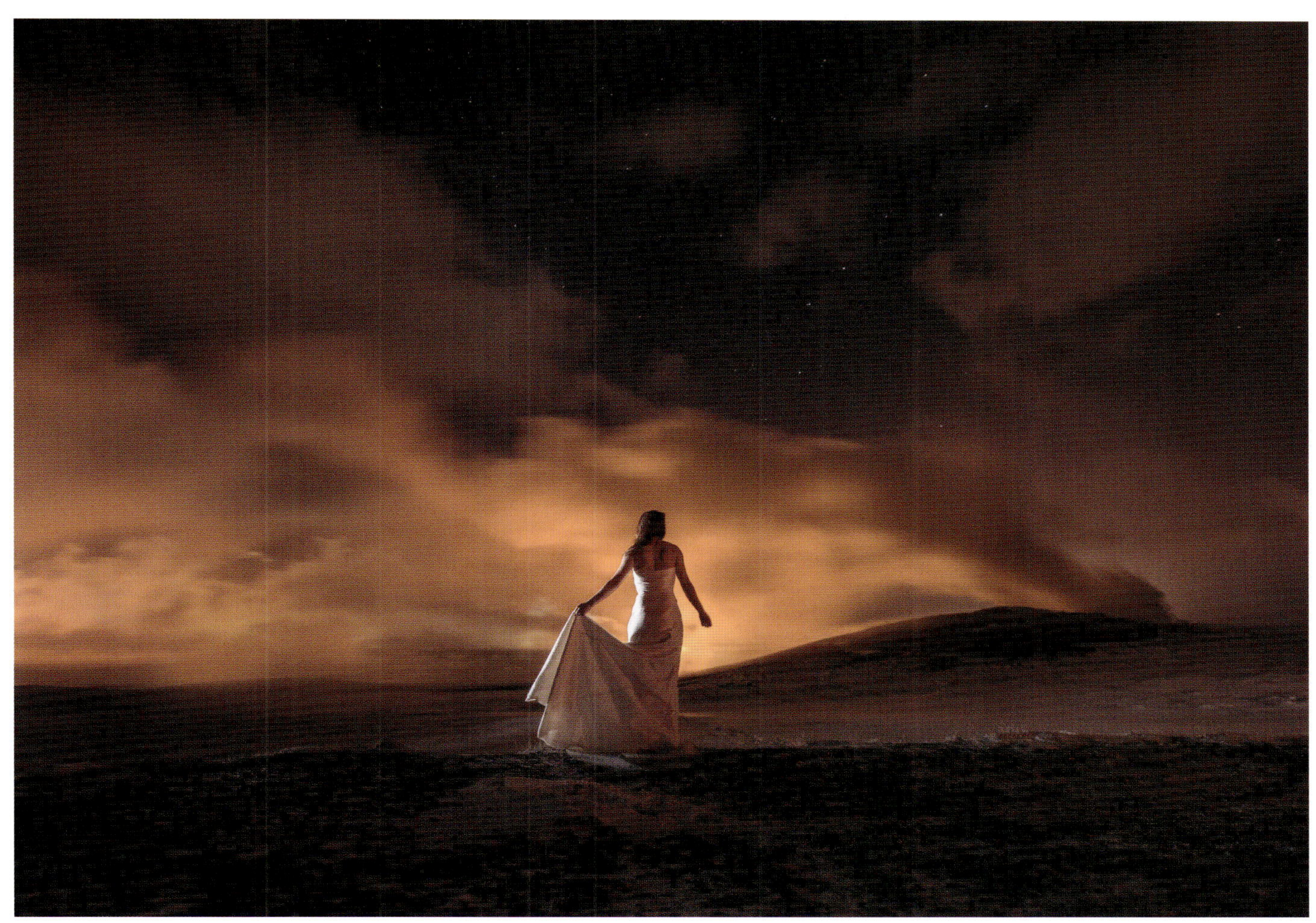

Into the Good Night

Maggie Hood at Gunnuhver, Iceland

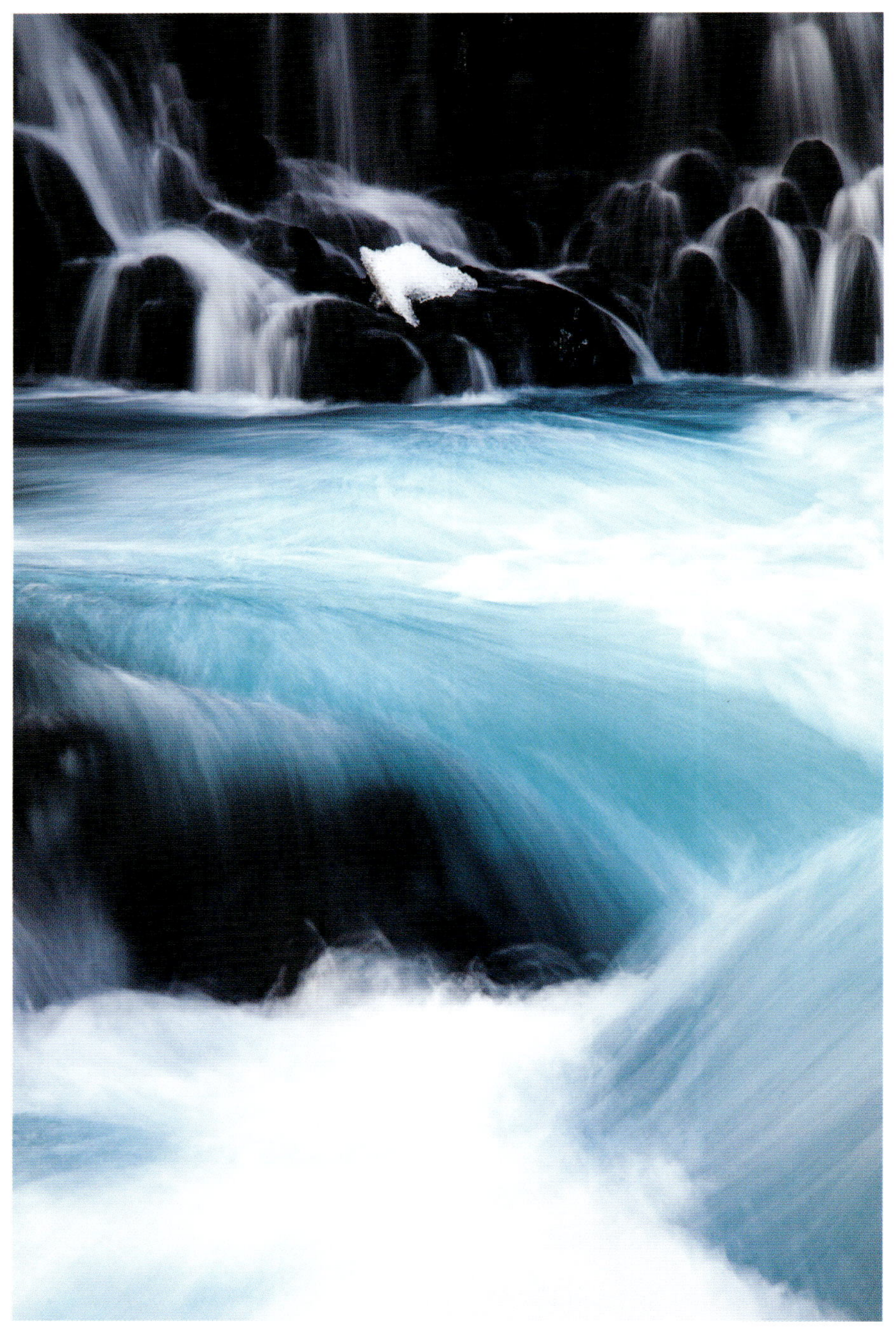

The Blue Pools
Brúarfoss, Iceland

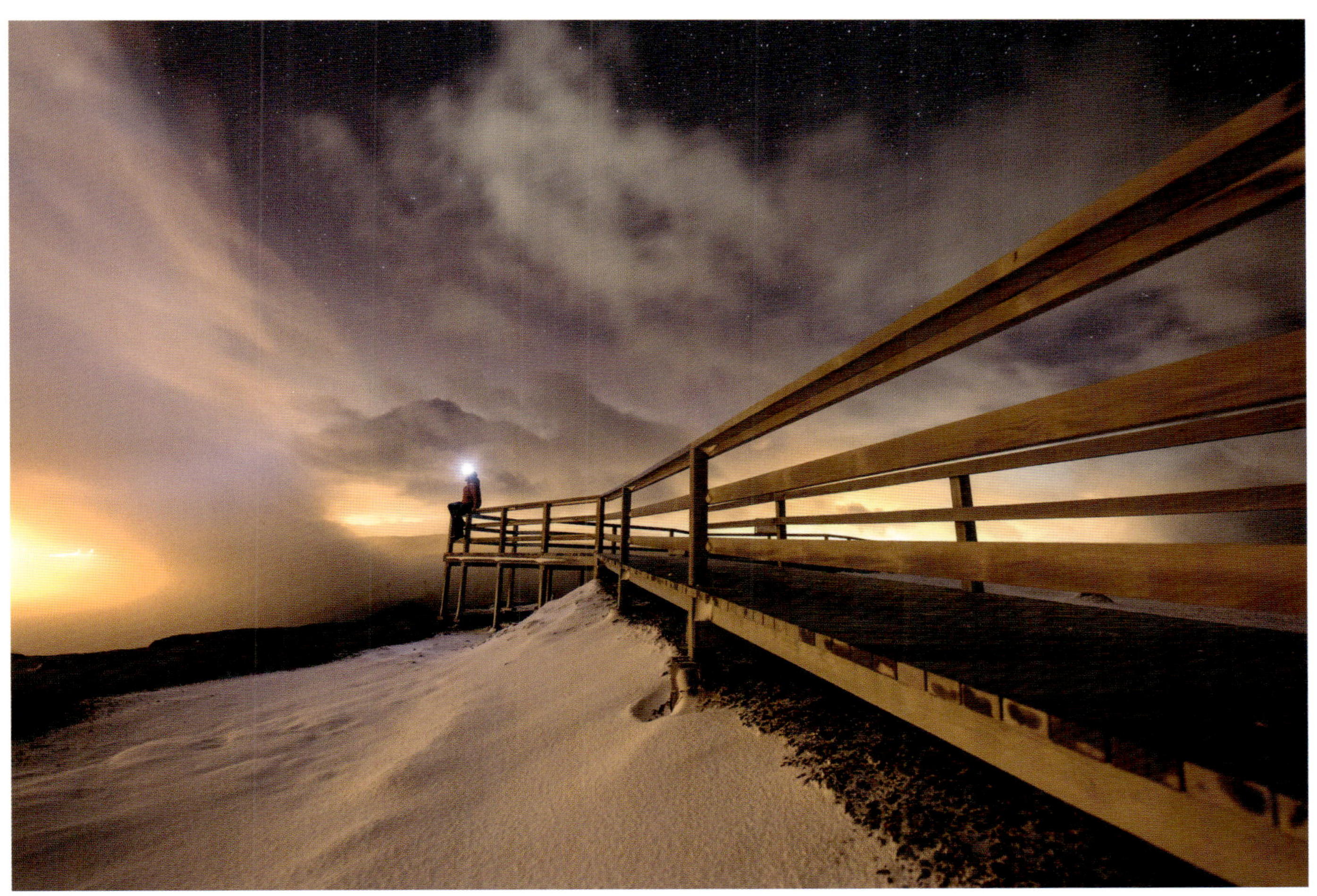

Night Life
Self-Portrait at Gunnuhver, Iceland

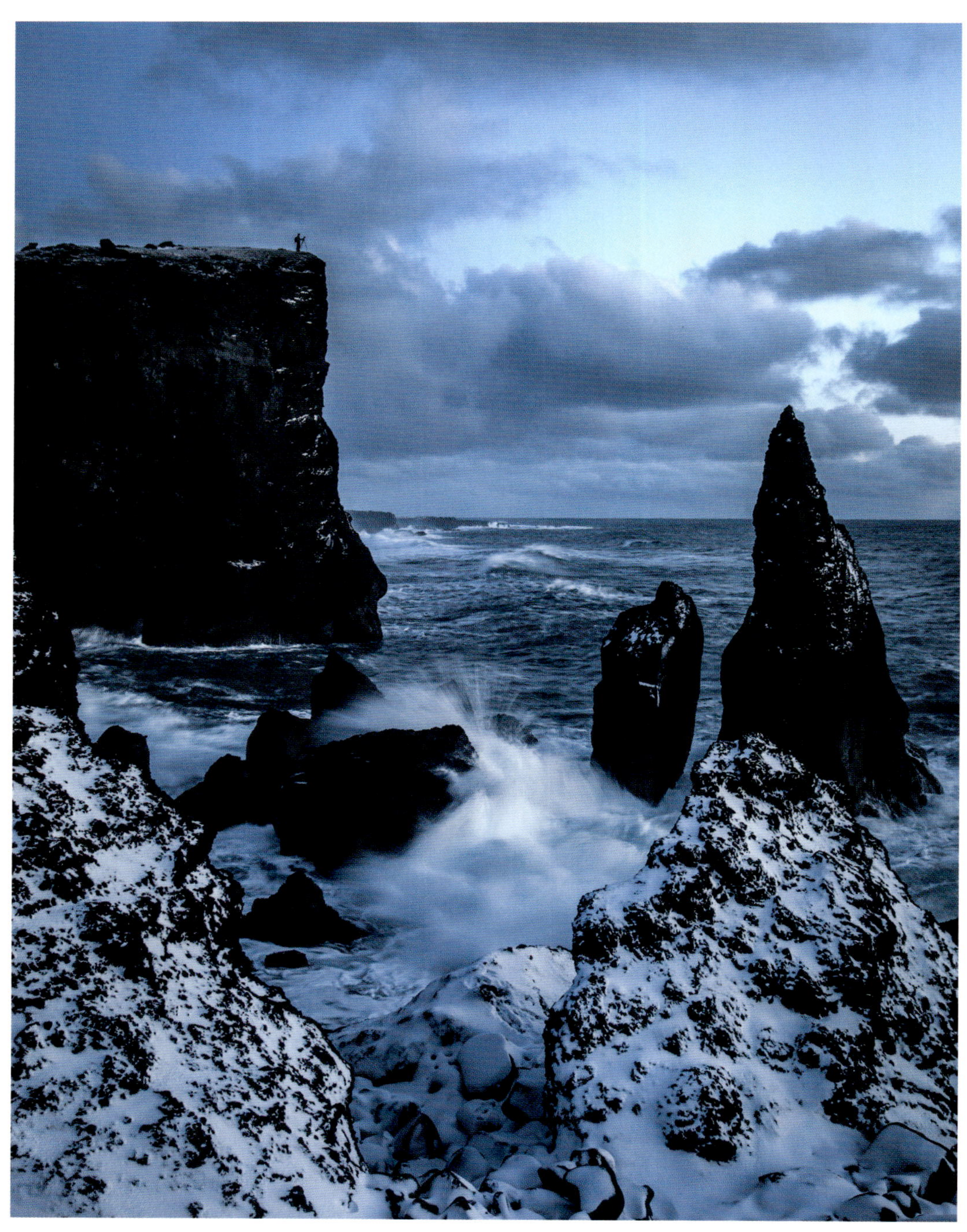

Such Great Heights

Paul Zizka at Valahnúkamöl, Iceland

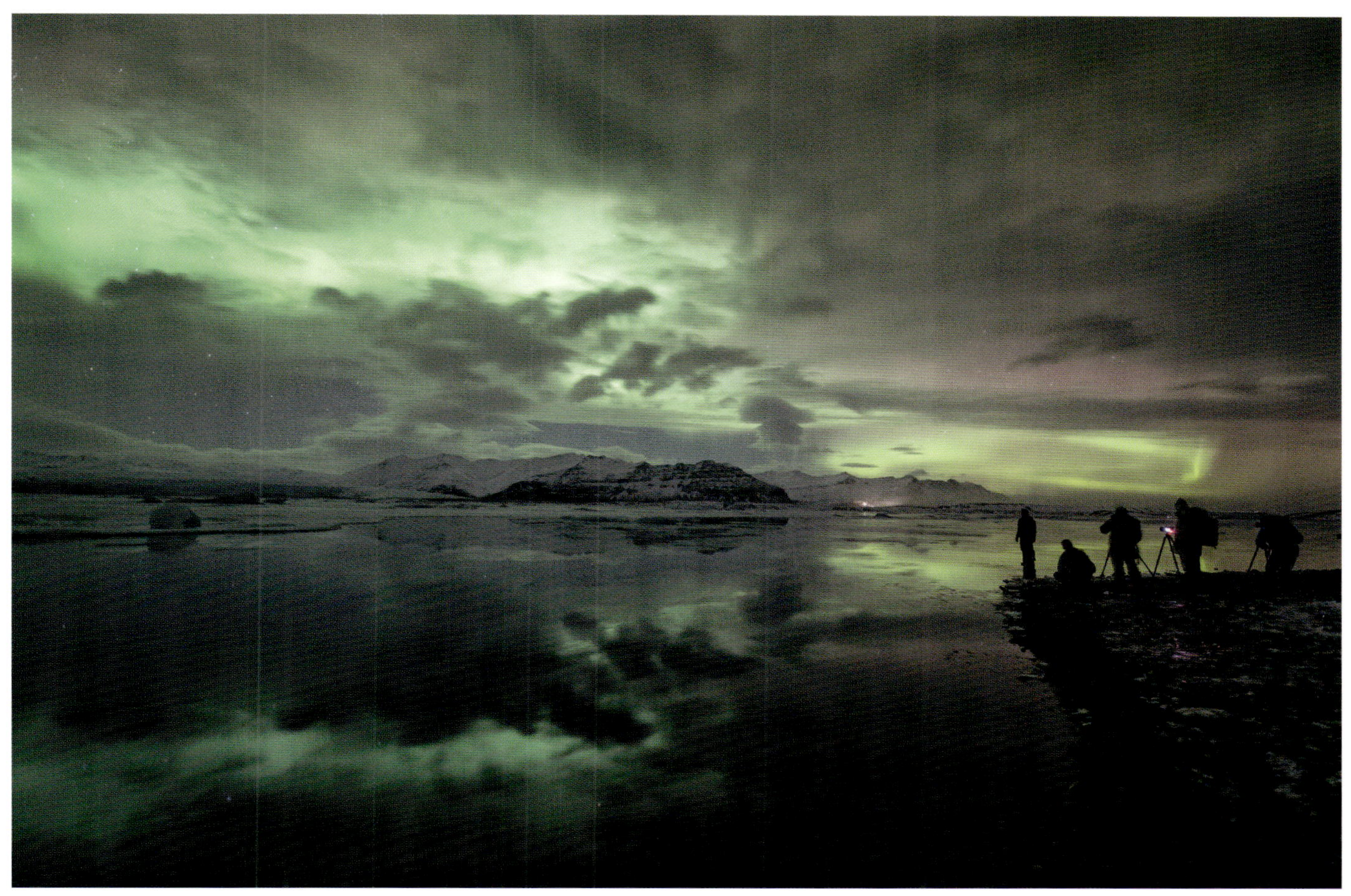

Front Row Seats
Jökulsárlón Glacier Lagoon, Iceland

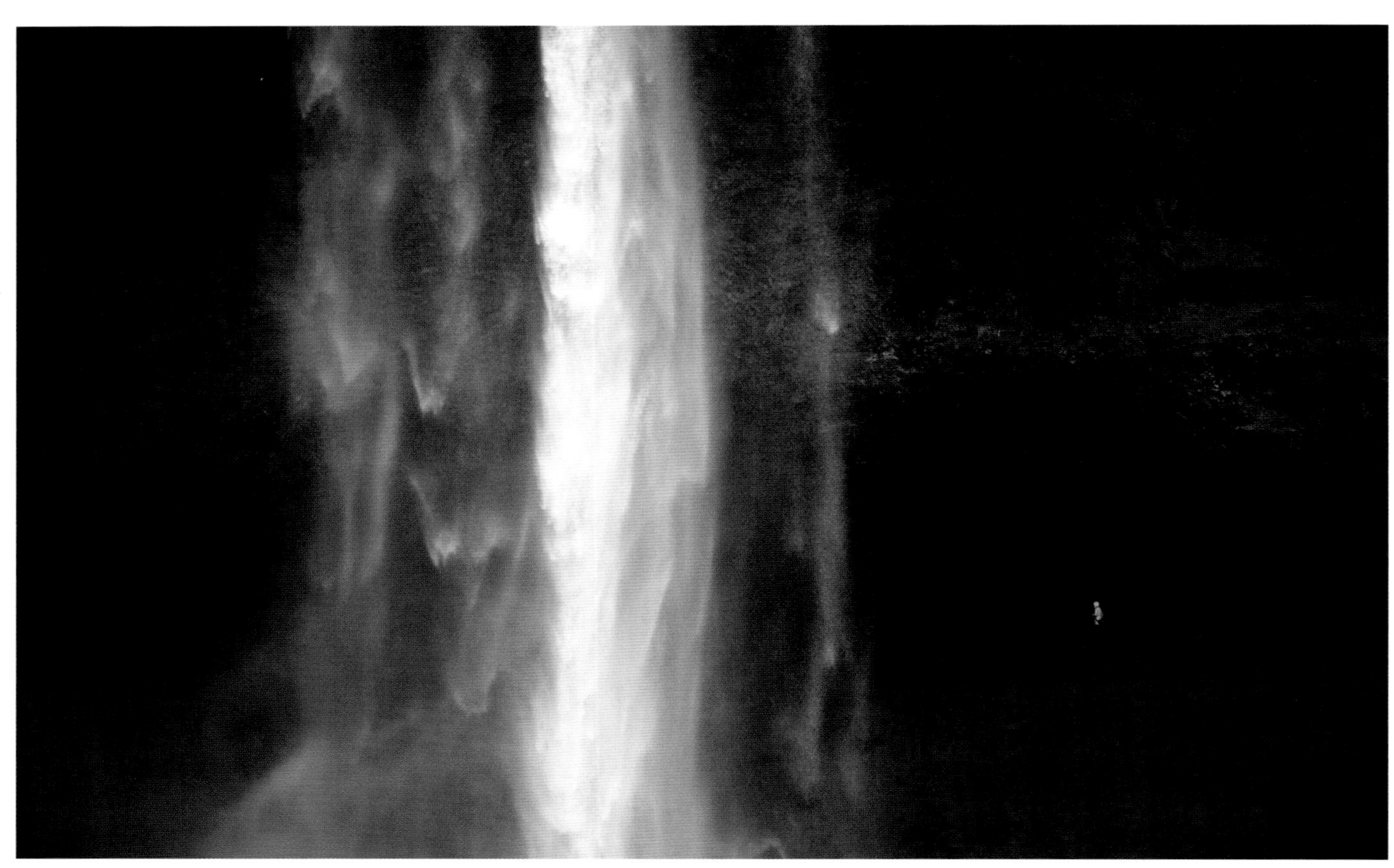

 The Visitor
Seljalandsfoss, Iceland

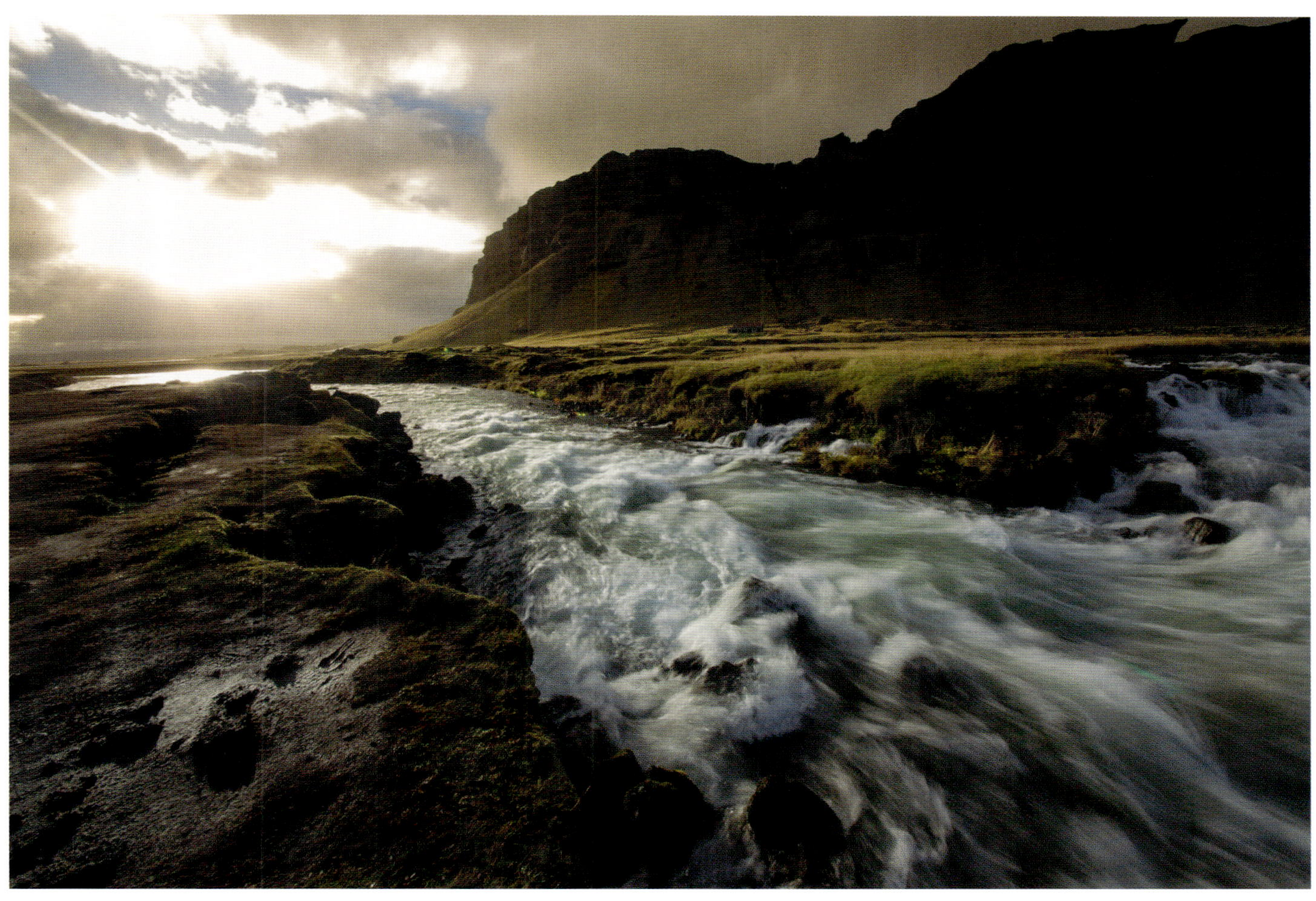

Into the Mystic
Southeast Iceland

The Spectacular Northwest Territories

The Northwest Territories is where I really became a photographer. It is where I discovered a community of creative people, where my love affair with the outdoors truly took root and where my photography was allowed to flourish as an actual career.

Erin and I moved "south" to the Northwest Territories from Nunavut in 2004 – we would often joke that we'd moved somewhere "warm and cheap" compared to Nunavut (even if the rest of Canada considered it cold and expensive). I moved because of my nine-to-five job, but within two short years I had established a small photography business on the side, a business that would eventually take off and allow me to pursue my photography full time.

In addition to heading out and shooting the lake-covered, rocky, barren and beautiful landscapes around Yellowknife – along with its world-famous night skies (Yellowknife is noted as being one of the prime places on the globe to view and photograph the aurora borealis) – I found myself shooting commercial photography, weddings and even family photography (despite Martin Hartley's early advice to "never shoot babies or puppies; it's a career-killer!"). In most places in Canada, photographers are forced to specialize to some degree to "make it" as a photographer; in Yellowknife I found the opposite. It was a community that embraced my love for shooting everything and helped immensely to nudge me to become the photographer I am today. Its creative circle is – in my mind – one of the strongest in all of Canada, and I'll forever be thankful for the many photographers, artists, writers, musicians and uniquely creative folks with whom I've shared countless conversations, coffees and collaborative field time in Yellowknife and many other parts of the Northwest Territories.

I love having the time to really dive into a geographic area. One of the most powerful components of living in a place is that you have greater opportunity to find beauty even in its less-appreciated locations: you don't simply travel to and document the "icons" of an area. You have the power to return to areas again and again under different conditions: mist, morning light, cloud cover, stars, sun… they all become your creative muse. Most of my favourite images from the Northwest Territories came out of observing simple moments of light or interesting conditions rather than being in the "tourism brochure" locations. They came out of observation and exploration and curiosity and simply wandering, looking – as The Tragically Hip famously sang – for a place to happen, making stops along the way.

The Northwest Territories is vast (1,144,000 square kilometres) and impossible to fully document. Like all the Northern areas I've explored, it fills me with appreciation for the locations I've had the chance to see, and with longing for the ones within its far-reaching borders that I have yet to see. Despite calling the Northwest Territories home for over a decade, I would need many lifetimes to properly see and photograph it. These, here, are some of my favourite moments and images from a place that I love.

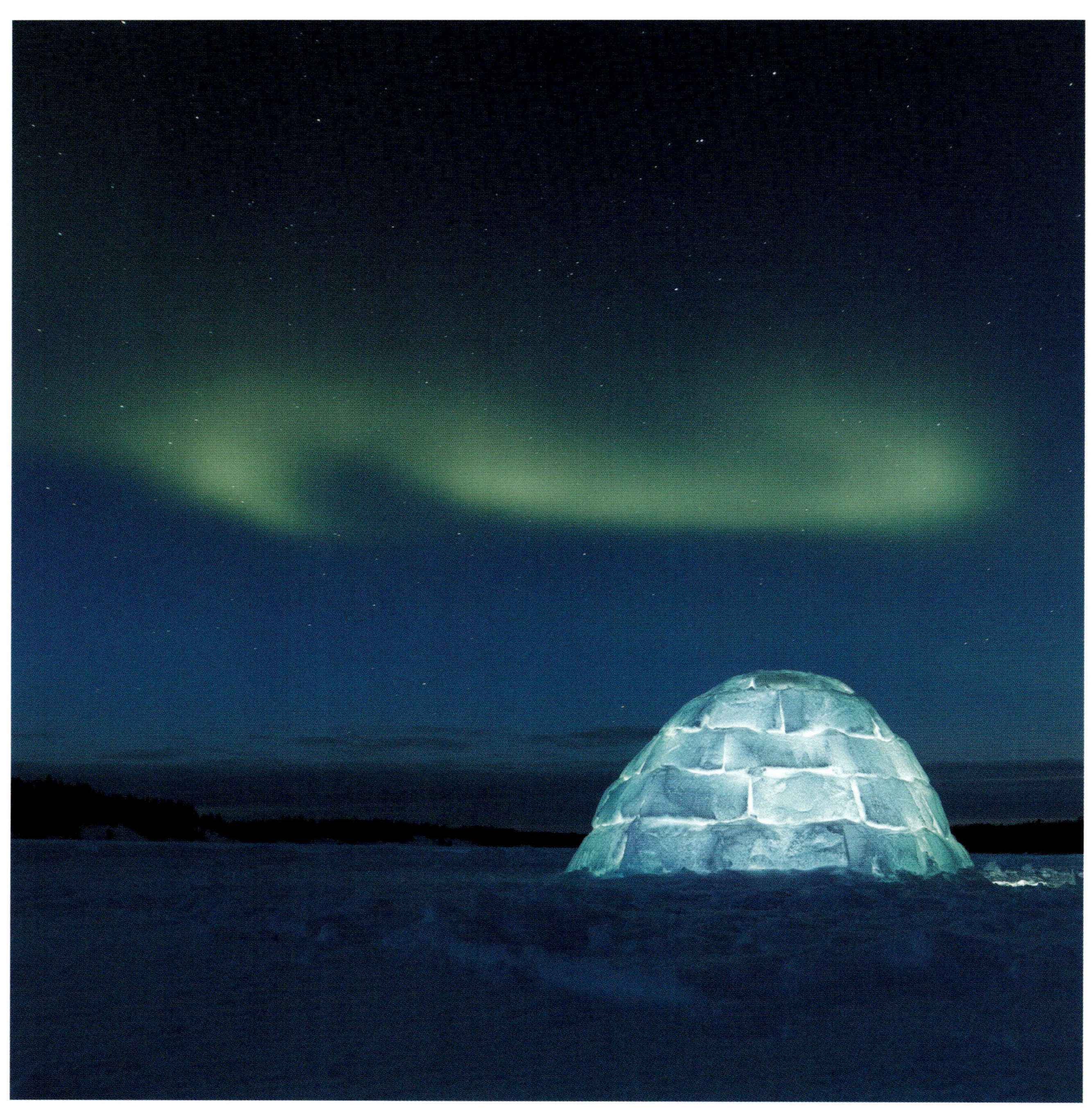

Peace

Vee Lake, Northwest Territories

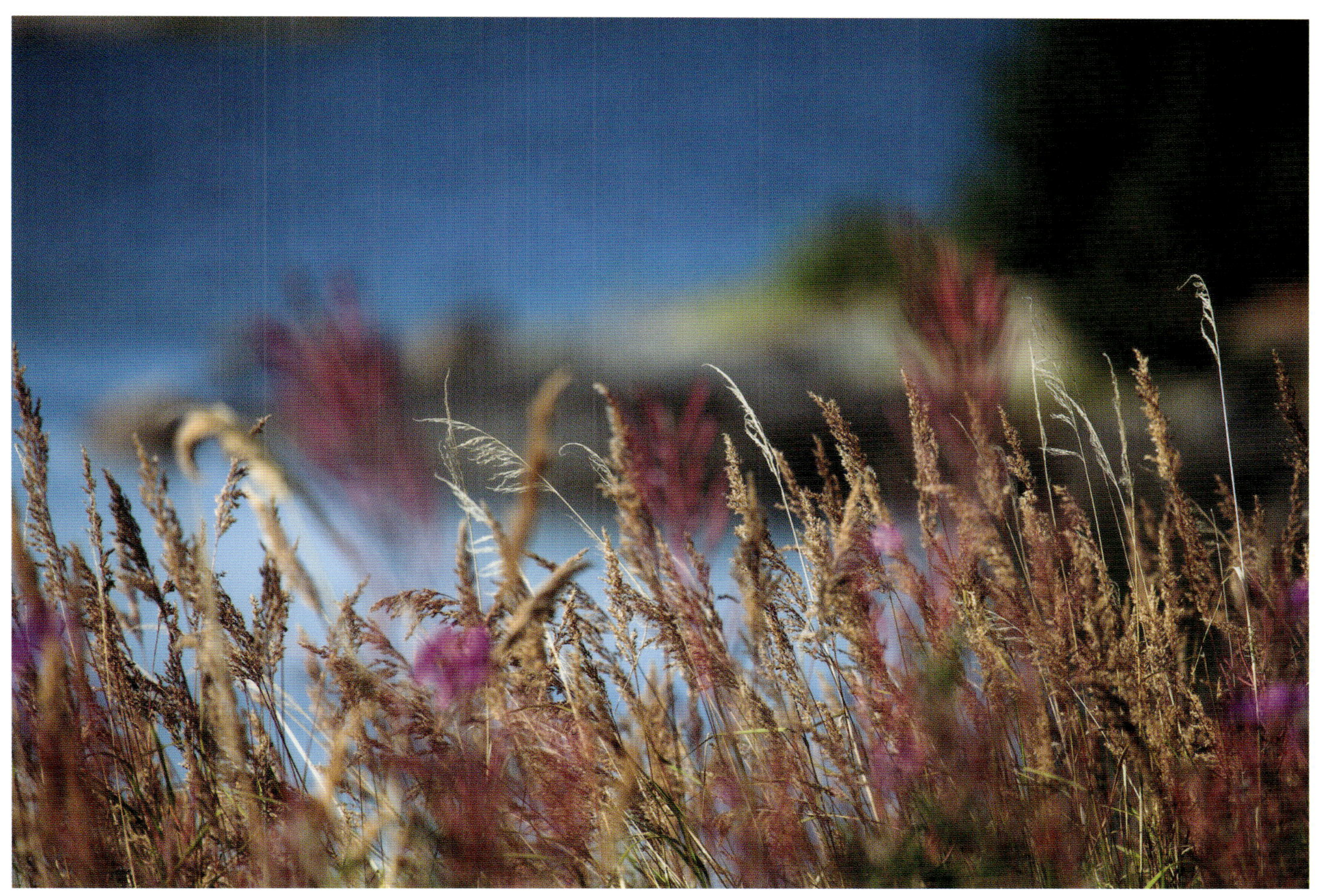

The Layers of Denendeh
Dettah, Northwest Territories

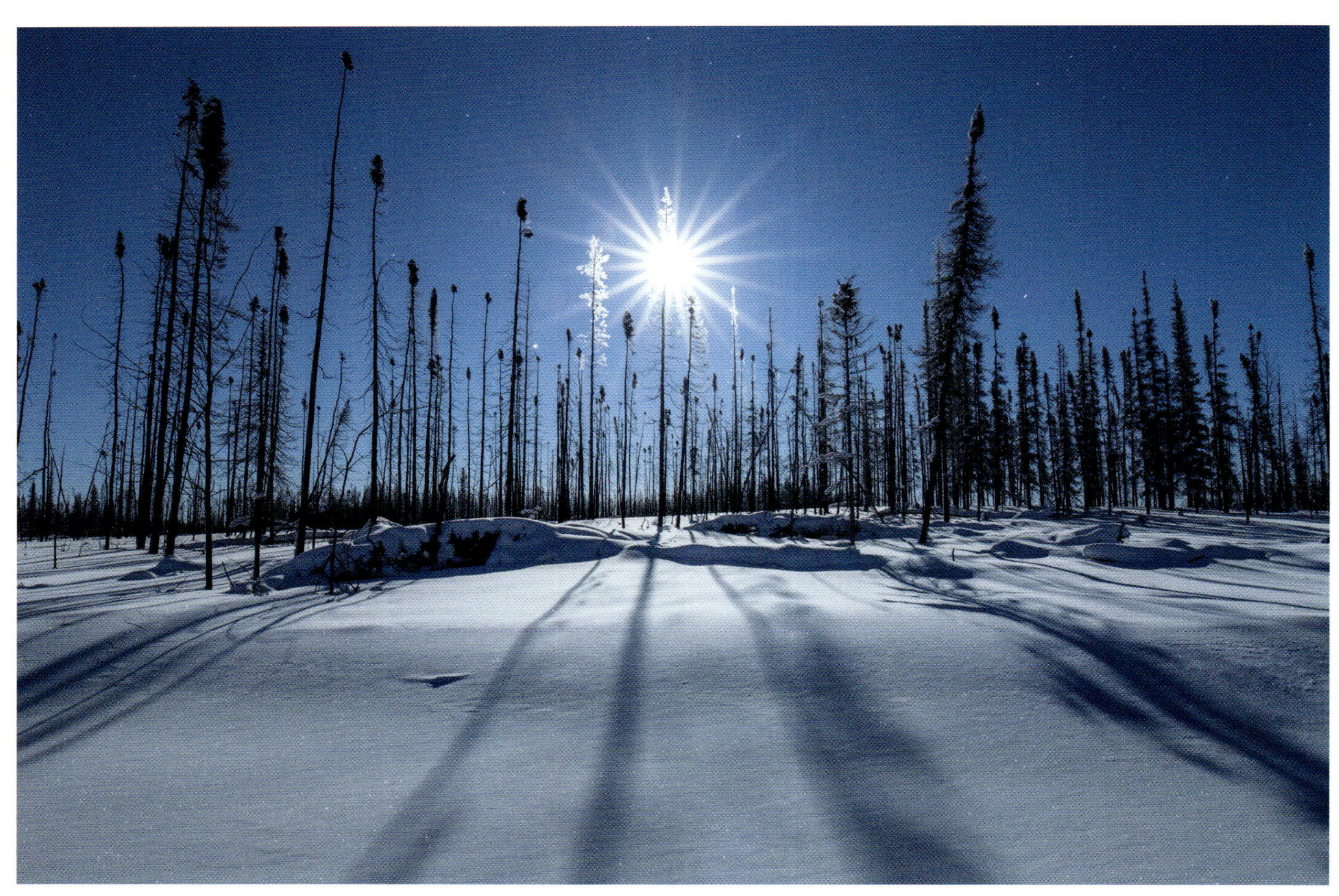

Moonshadow

Behchokǫ̀, Northwest Territories

Winter Home

Yellowknife, Northwest Territories

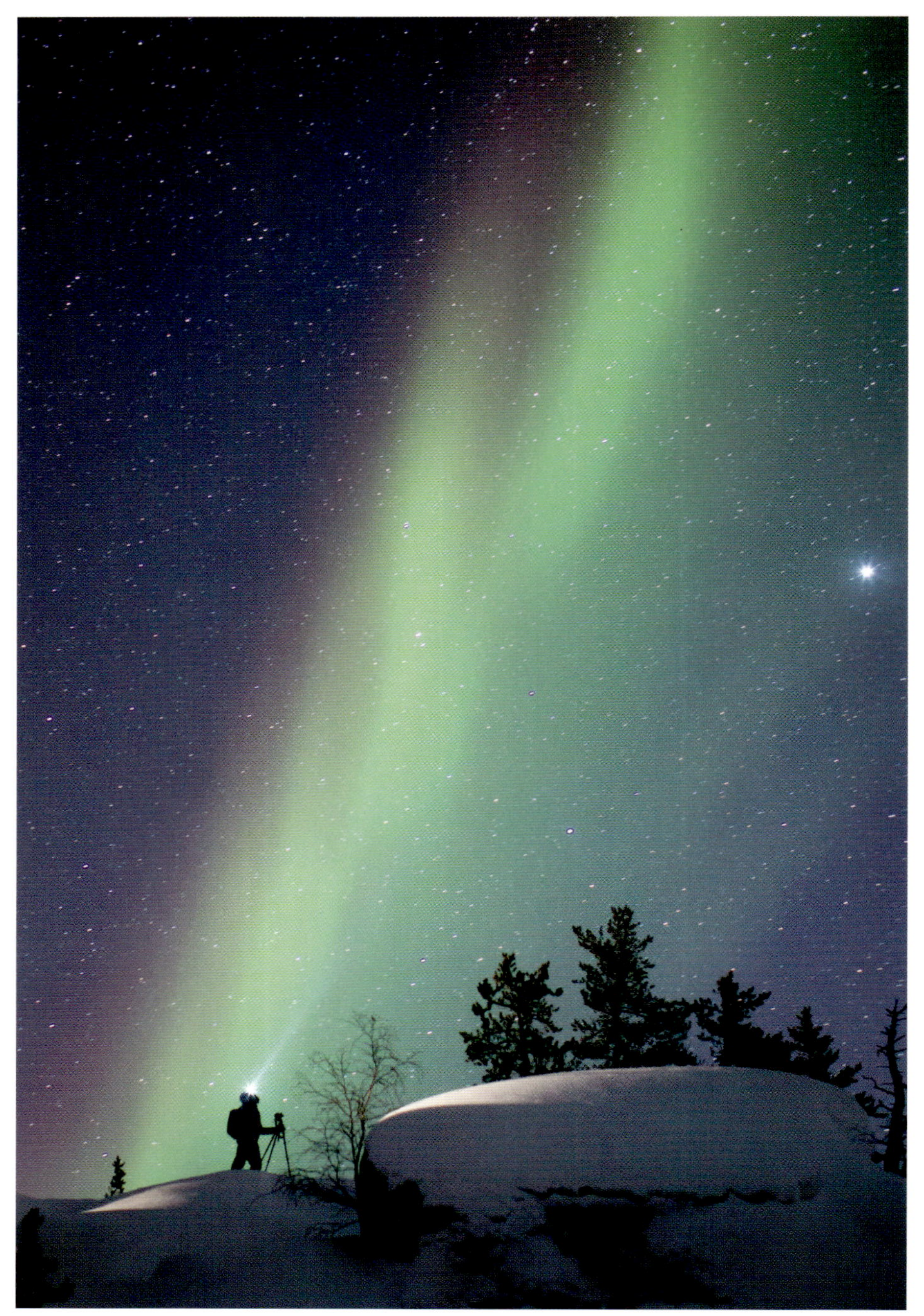

Nights of Wonder
Paul Zizka at Vee Lake, Northwest Territories

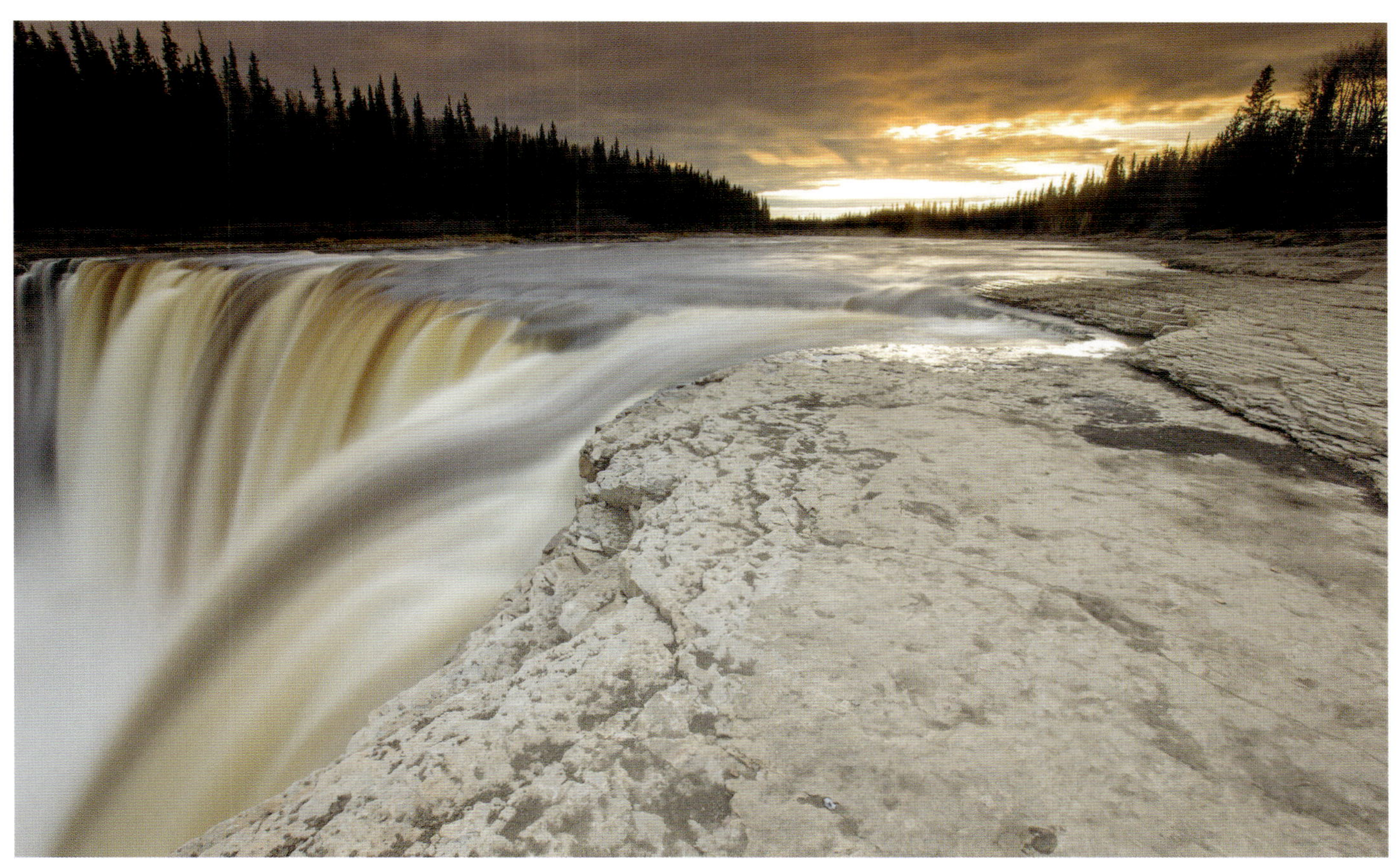

Alexandra in Fall
Alexandra Falls, Northwest Territories

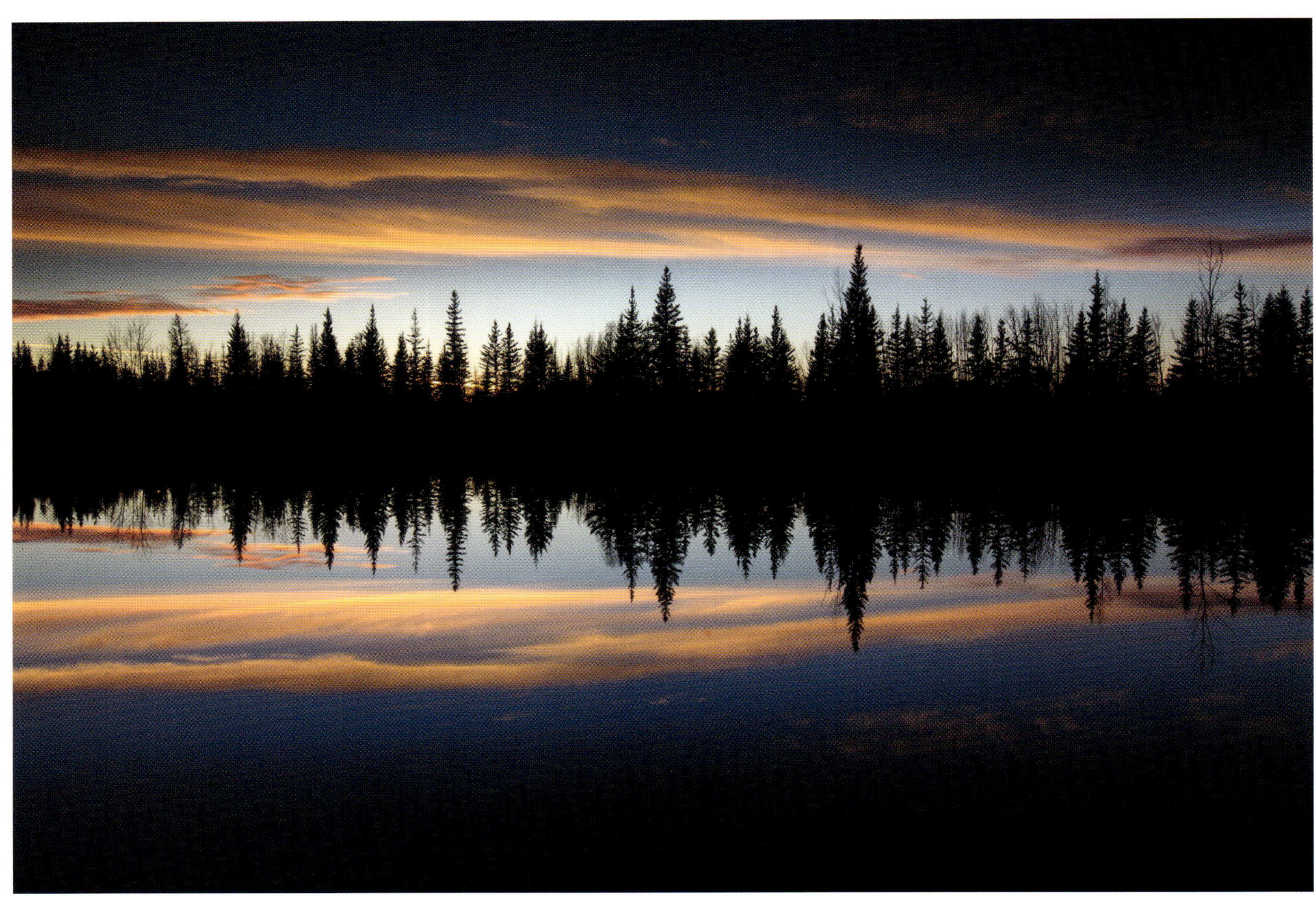

Northern Frequency
Enterprise, Northwest Territories

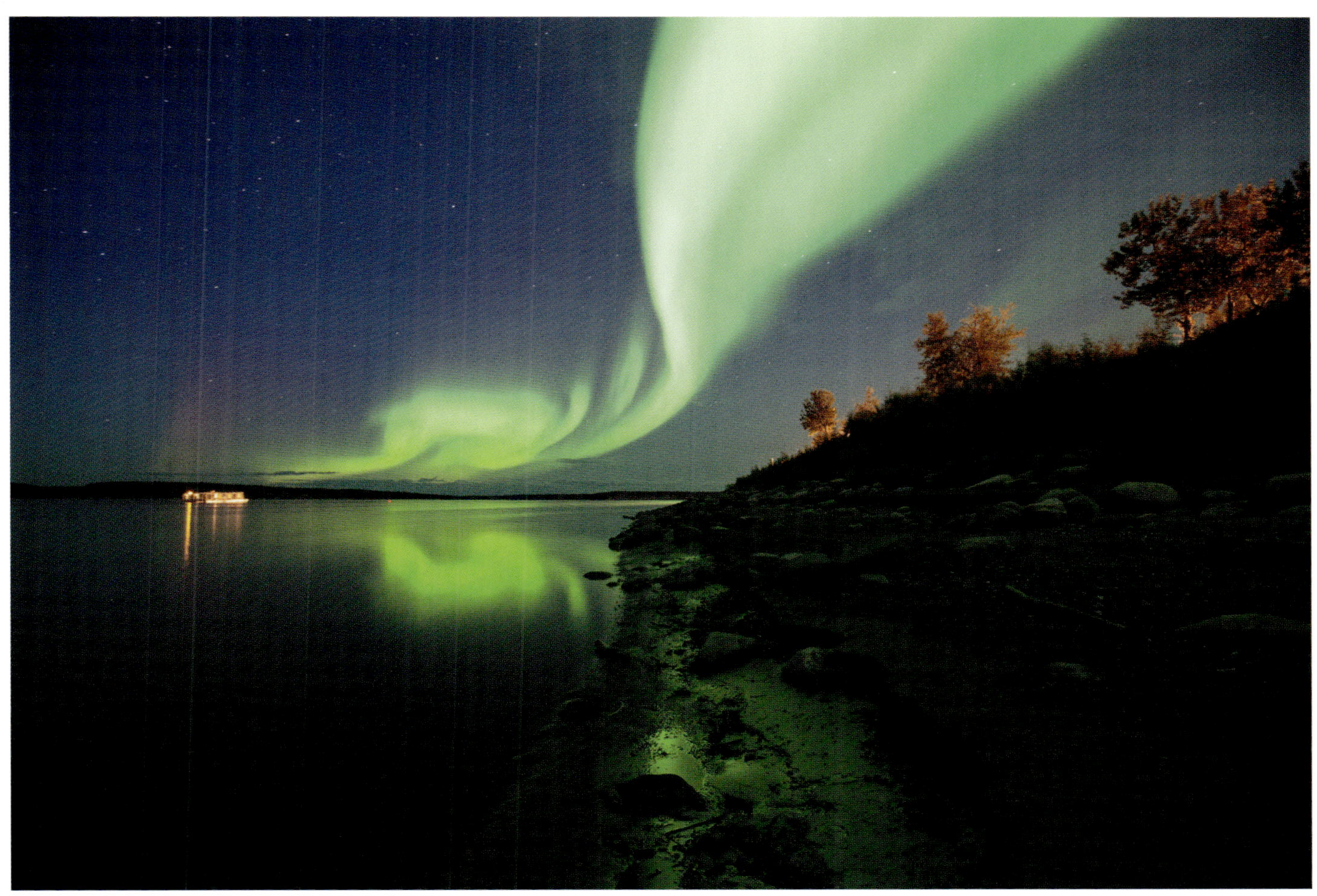

Simpson Sings a Green Song

Fort Simpson, Northwest Territories

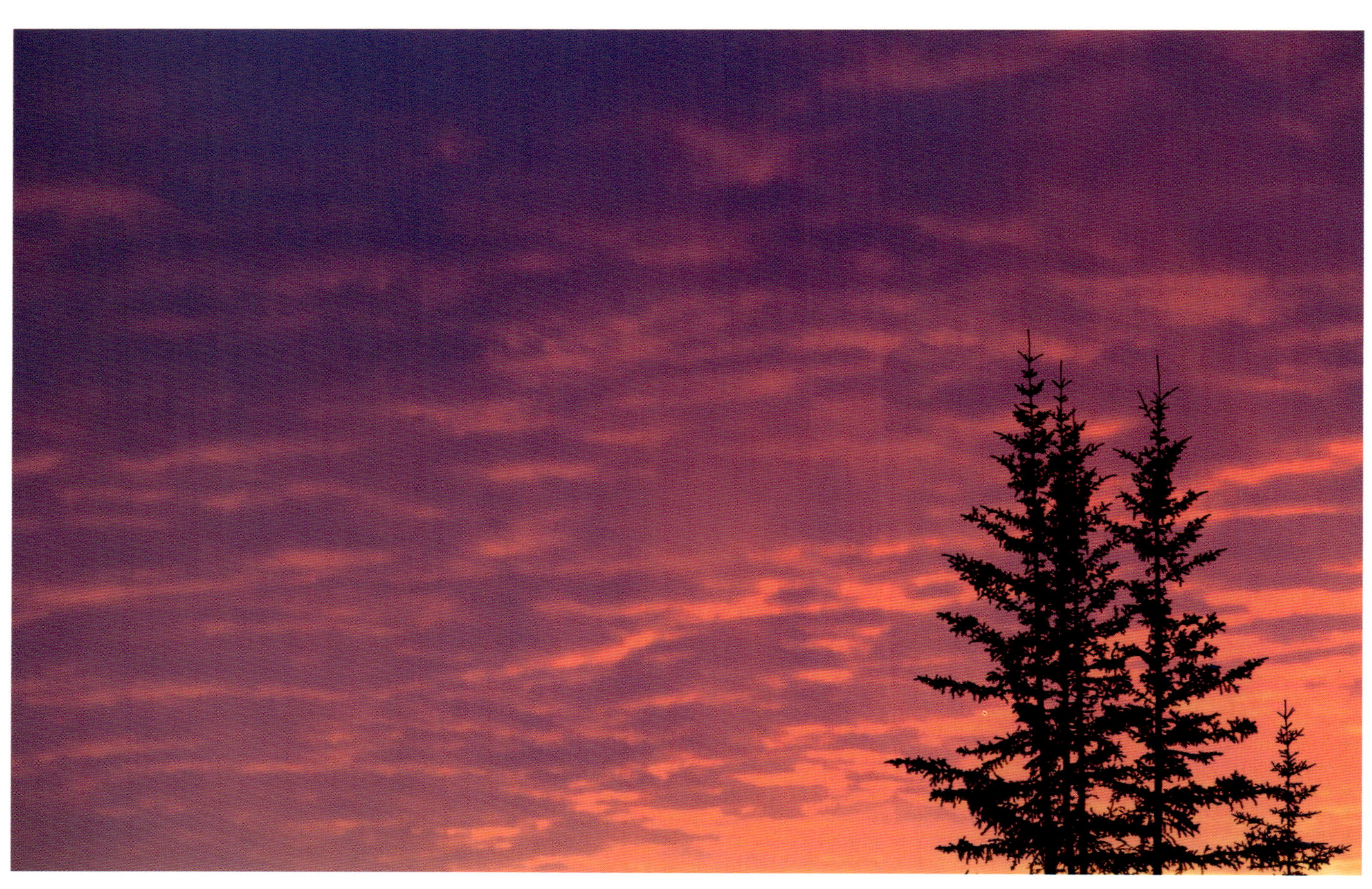

Morning Sky

Yellowknife, Northwest Territories

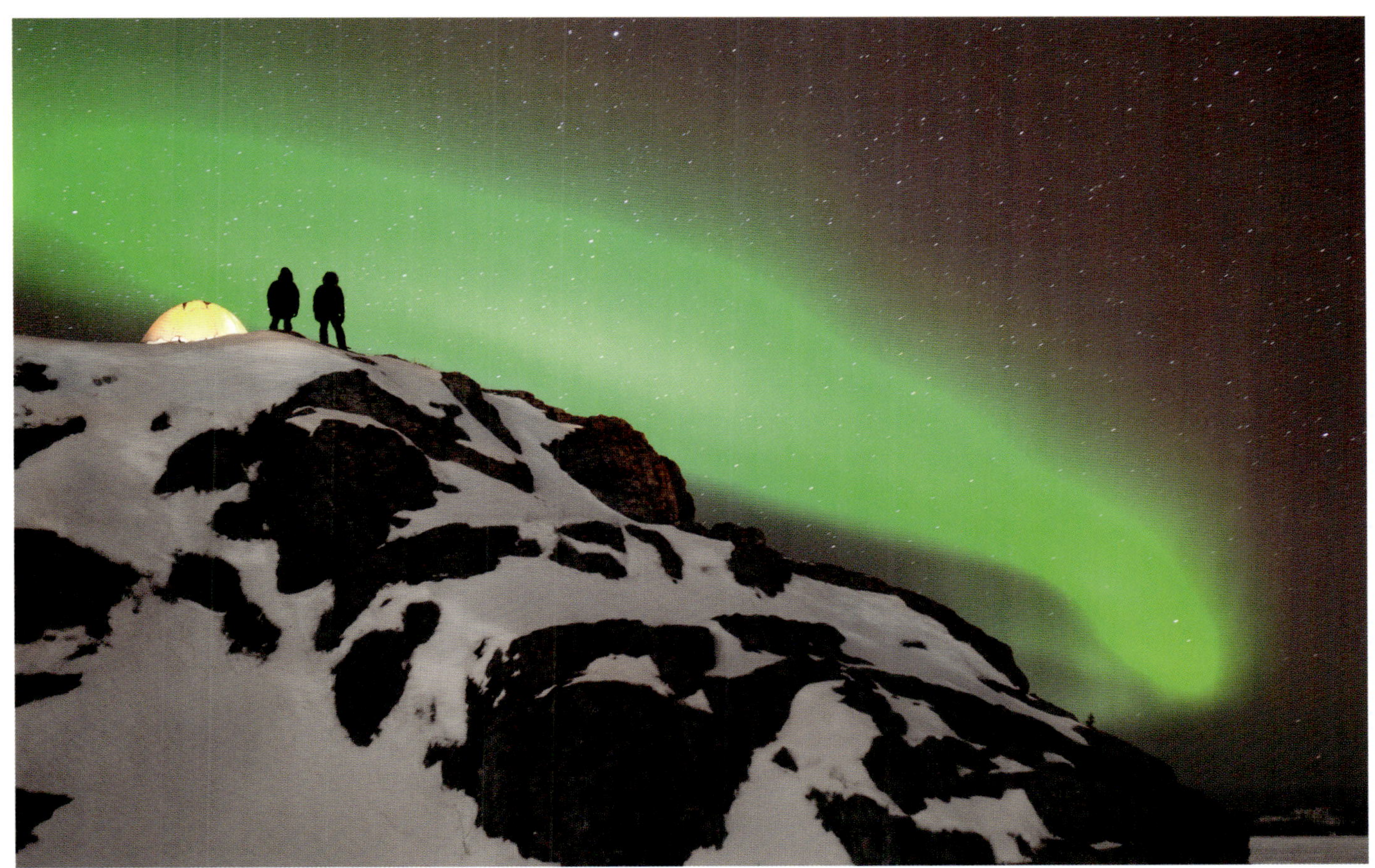

Call of the North

Robbie Craig and Greg Morrison at Great Slave Lake, Northwest Territories

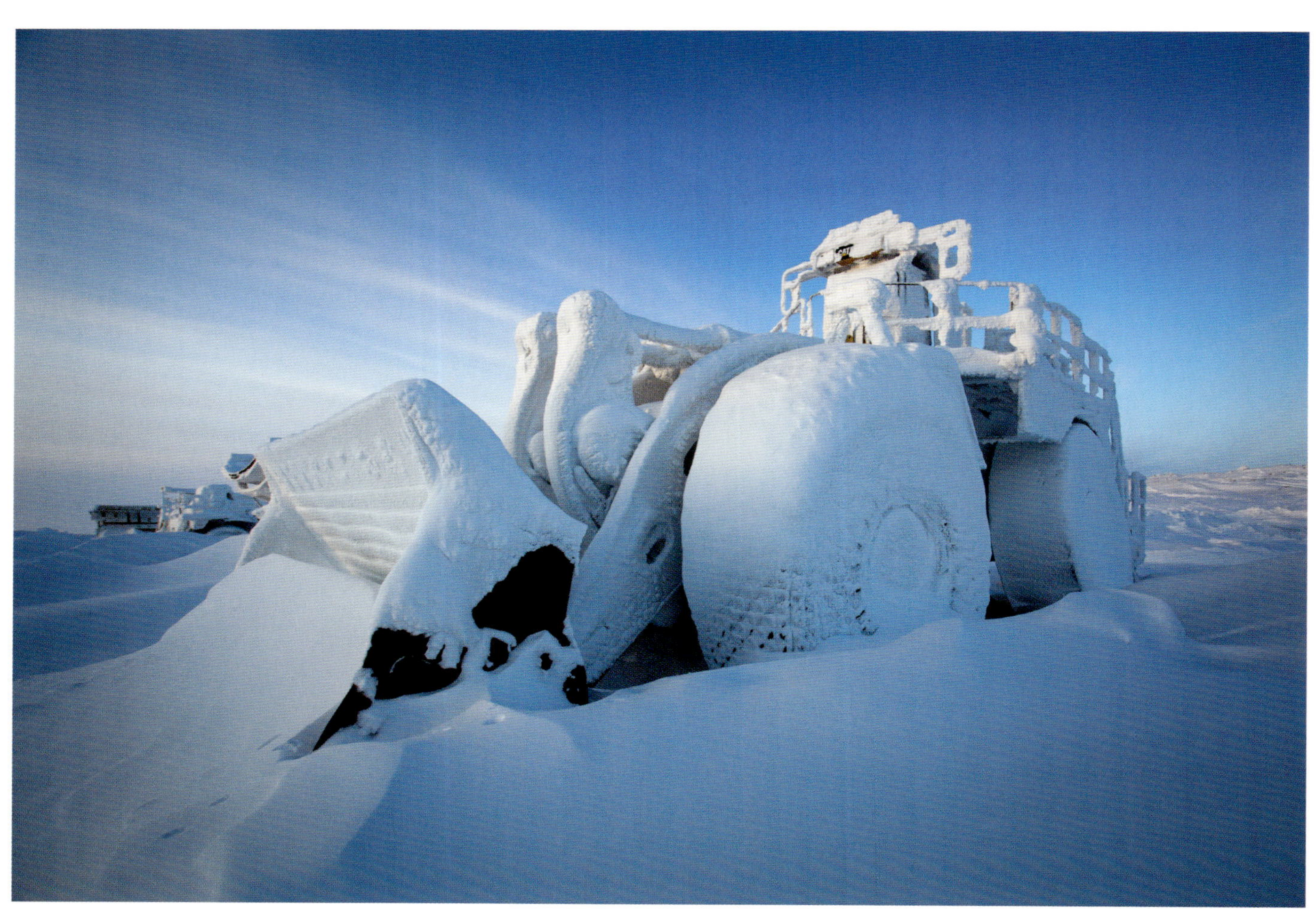

Shutdown

The Barrenlands, Northwest Territories

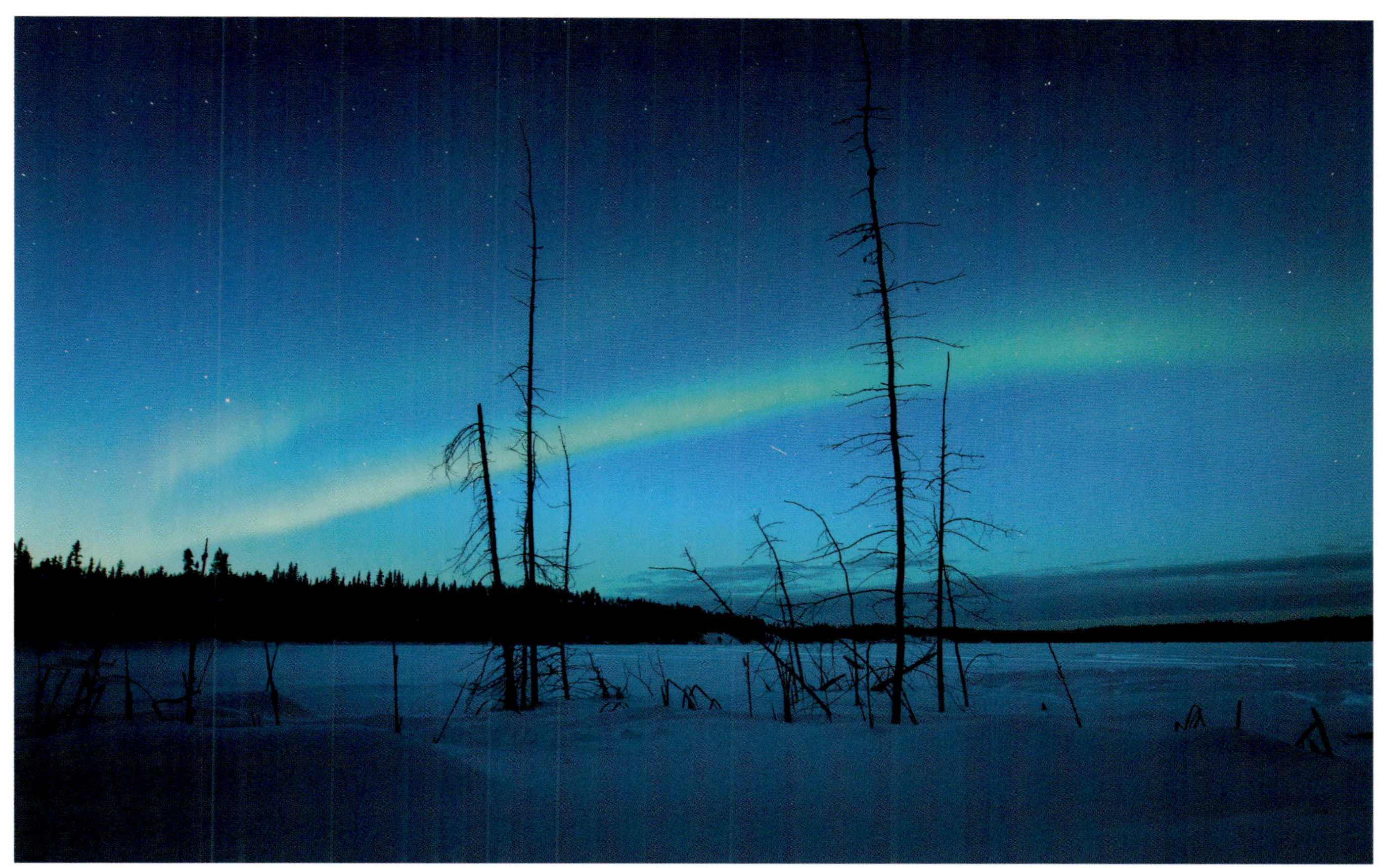

Taiga Calm
Vee Lake, Northwest Territories

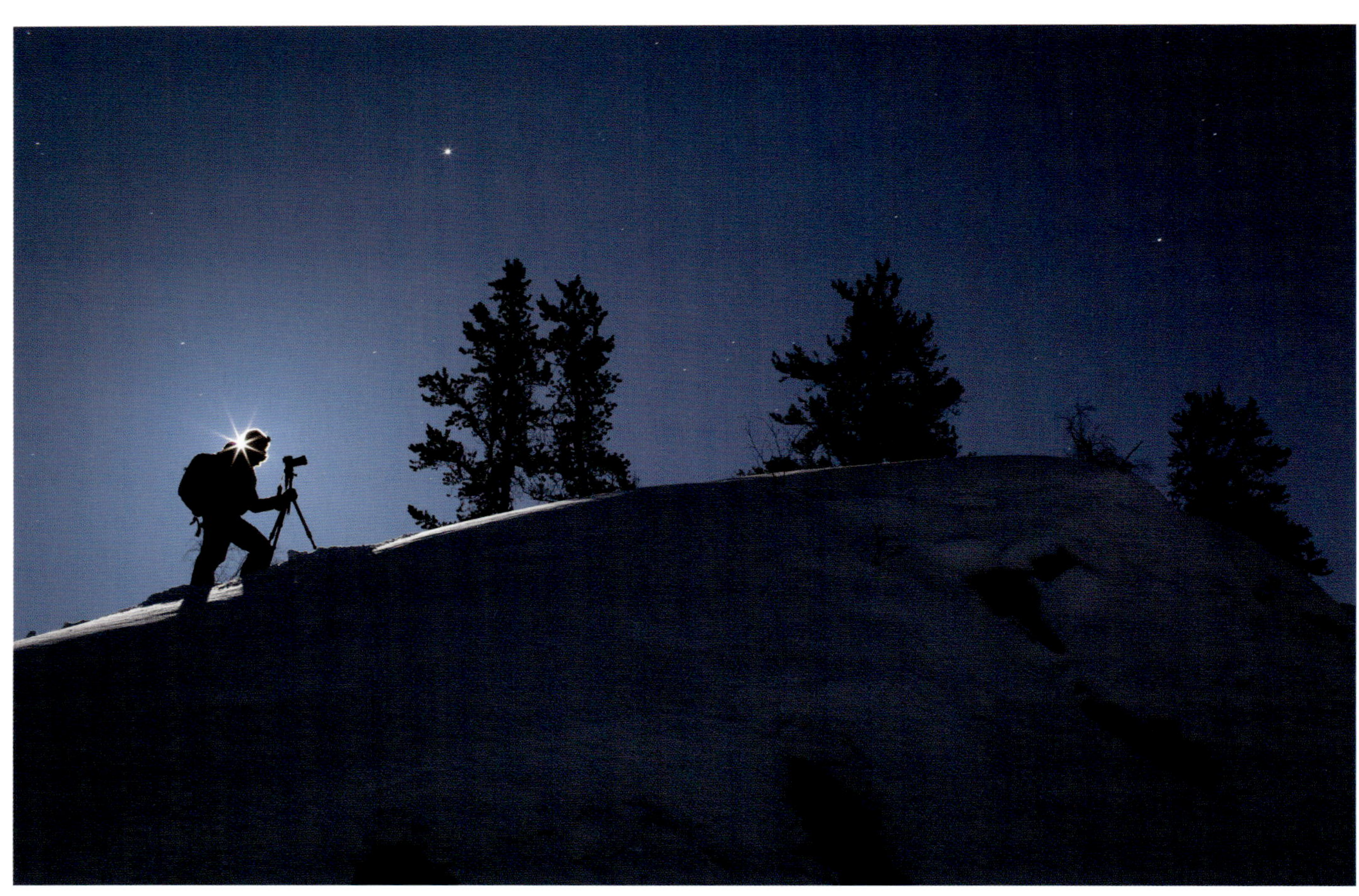

The Night Master

Paul Zizka at Vee Lake, Northwest Territories

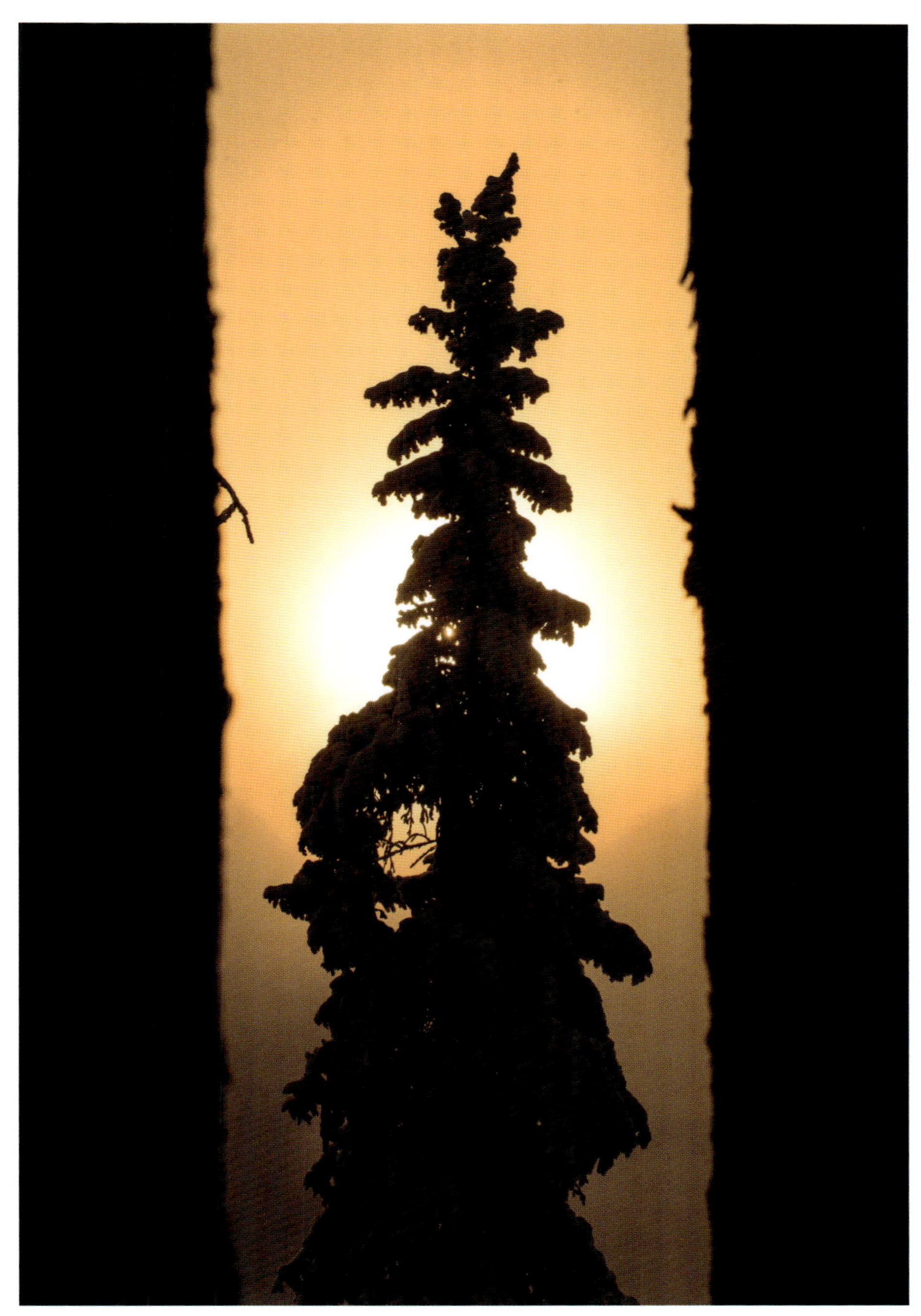

The Morning Frame
Yellowknife, Northwest Territories

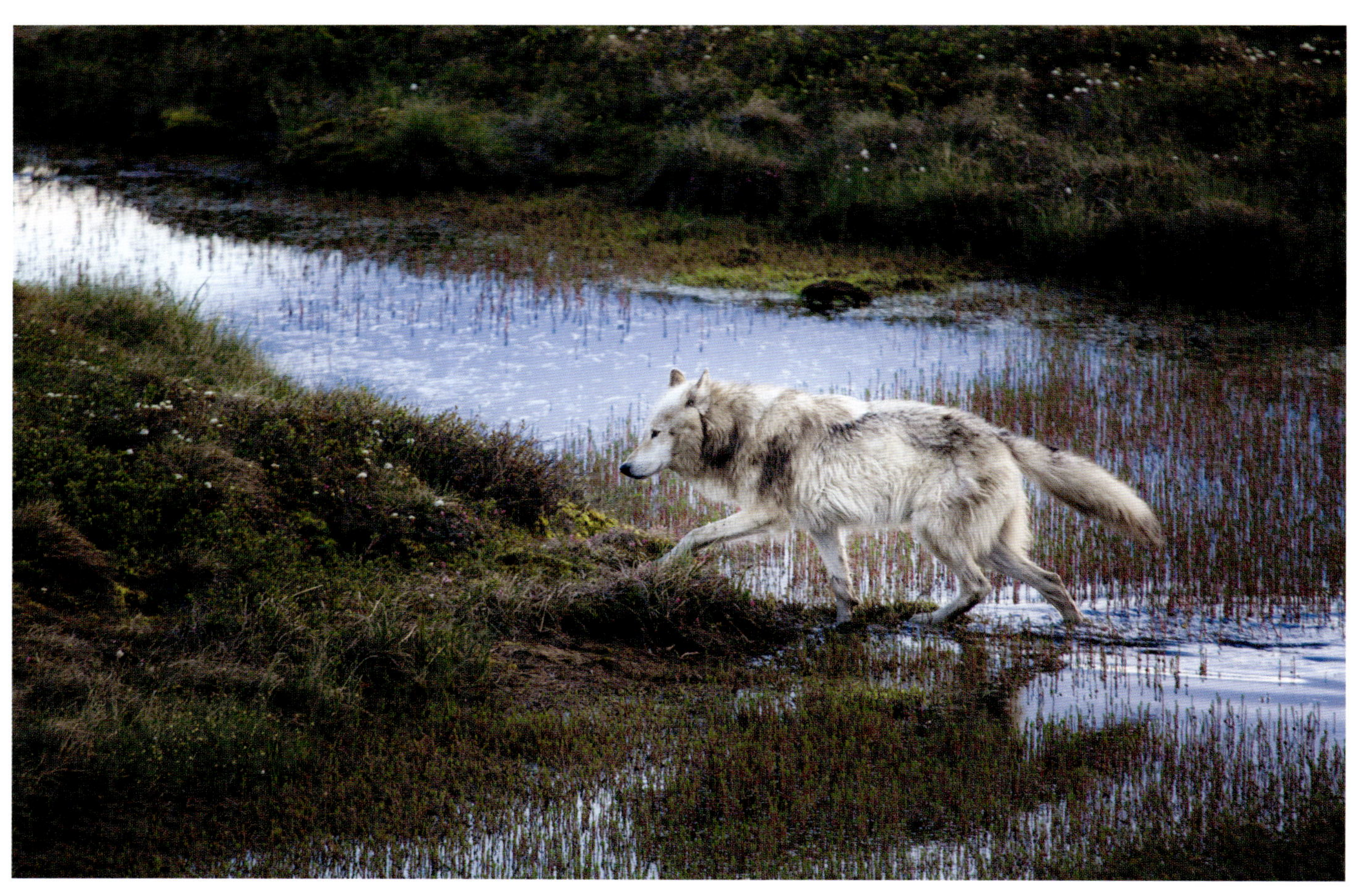

The Legend of the Subarctic

The Barrenlands, Northwest Territories

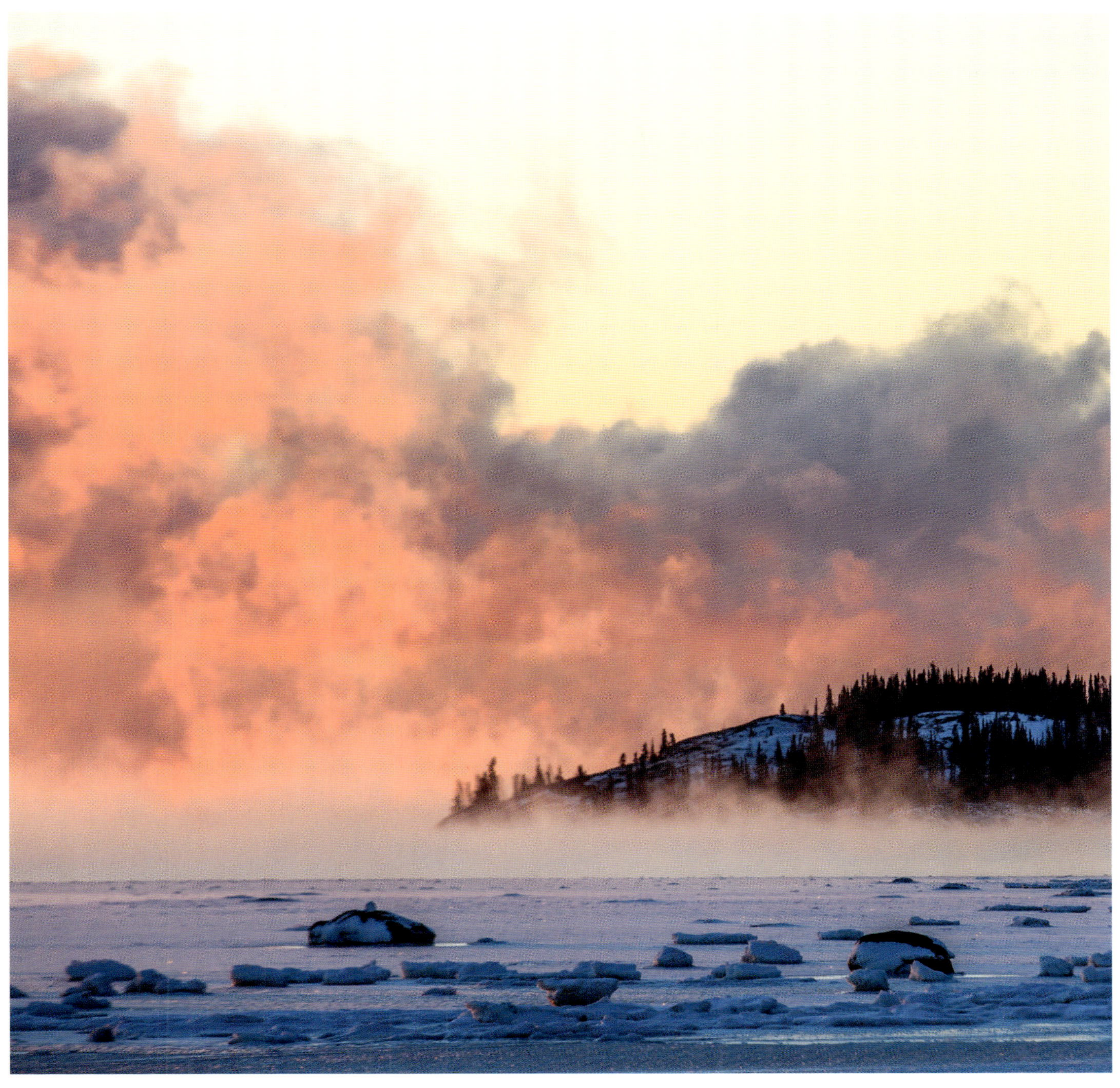

Fog Flames
Yellowknife Bay, Northwest Territories

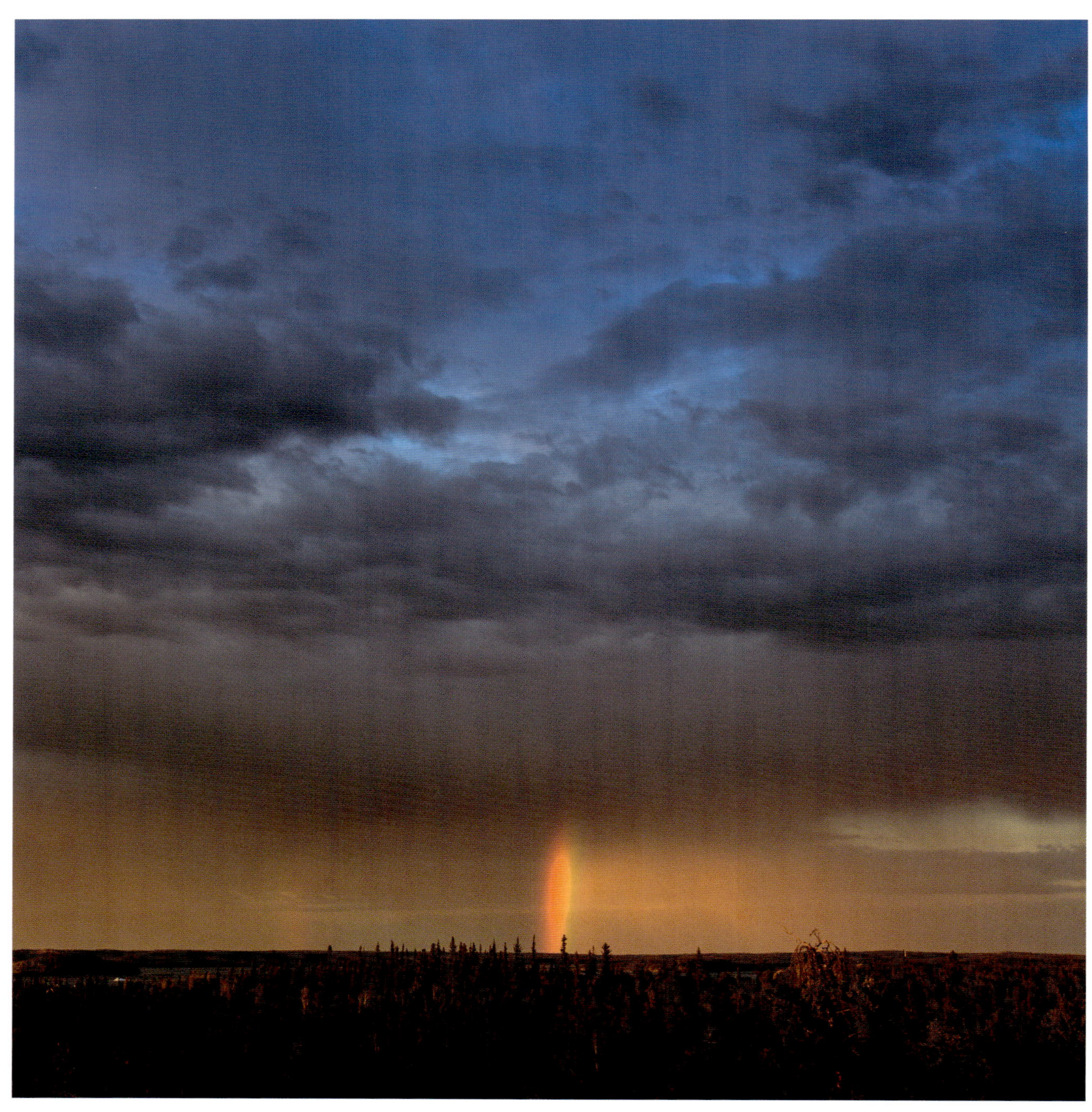

Painting With Light

Prelude Lake, Northwest Territories

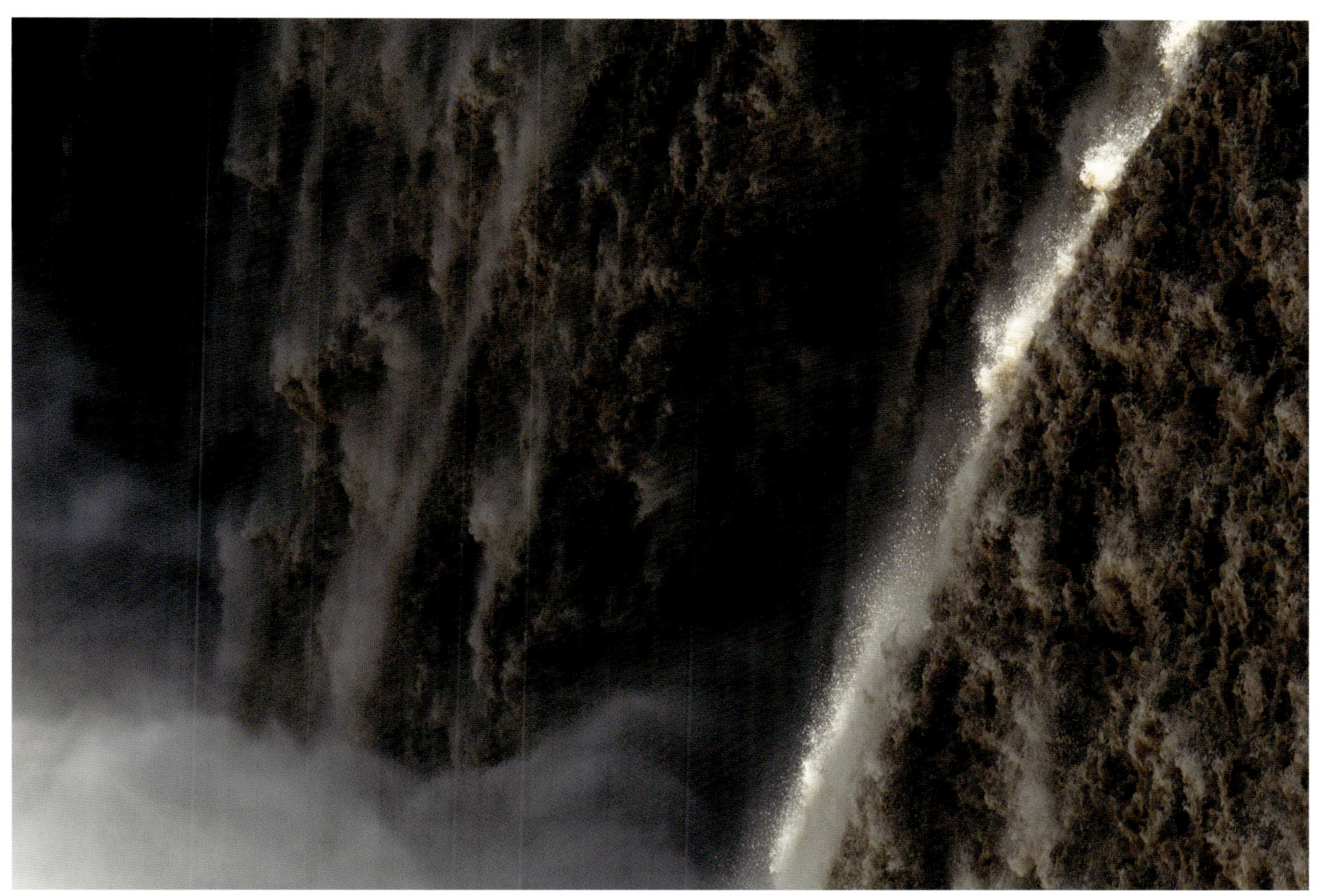

The Alexandra Strand

Alexandra Falls, Northwest Territories

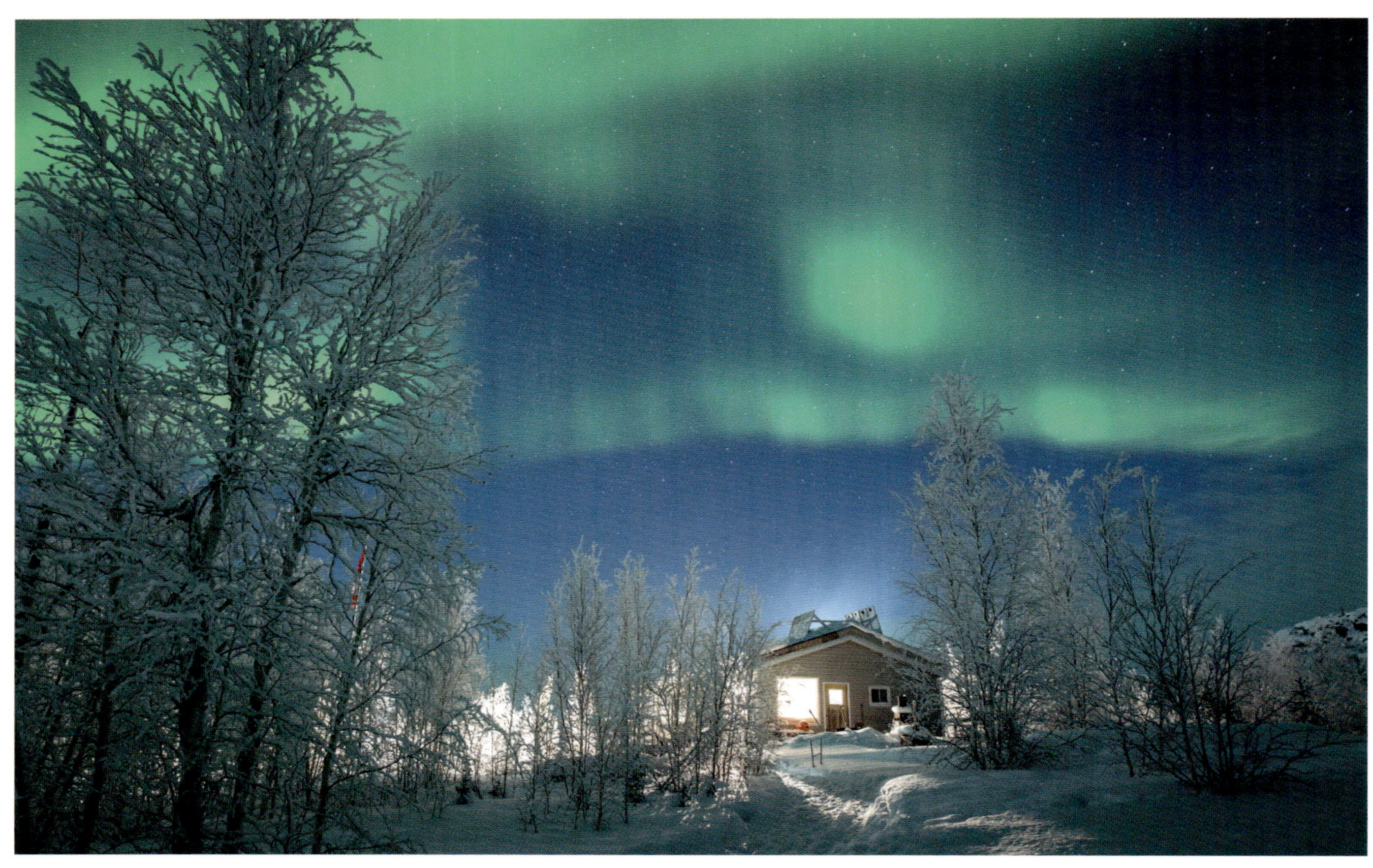

Heaven on Earth #4

Tibbitt Lake, Northwest Territories

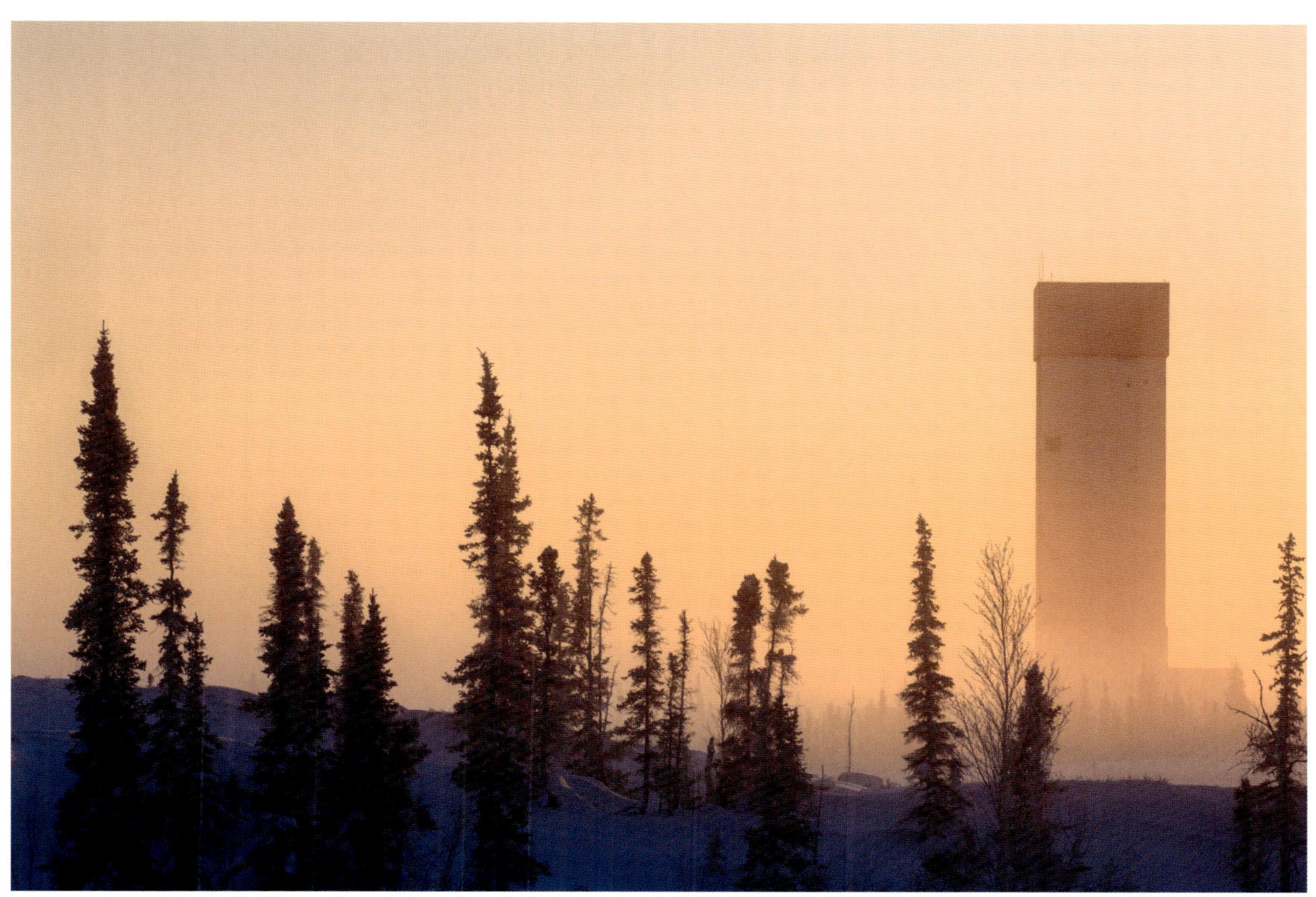

The Headframe

Yellowknife, Northwest Territories

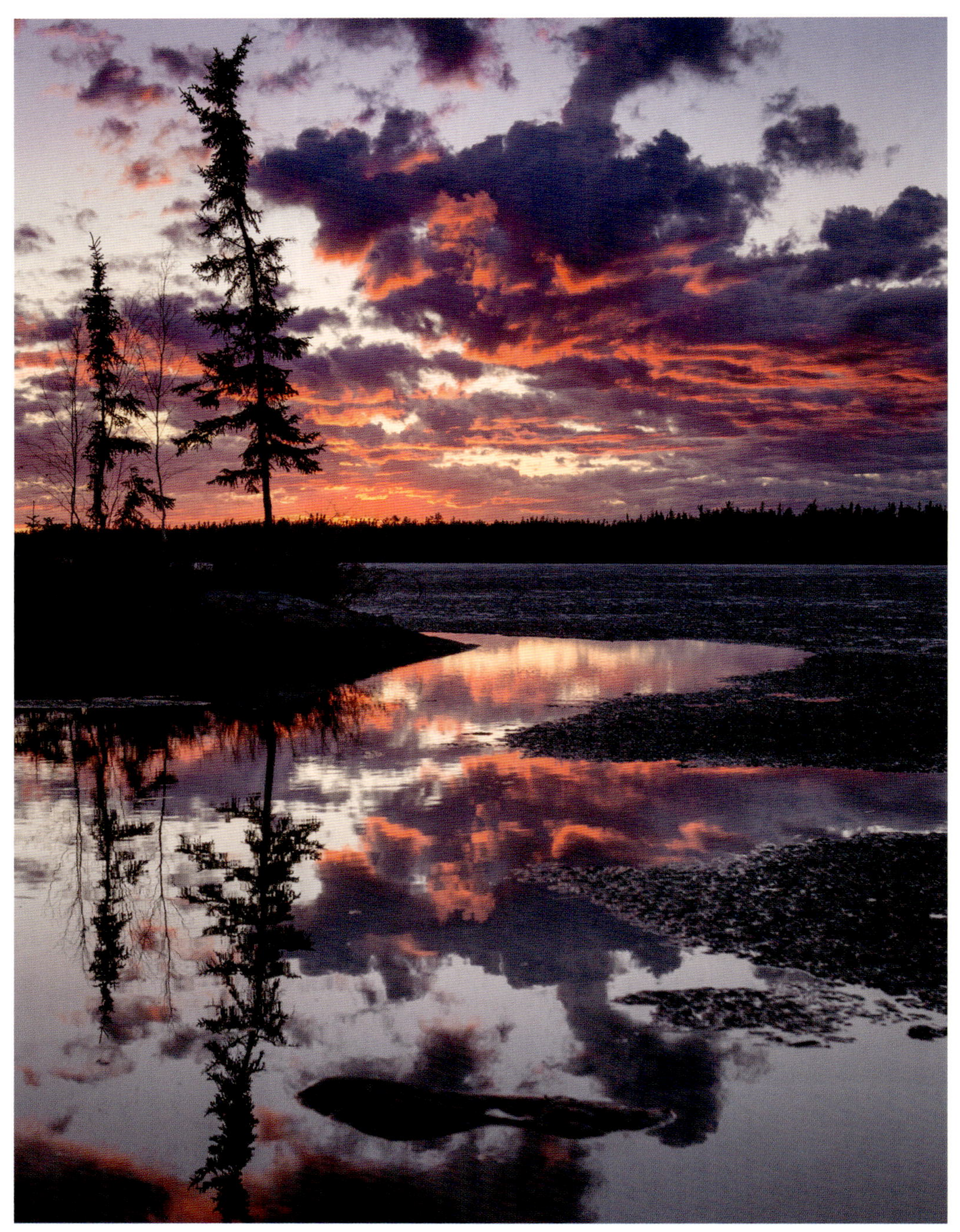

Galenlight

Long Lake, Northwest Territories

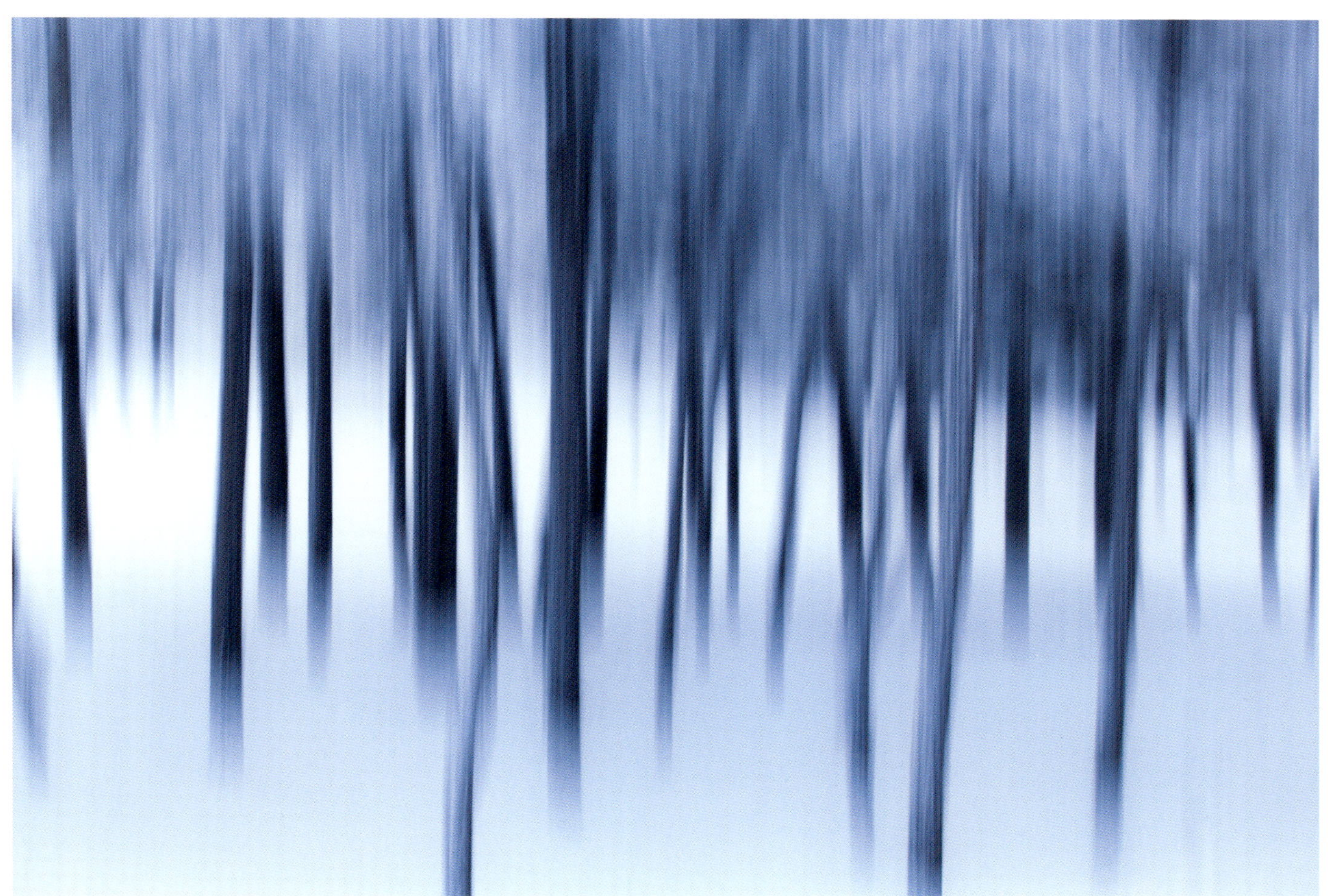

Winterlight

Yellowknife, Northwest Territories

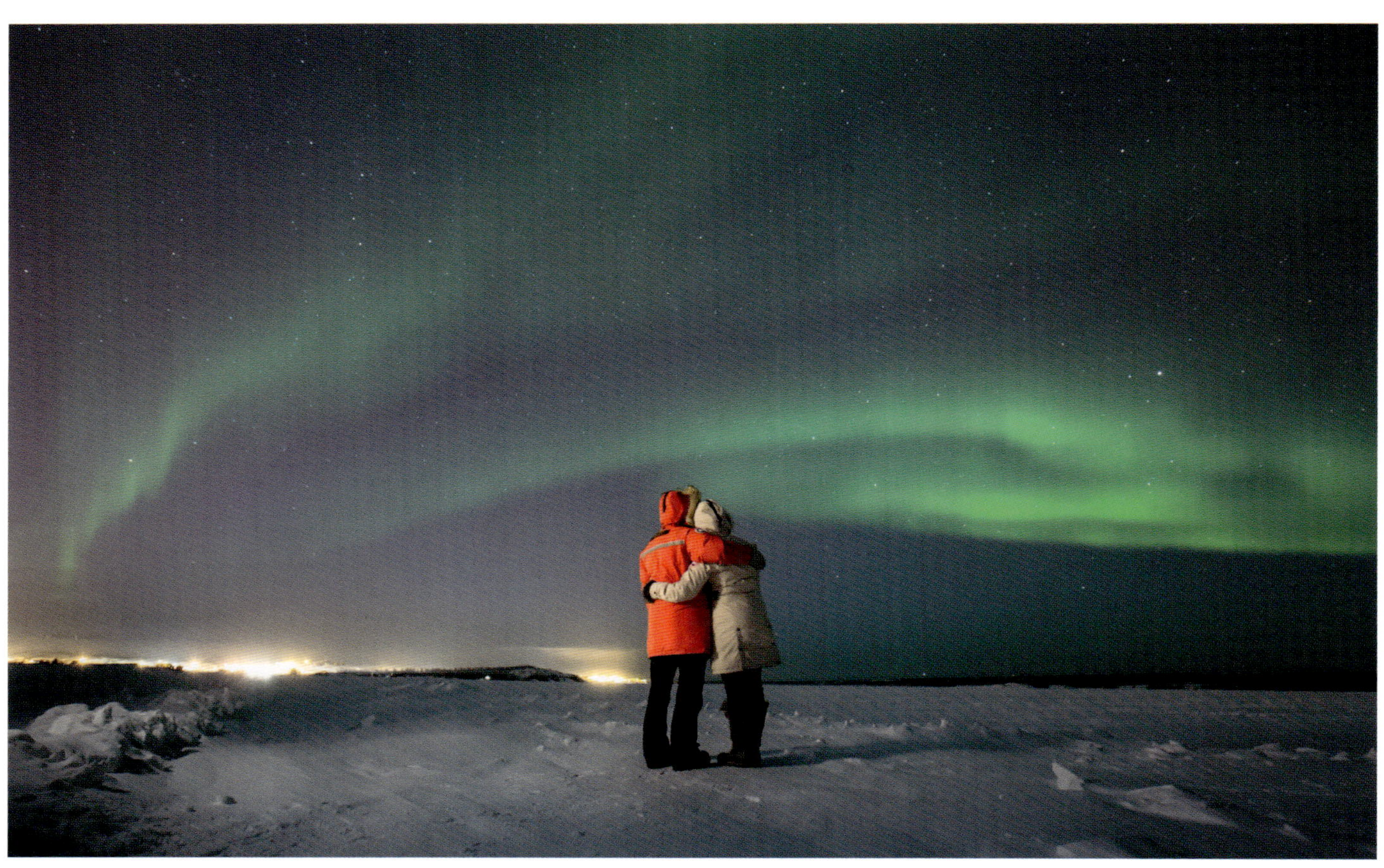

 A Love Song for Yellowknife
Yellowknife, Northwest Territories

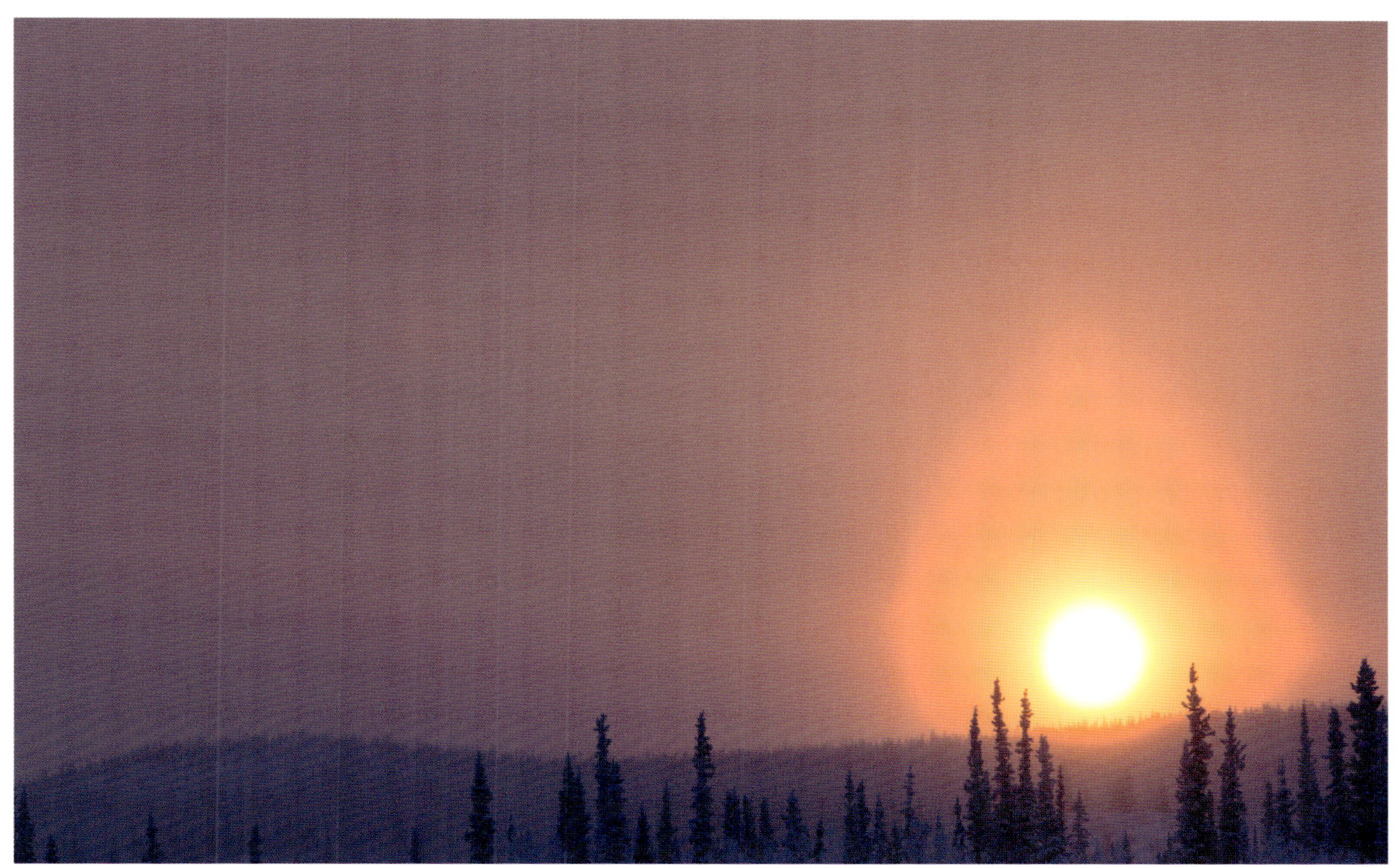

Touchdown

Whatì, Northwest Territories

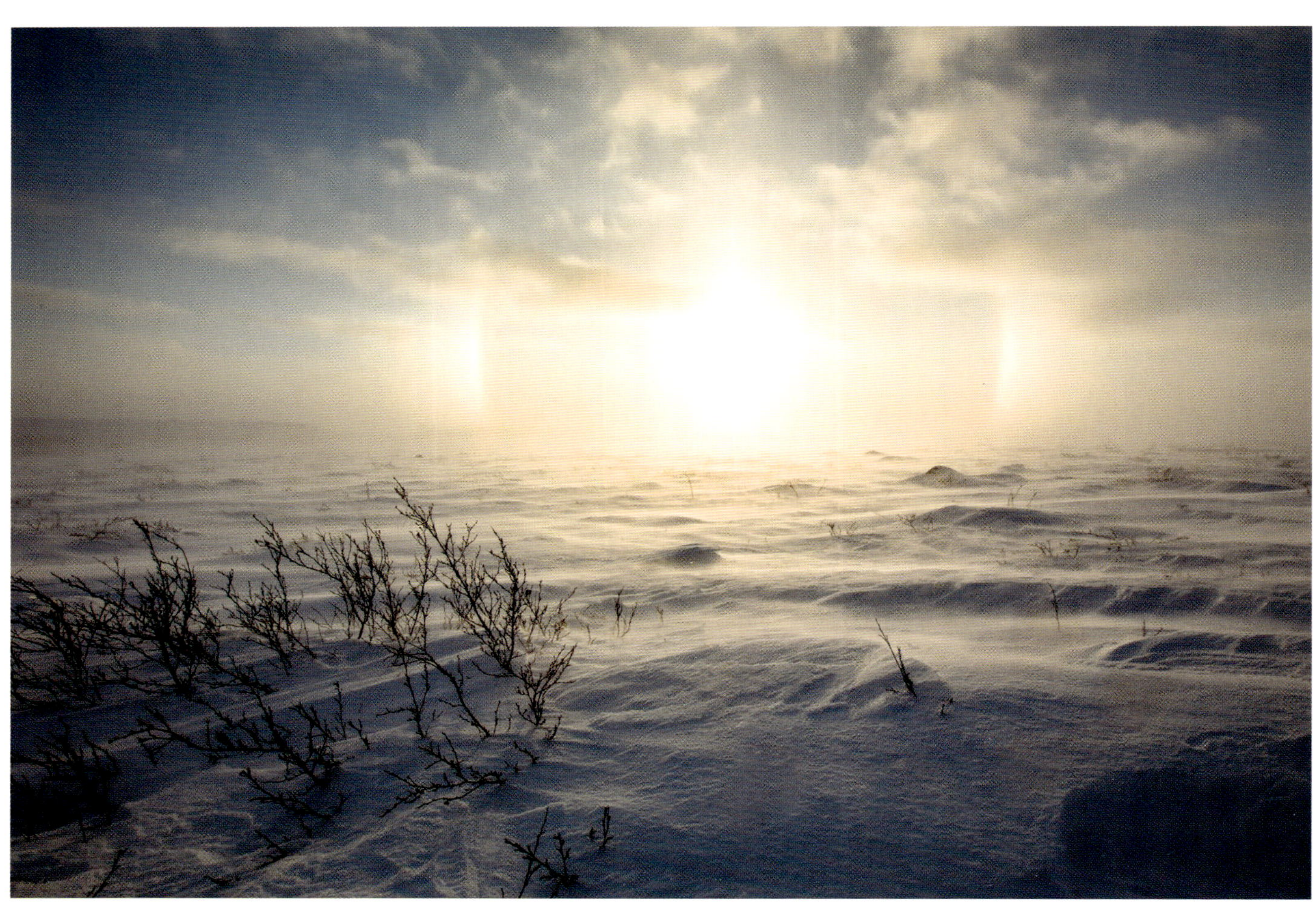

Tundra Angel, Rise
The Barrenlands, Northwest Territories

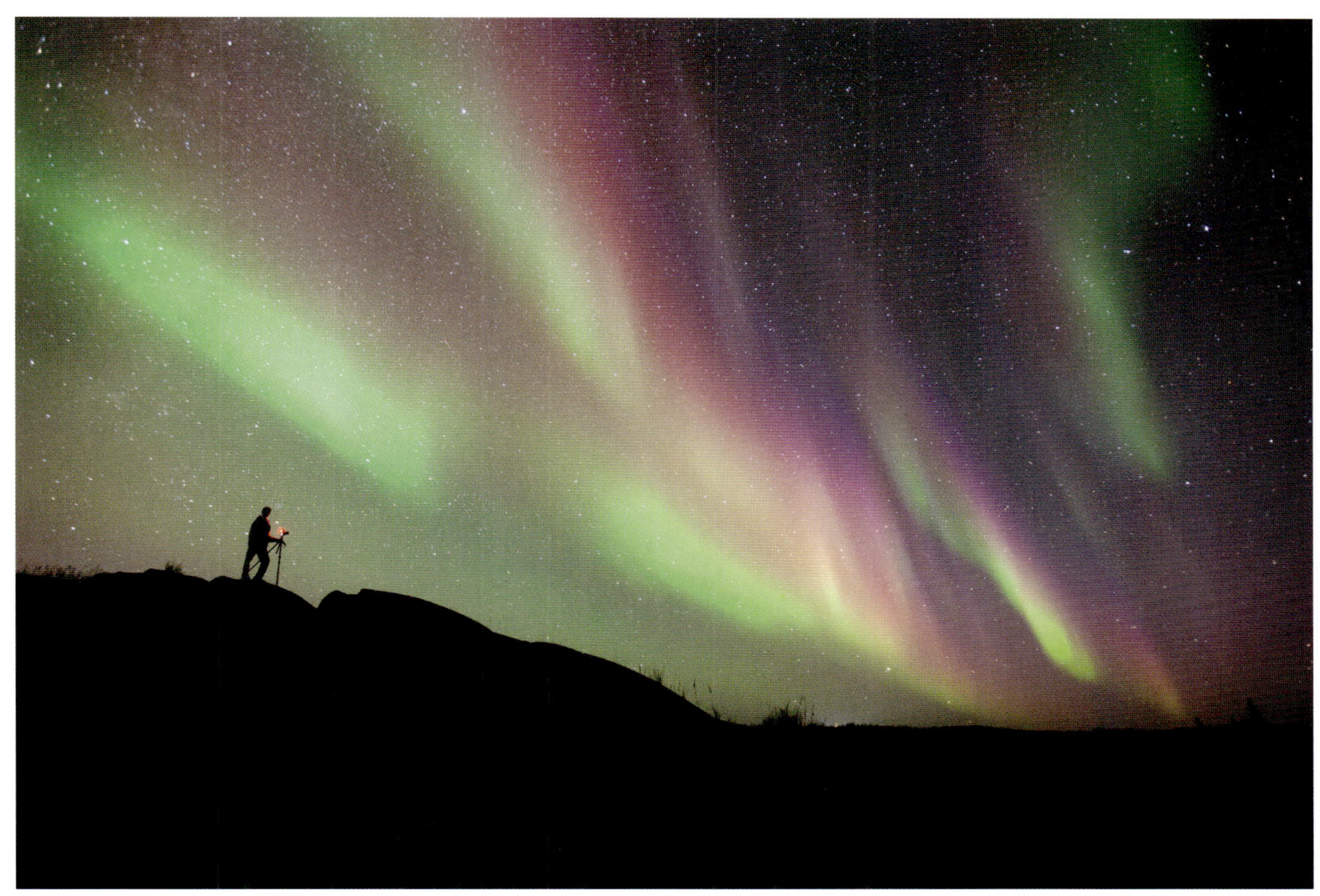

The Composer

Karl Johnston at Yellowknife River, Northwest Territories

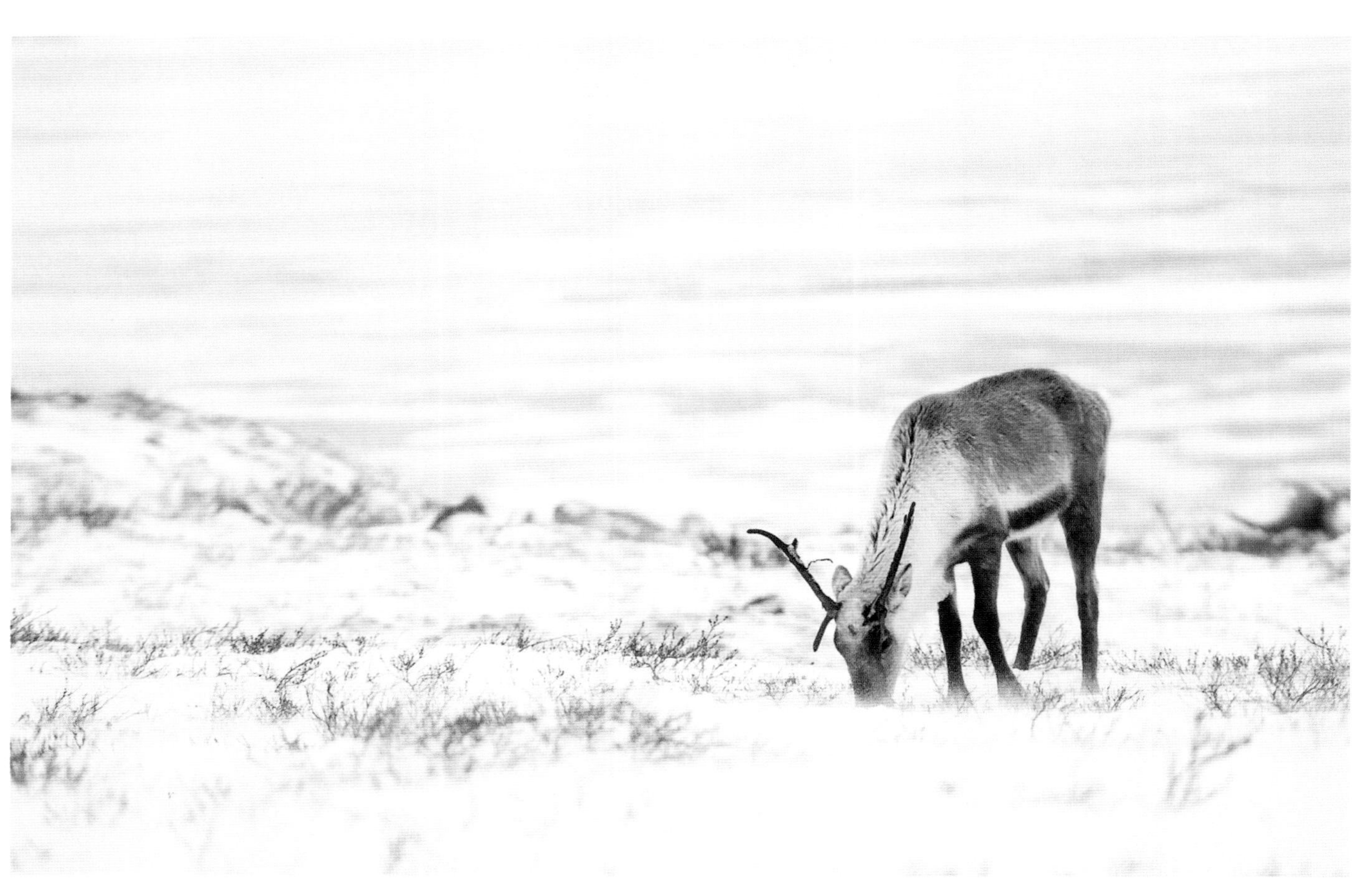

Winter Walker

The Barrenlands, Northwest Territories

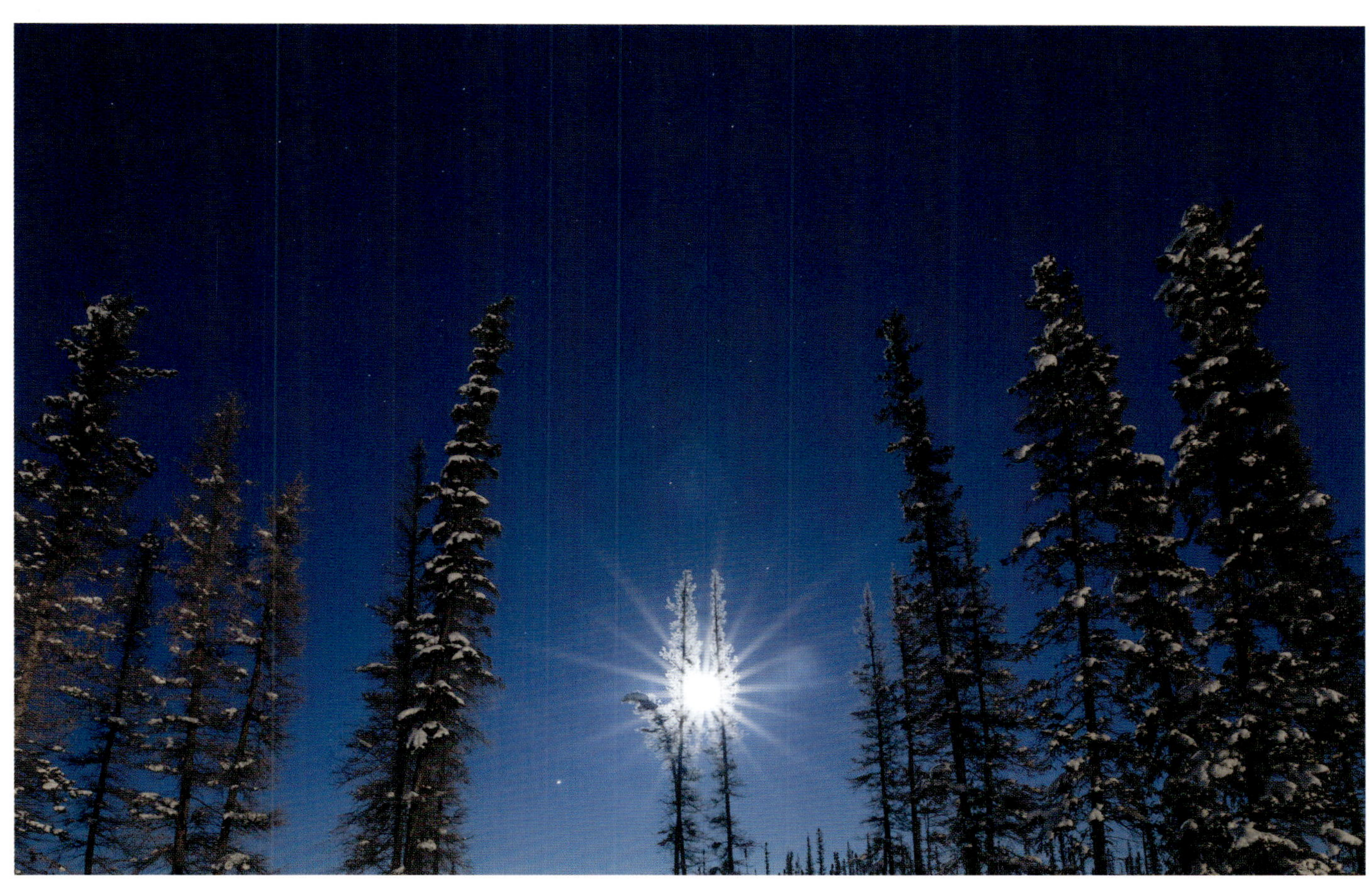

We Are All Made of Stars
Behchokǫ̀, Northwest Territories

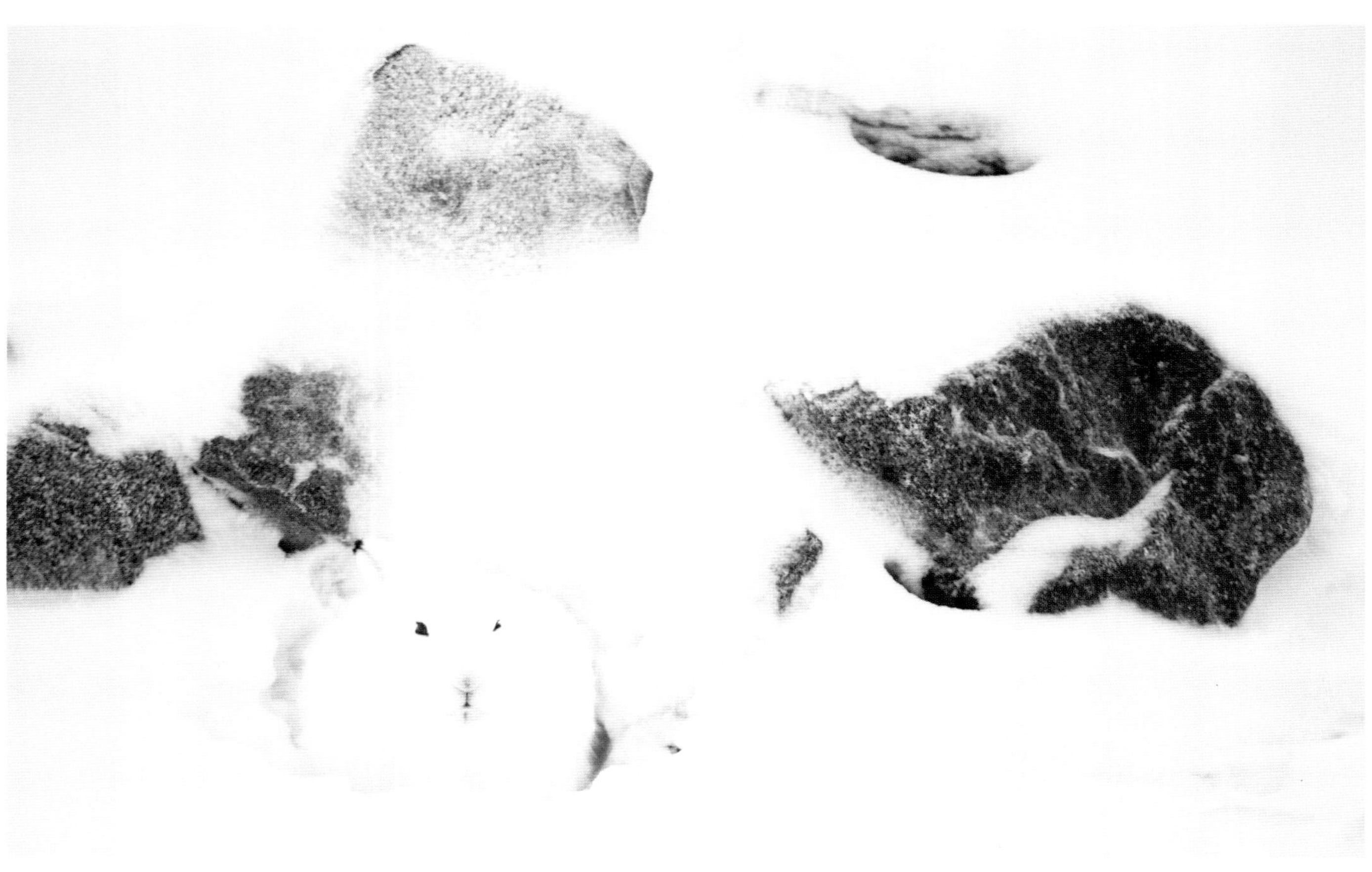

Winter Camouflage
The Barrenlands, Northwest Territories

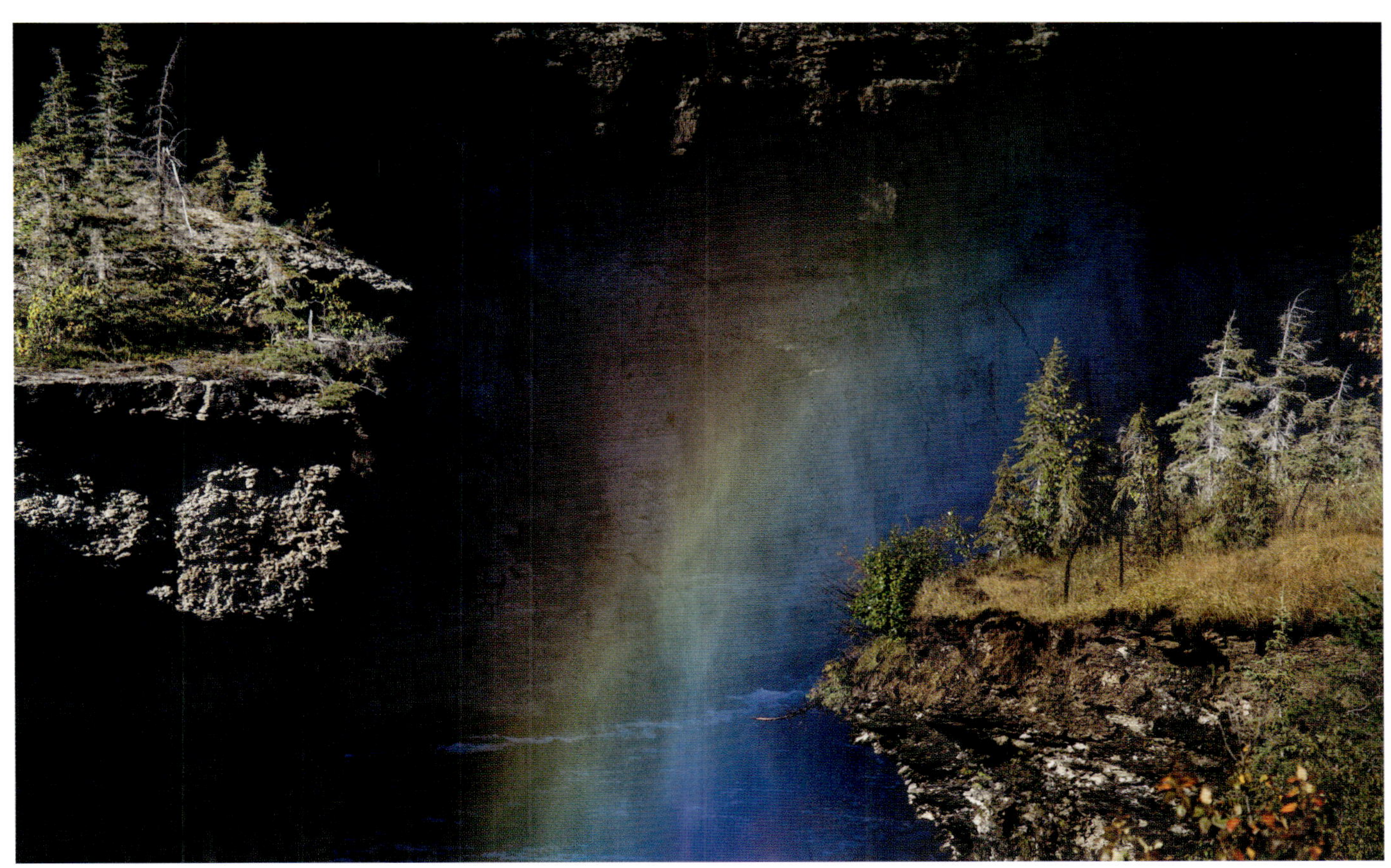

Sambaa Deh

Sambaa Deh Falls Territorial Park, Northwest Territories

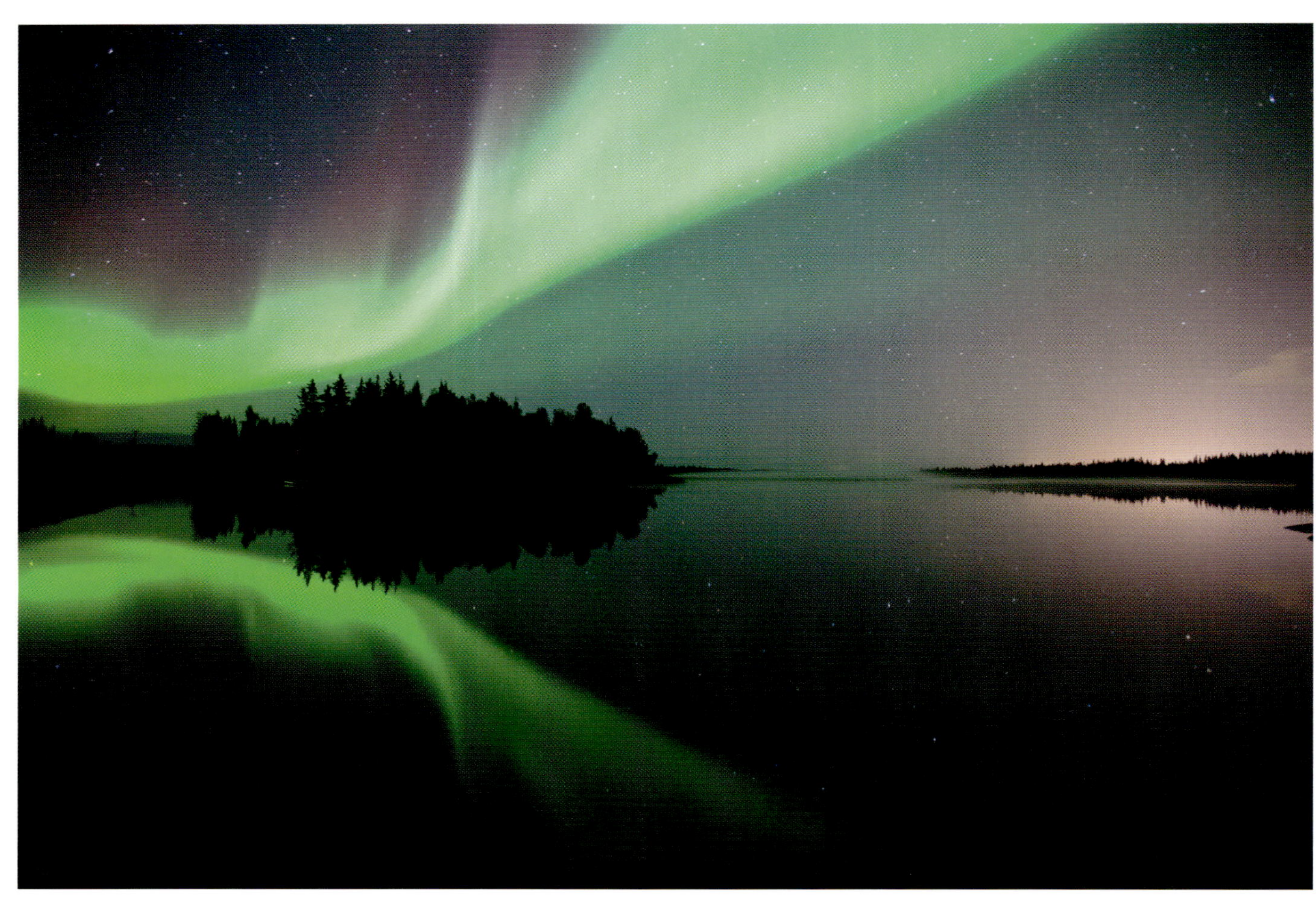

August Adrift

Yellowknife River, Northwest Territories

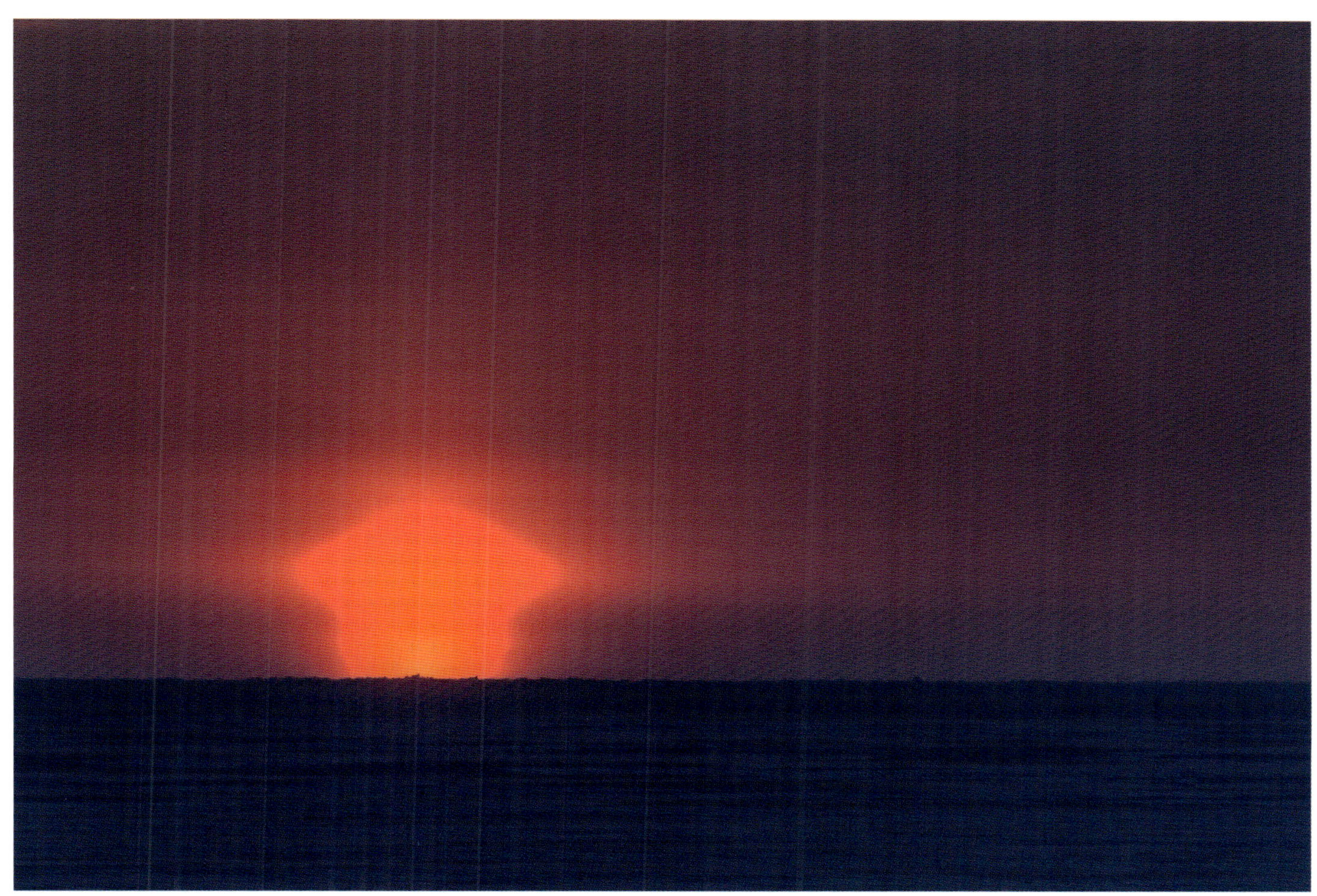

Atomic Dawn

Ulukhaktok, Northwest Territories

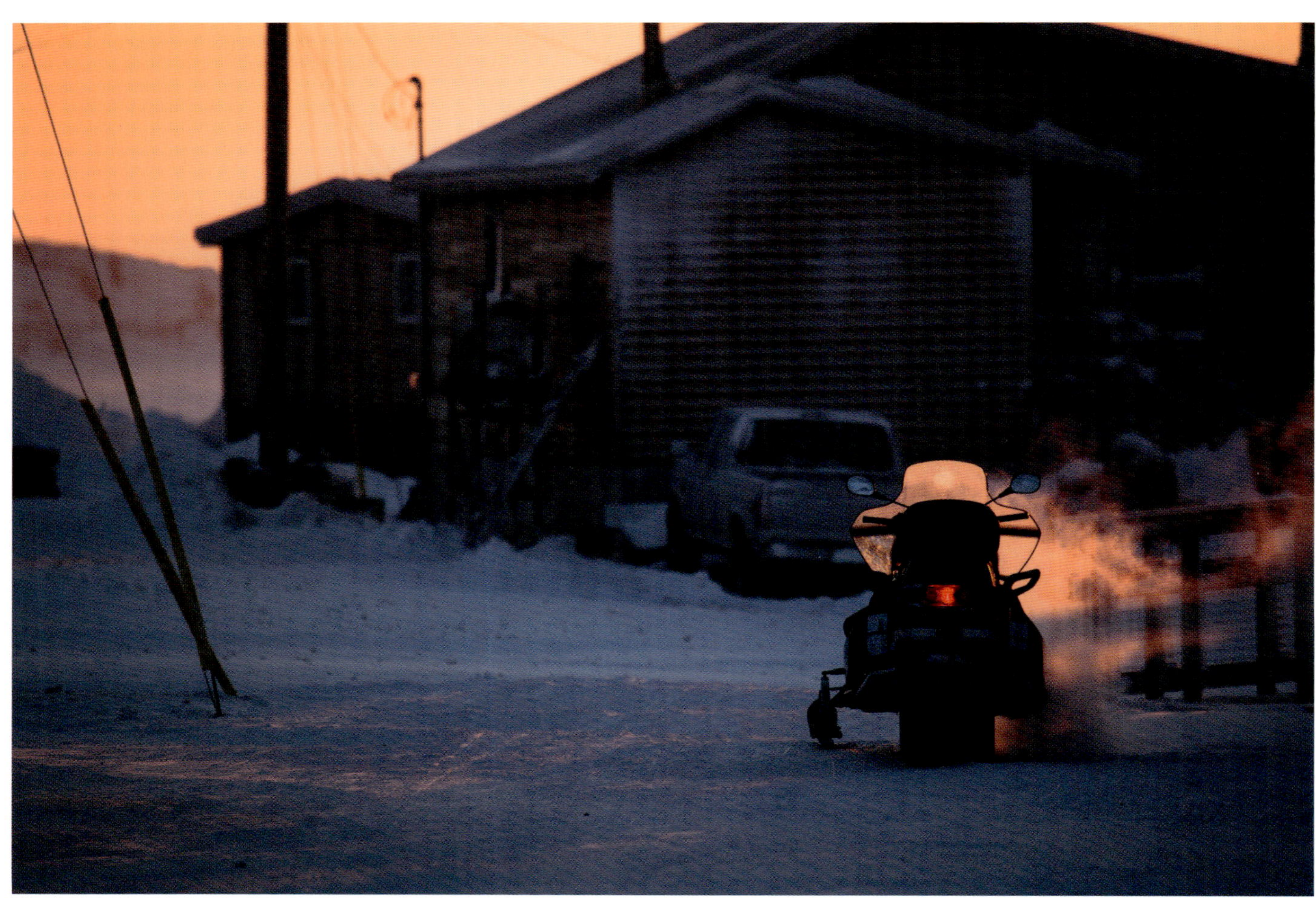

Ulukhaktok Light
Ulukhaktok, Northwest Territories

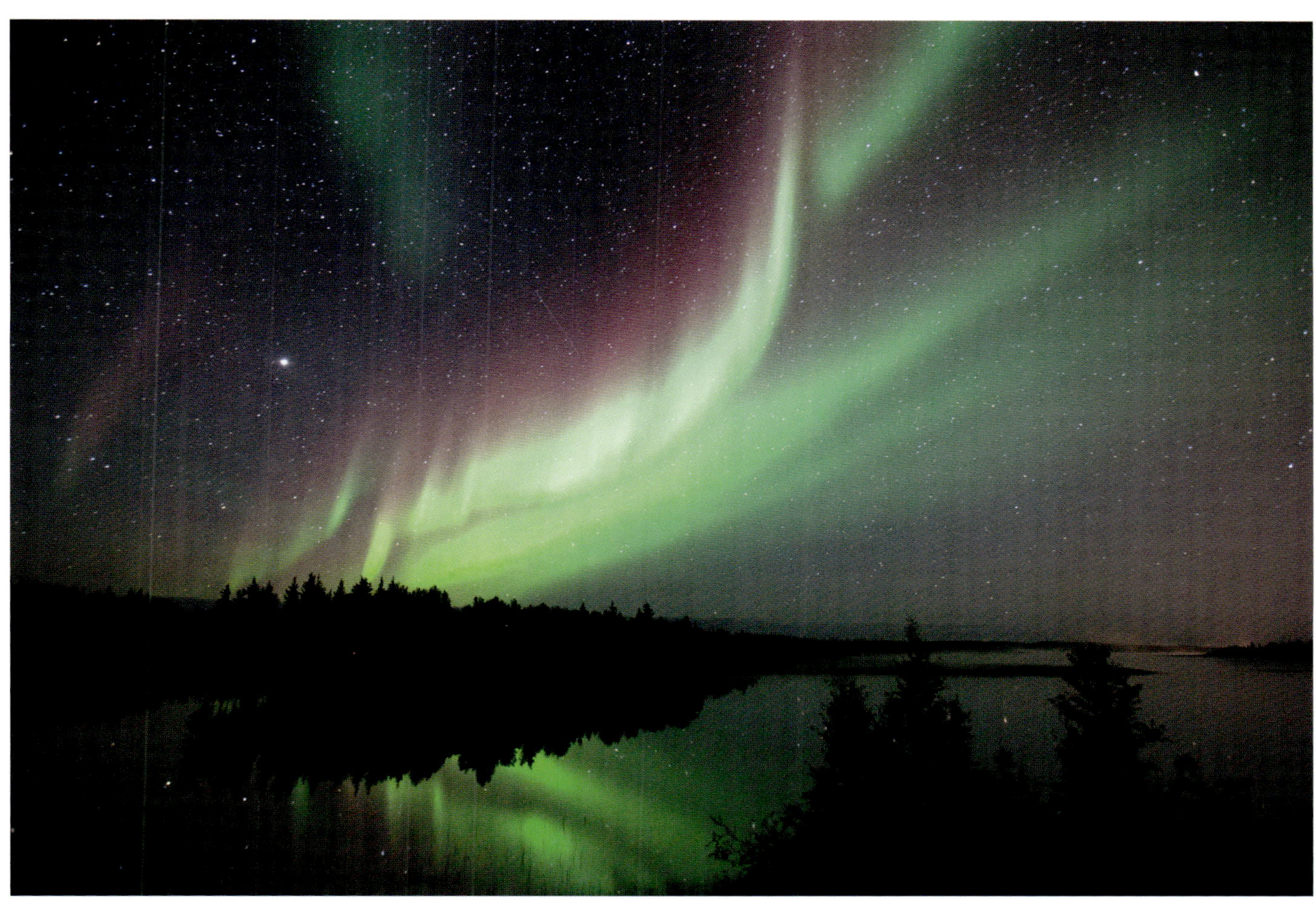

The Painter's Palette

Yellowknife River, Northwest Territories

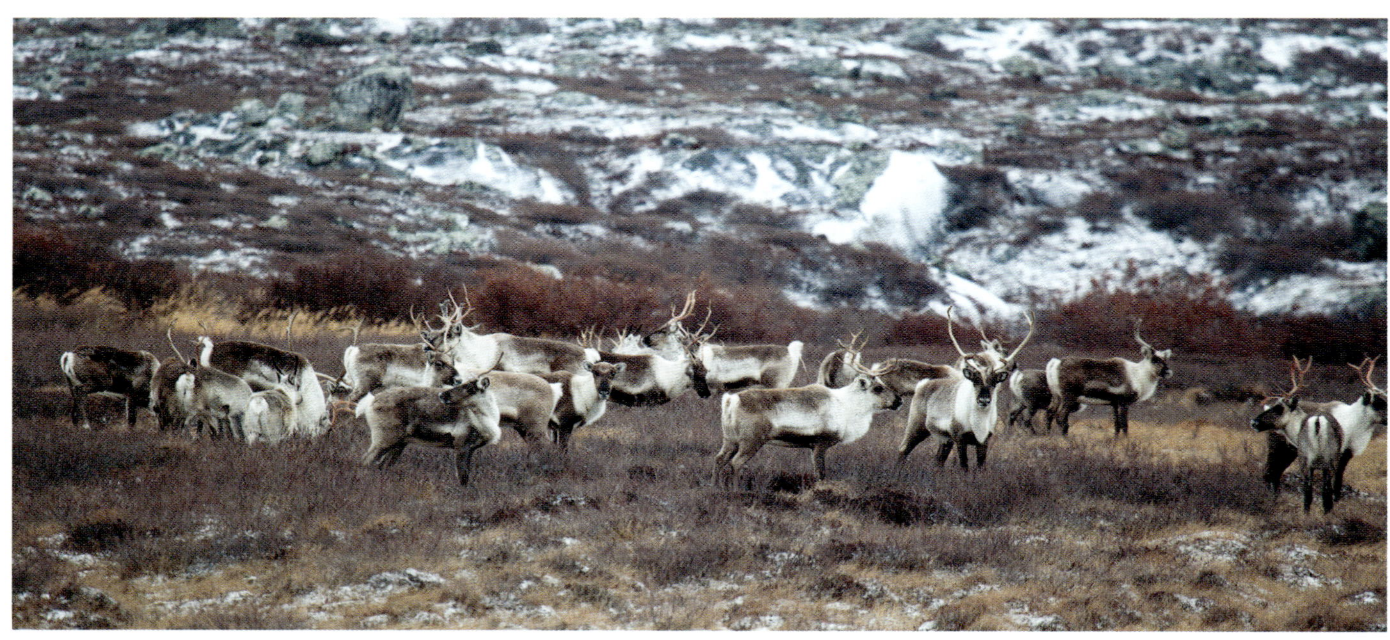

 The Herd
The Barrenlands, Northwest Territories

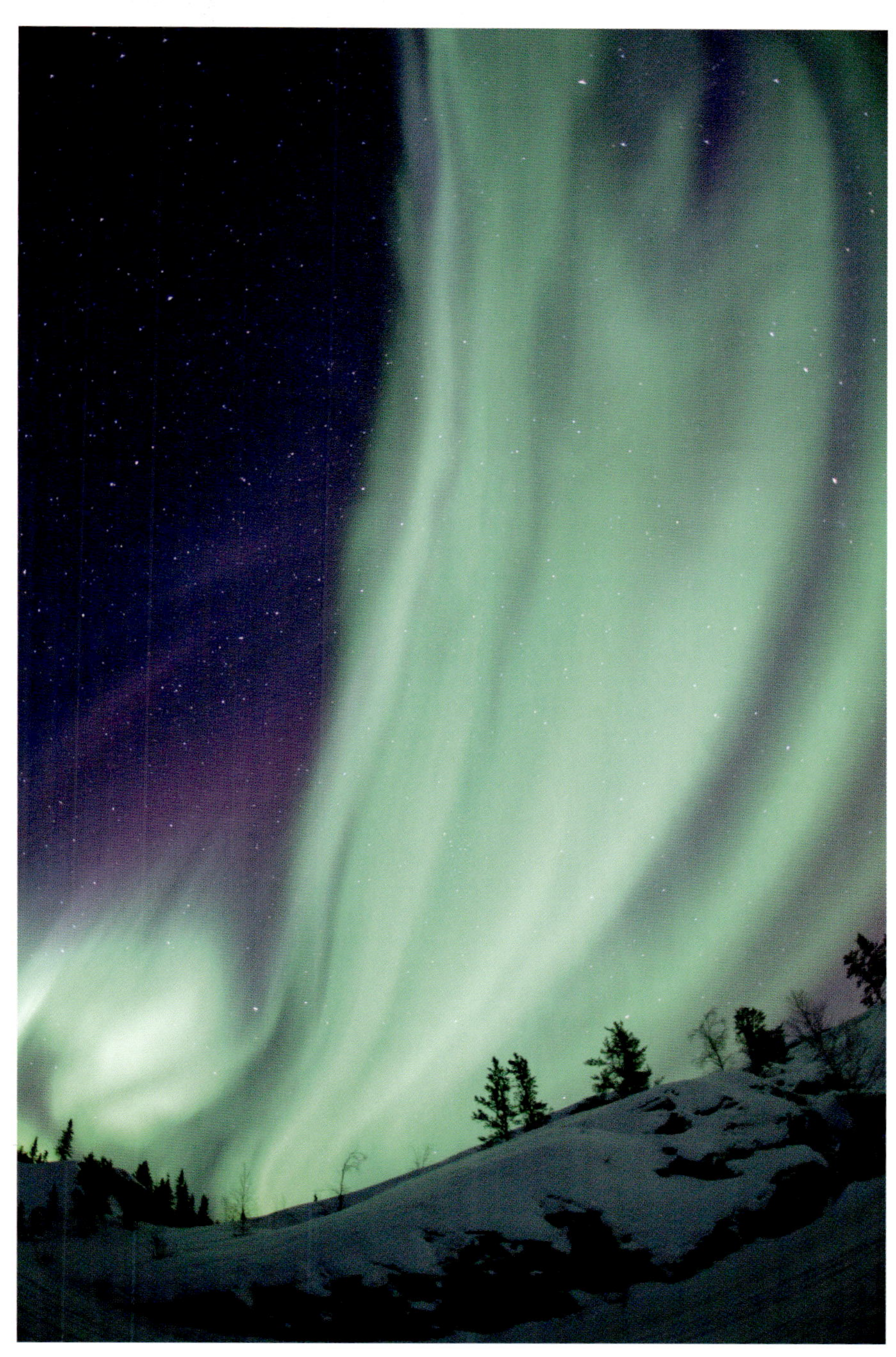

The Canvas
Yellowknife, Northwest Territories

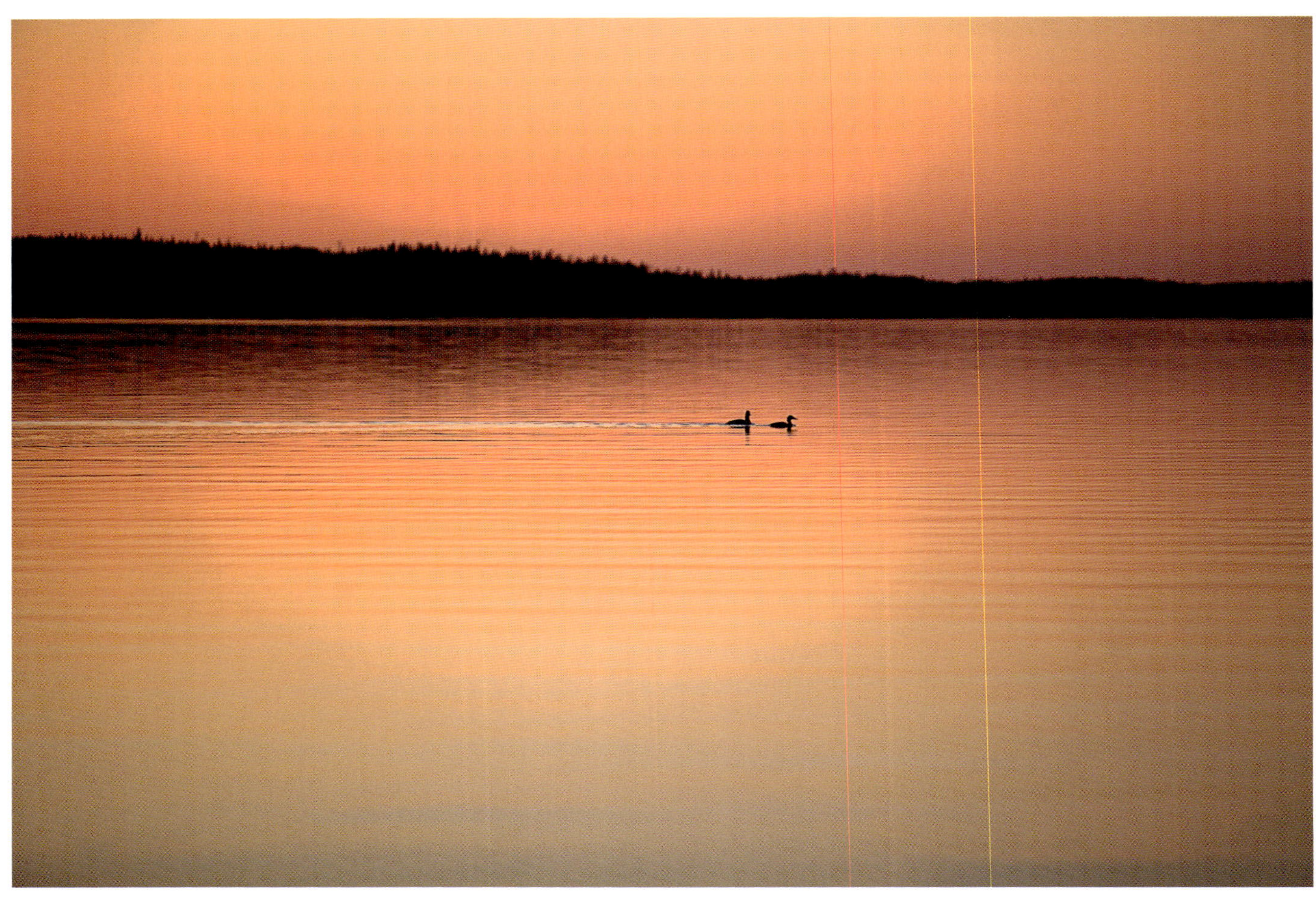

Back Bay, 401

Yellowknife, Northwest Territories

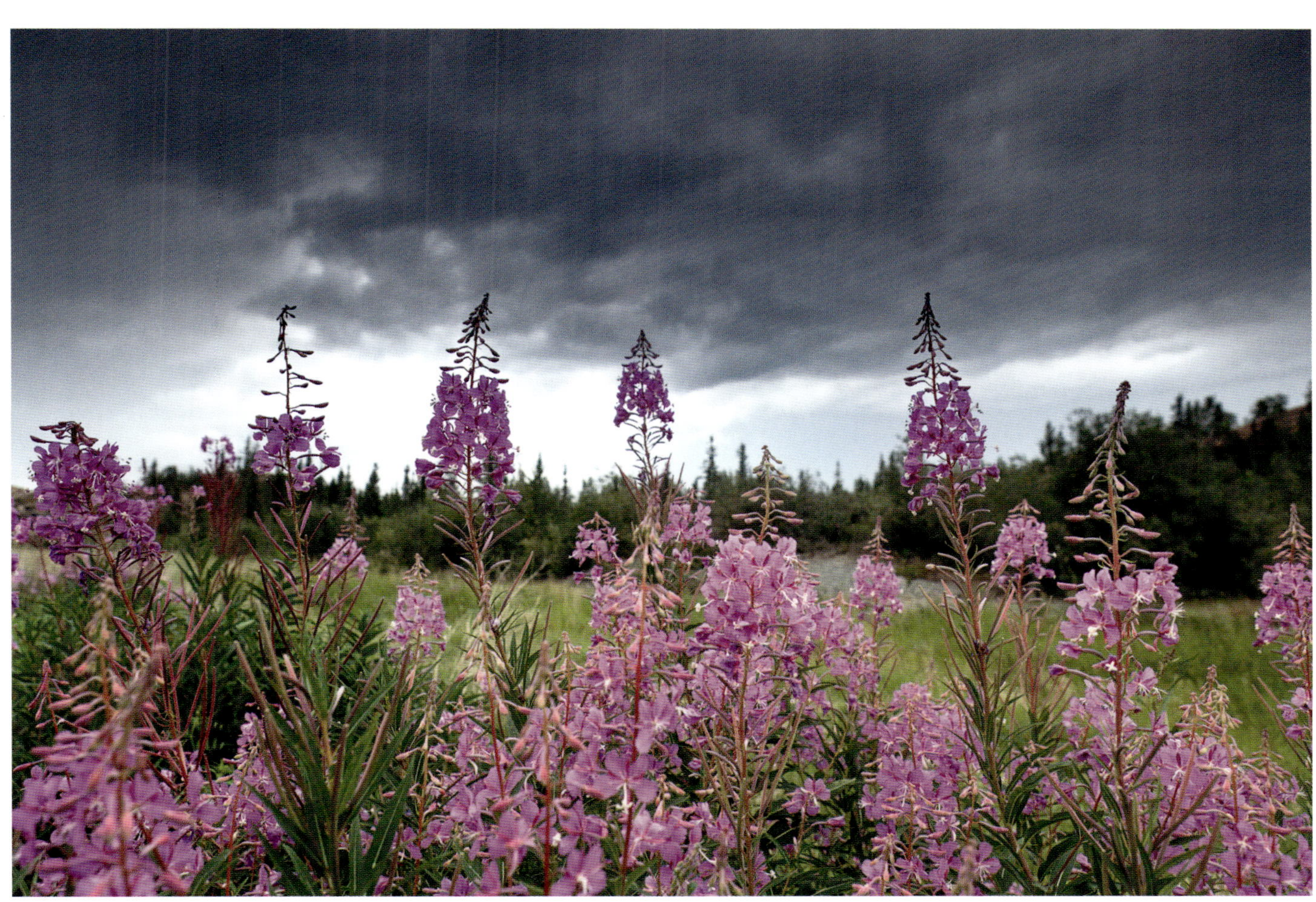

Northern Balance

Yellowknife, Northwest Territories

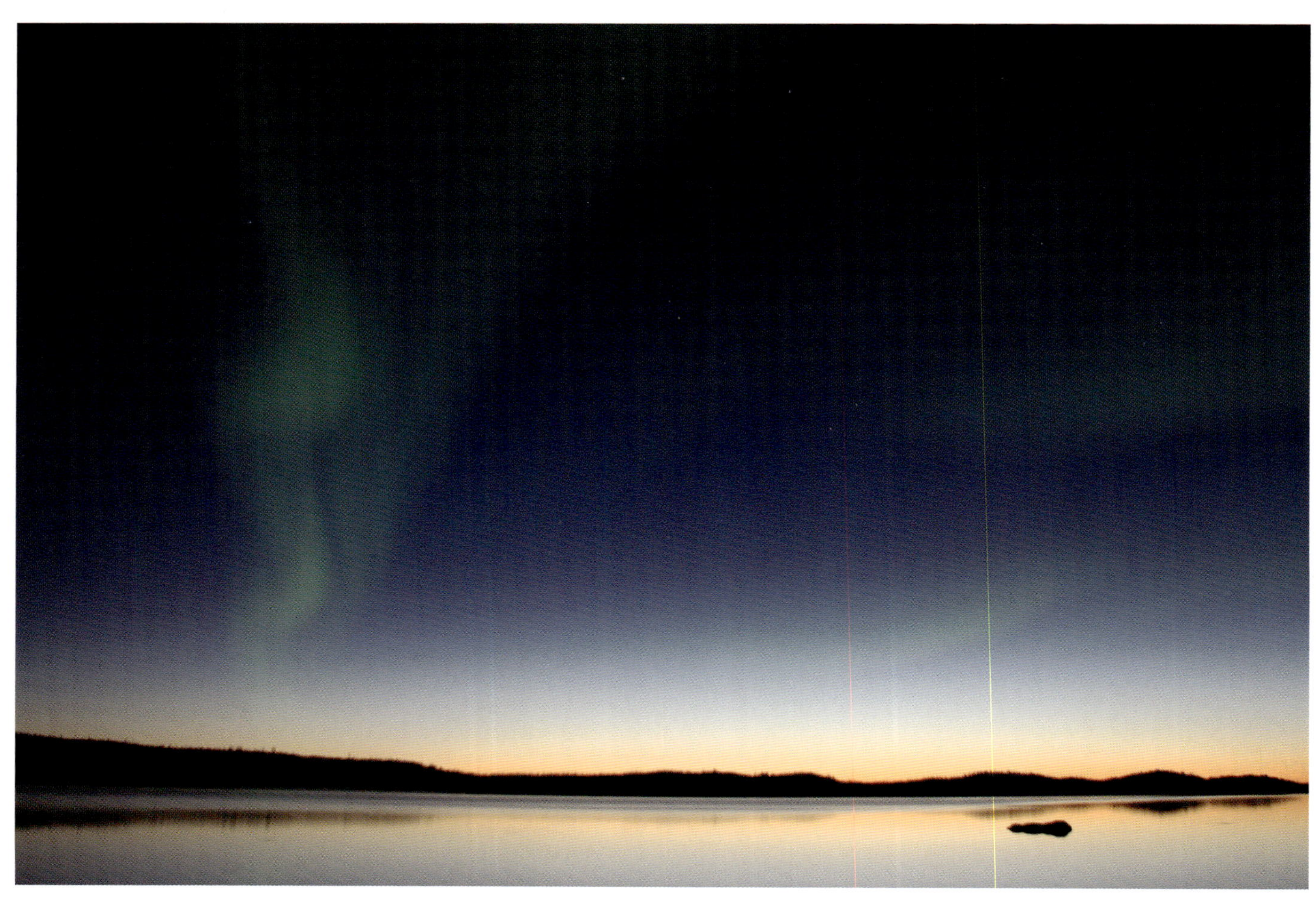

Northern Calm

Prosperous Lake, Northwest Territories

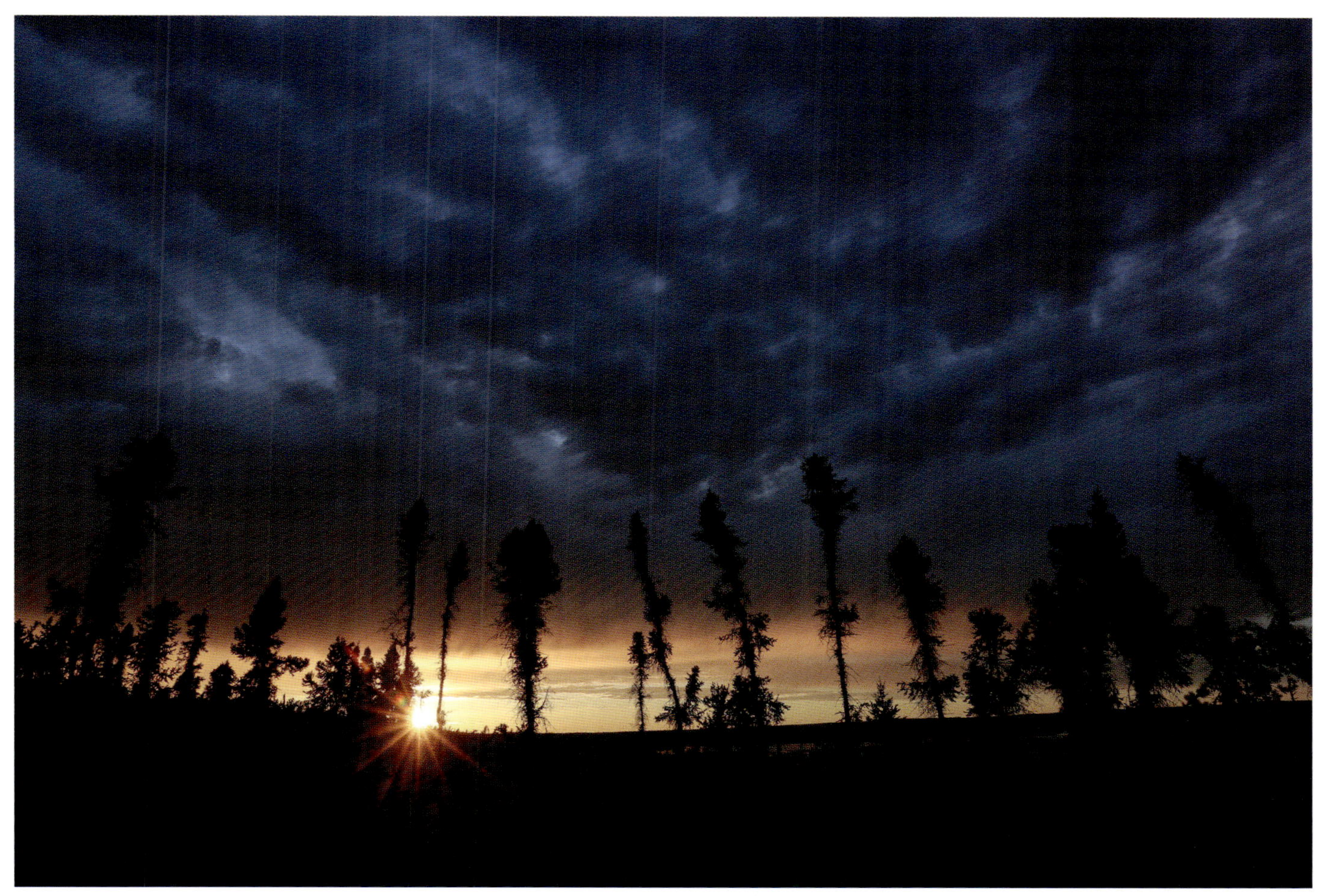

Fire/Rain

Prelude Lake, Northwest Territories

Land Before Time

THE TORNGATS

"Dave, we have to get to the Torngats!"

This is Paul Zizka. Business partner, shooting companion, creator, friend. As with many of the location suggestions that Paul routinely throws at me, I just smiled, nodded... and then secretly went off to Google "What are the Torngats?" Paul's got an encyclopedic brain when it comes to geography, and I can't keep up.

In all seriousness, though, I had heard of the Torngats before. A friend, Arthur Boutilier, had been part of the Parks Canada team that did some of the initial park survey work in the late '70s – 9700 square kilometres are now officially designated as the Torngat Mountains National Park – and sometime around 2010 I watched a private slide show he presented to me on the beauty of the park. I was stunned. This was in Labrador? In eastern Canada? How come I had never heard of this place of fjords and bays and towering mountains and rich marine wildlife and polar bears and light and shadow? A seed had been planted, watching those beautiful images he shared, to somehow, someday, get there.

When Paul brought up the Torngats many years later, my interest was immediately piqued. Northern Labrador seemed about as remote and inaccessible a place you can get in Canada. My kind of place.

It was challenging, logistically, to get and travel there. Weather delays and sea swells (most of the exploration out of Torngat Mountains National Park is done by water) hampered some of our efforts, but when the weather gods finally cooperated, I could see why this area was so revered by the few people who'd had the chance to visit. Despite being one of Canada's least-visited national parks, it has to be one of the most spectacular.

One of my personal discoveries was just how rich the area is in culture and history; like so many of the world's Northern locales, it isn't just another "pretty place." Our planet's indigenous people travelled, lived and flourished across the North for thousands of years, and the Torngats area is no exception: it is rich with traditional Inuit sites, and we learned a lot from our Inuit guides, bear guards and elders during our time in the Torngats and nearby Hebron.

Compared with my exploration through much of the rest of the North, my time in northern Labrador has still been somewhat limited, but I yearn to return and spend more time exploring its endless coastline and silently observing its many treasures.

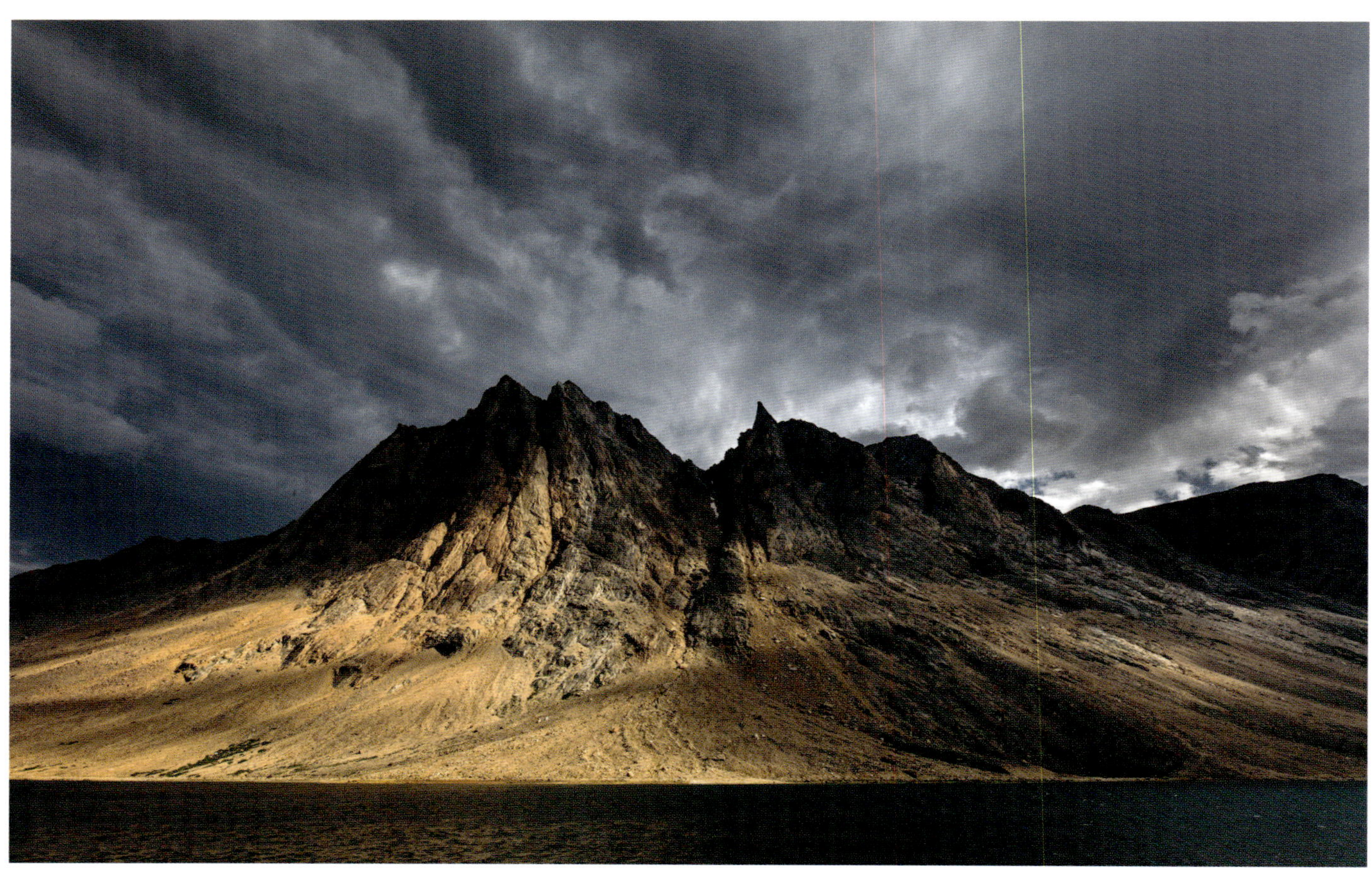

Land before Time

The Torngats, Labrador

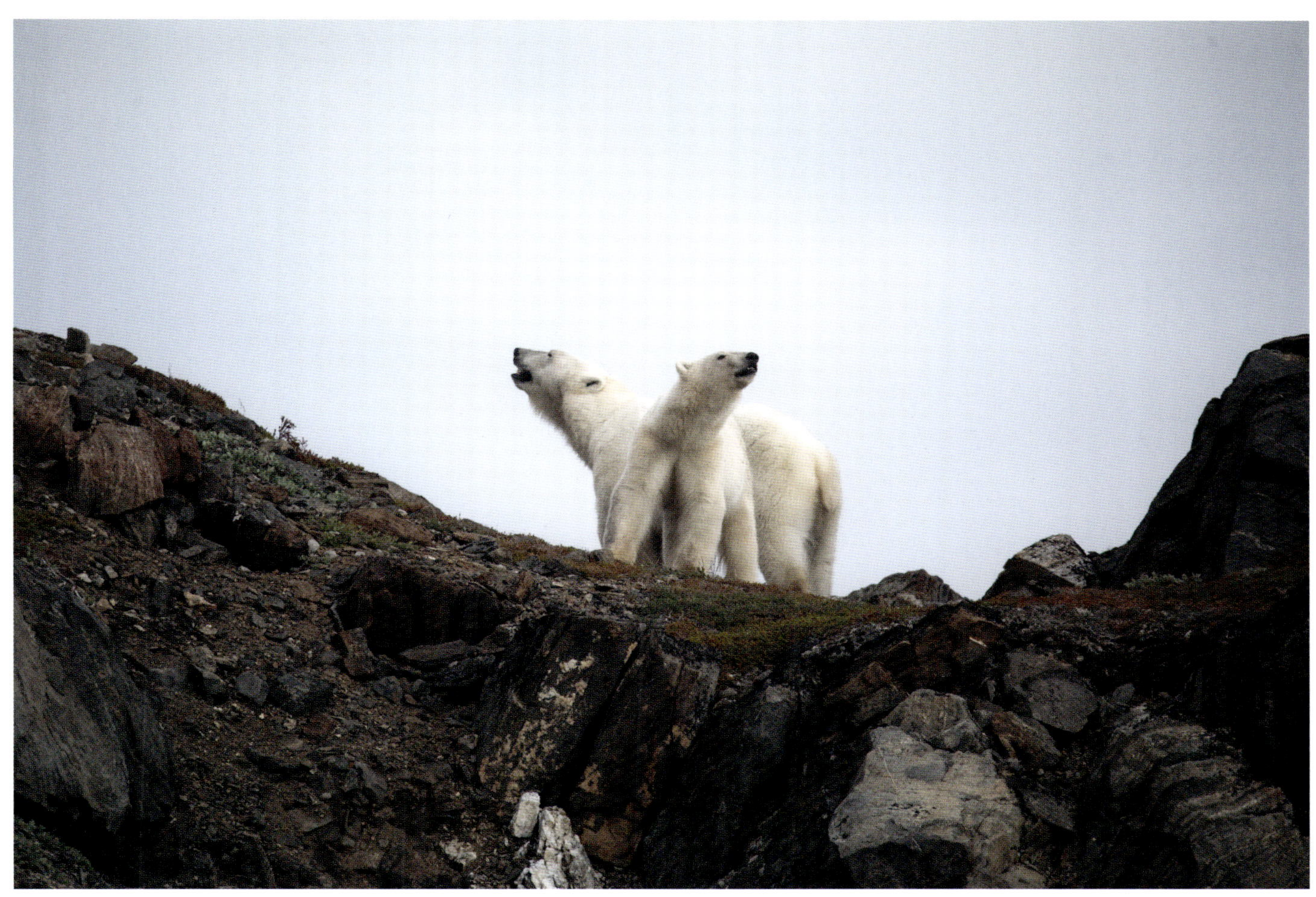

Two-Spirited
The Torngats, Labrador

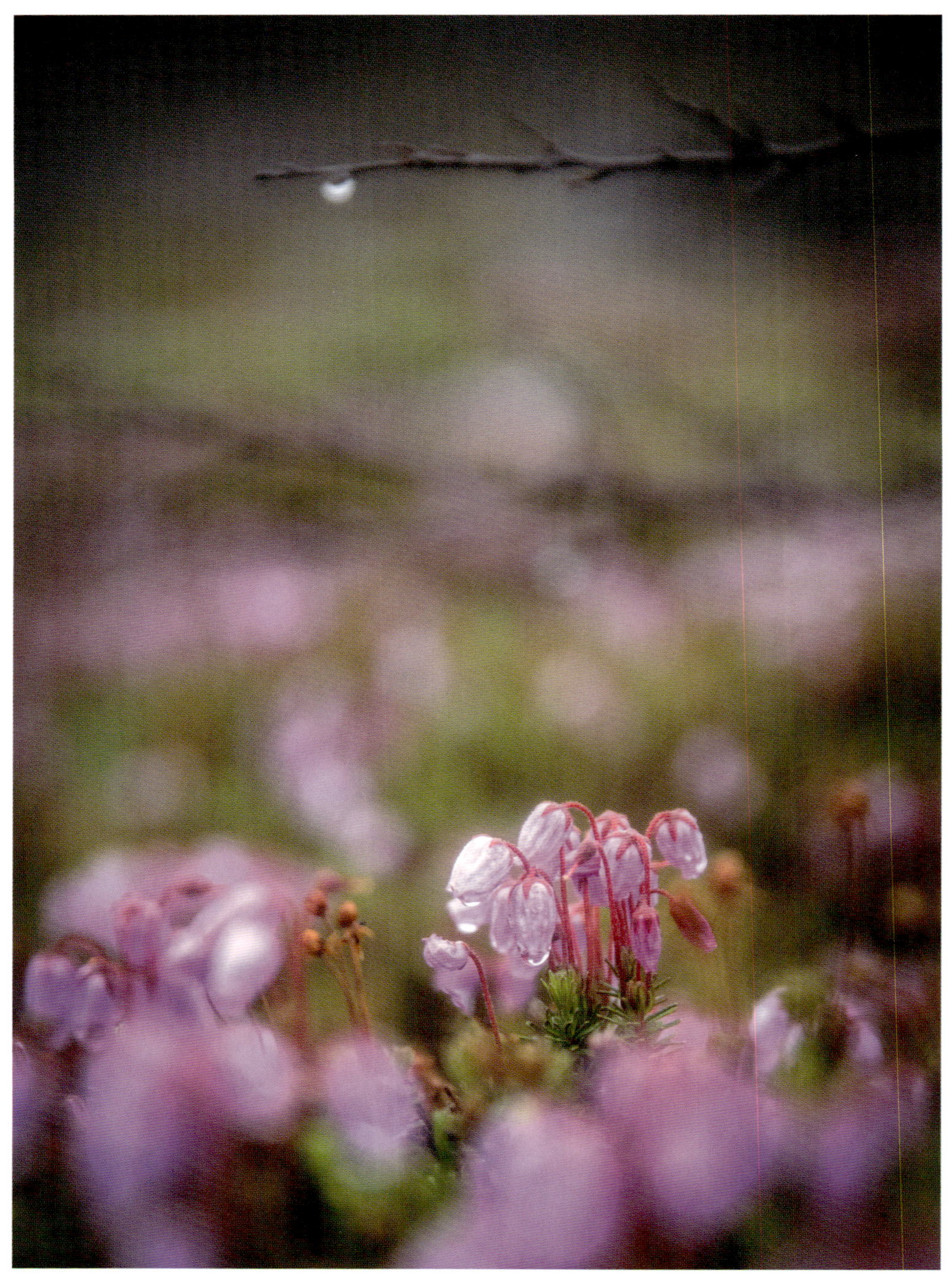

The World Below
The Torngats, Labrador

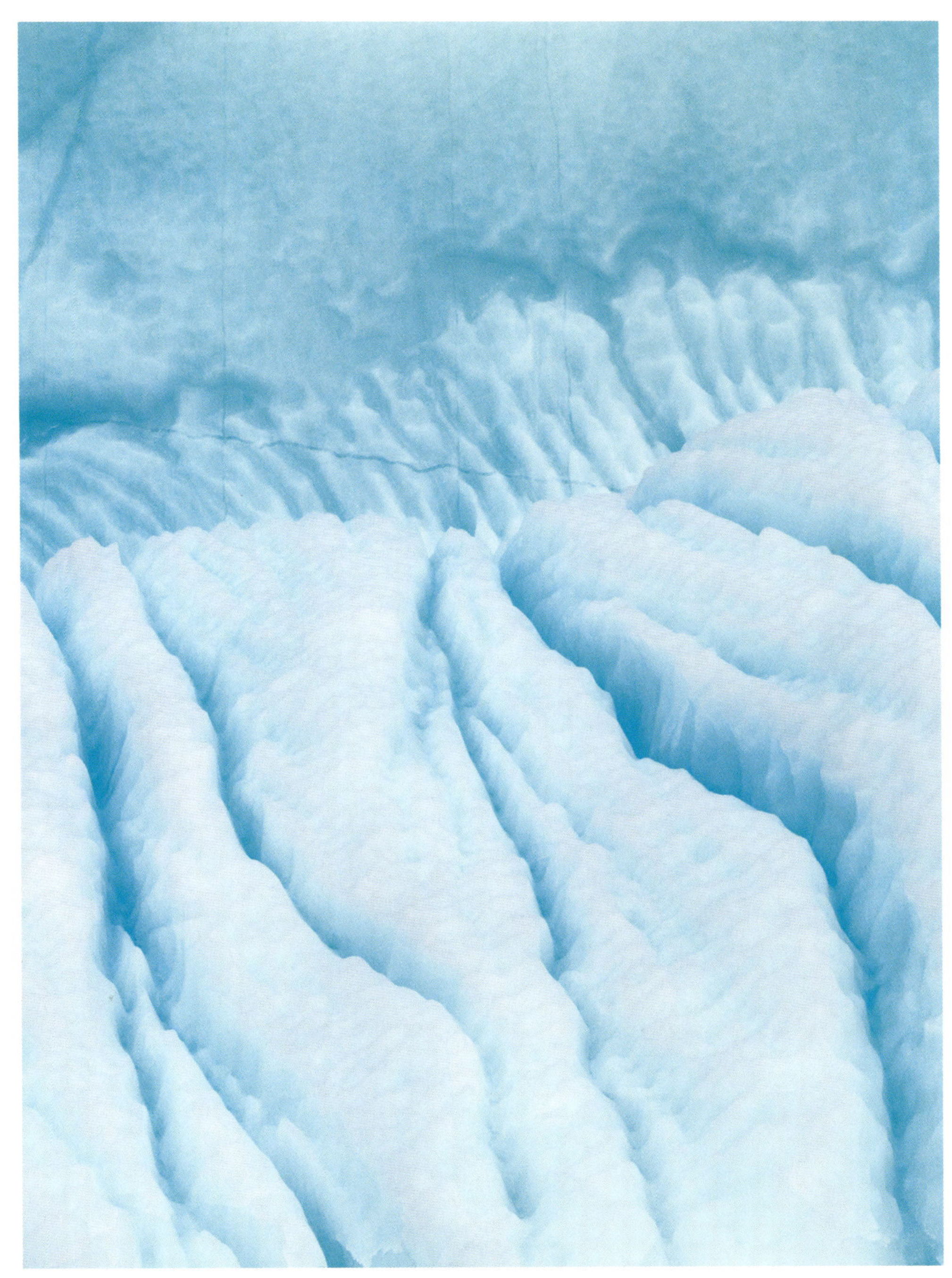

Puzzle Pieces
The Torngats, Labrador

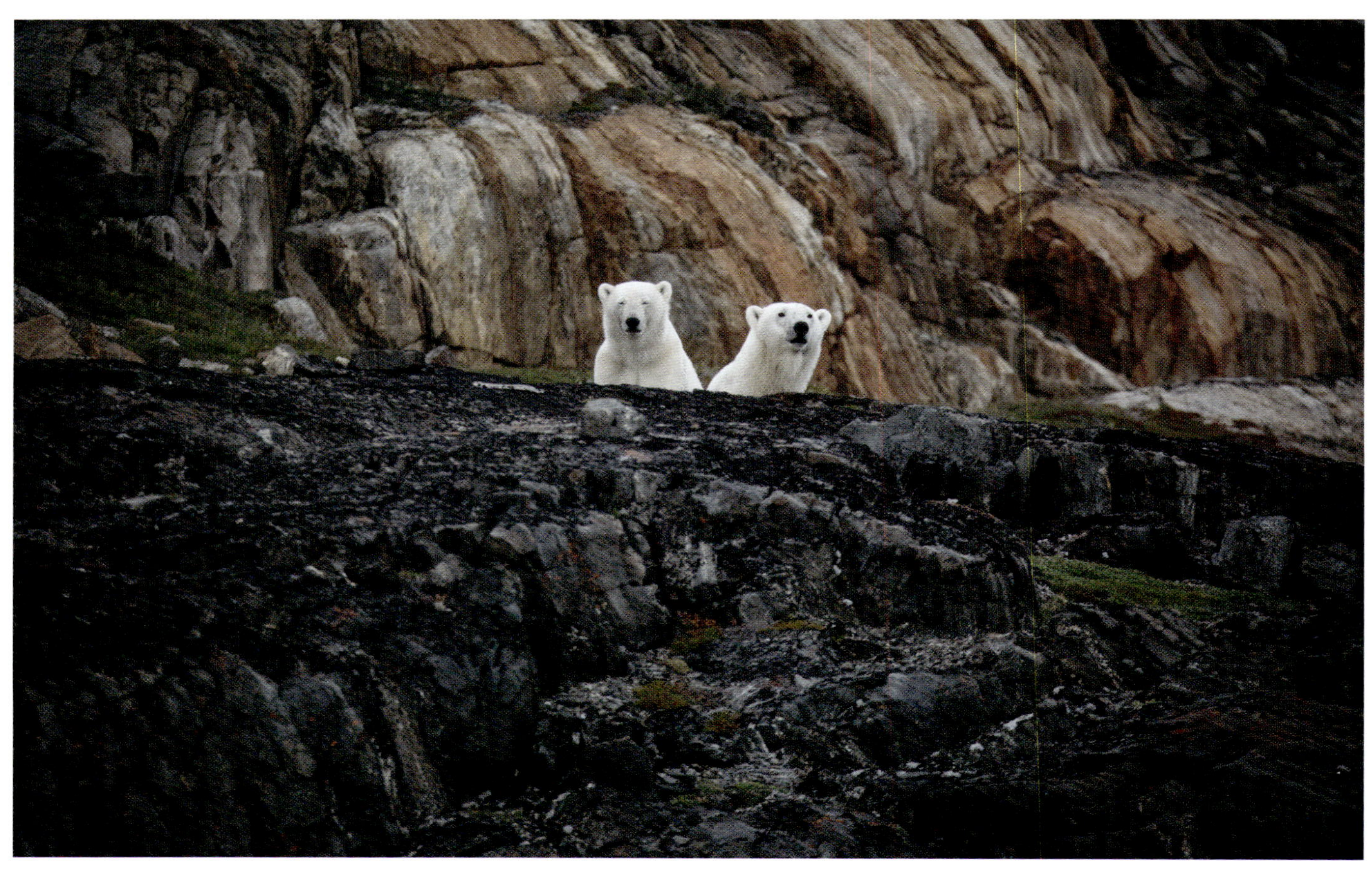

Who Goes There?
The Torngats, Labrador

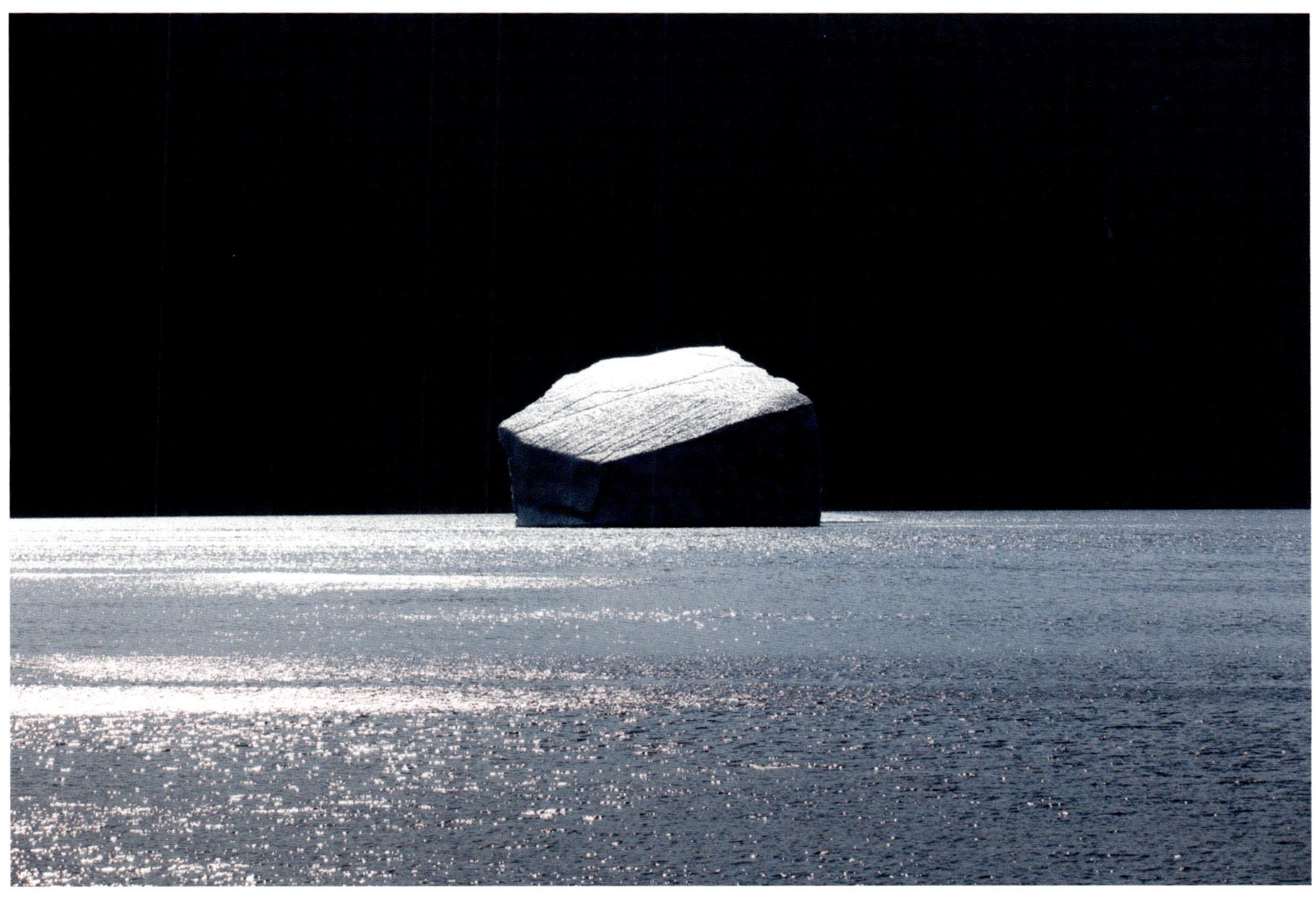

The Arctic Balance
The Torngats, Labrador

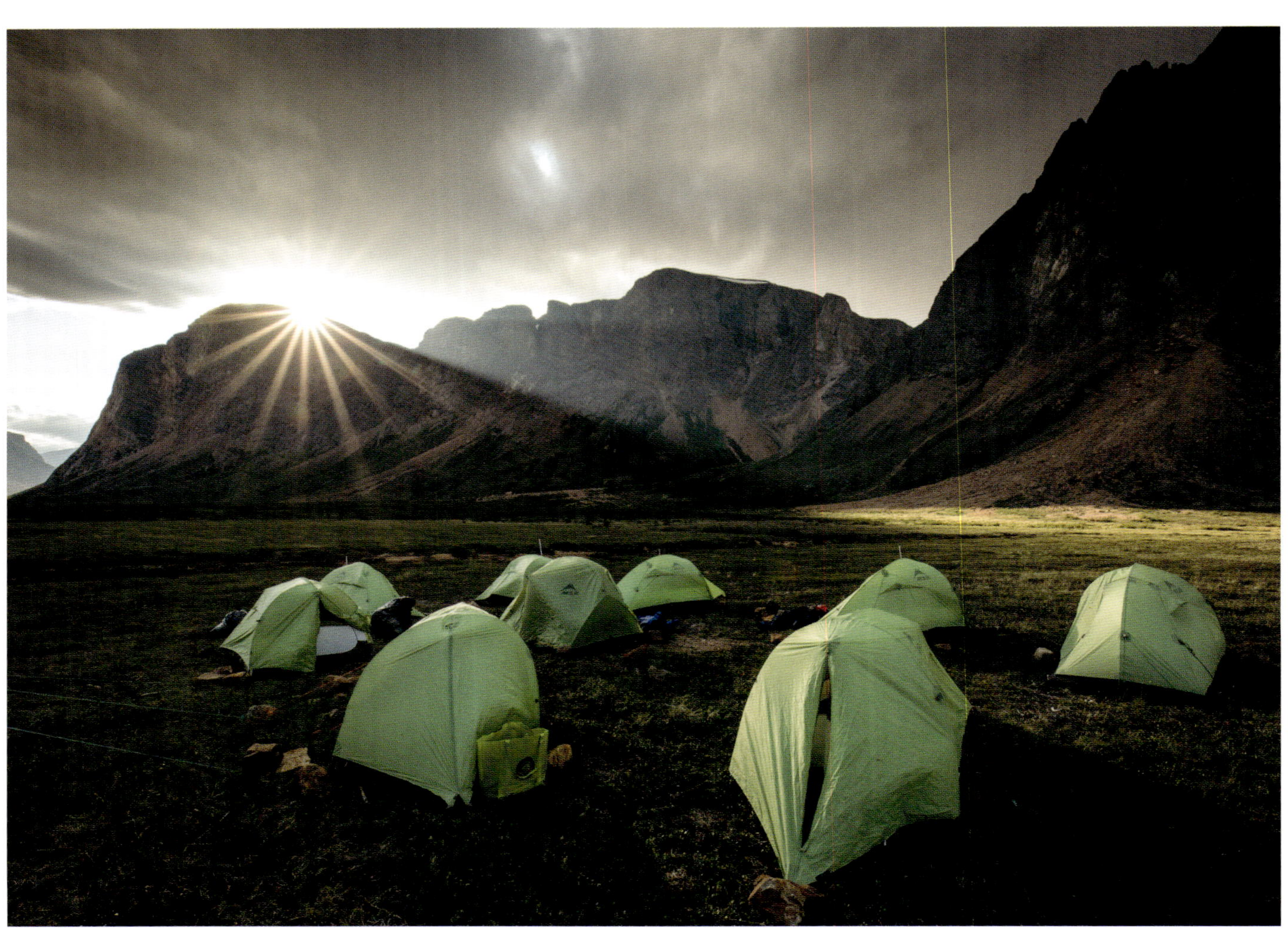

162 *Base Camp*
The Torngats, Labrador

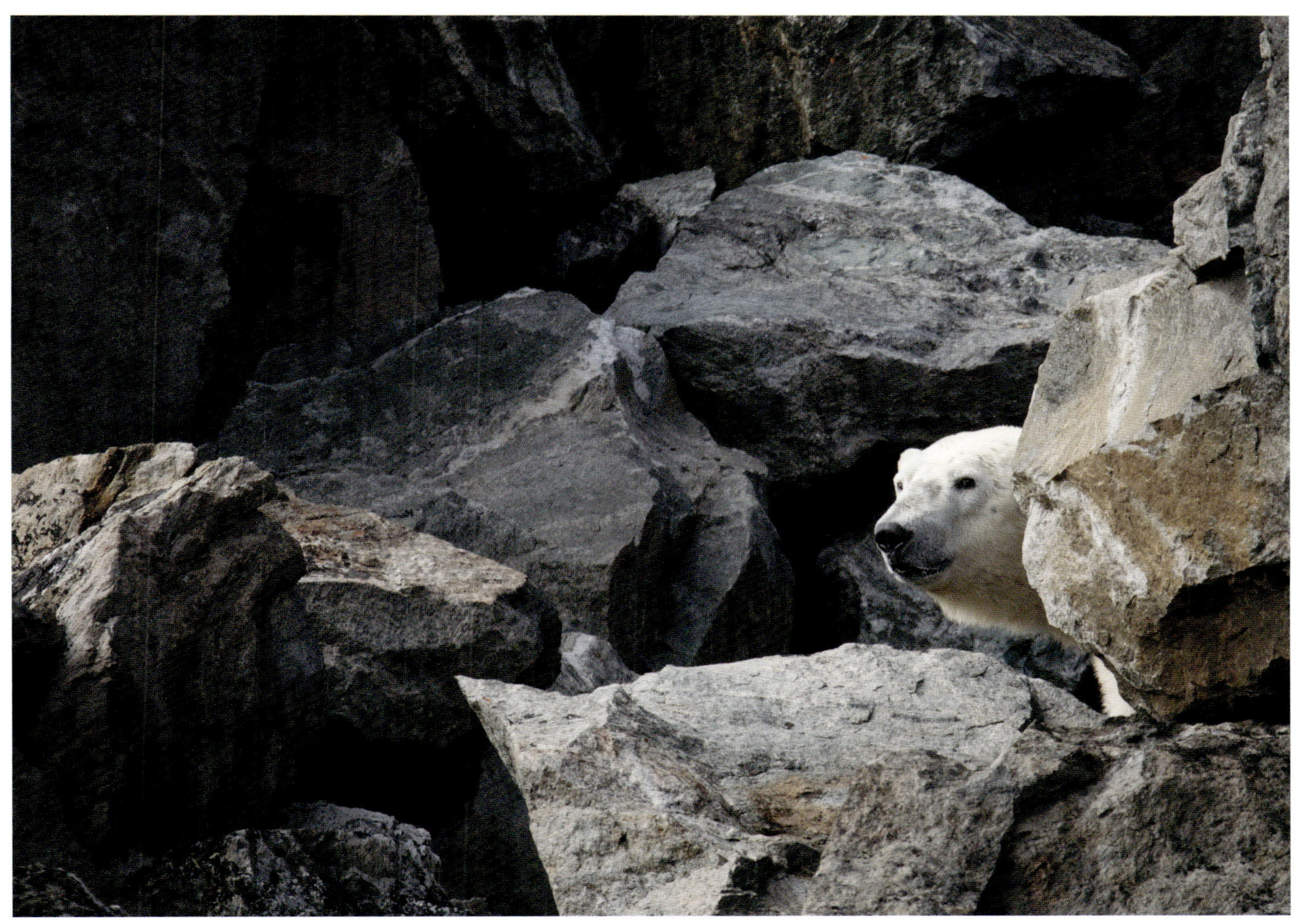

Room with a View
The Torngats, Labrador

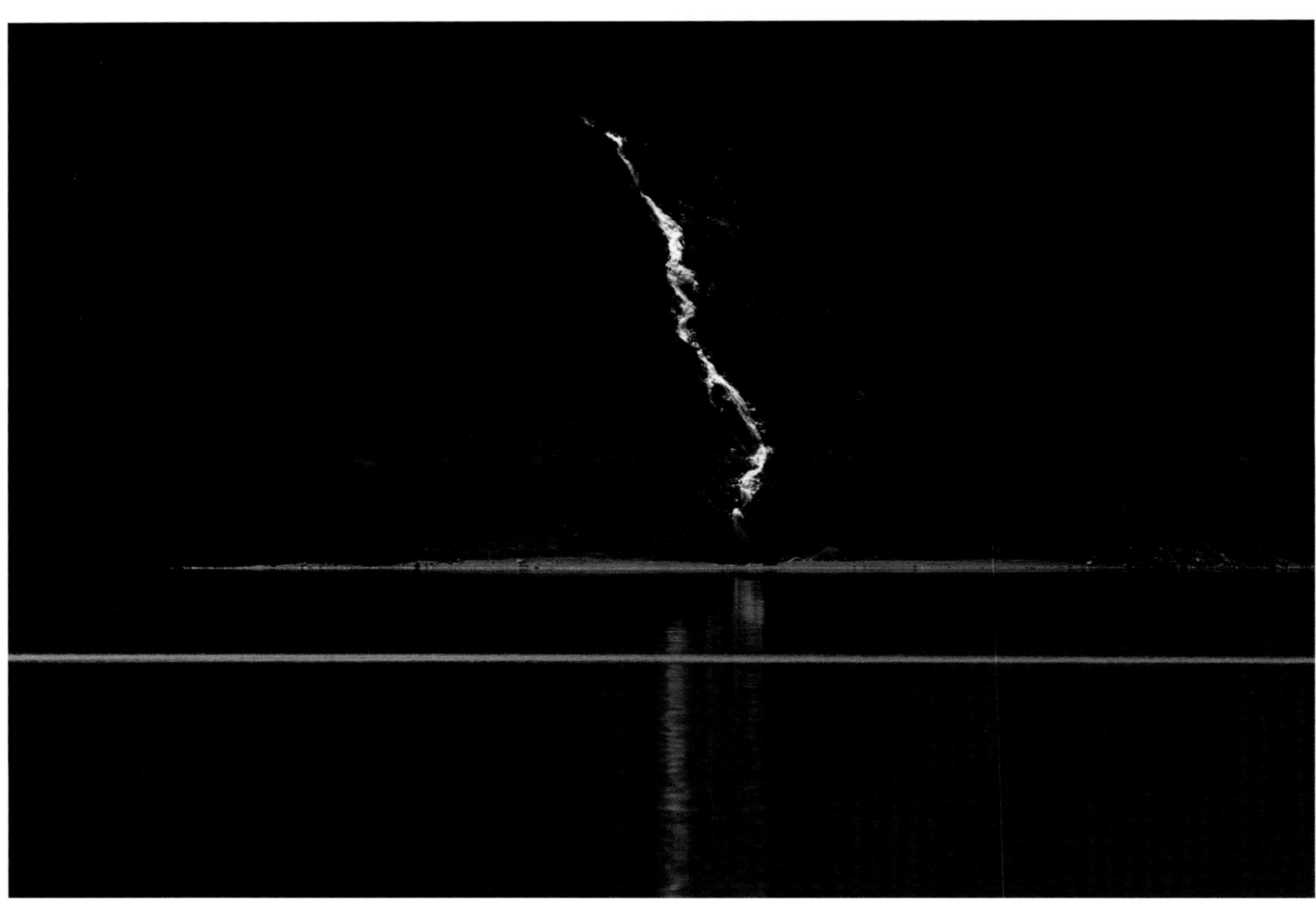

Lines

The Torngats, Labrador

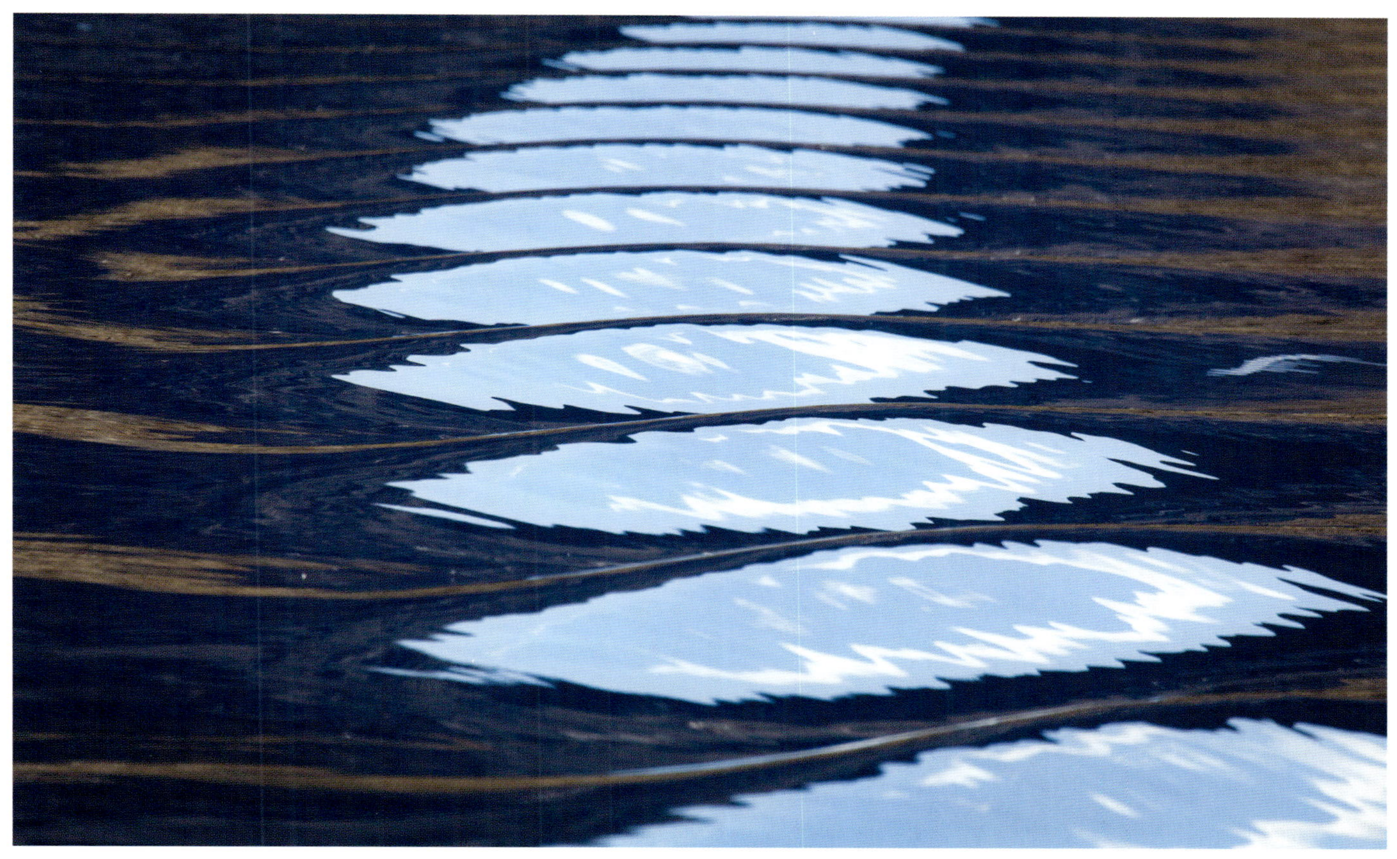

Down in the Valley
The Torngats, Labrador

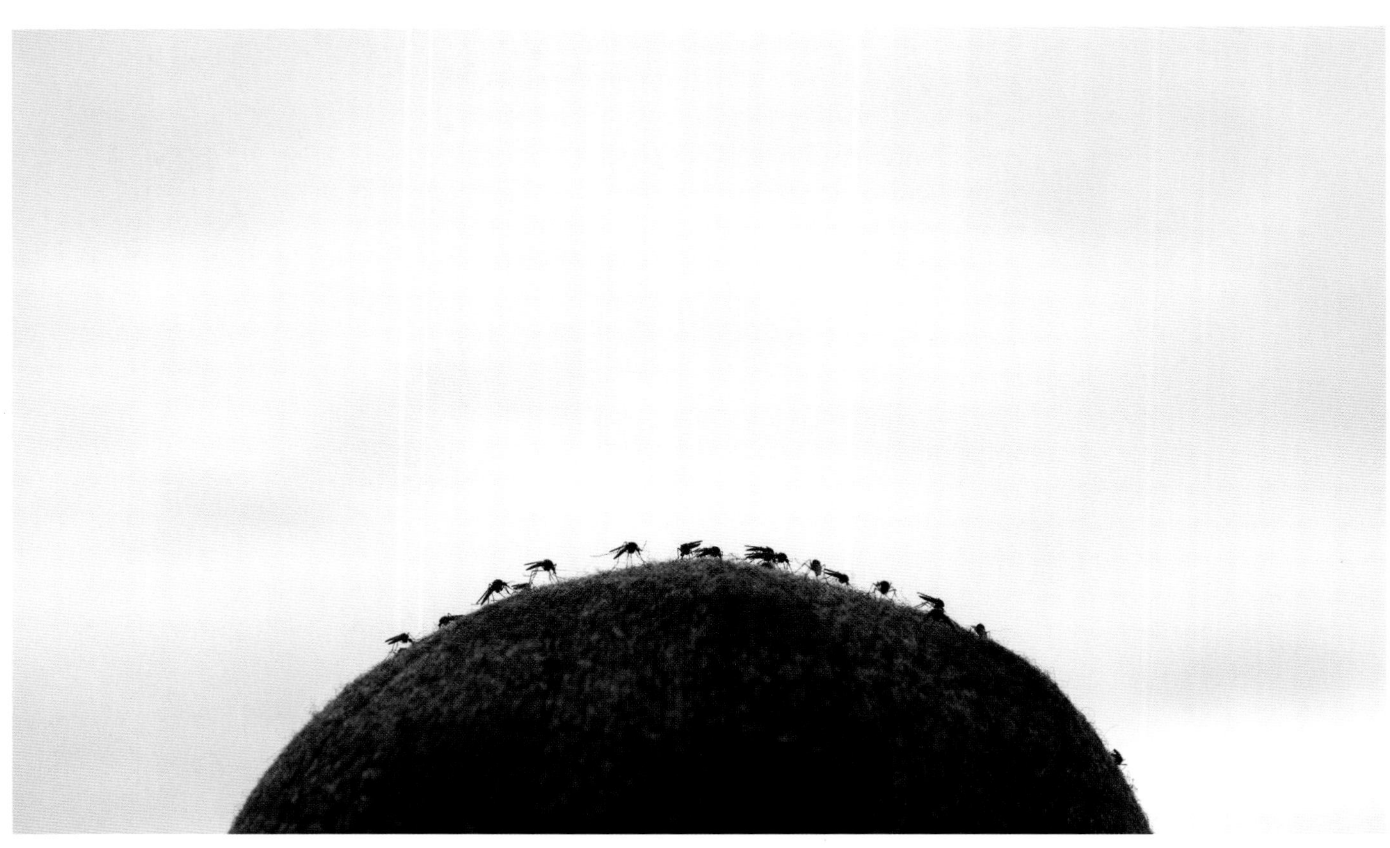

Canadian Wildlife
The Torngats, Labrador

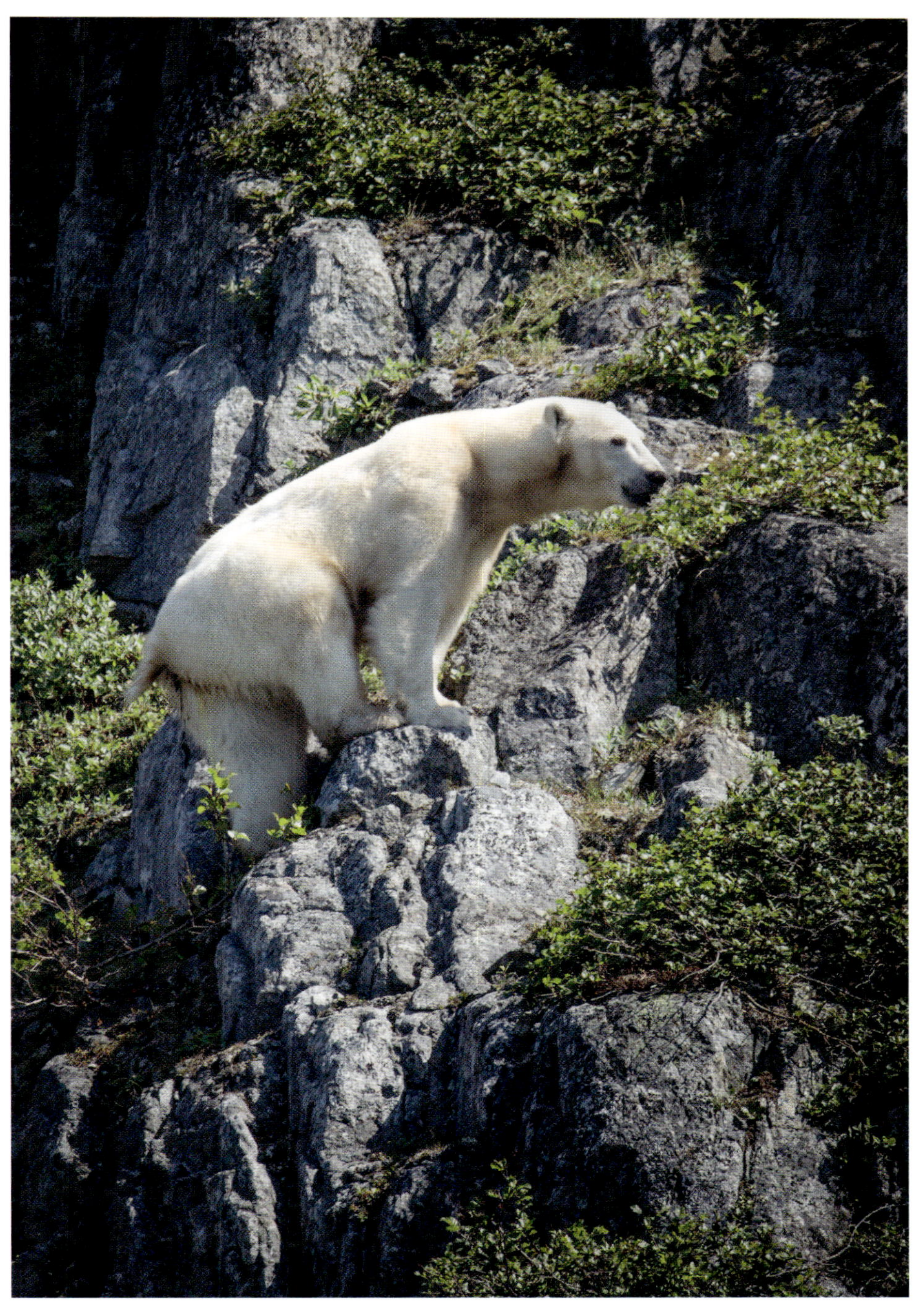

The Catwalk
The Torngats, Labrador

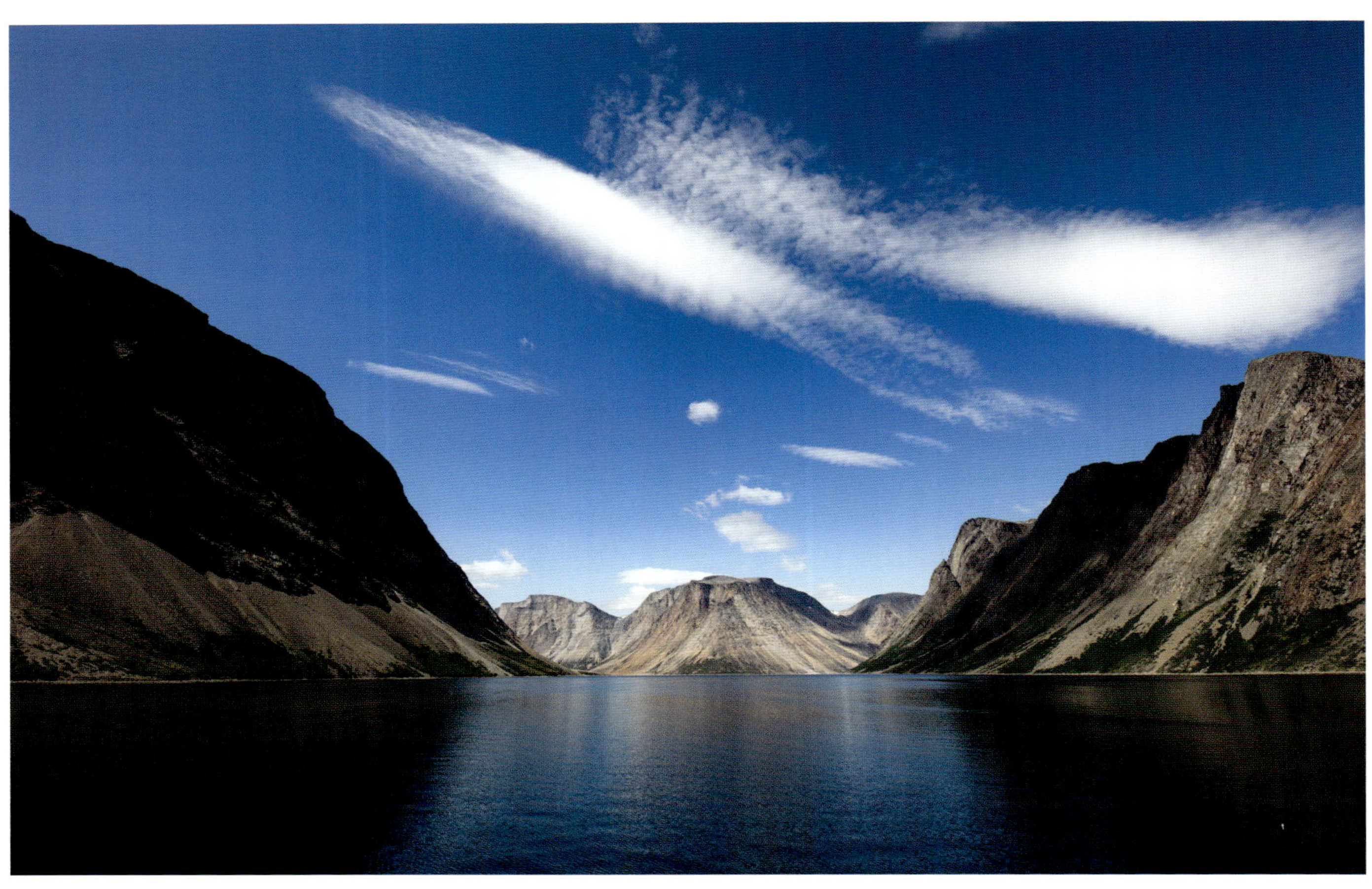

Summer Solitude

The Torngats, Labrador

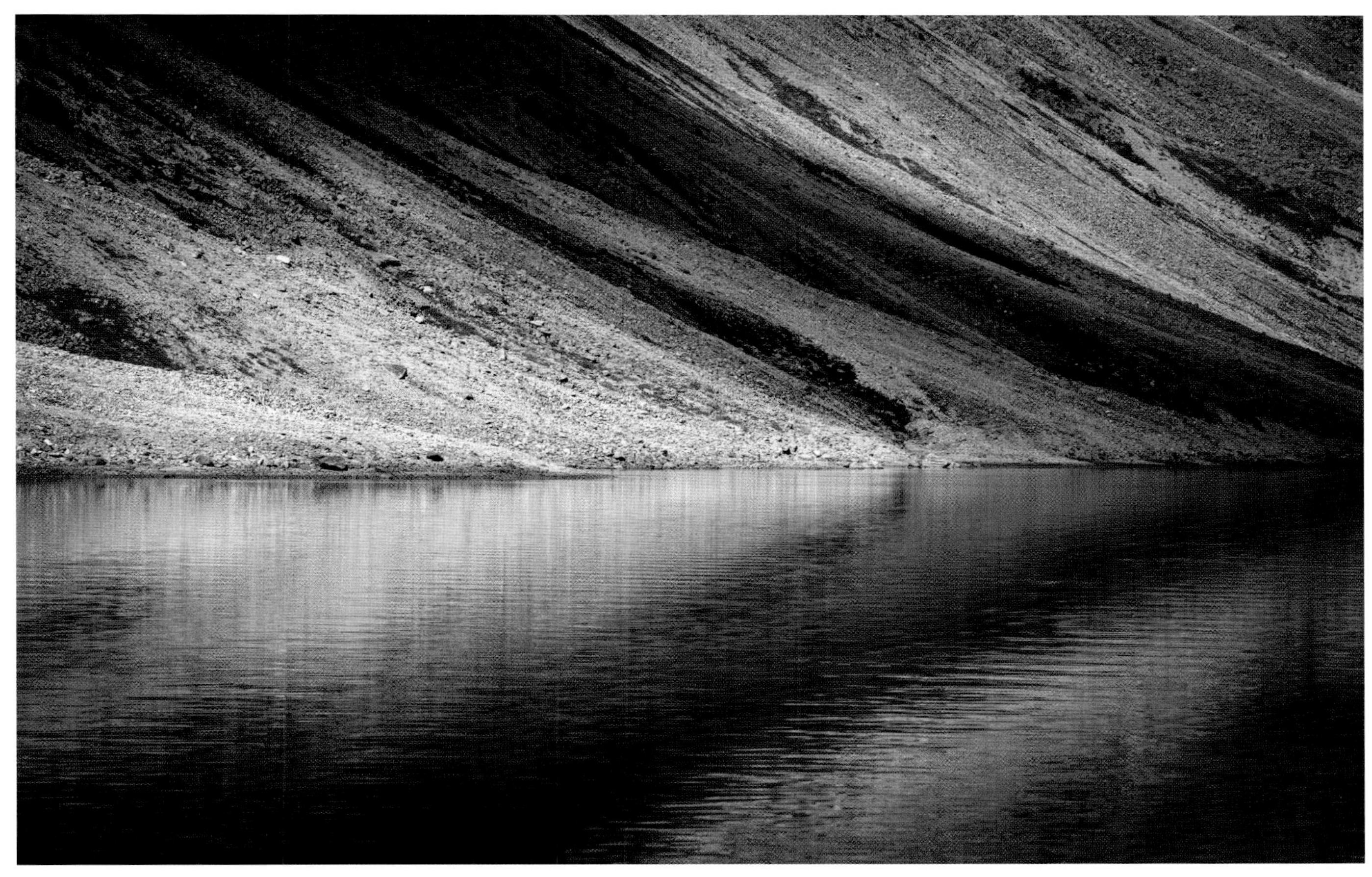

Broken Arrow
The Torngats, Labrador

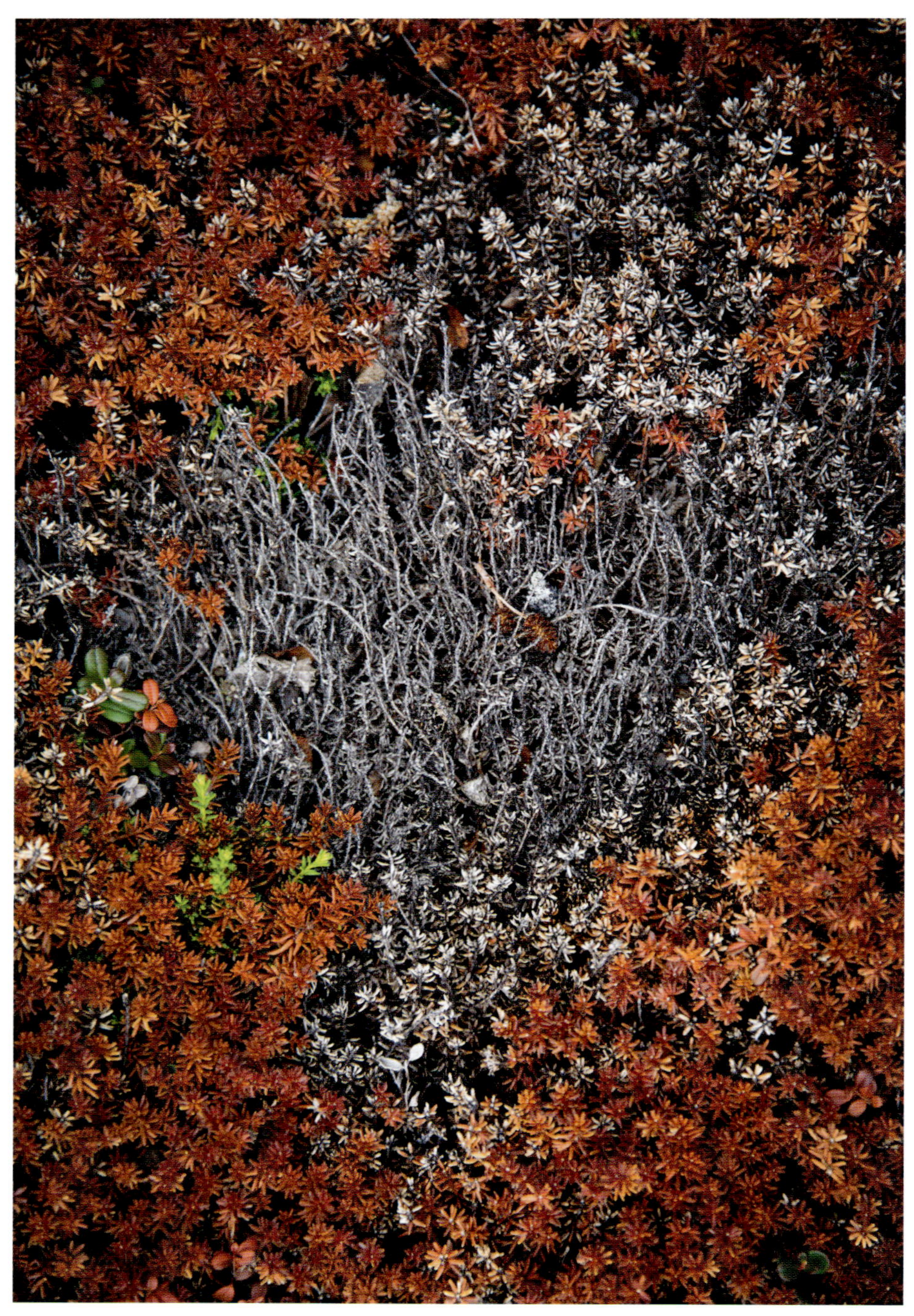

A Closer Look
The Torngats, Labrador

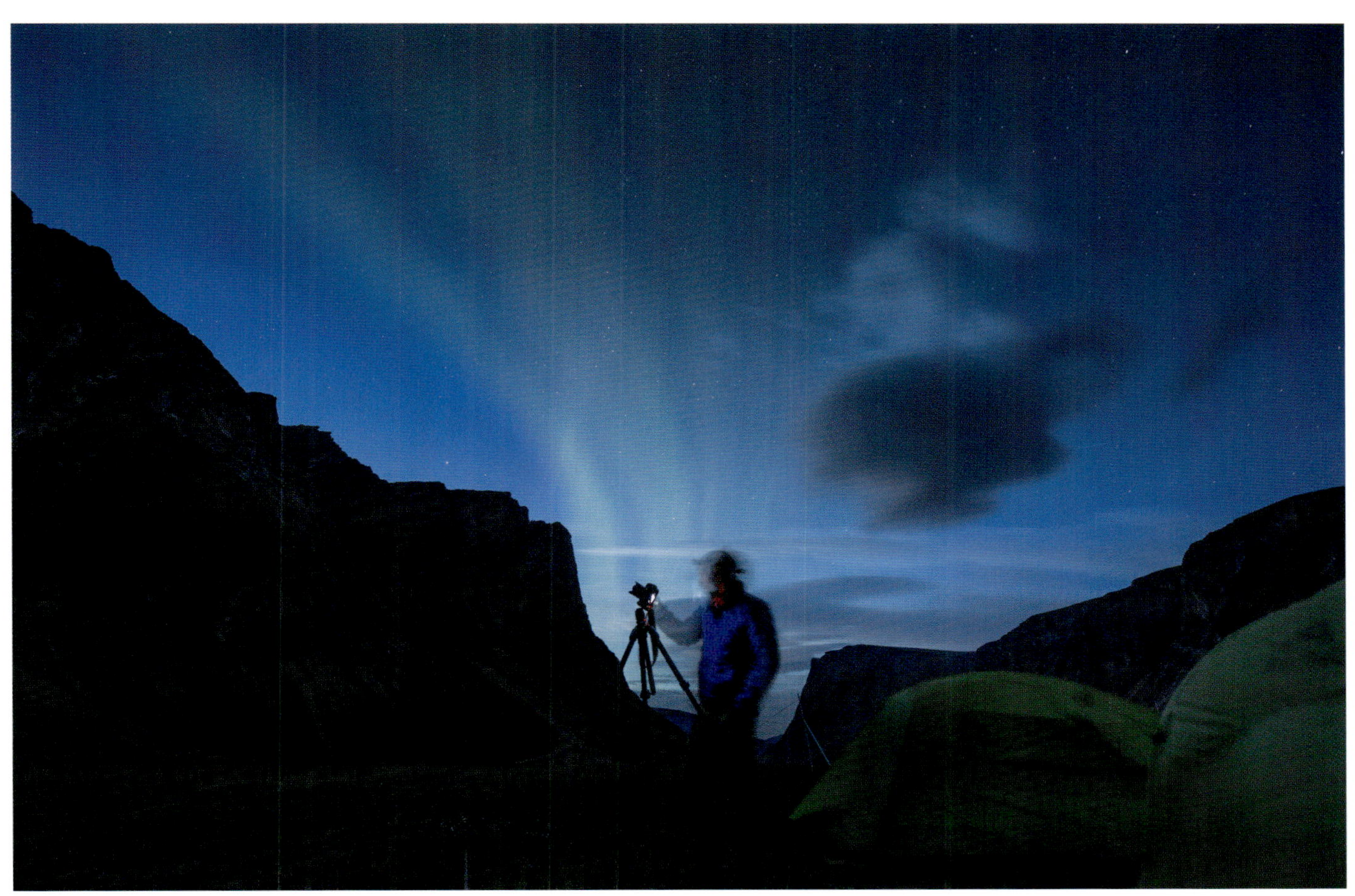

Night Lights

Paul Zizka in The Torngats, Labrador

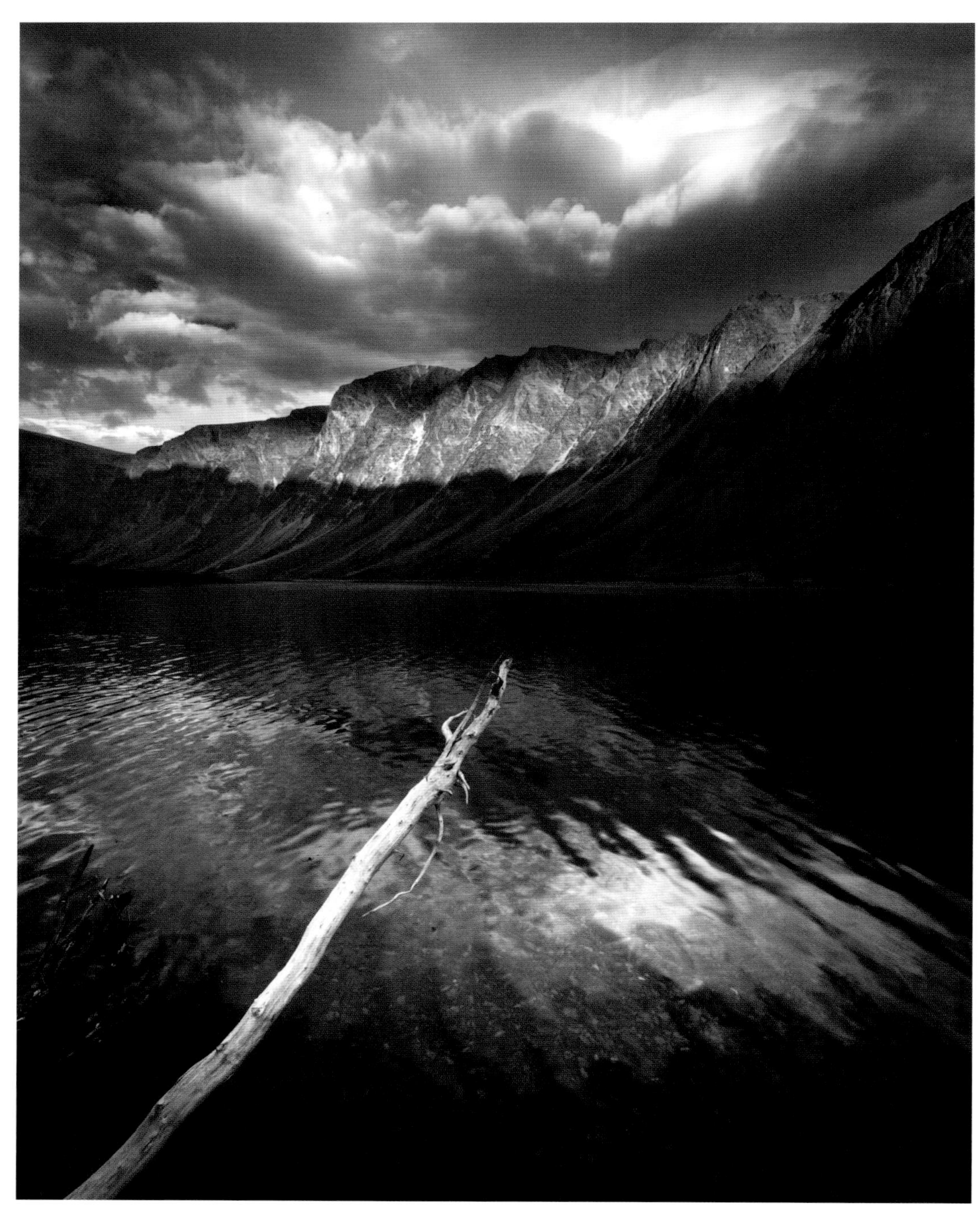

Into the Wild
The Torngats, Labrador

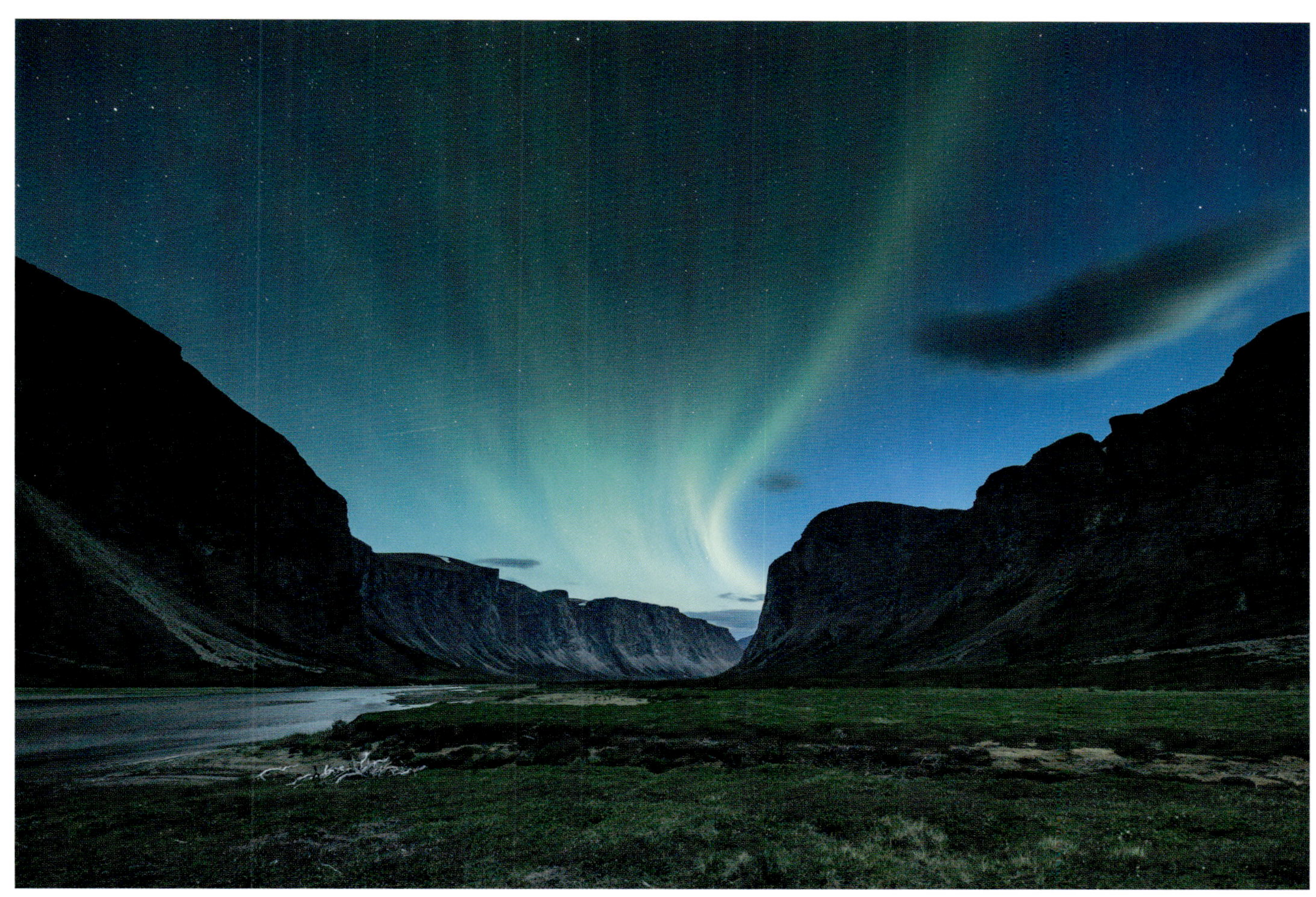

Night Song
The Torngats, Labrador

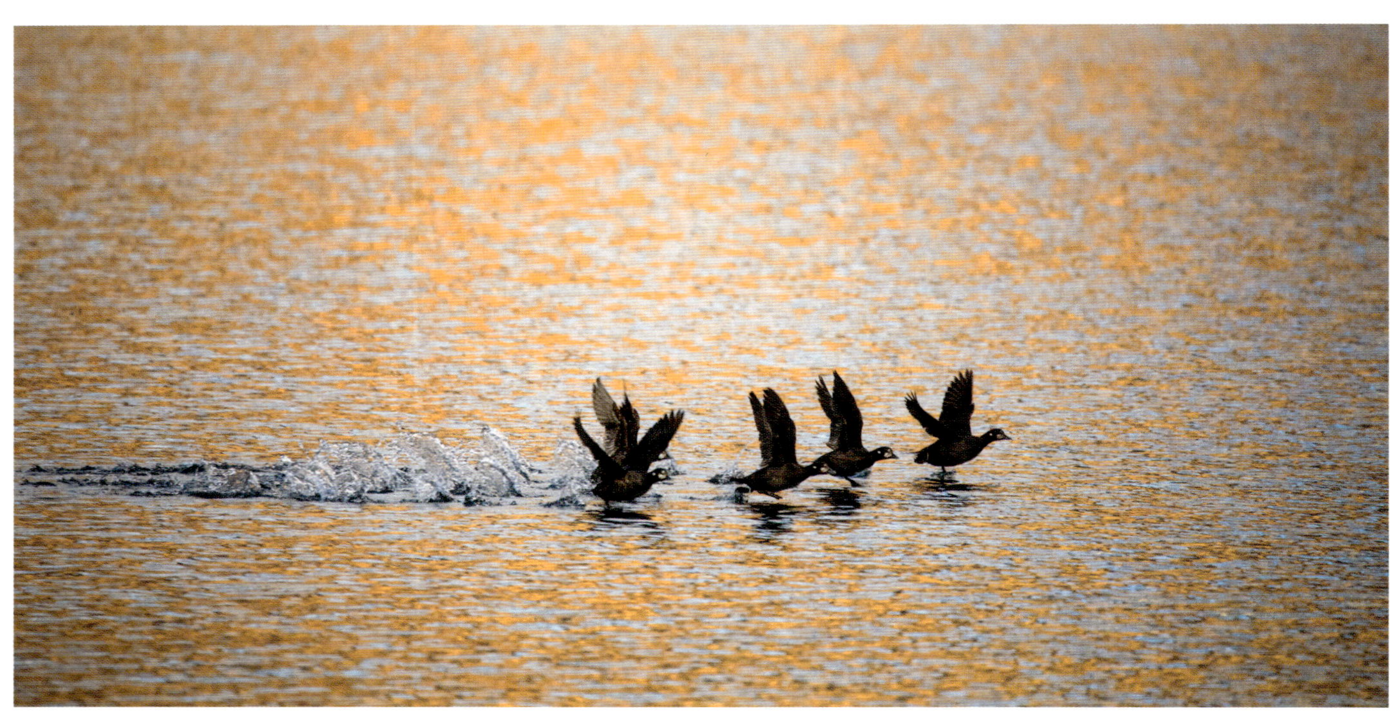

Sundown Ballet

The Torngats, Labrador

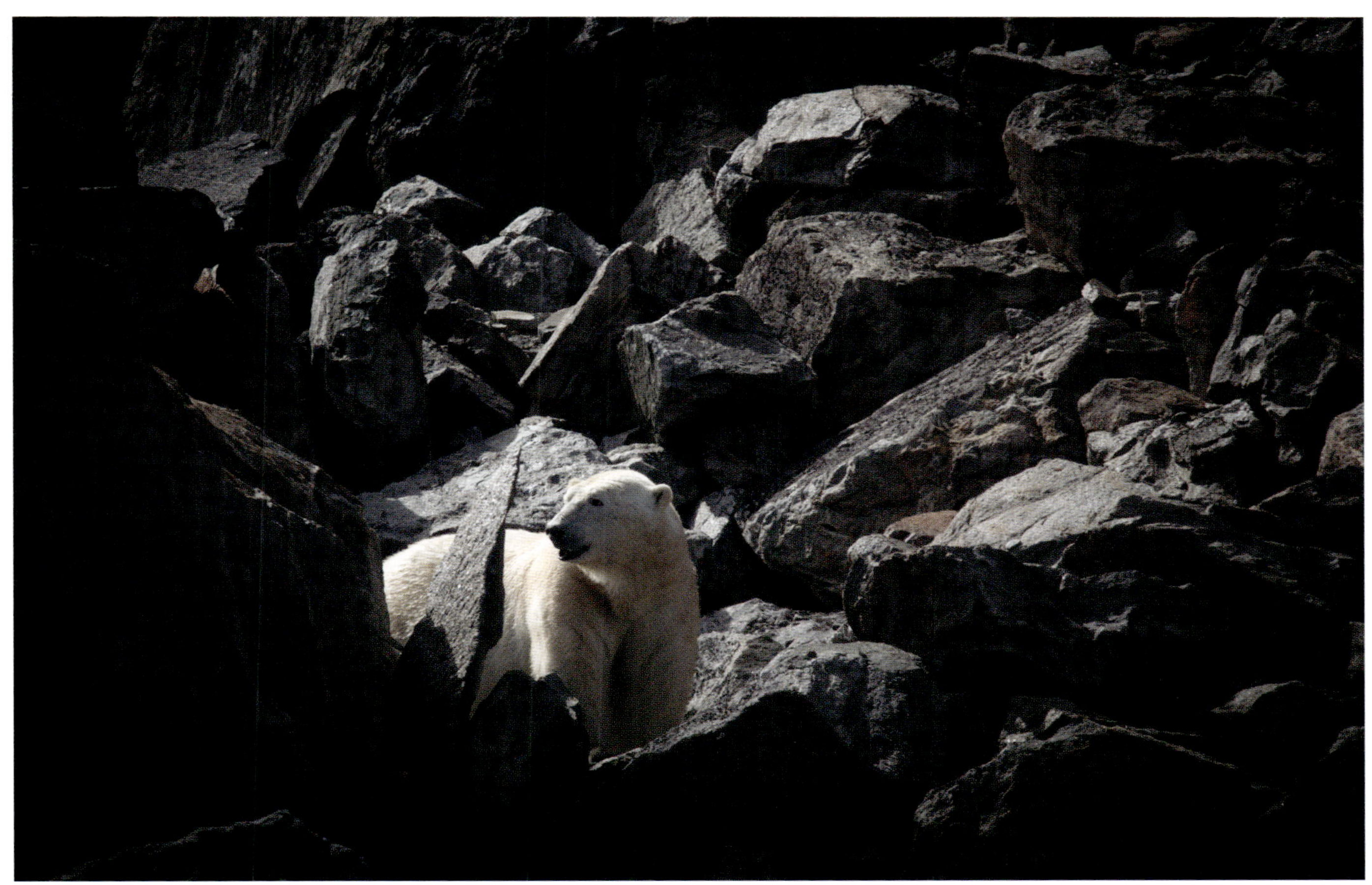

Nanook
The Torngats, Labrador

Yukon Gold

What can I say about Canada's Yukon that doesn't make me sound like a kid in a candy shop with his head on a swivel, mouth agape at all the delights and sensations around him?

I can remember the first time I travelled to the Yukon. It was in the mid-2000s, and I was still working a full-time job in Yellowknife; full-time photography was still a few years away. My boss had come up to me and said, "Hope you don't mind – we need you to go to Whitehorse for a training course. You'll be gone about a week."

Oh, yeah.

The Yukon. The final piece in the mindless little quest I had back then to travel to each of Canada's provinces and territories. Little did I know that I would not only visit the Yukon at least a dozen more times but would also visit every province and territory many more times – sometimes all within a span of nine months. Our country is vast and its lands beautiful and most of its regions memorable, but I had always dreamed of being able to explore the Yukon.

Flying into the Yukon, for those who love mountainous areas, is like flying into a dream. Far-flung, snow-capped peaks rise above the clouds, and numerous valleys snake in every direction, filled with an impossible number of lakes, rivers and streams. Some of Canada's highest mountains are found in the Yukon, including our highest: Mount Logan, which stands at almost 6000 metres.

On that first trip to Yukon, I had – along with several co-workers – a free day or two that we used to full advantage. We rented a car and travelled north from Whitehorse to the remarkable Kluane National Park. *Now these are mountains*, I thought. We made numerous stops, but one place in particular, Sheep Mountain, got into my psyche and has never left. We stopped and spent the afternoon enjoying the area. I hiked above most of the trees and sat on a rock and took it all in: sweeping views of Kluane Lake and the mountains surrounding its junction with the Slims River, scree slopes and even a herd of Dall sheep who lazily sat in their habitat, enjoying a spring day. I can remember thinking, as I sat up on that mountain, *This is what life's all about.* I felt so alive in that cool breeze; taking photographs in many of these Northern locations almost feels secondary to just being there, and I think that's how it should be.

From that first trip in the mid-2000s, I have returned to the Yukon almost every two years and have photographed countless images of its wild beauty, mainly around Kluane. Despite my numerous trips, however, I still feel like I've only scratched the surface of this special place, and I look forward to documenting its treasures as long as life and circumstance allow.

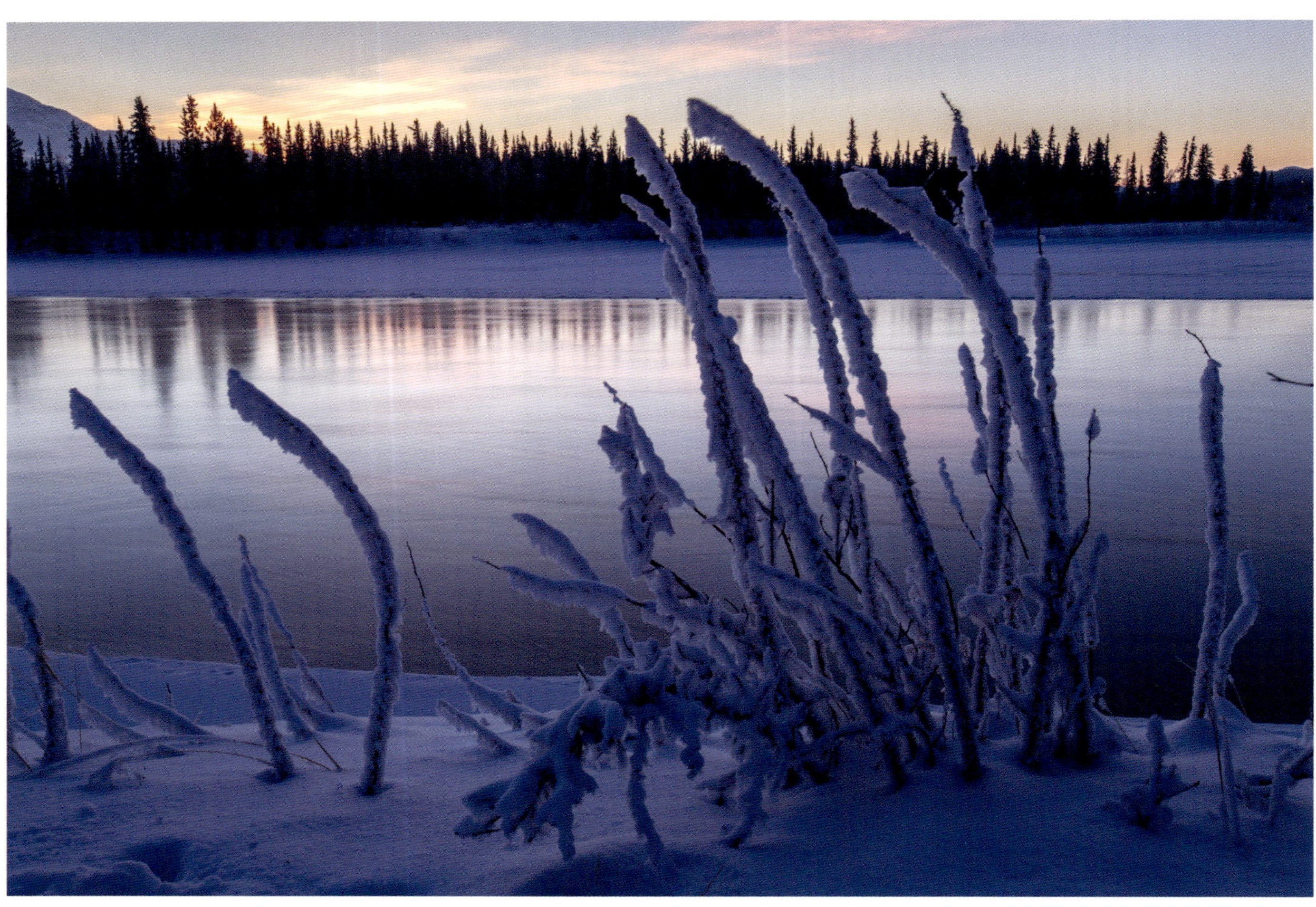

Winter Rise

Whitehorse, Yukon

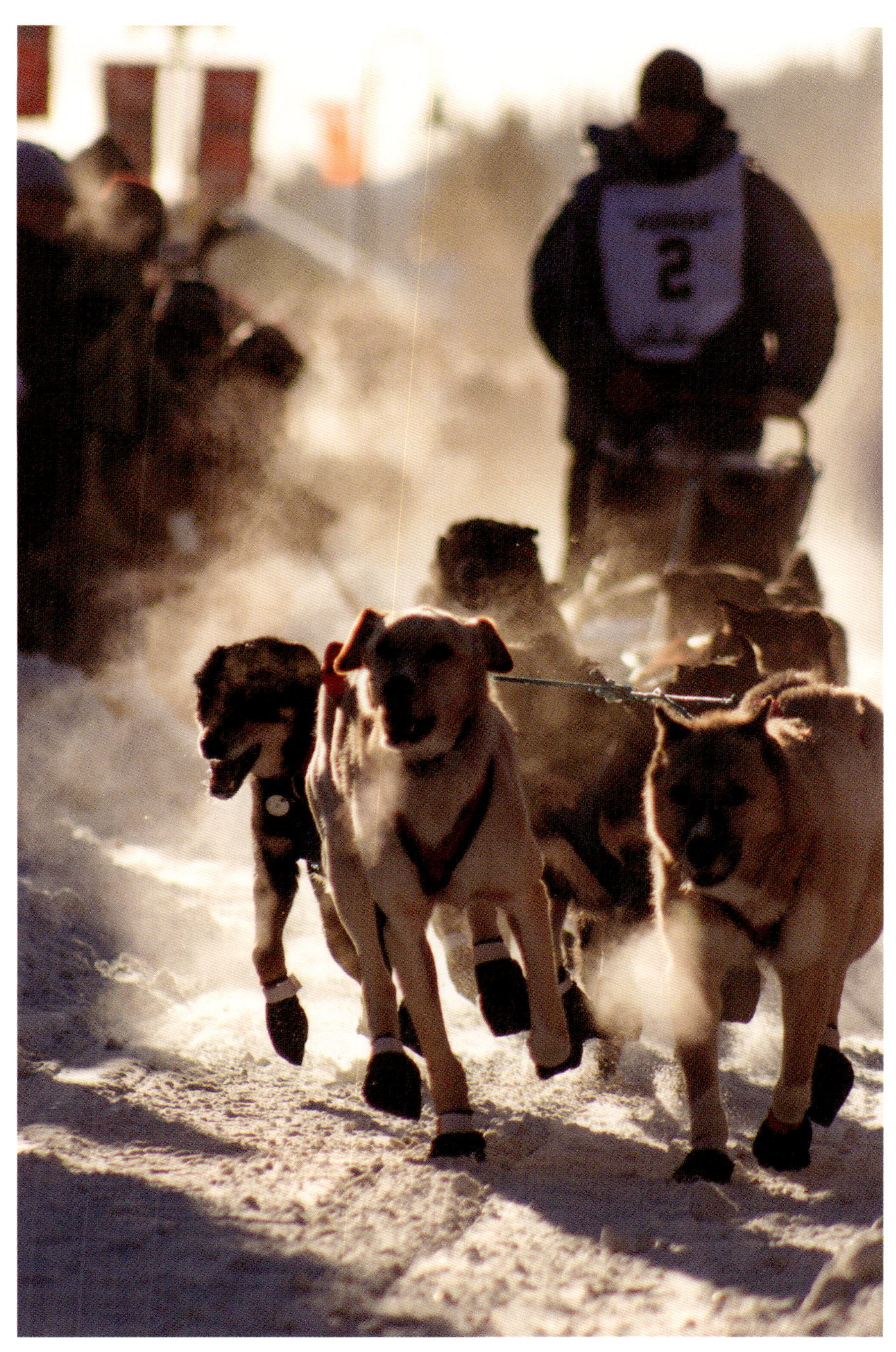

Quest
Whitehorse, Yukon

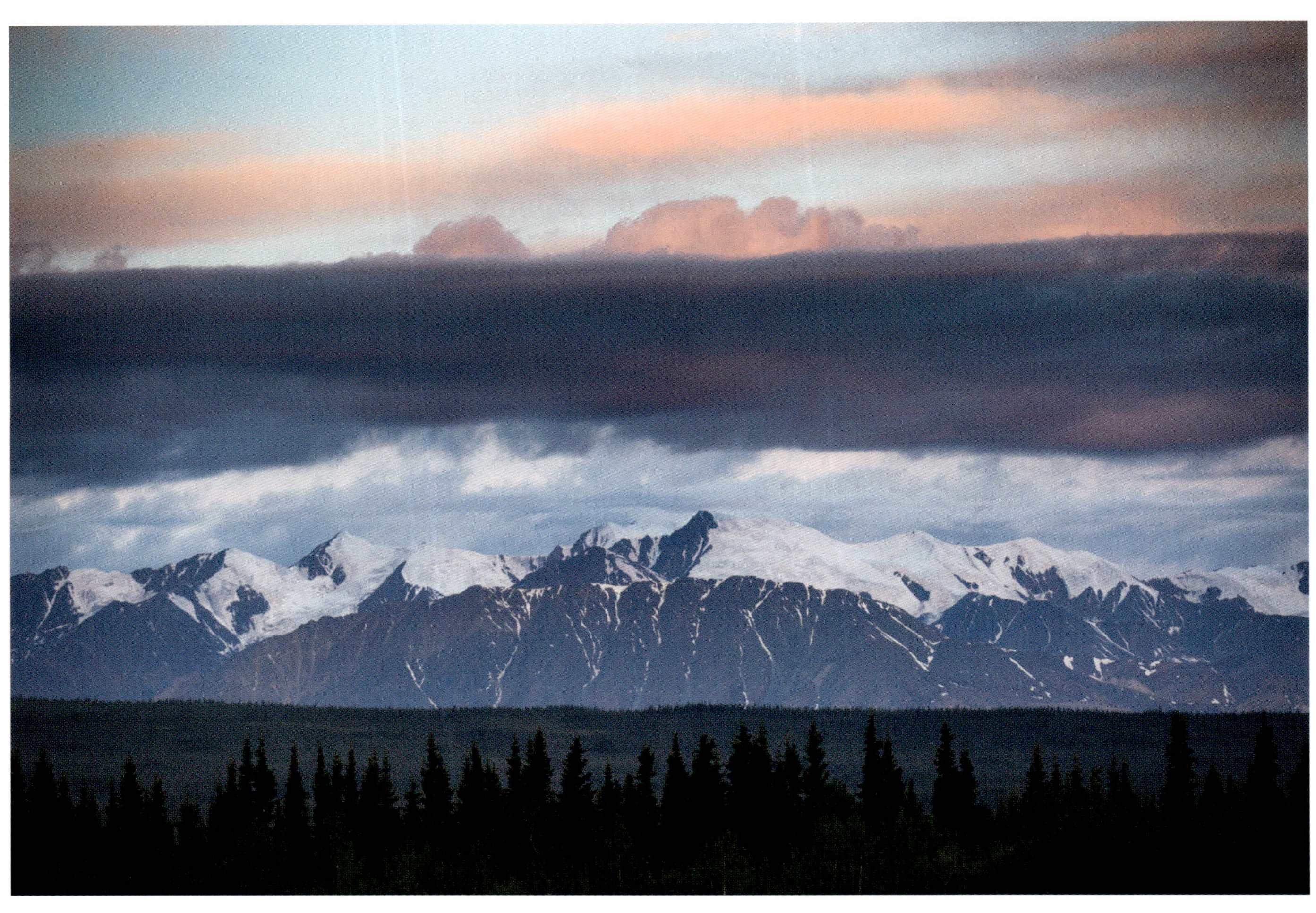

The Yukon Layers
Burwash Landing, Yukon

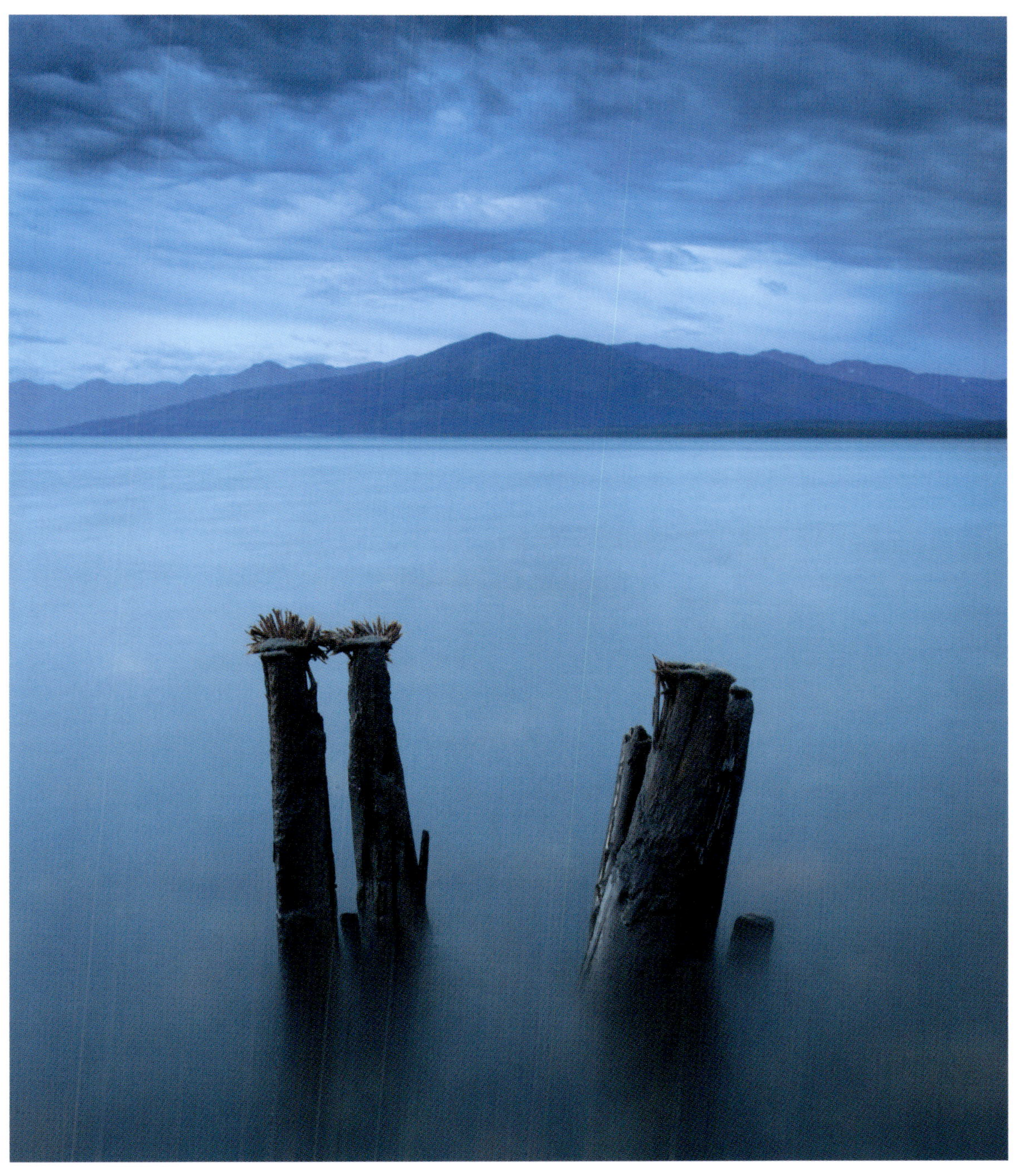

The Blue Hour
Whitehorse, Yukon

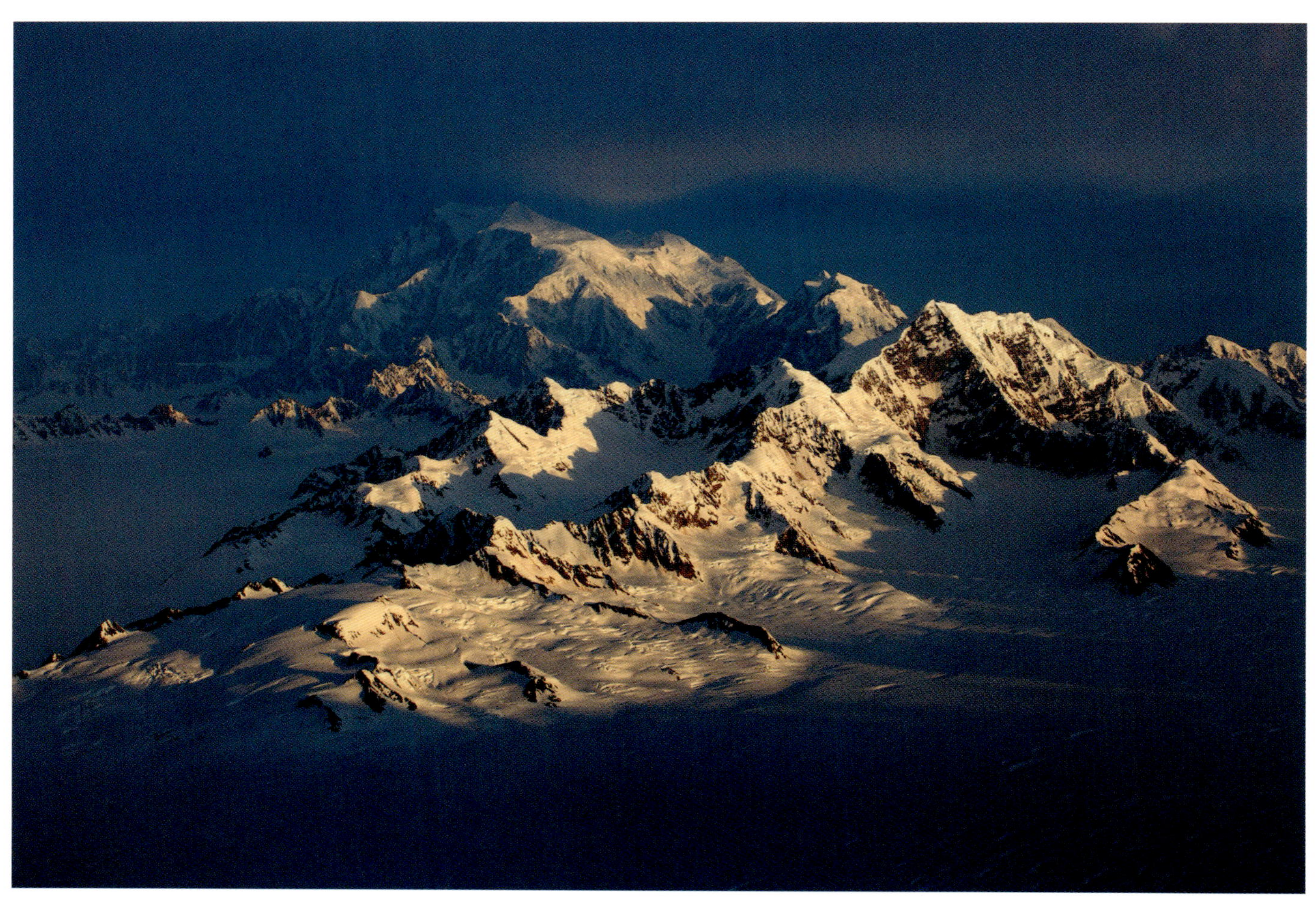

Yukon Gold

Mount Logan, Yukon

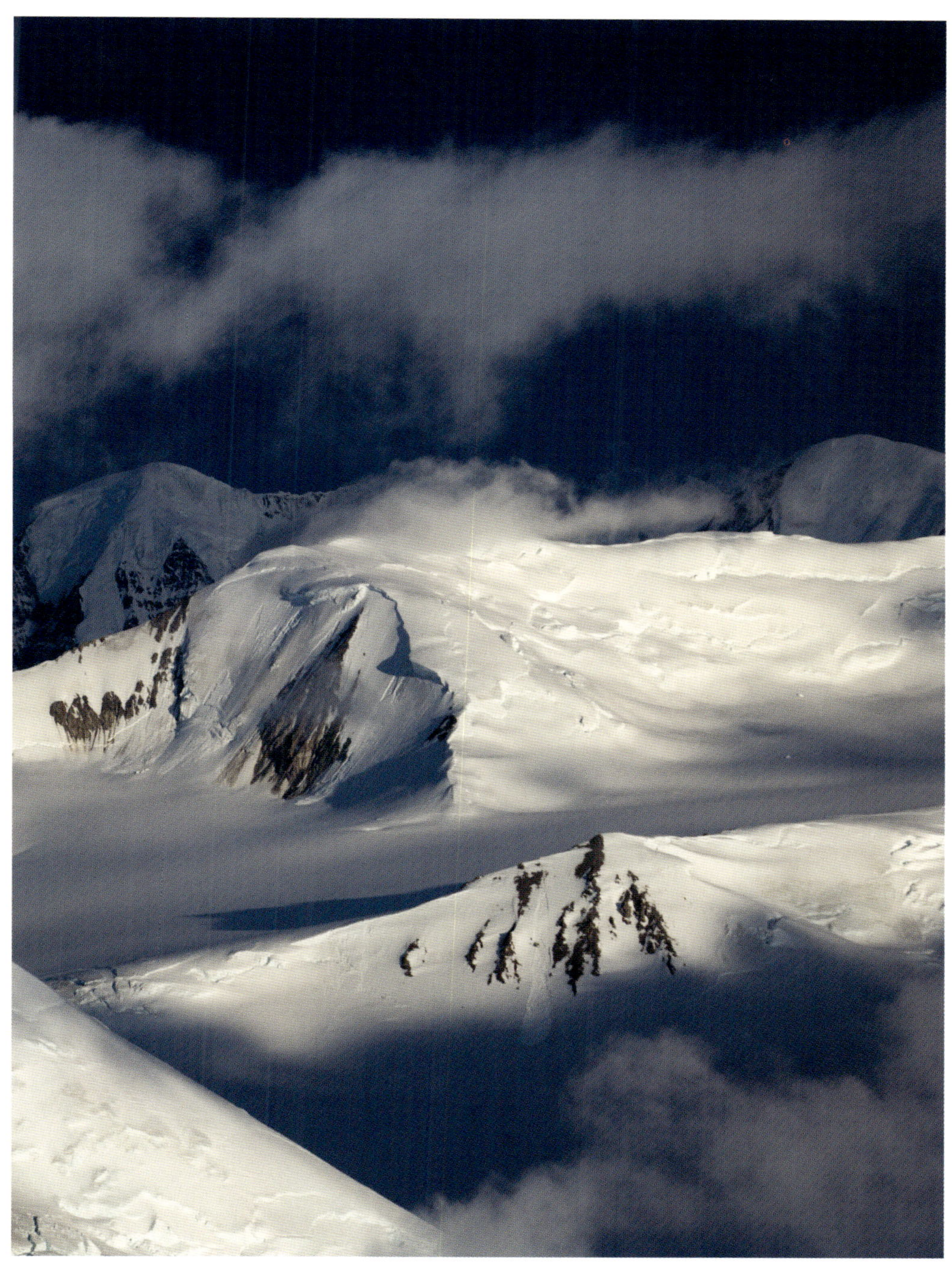

Cut-Out

Saint Elias Mountains, Kluane National Park, Yukon

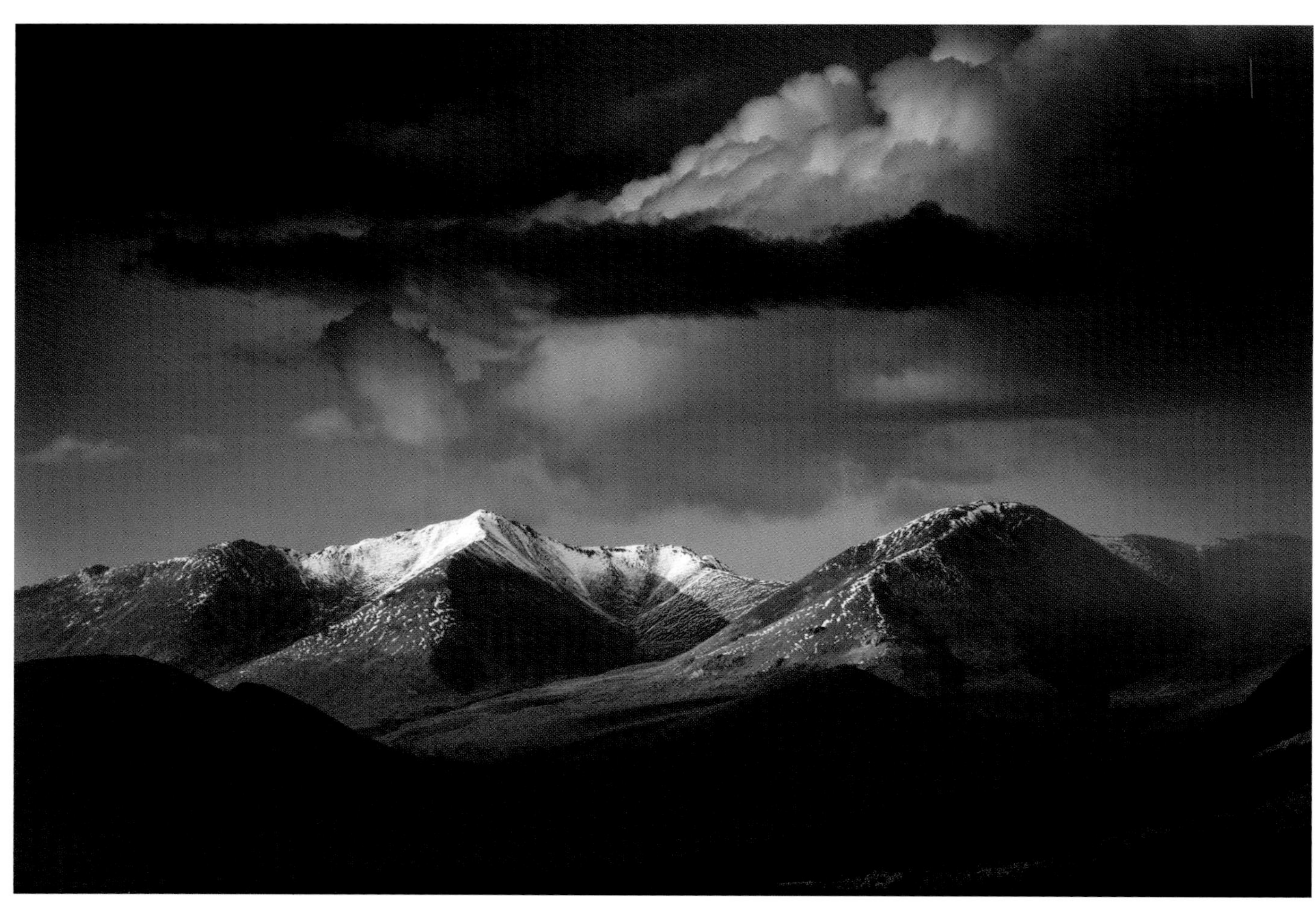

A Moment of Light and Shadow
Kluane National Park, Yukon

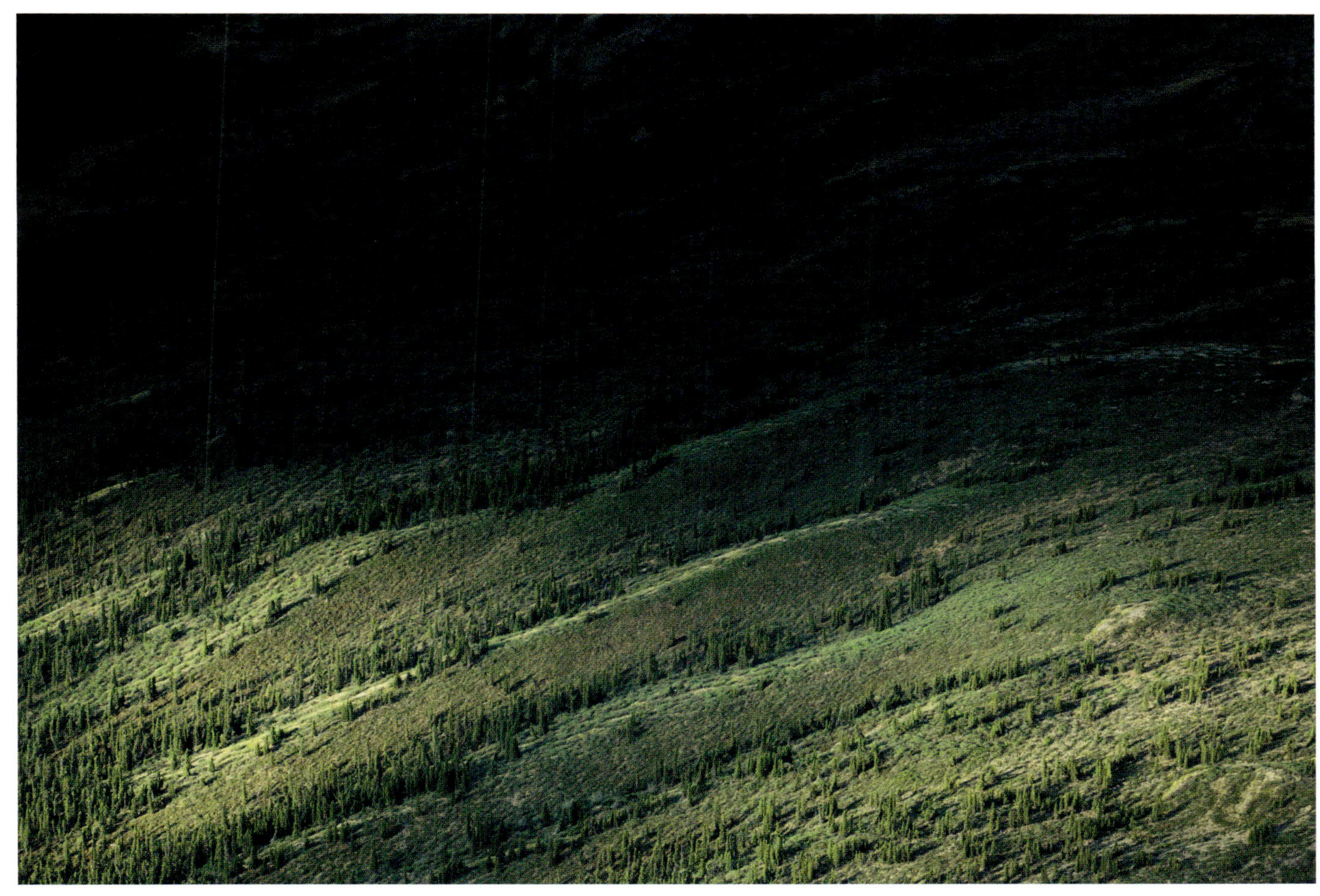

Giant's Edge
Kluane National Park, Yukon

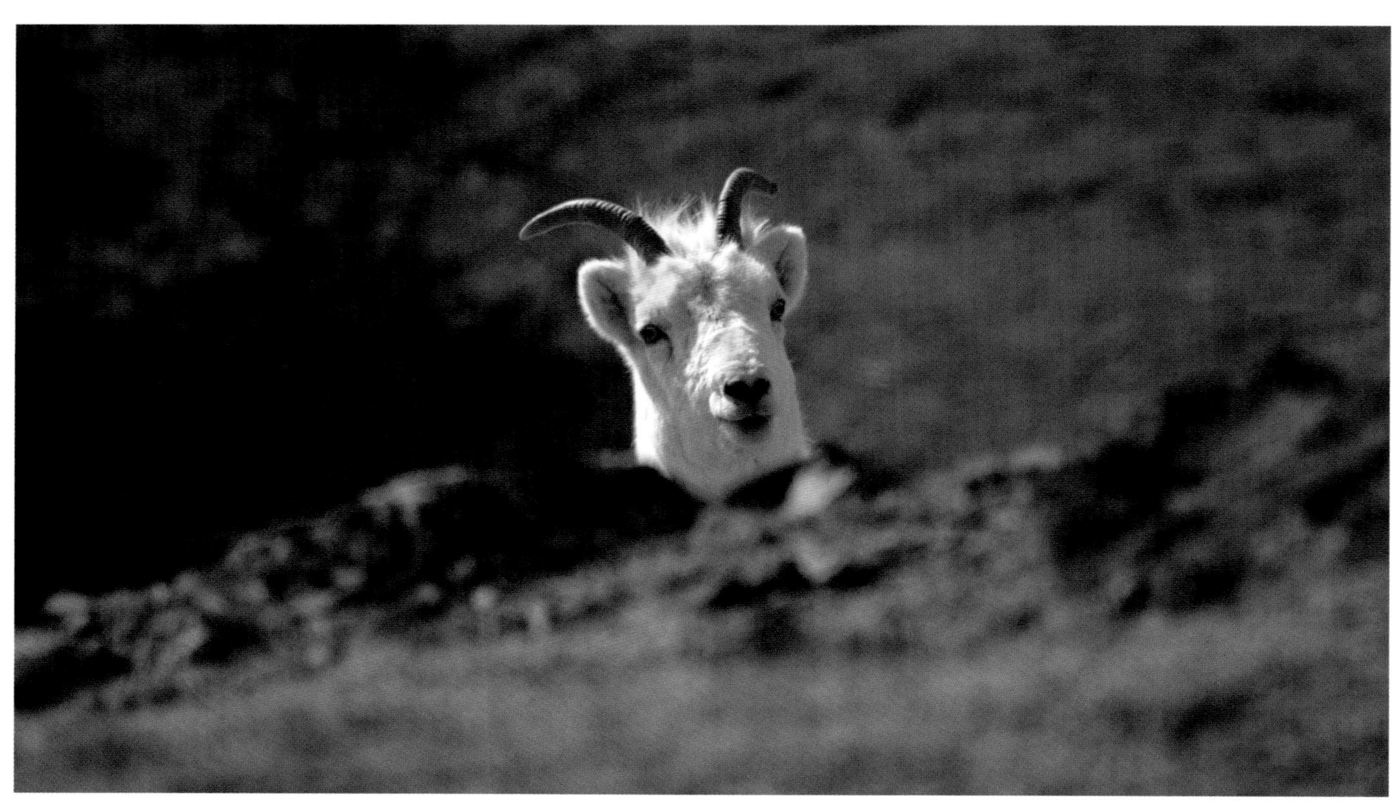

Sheep Mountain
Kluane National Park, Yukon

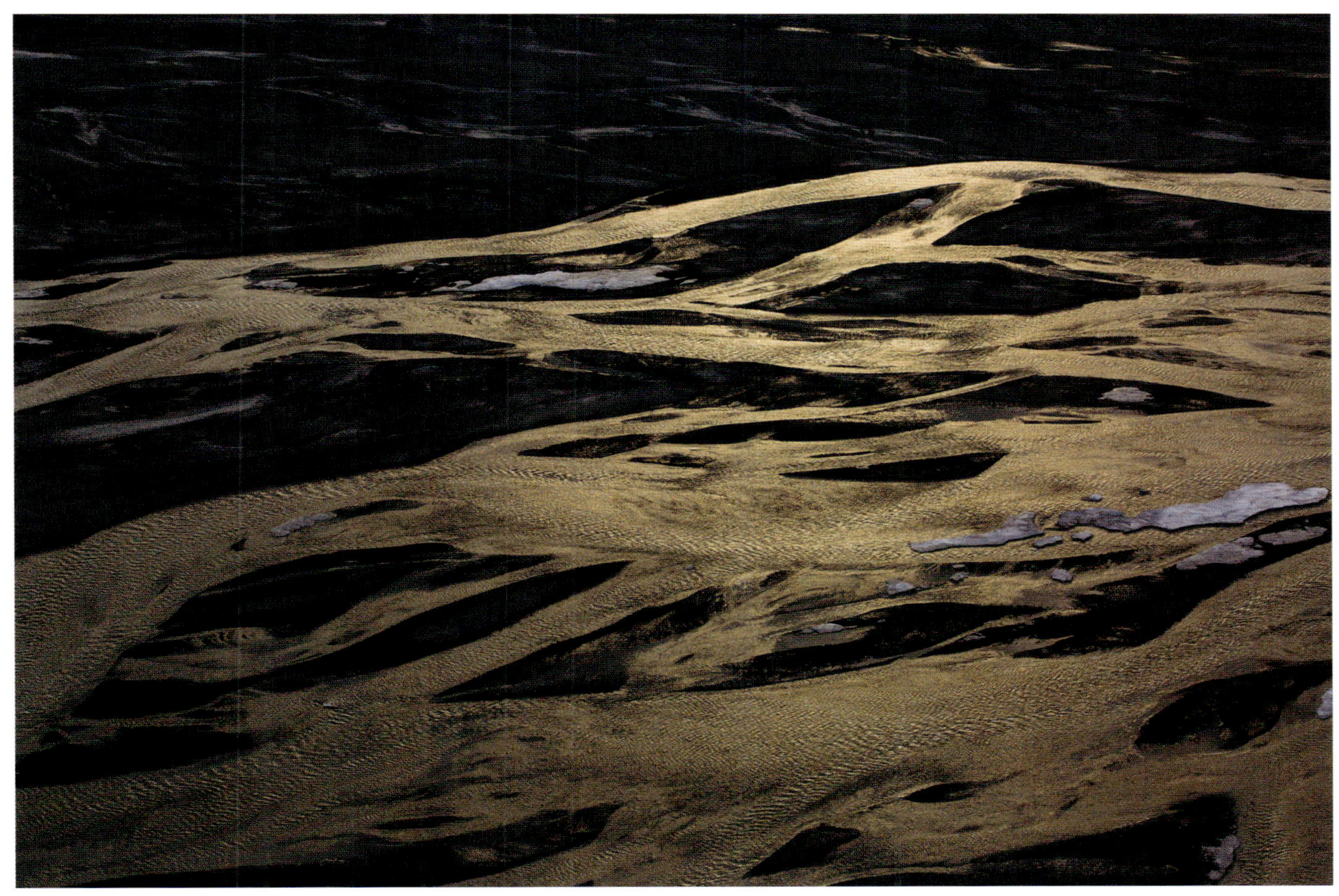

Golden Hour
Kluane National Park, Yukon

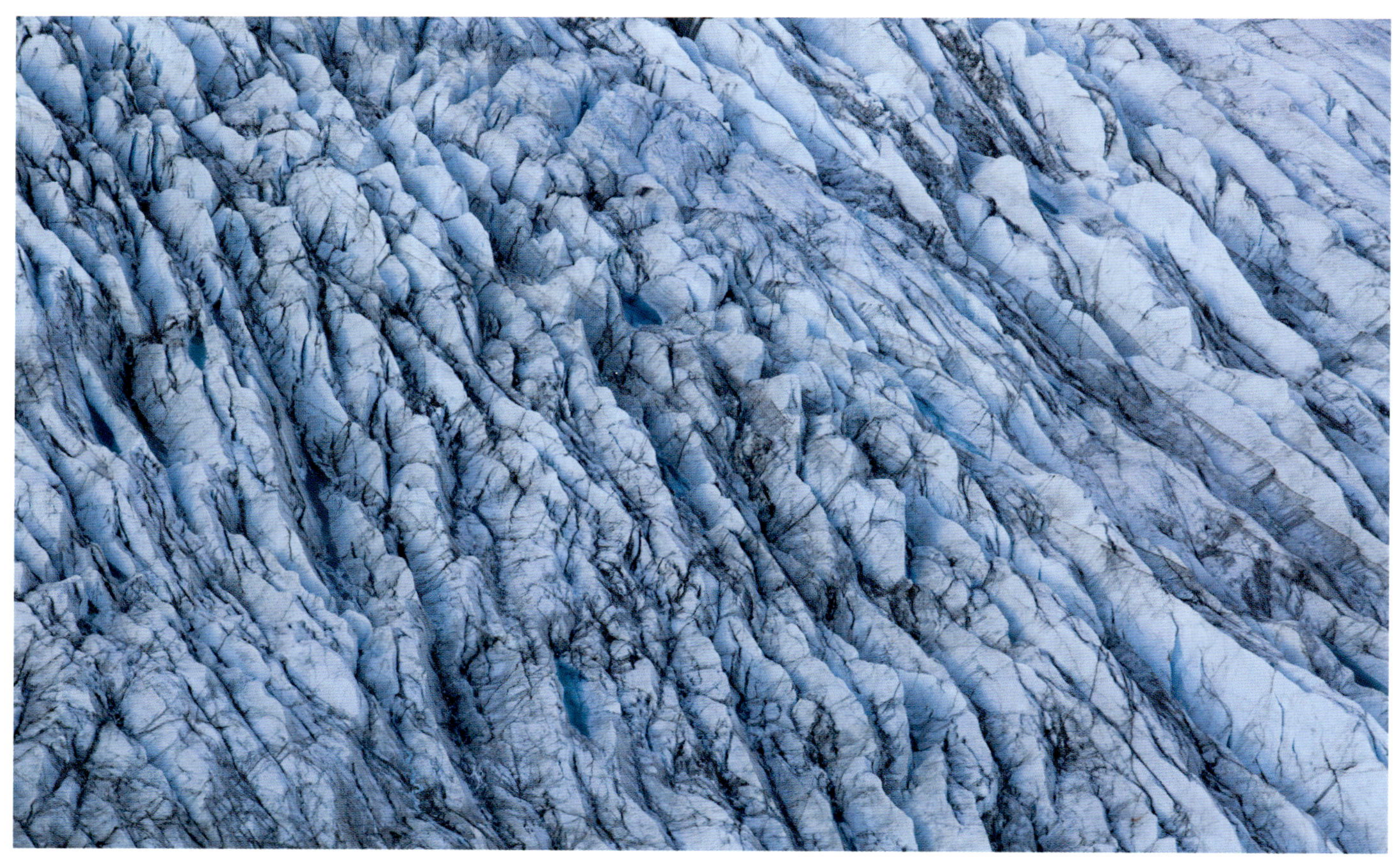

Glacial Remedy
Kluane National Park, Yukon

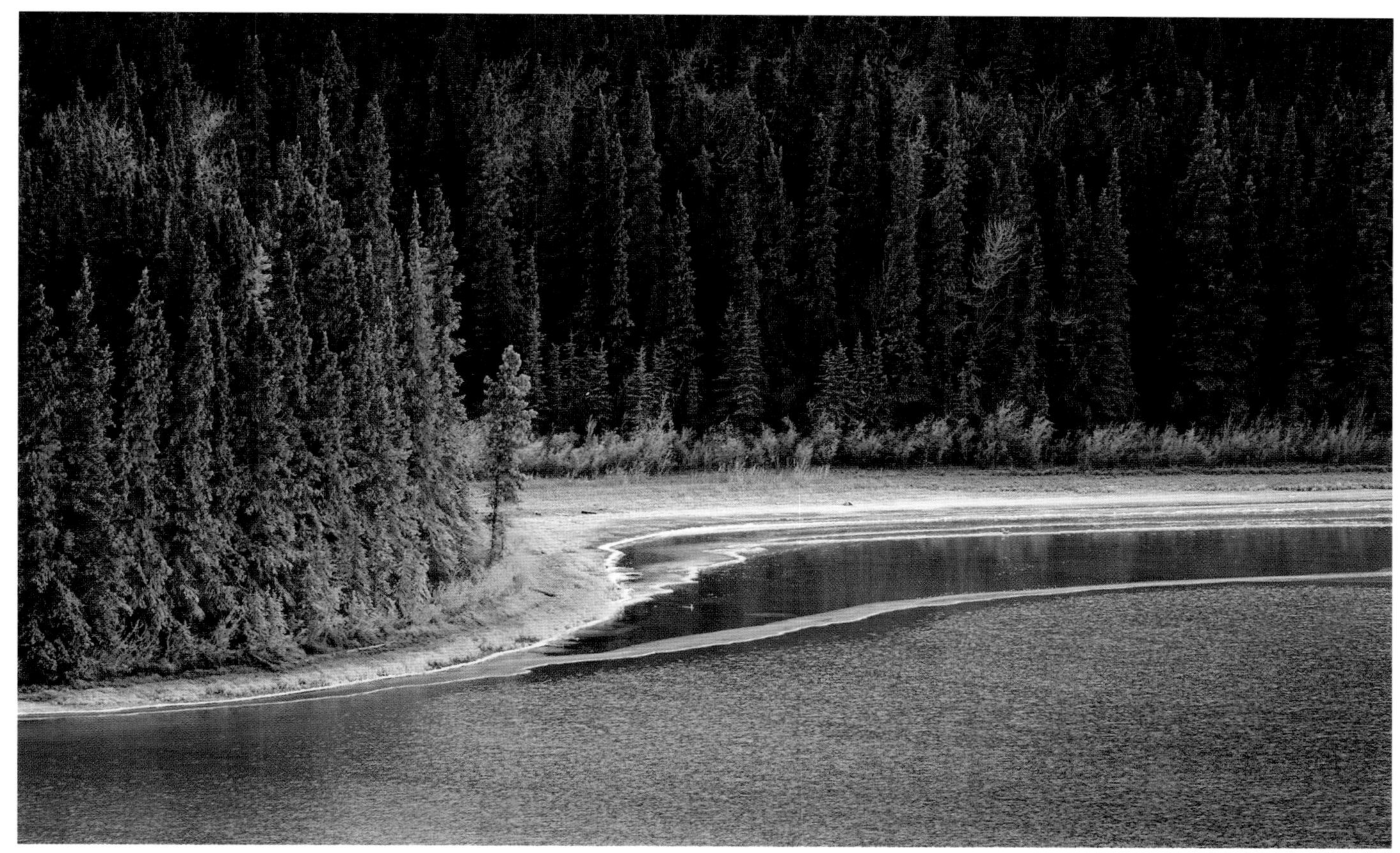

Transitions
Emerald Lake, Yukon

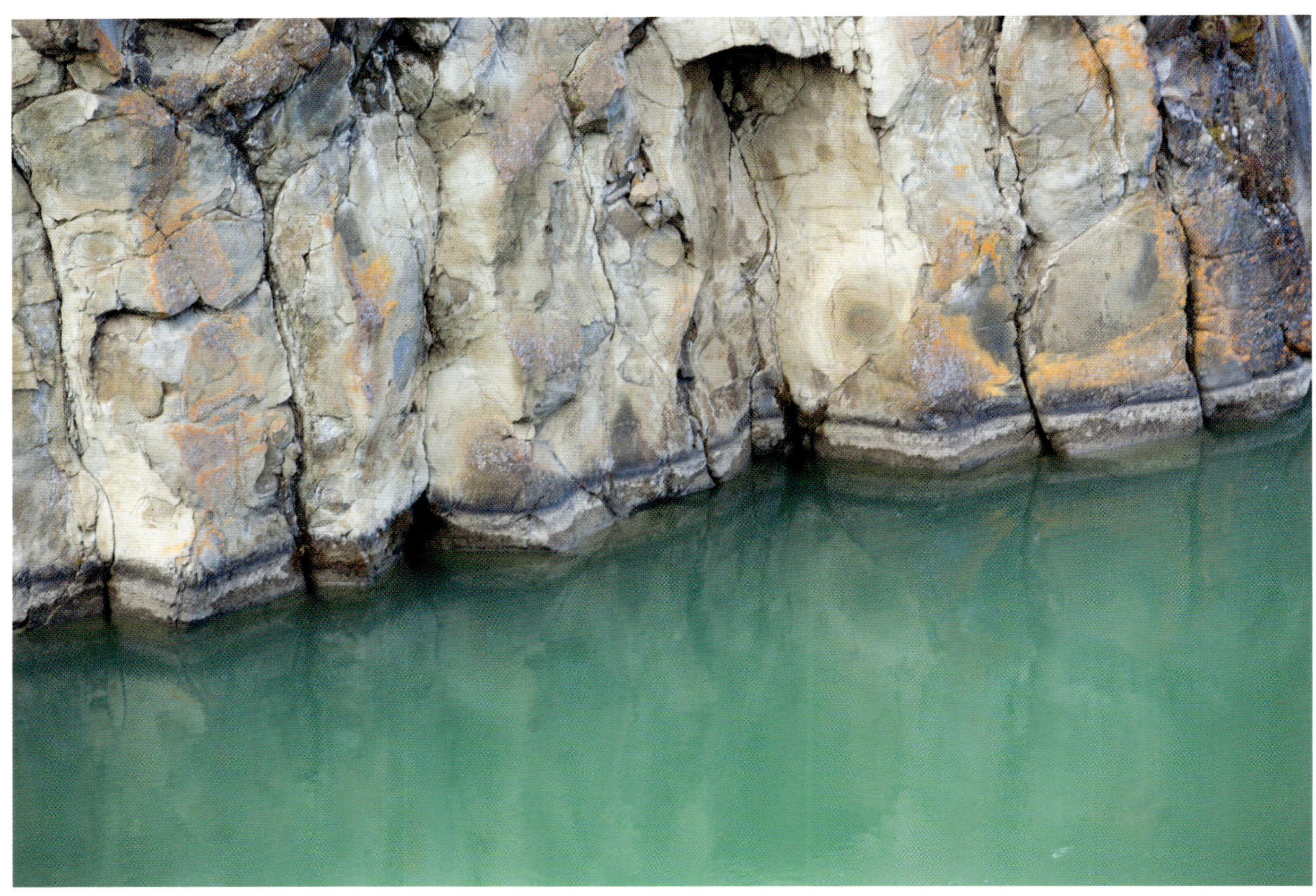

Miles Canyon Study

Miles Canyon, Yukon

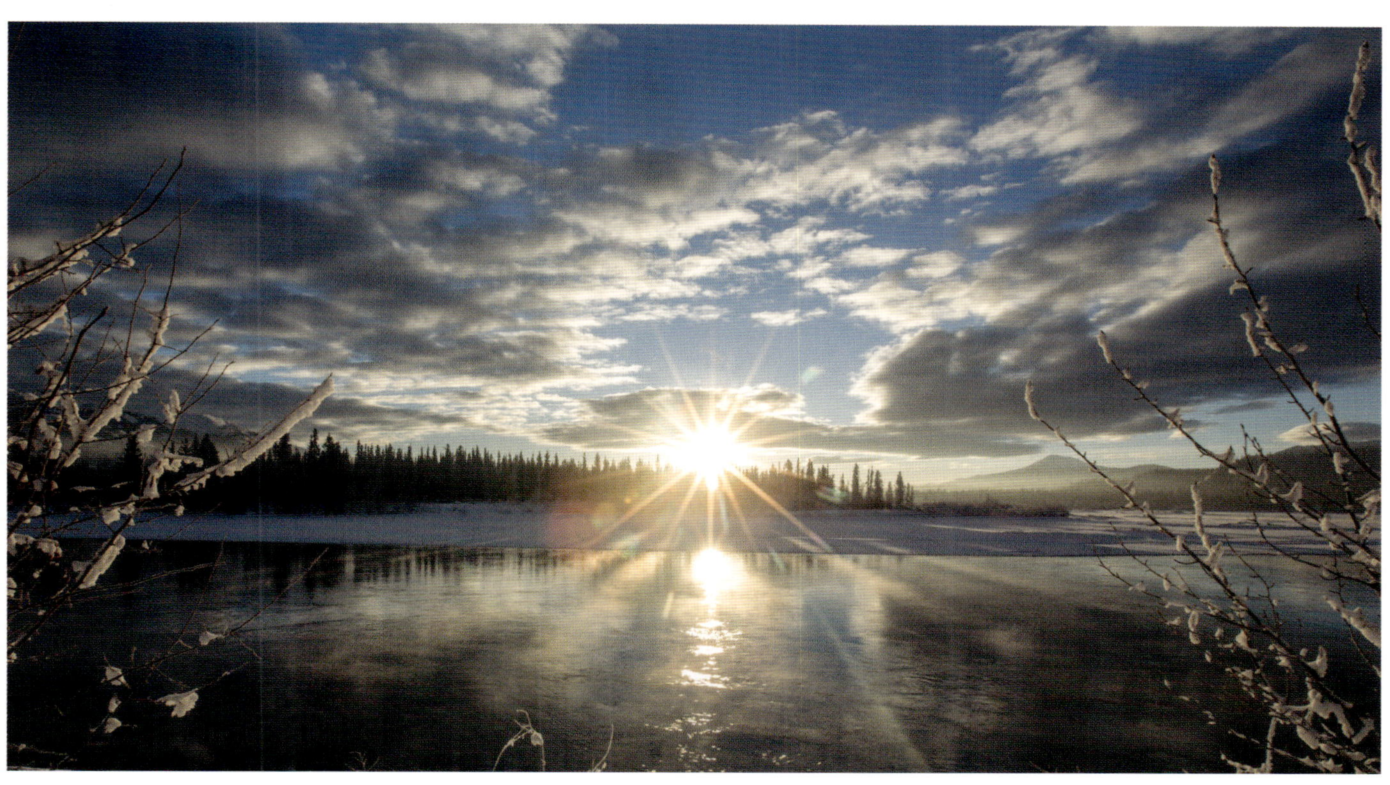

A Breath of Fresh Air
Whitehorse, Yukon

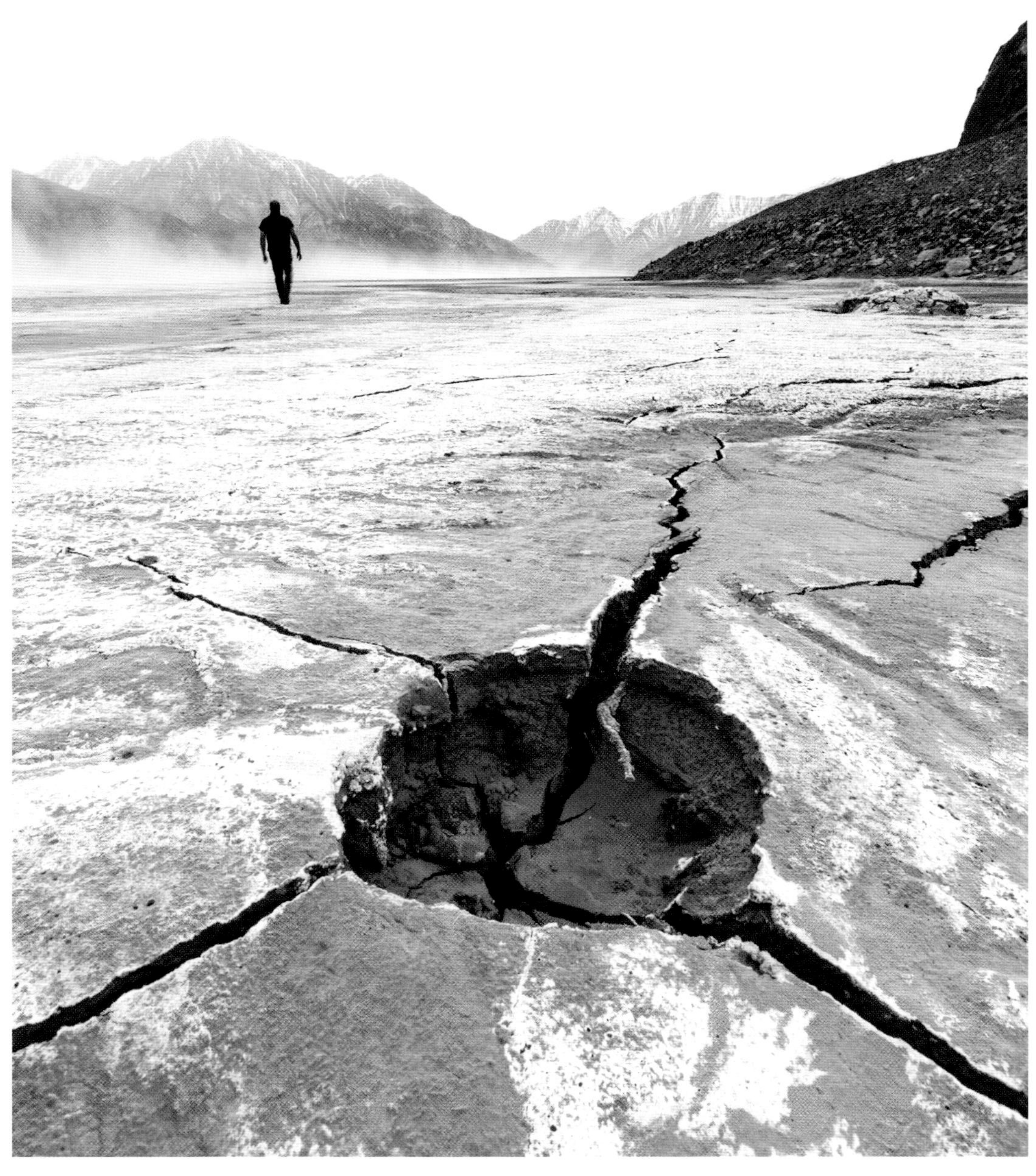

Moonscape

Kluane National Park, Yukon

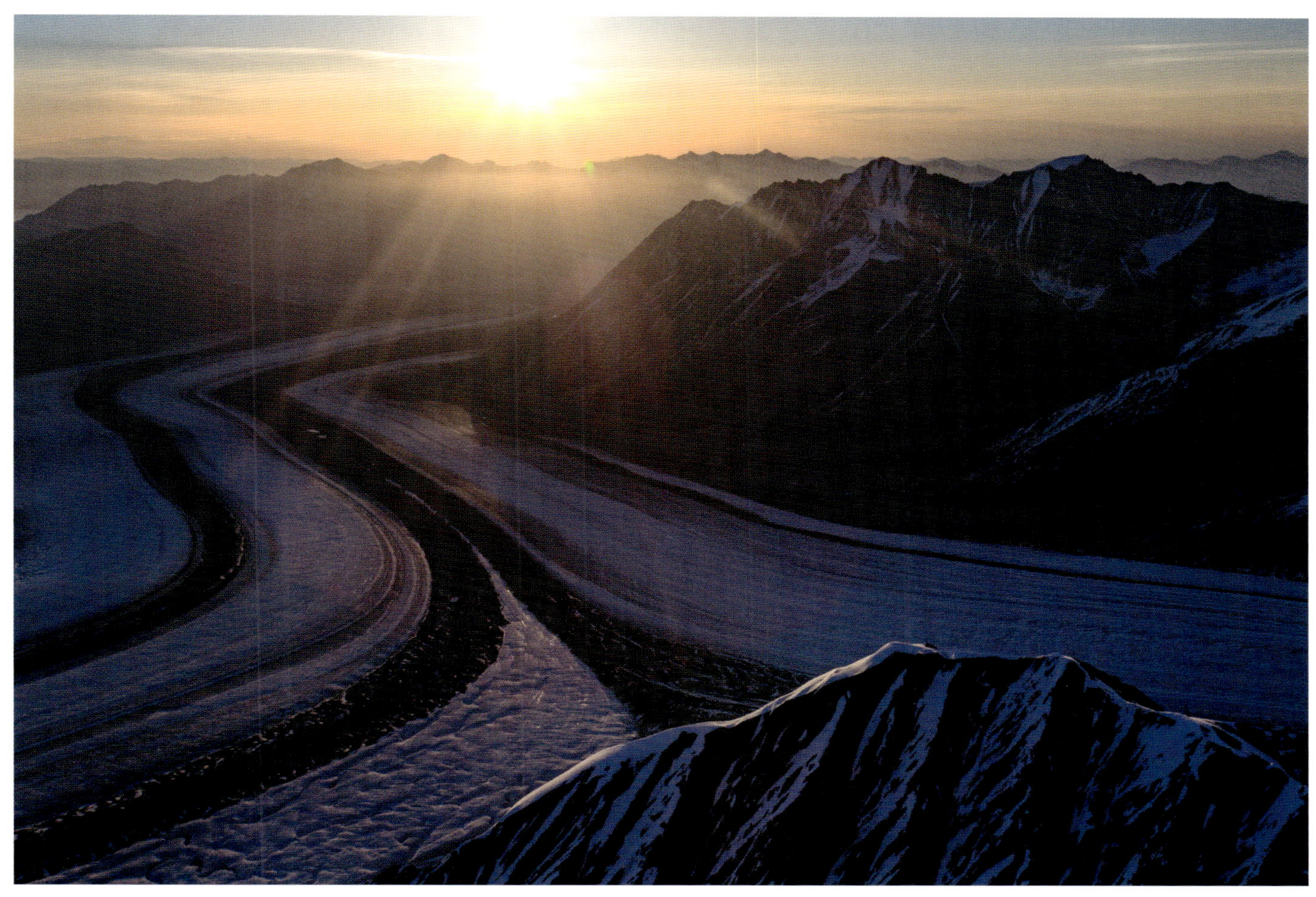

Morning's Reach
Kluane National Park, Yukon

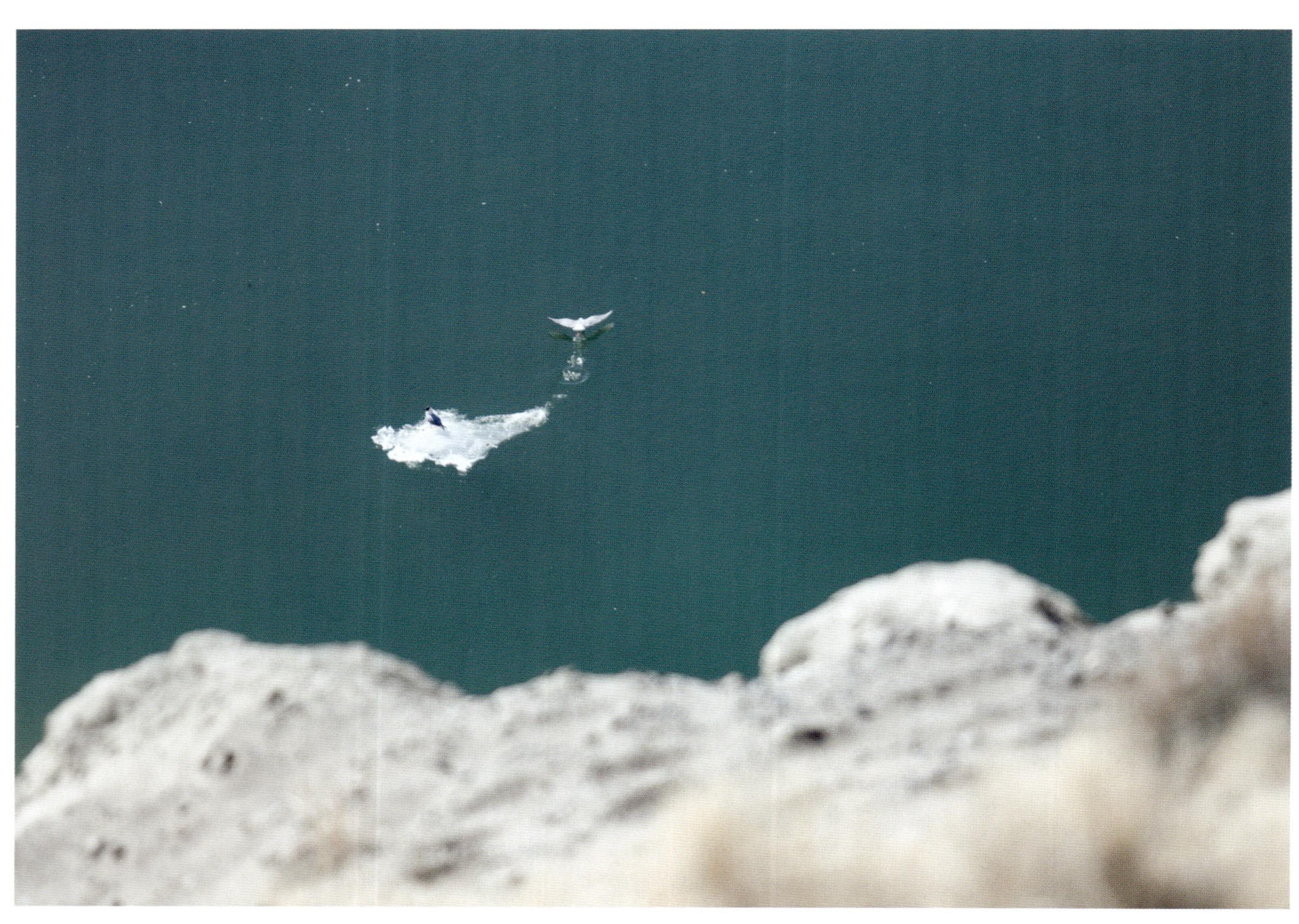

194 *A Whale Tale*
Whitehorse, Yukon

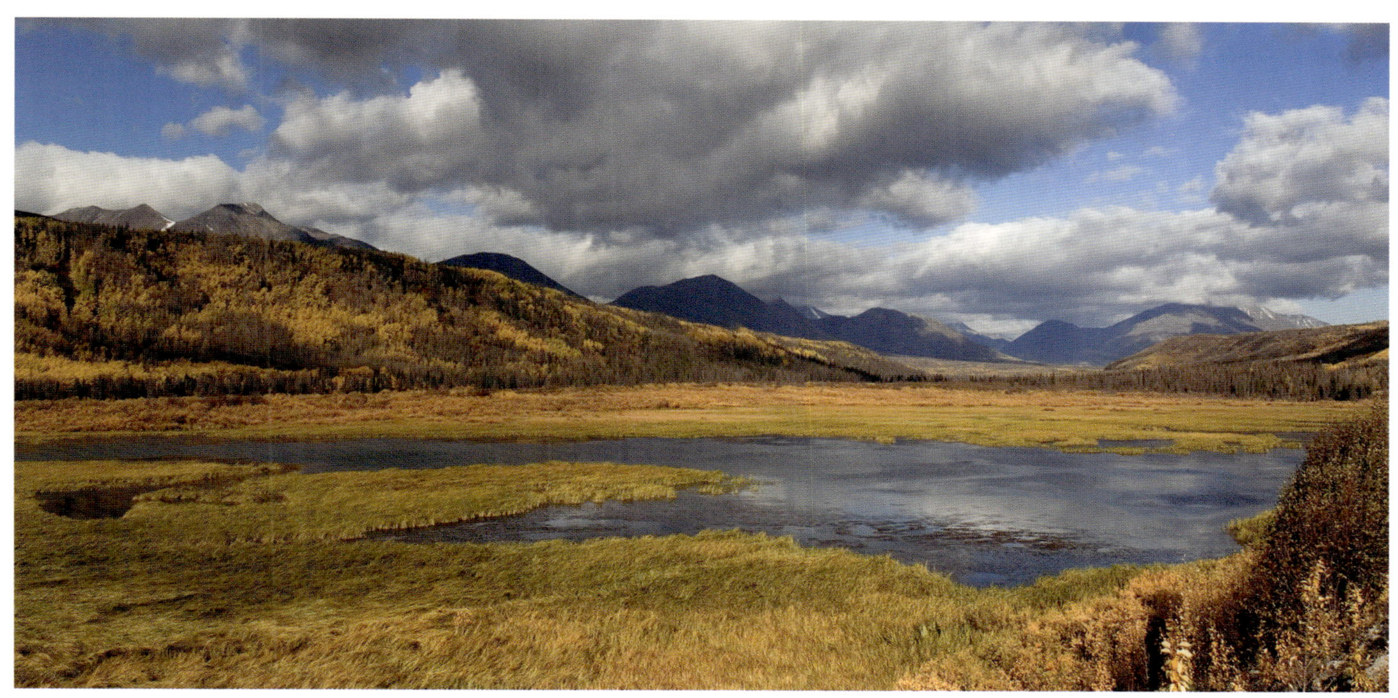

Kluane Autumn

Kluane National Park, Yukon

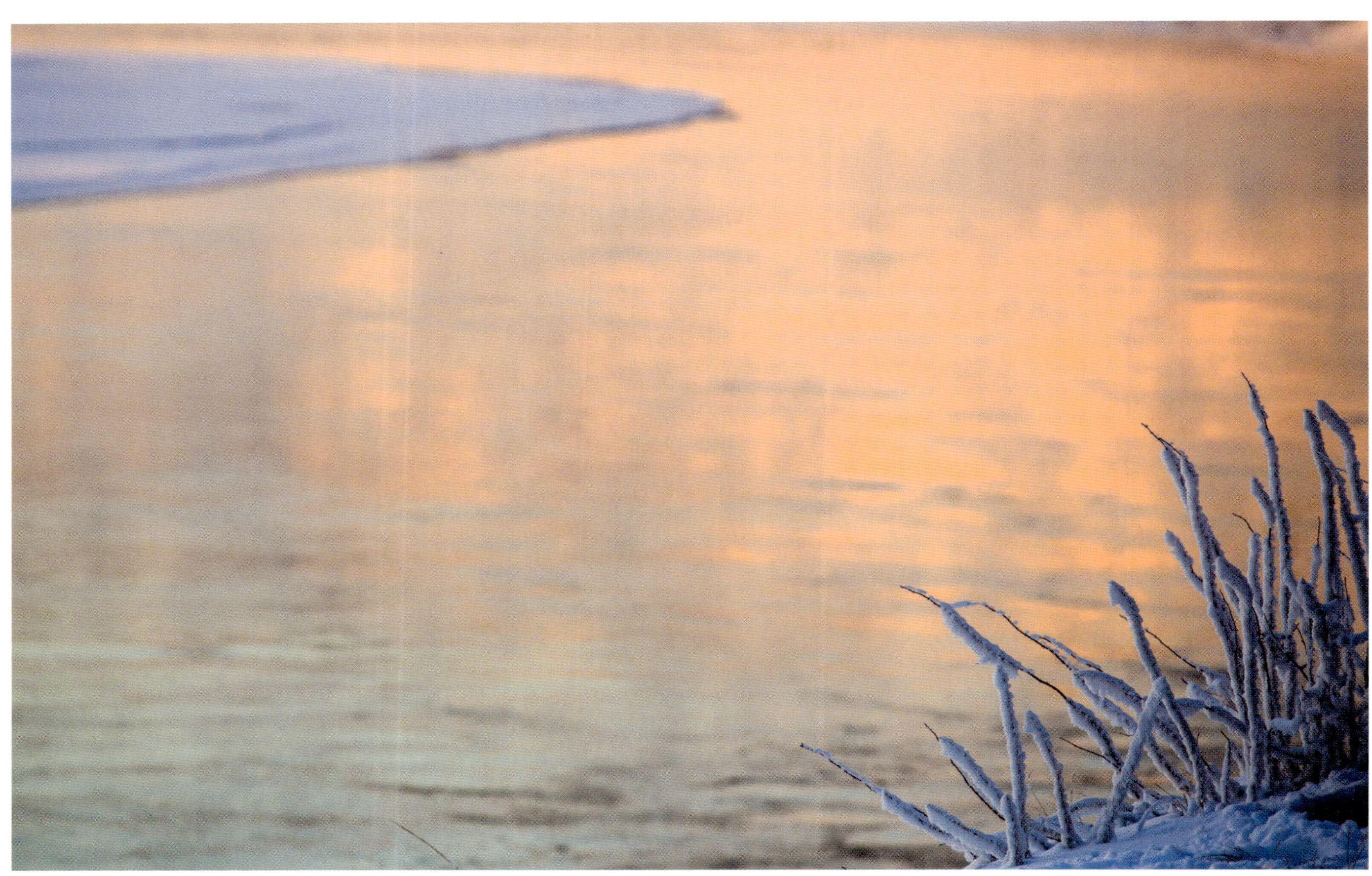

196 *Sum of Its Pieces*
Whitehorse, Yukon

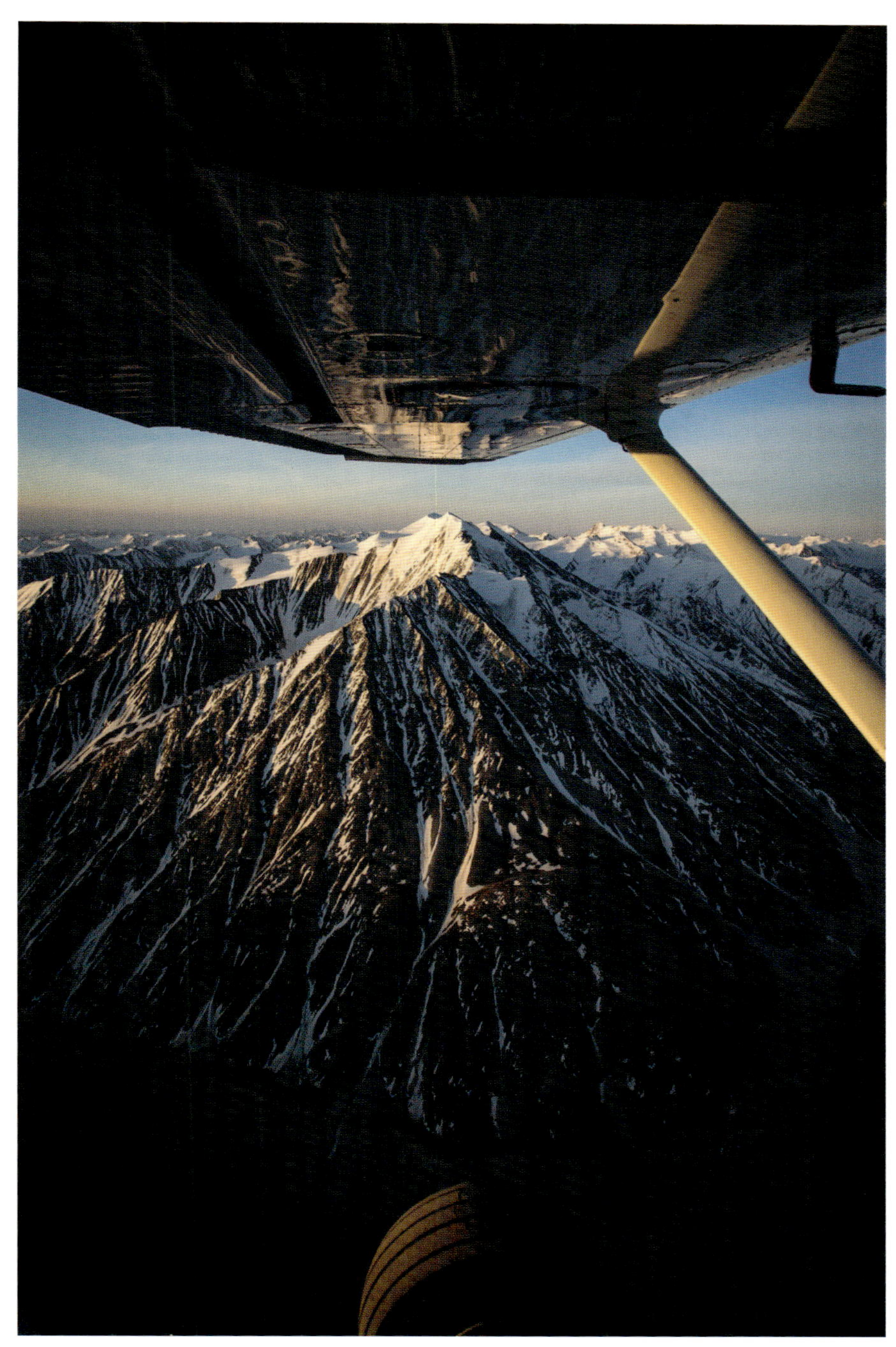

Morning Flight
Kluane National Park, Yukon

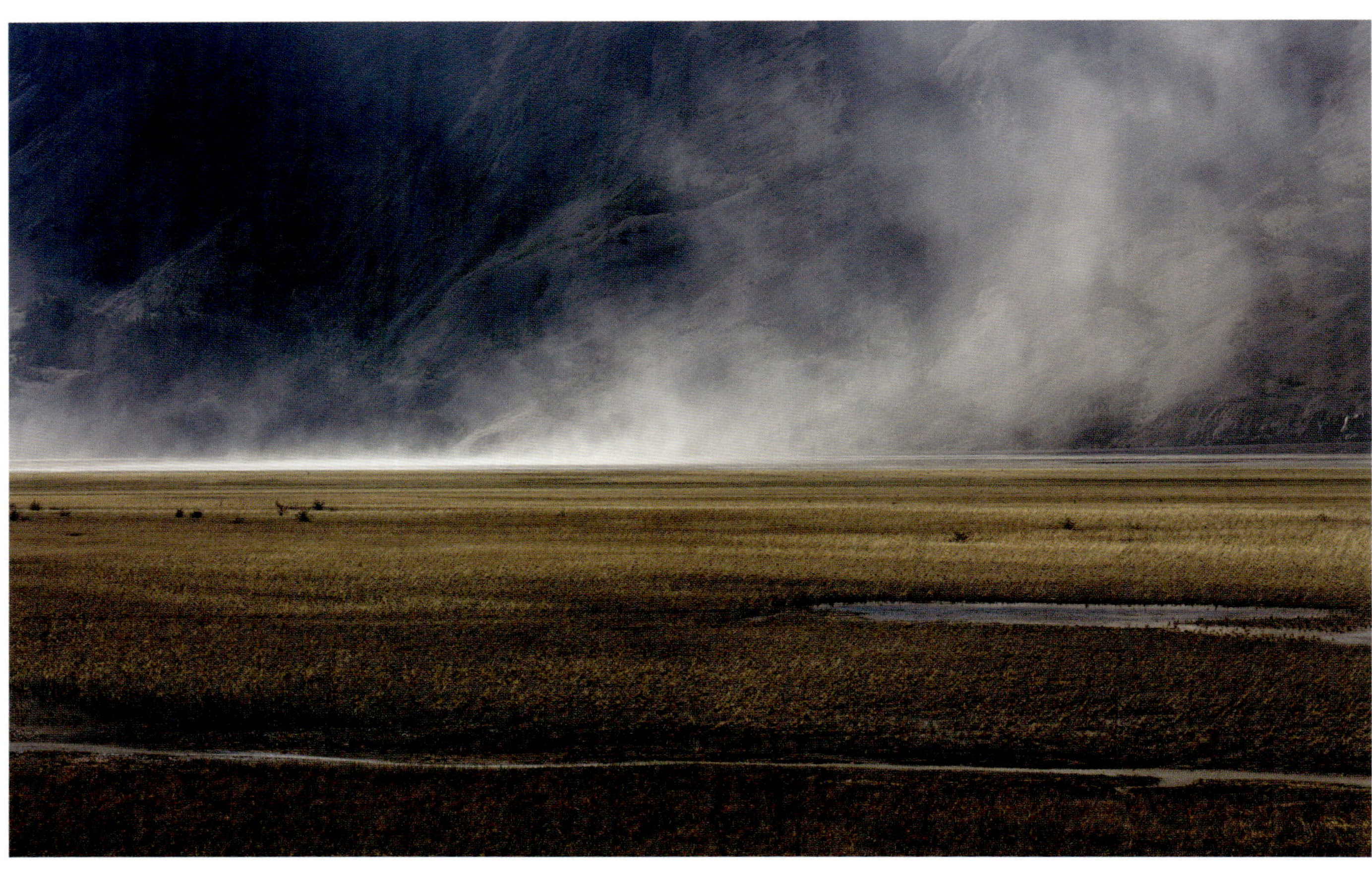

Dust on the Horizon
Kluane National Park, Yukon

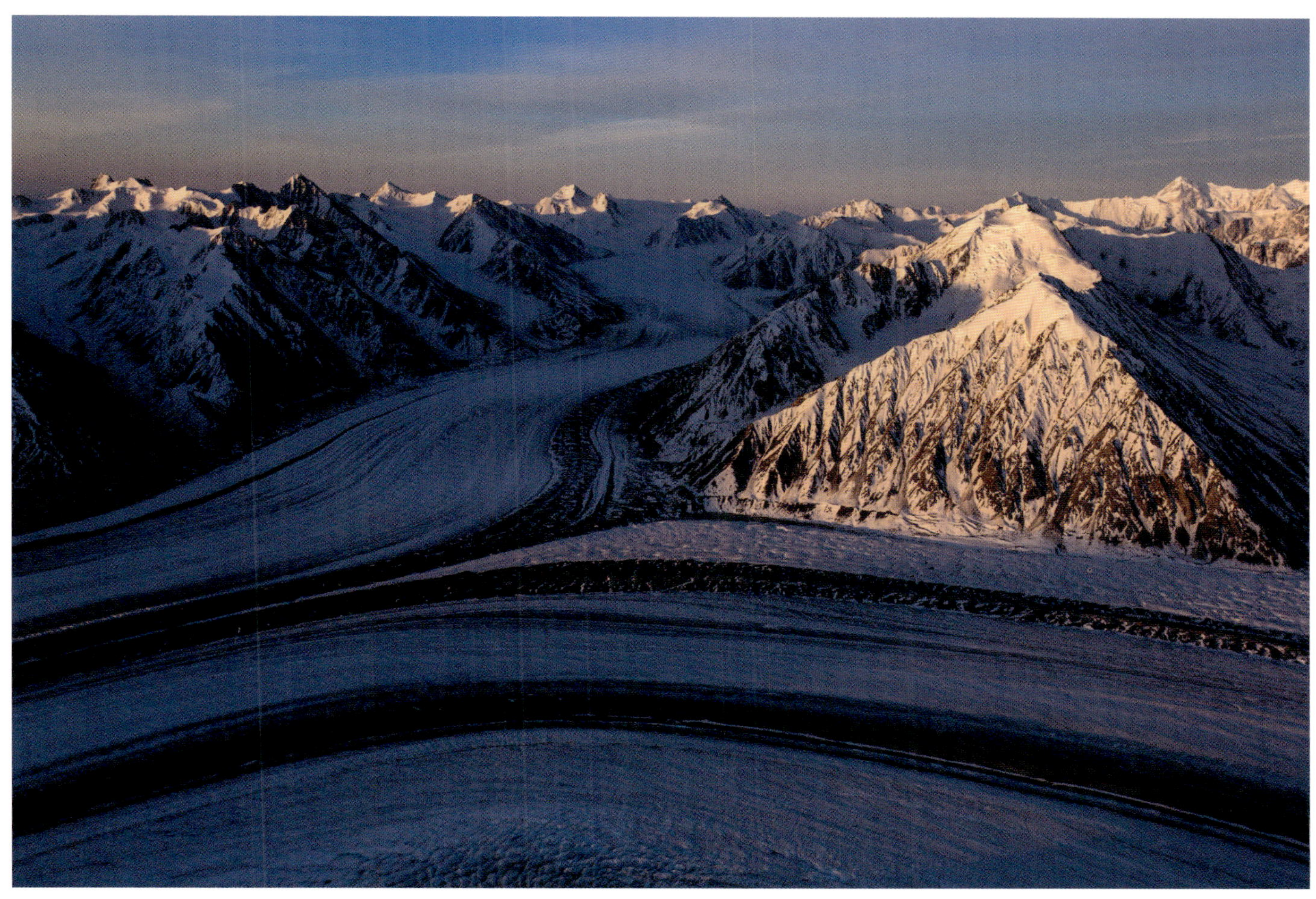

Divided
Kluane National Park, Yukon

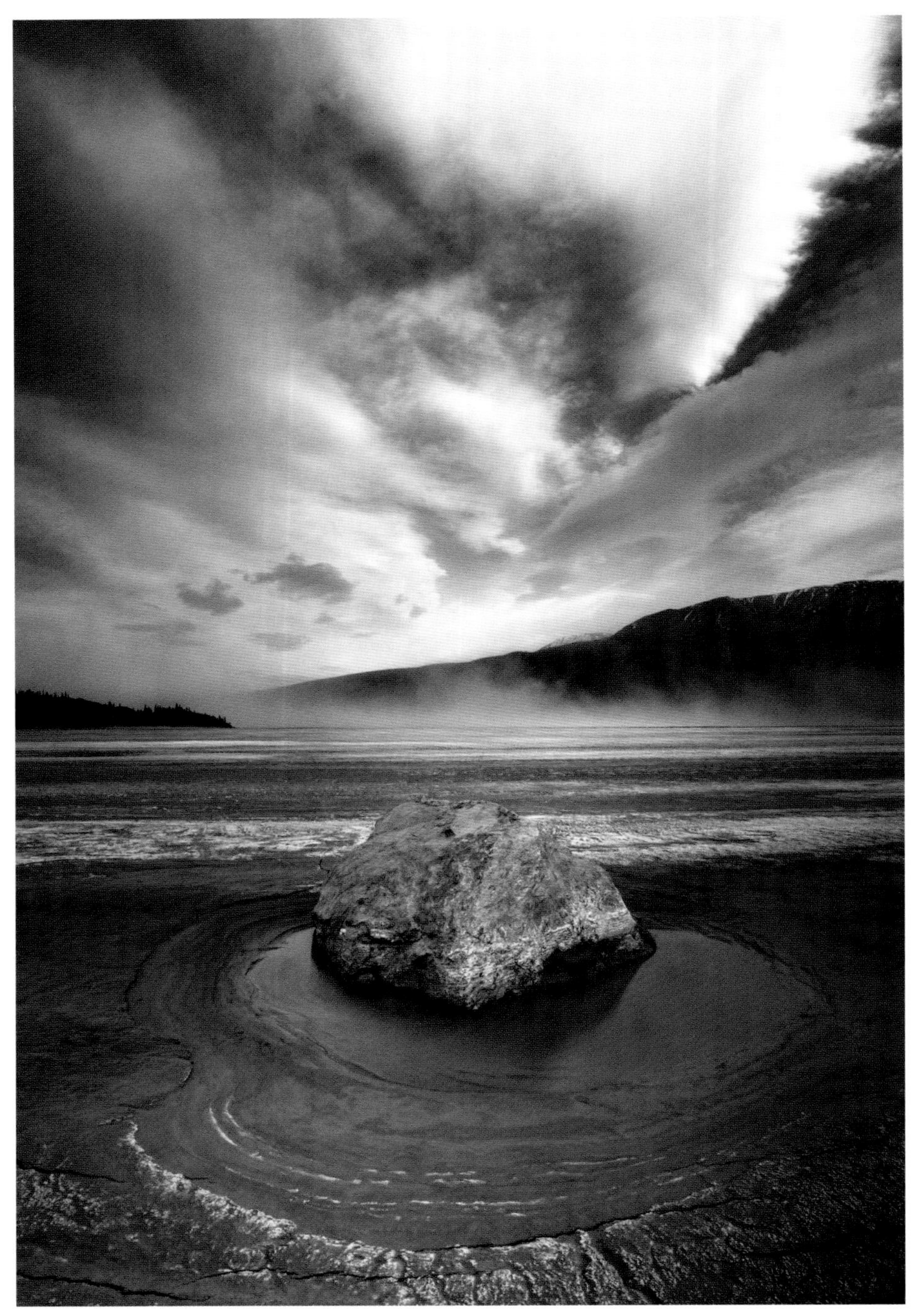

World Goes Round

Kluane National Park, Yukon

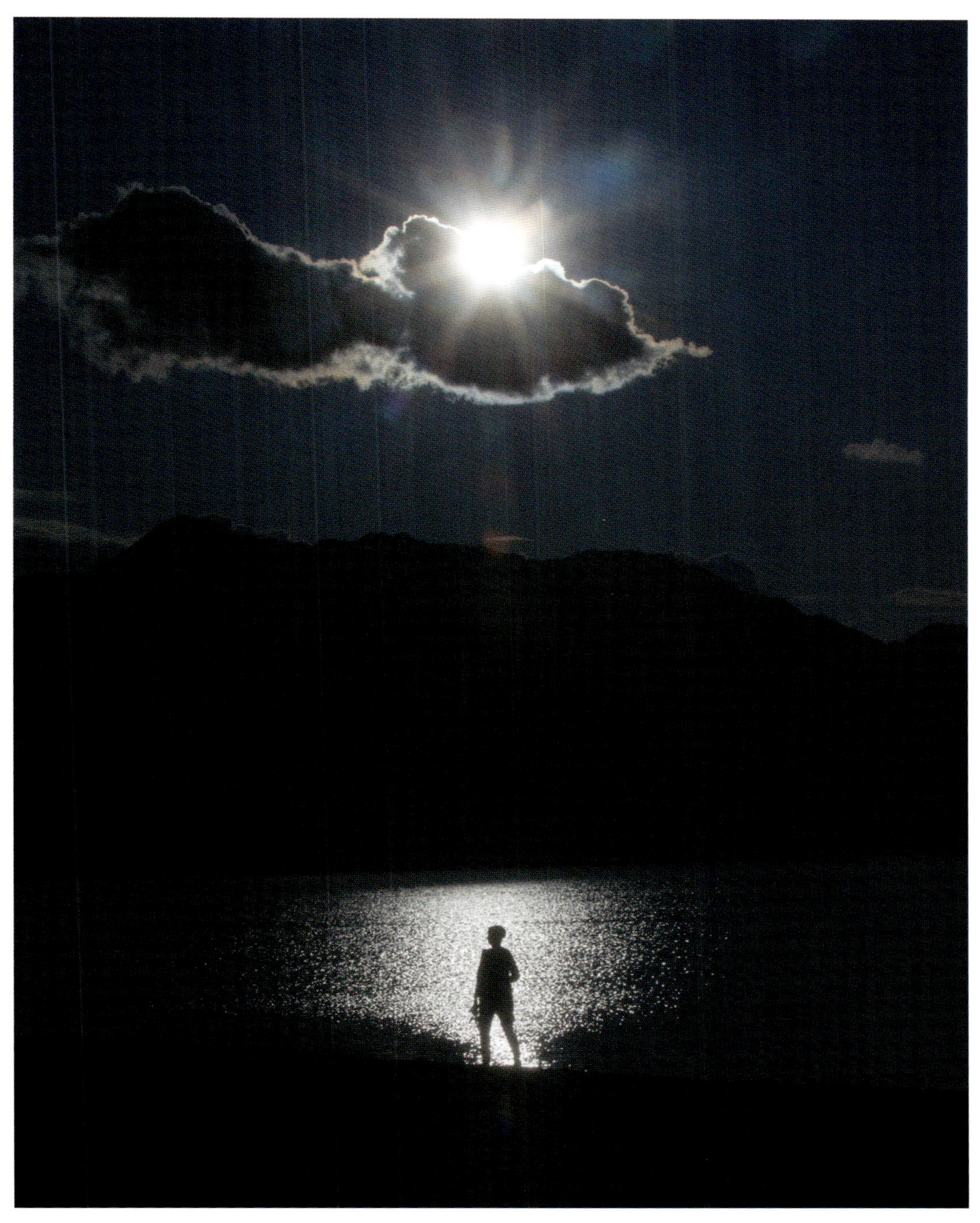

The Spotlight
Silver City, Yukon

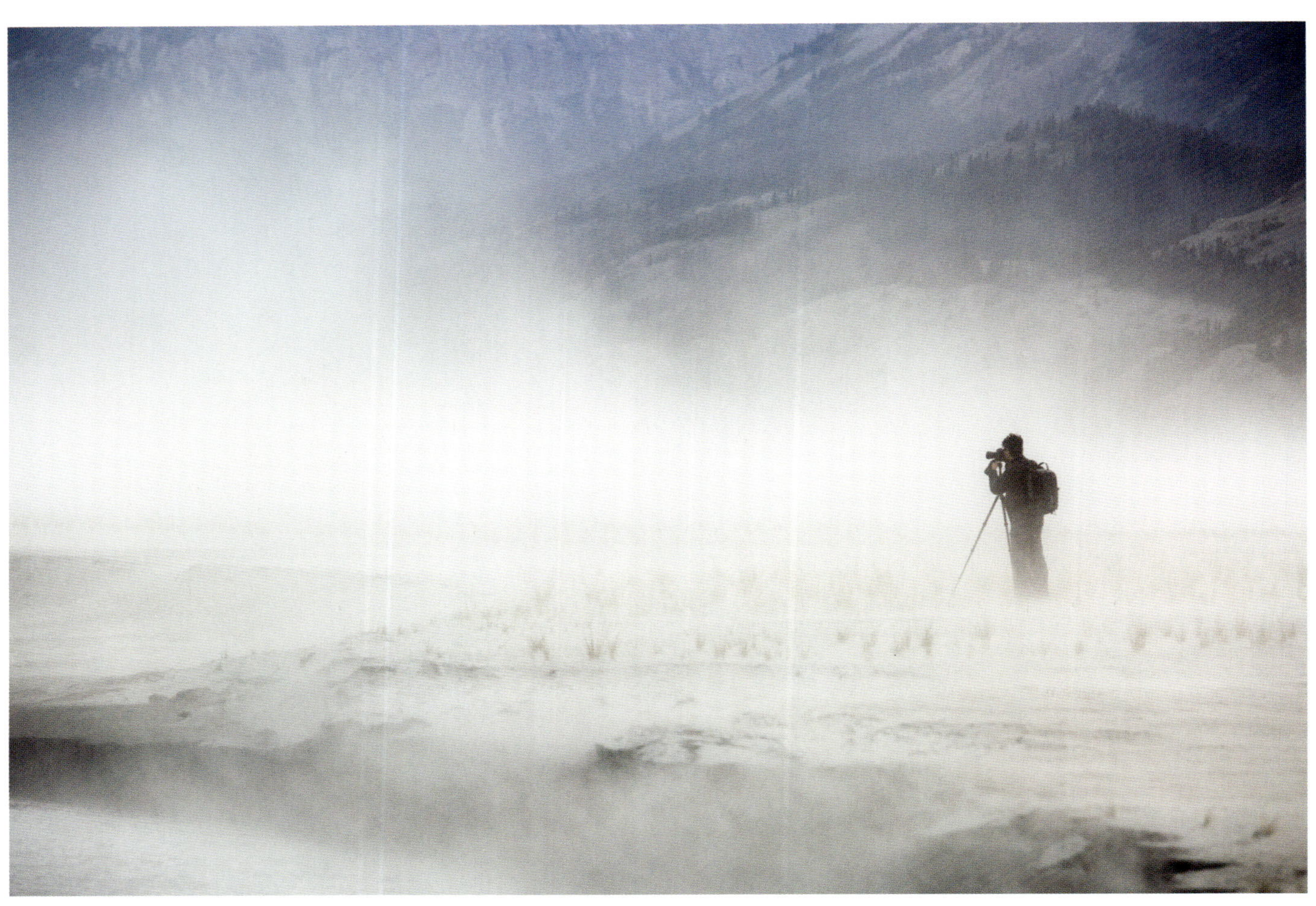

Dust Devils

Paul Zizka in Kluane National Park, Yukon

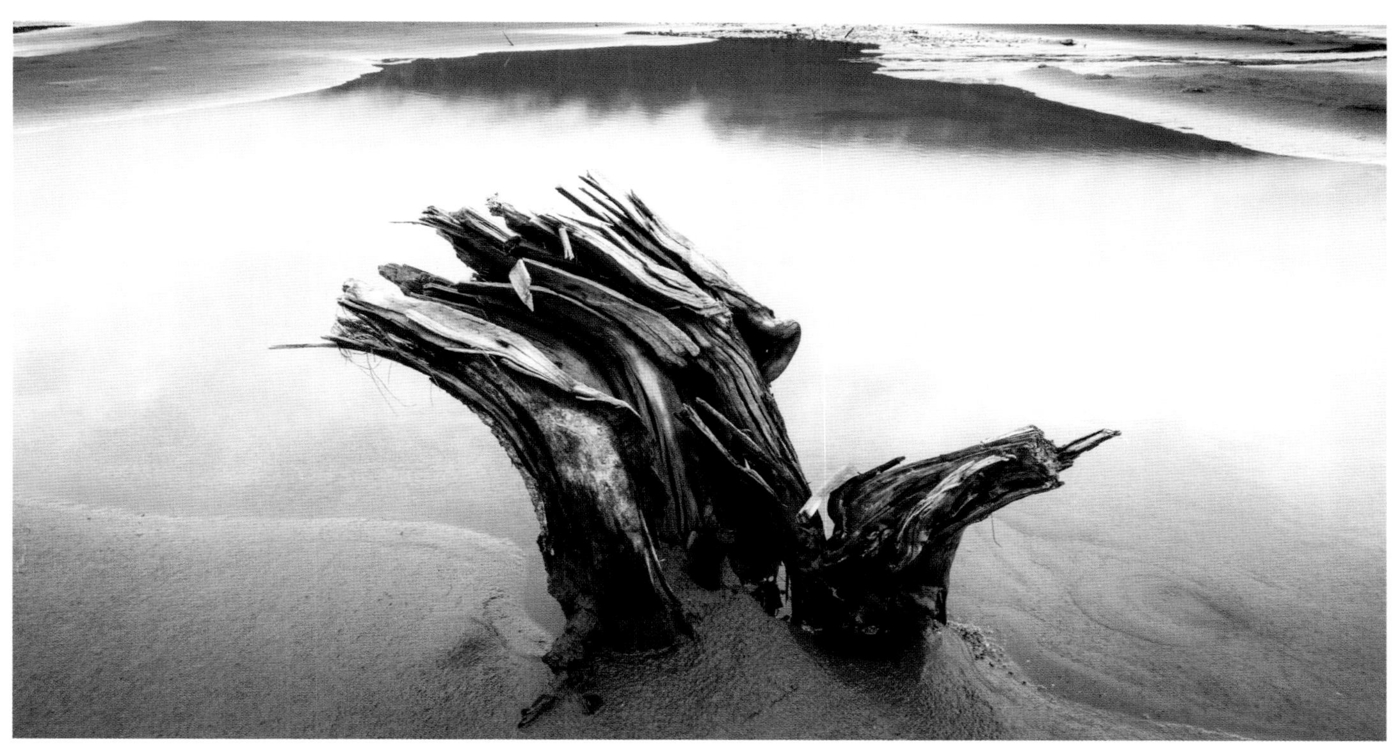

Outreach
Kluane National Park, Yukon

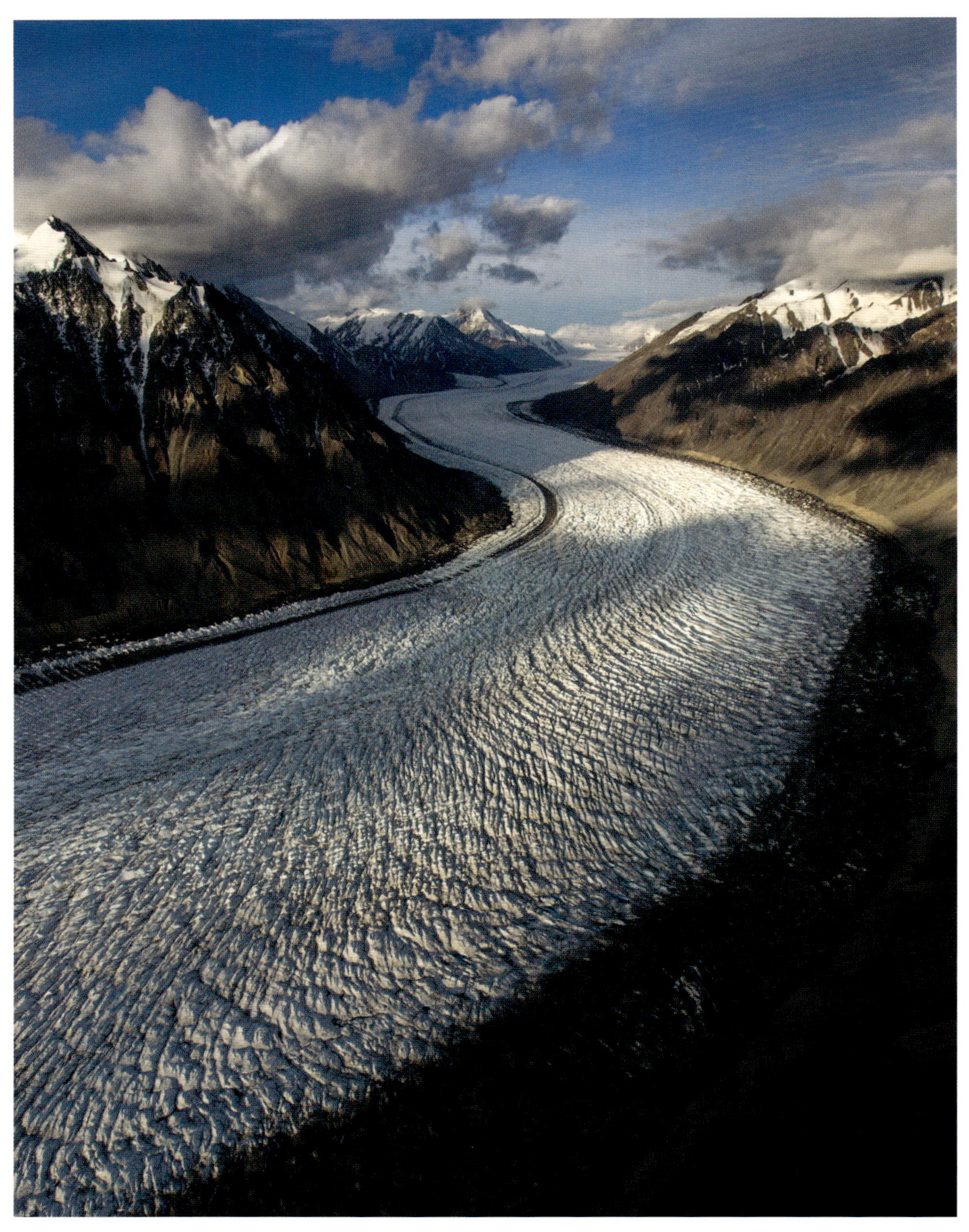

Great Bend

Kluane National Park, Yukon

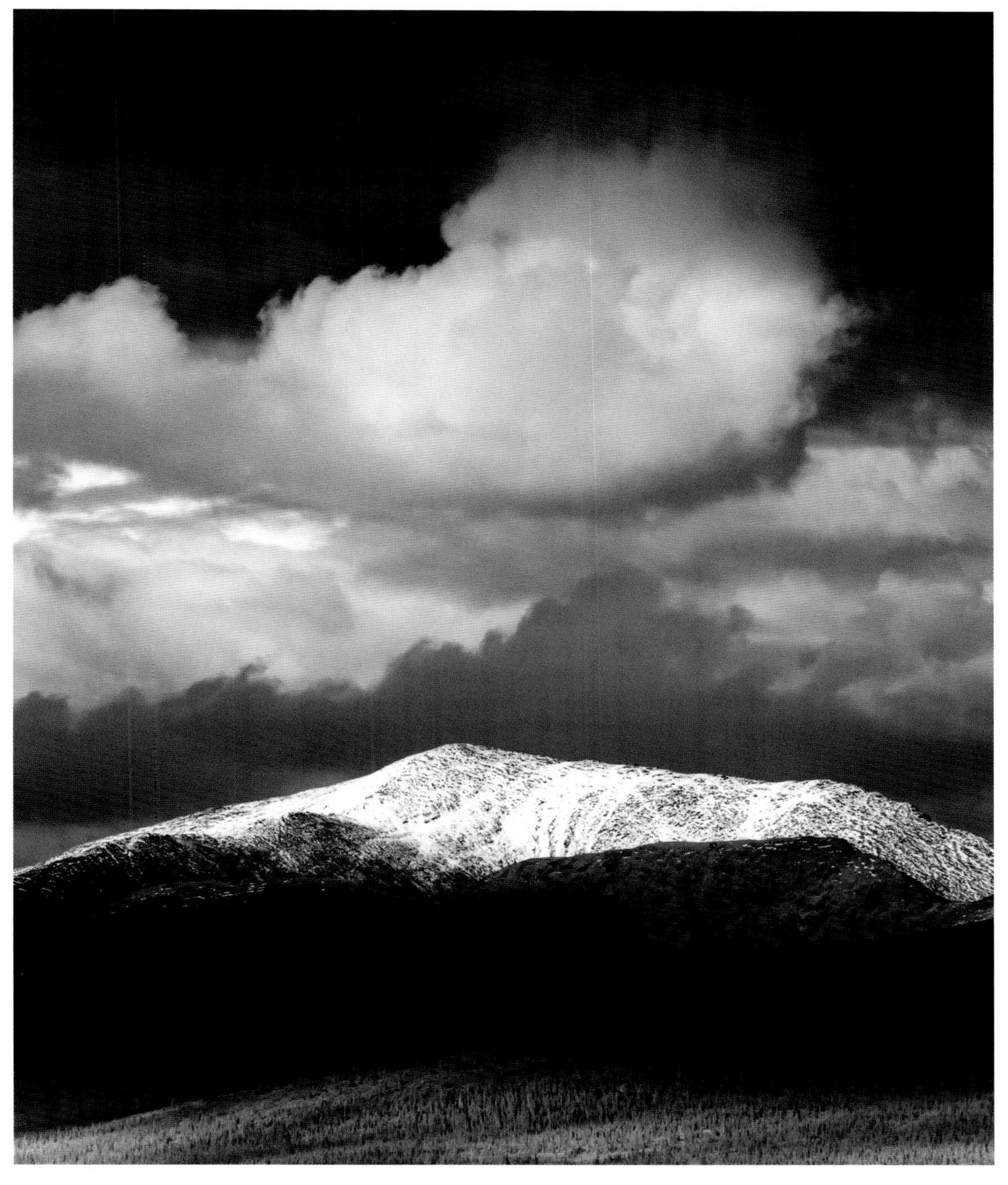

As It Should Be
Kluane Lake, Yukon

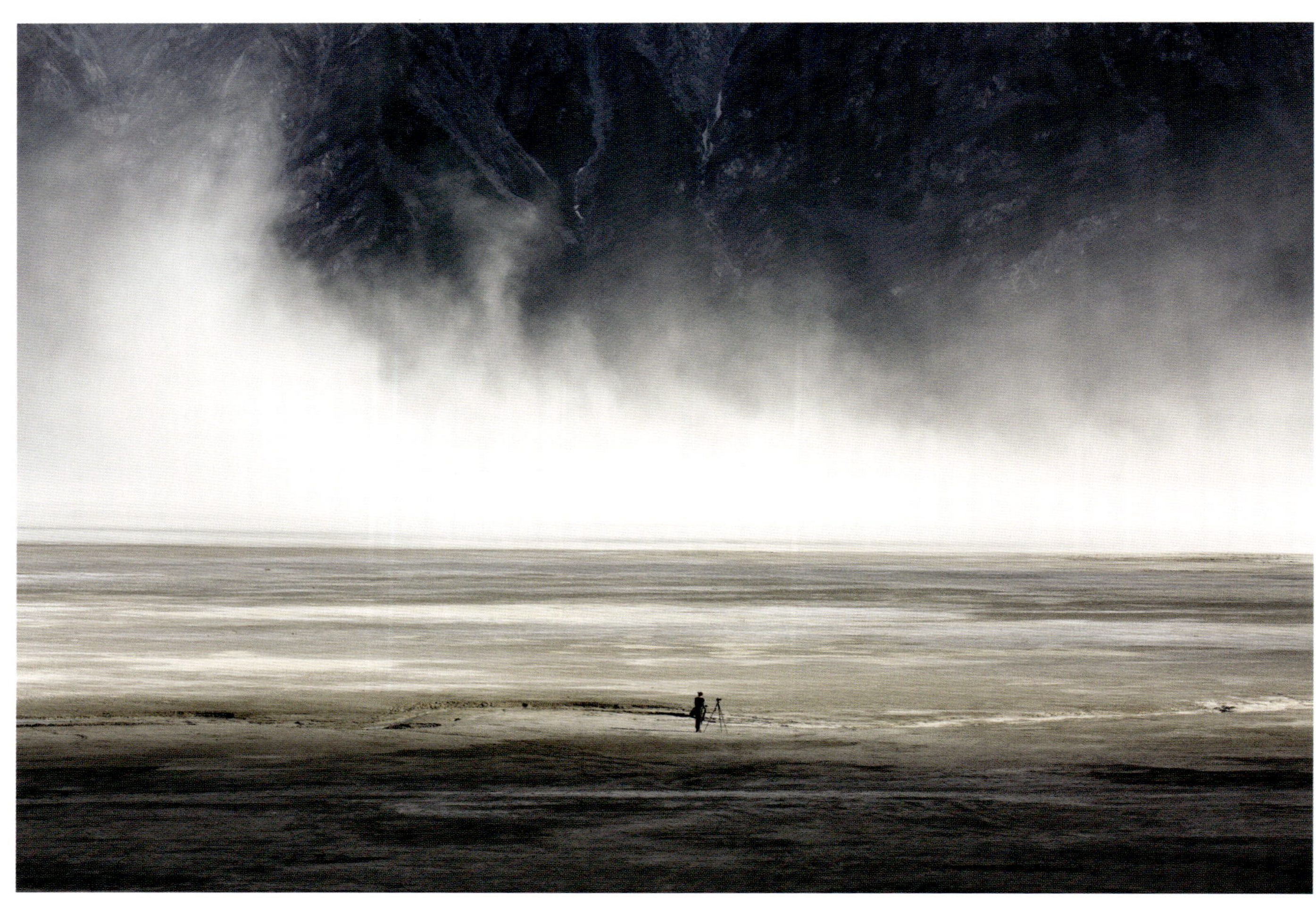

Set Adrift / Memory Bliss

Kluane National Park, Yukon

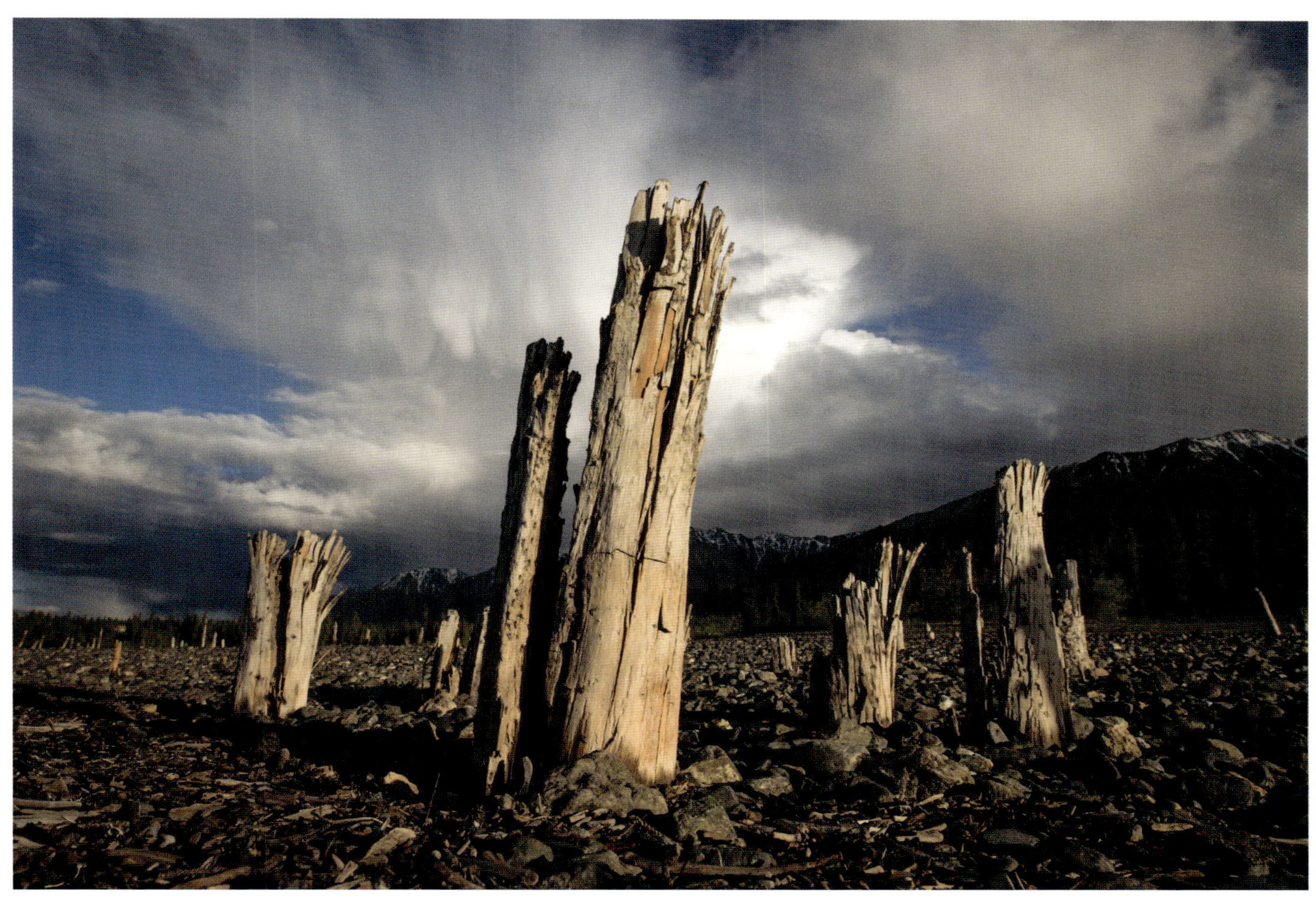

Stand Tall
Destruction Bay, Yukon

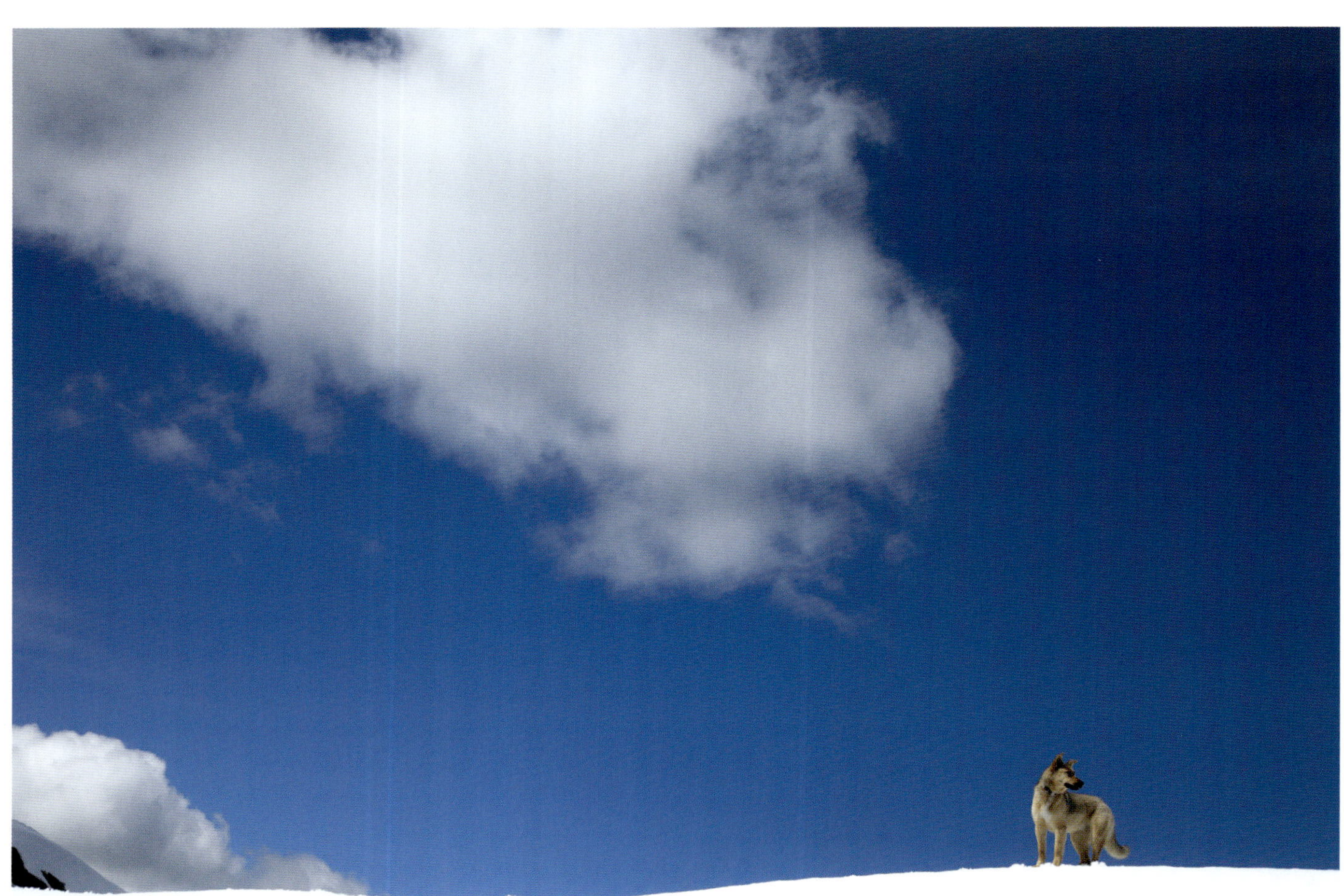

Northern Protector

King's Throne, Kluane National Park, Yukon

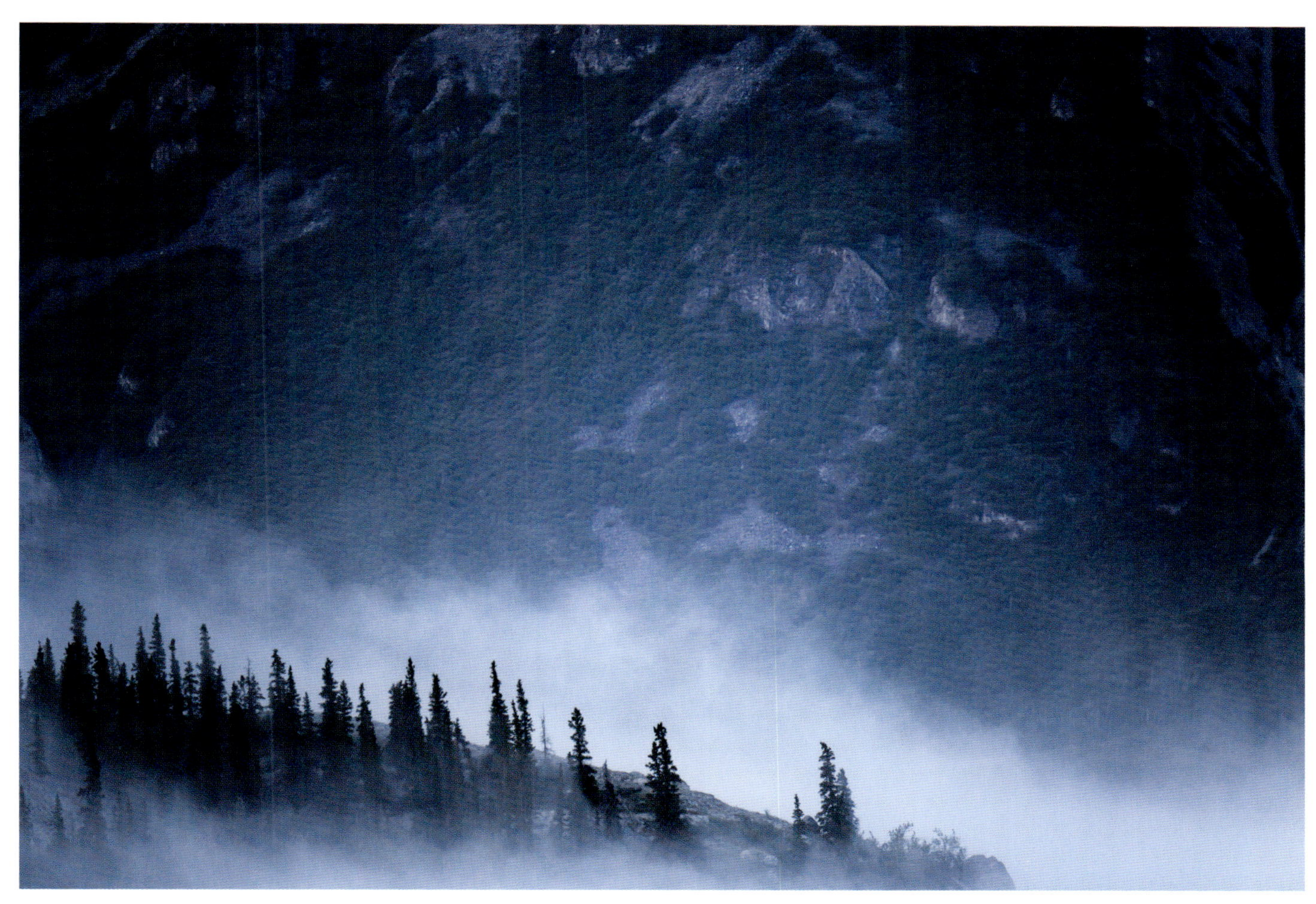

The Blue Notes

Kluane National Park, Yukon

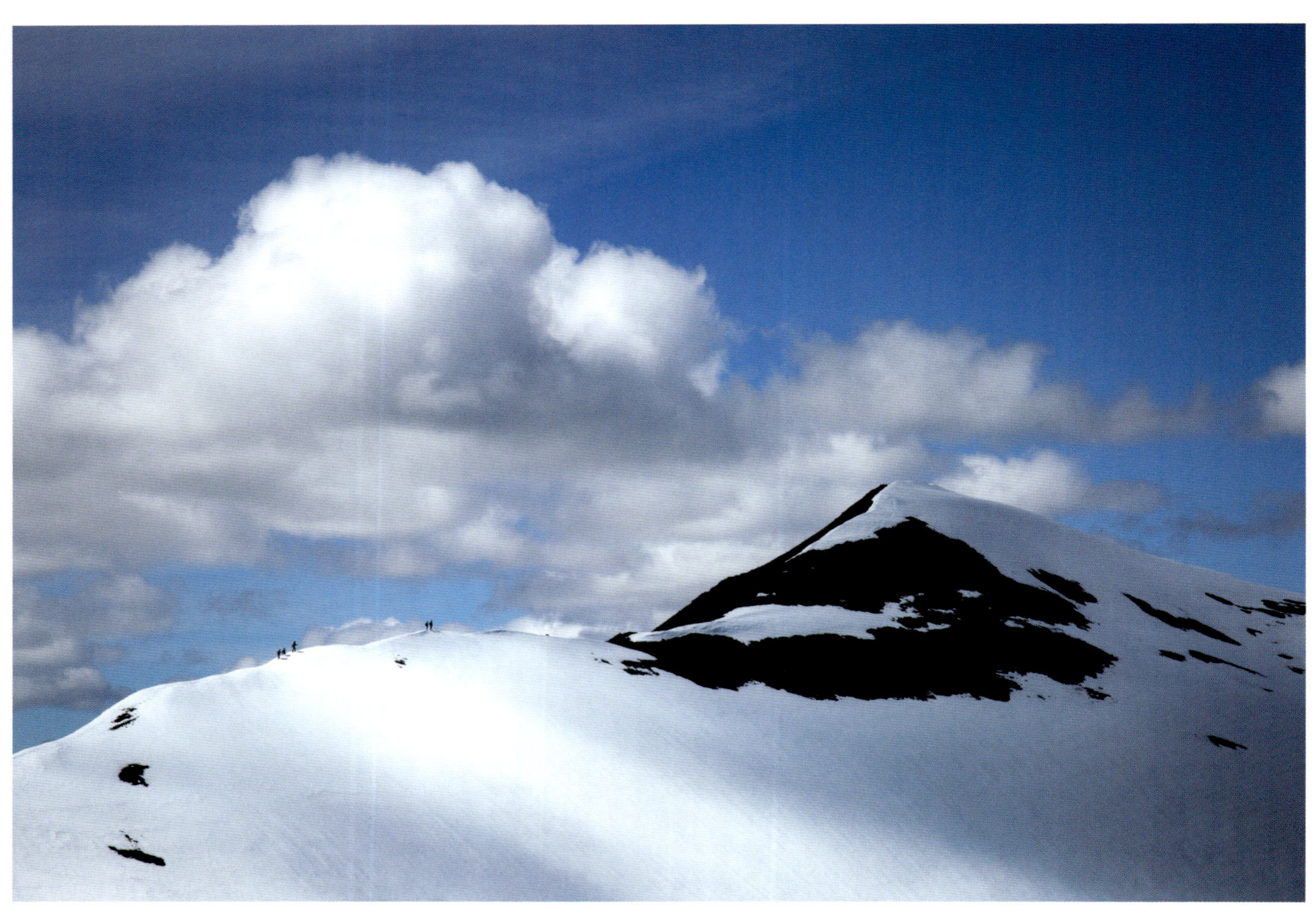

210 *Summit Push*
King's Throne, Kluane National Park, Yukon

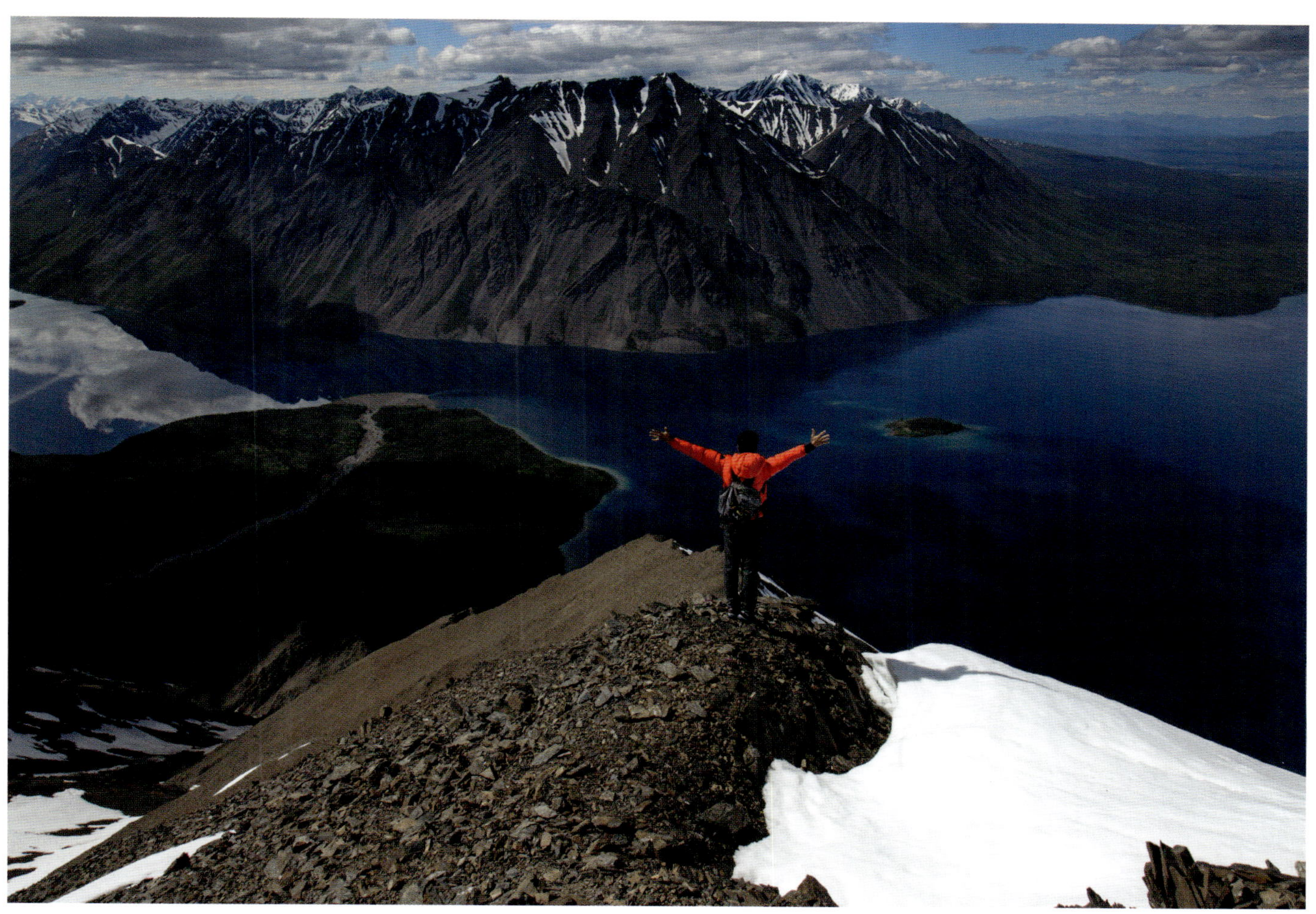

Yukon Glory

King's Throne, Kluane National Park, Yukon

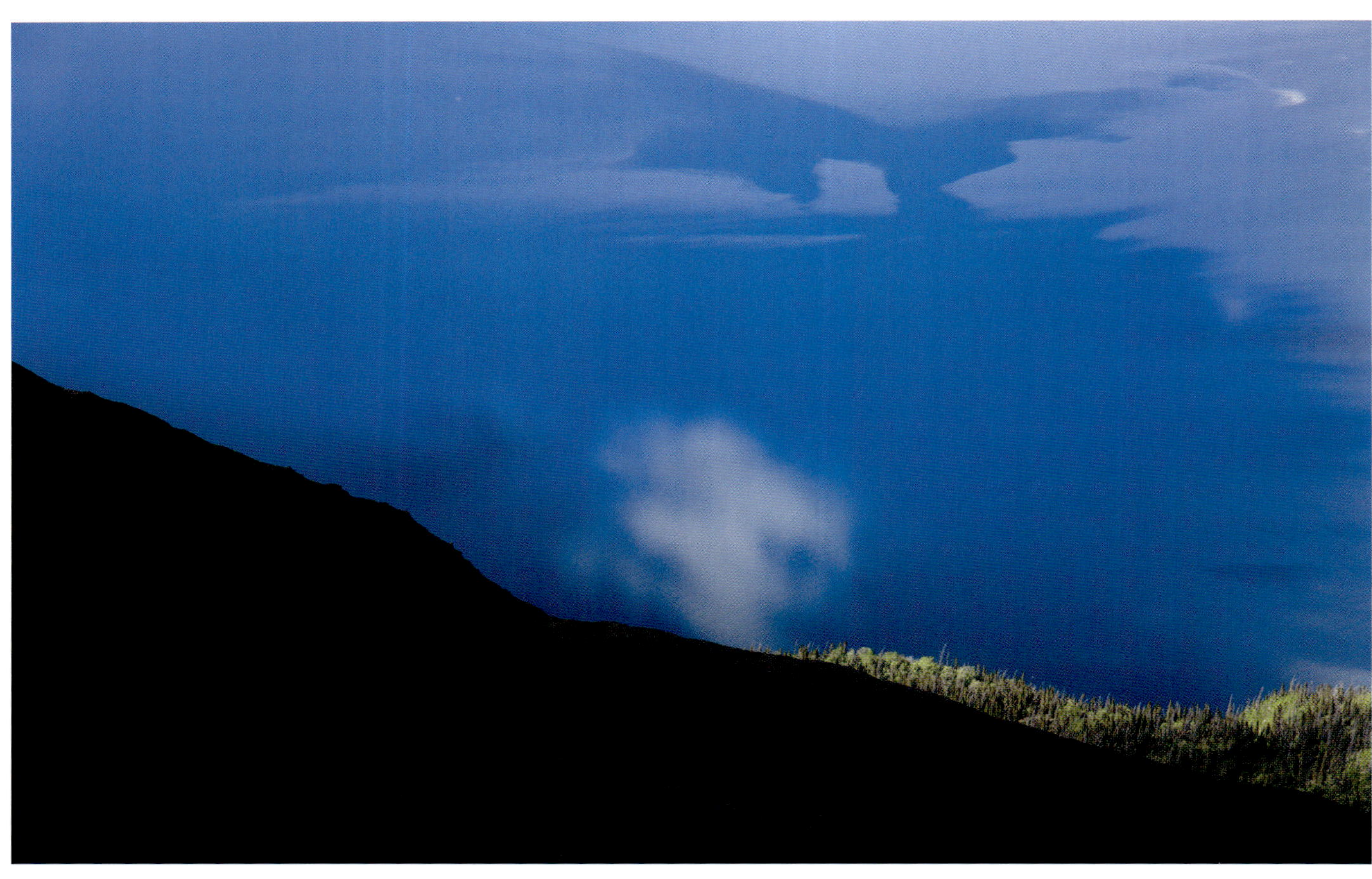

Exodus

Kathleen Lake, Kluane National Park, Yukon

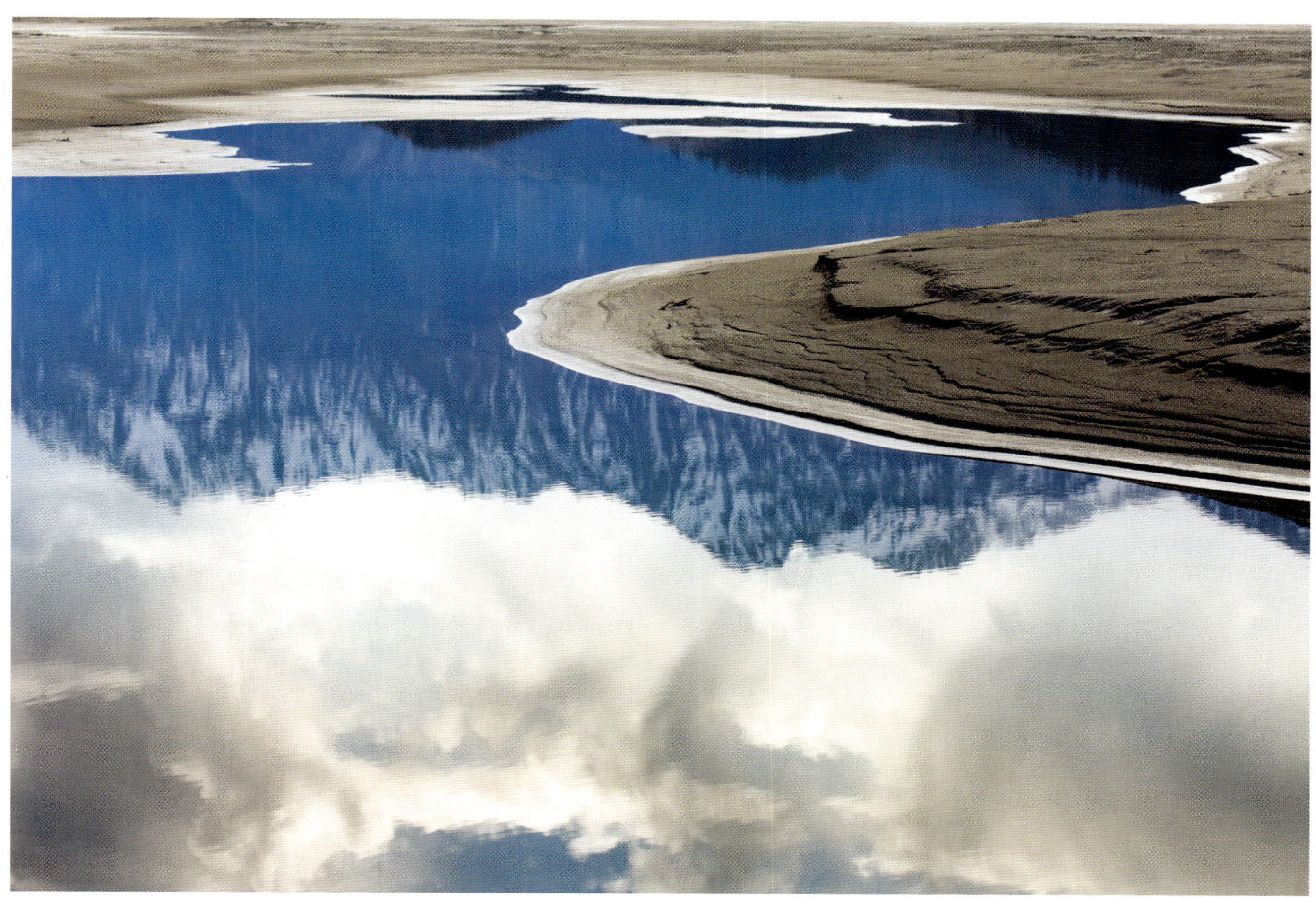

Better Side of Me
Kluane National Park, Yukon

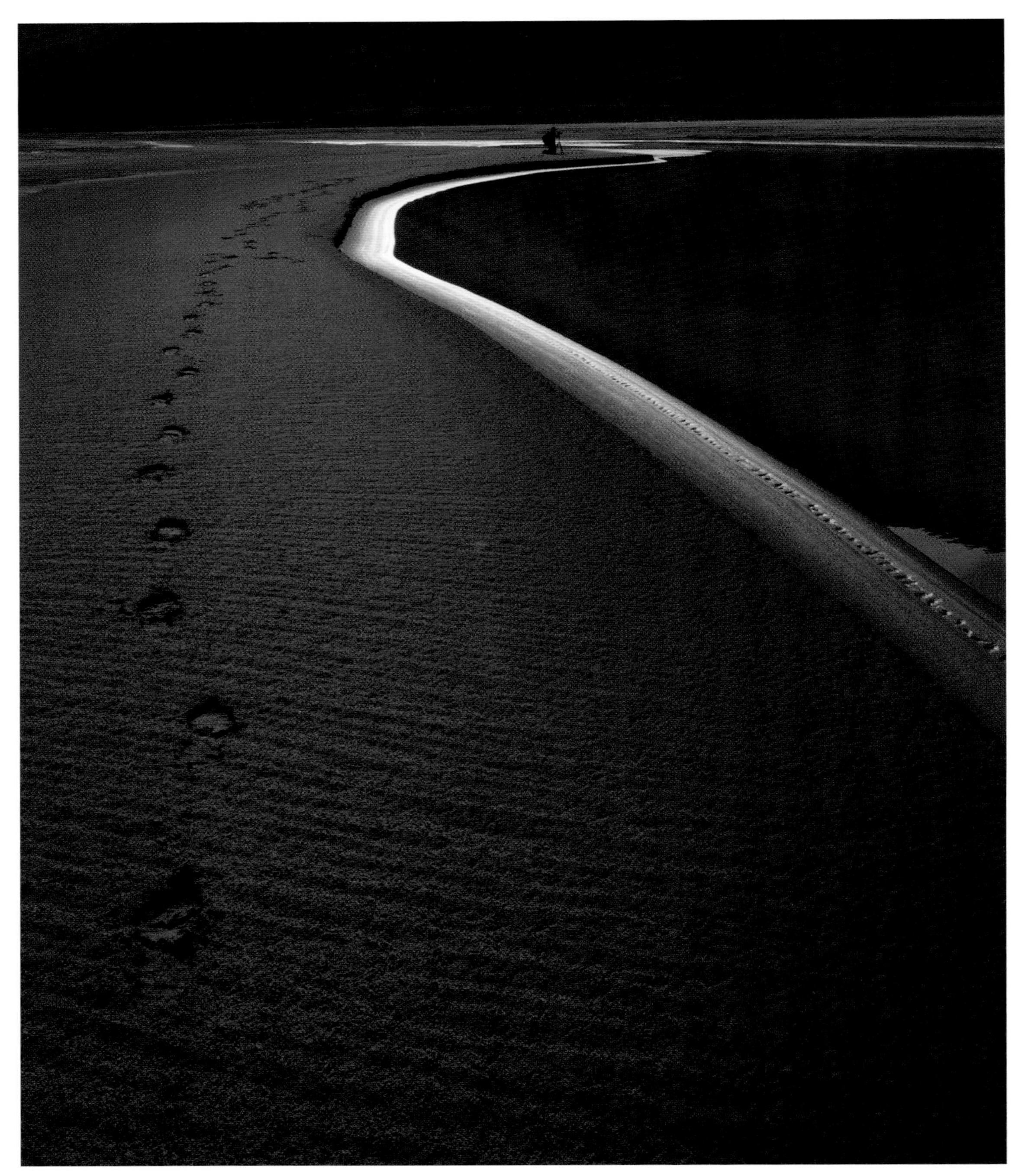

Pathways

Kluane Lake, Kluane National Park, Yukon

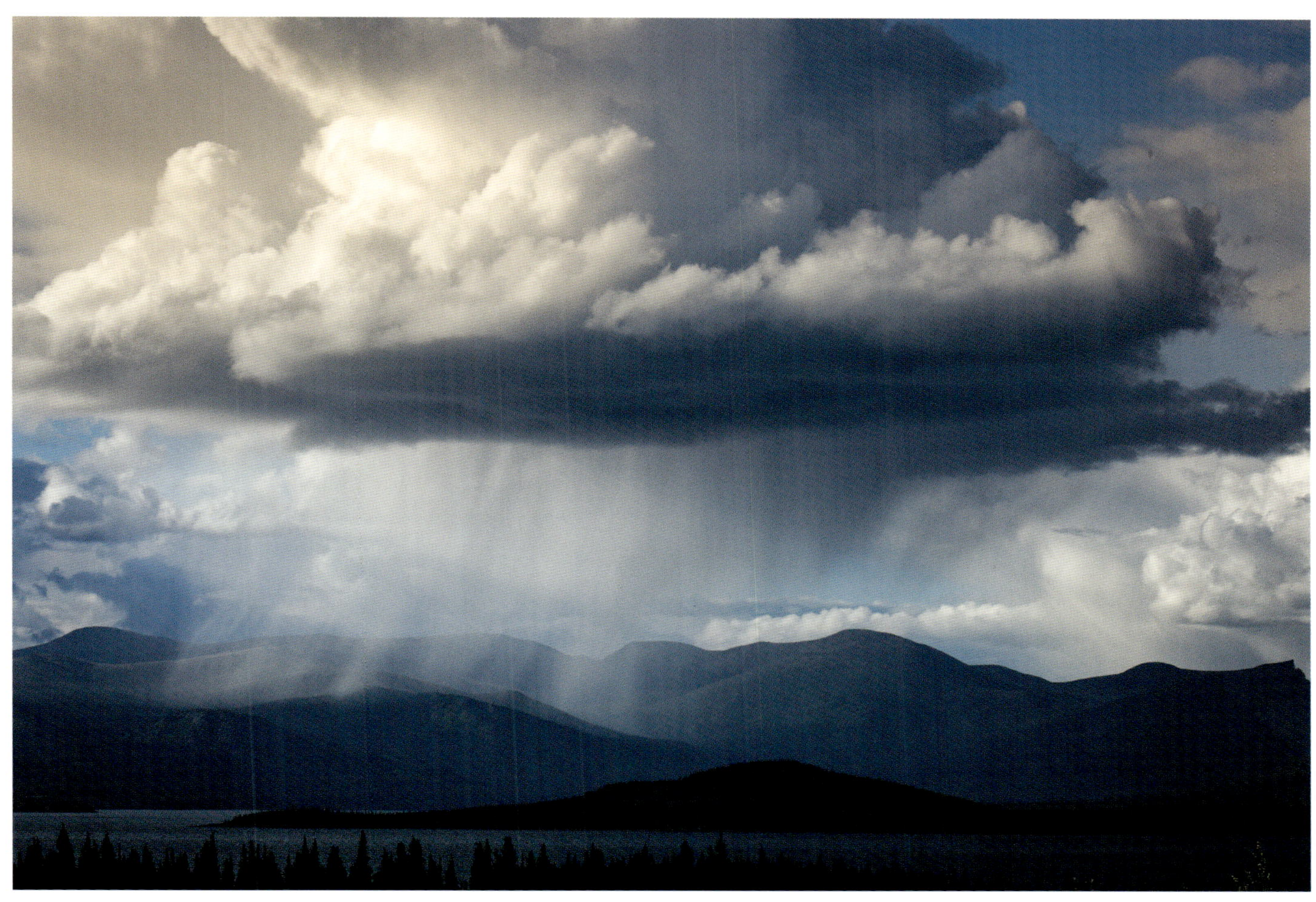

Passing Through

Kluane Lake, Kluane National Park, Yukon

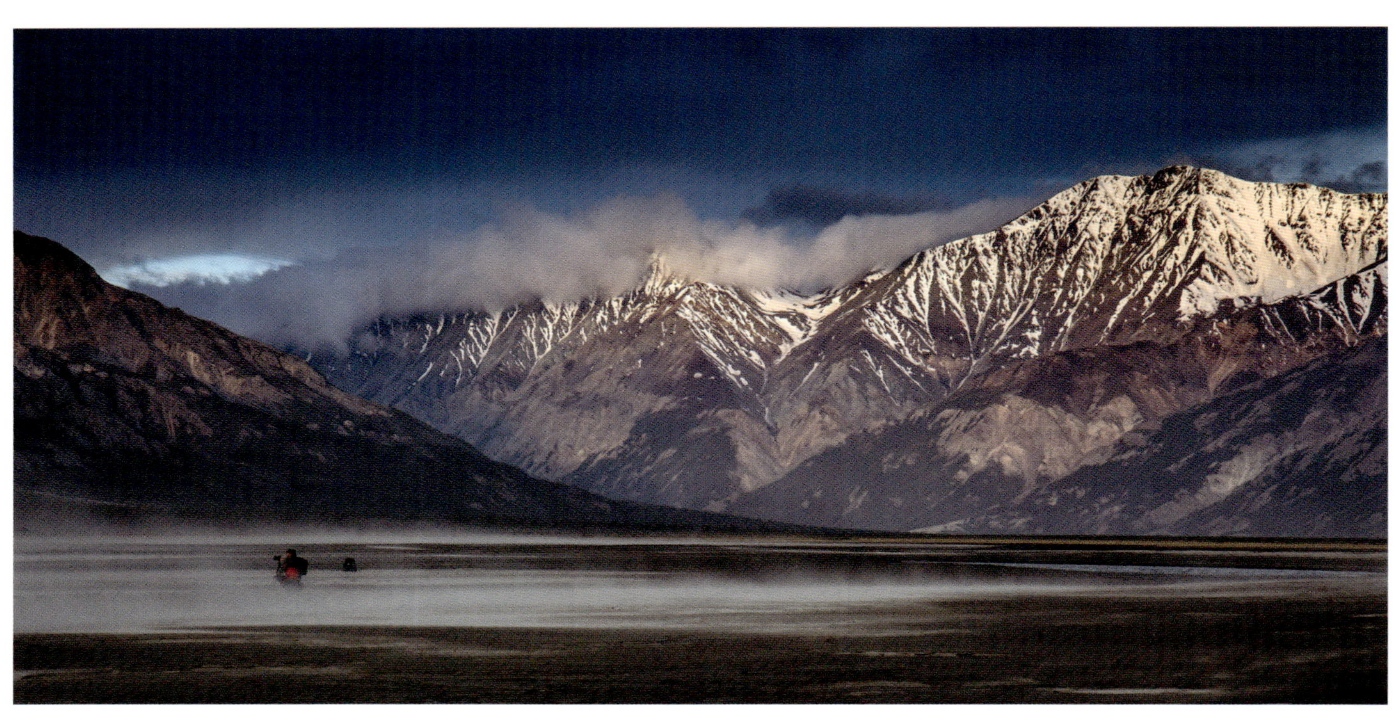

Morning Majesty
Kluane National Park, Yukon

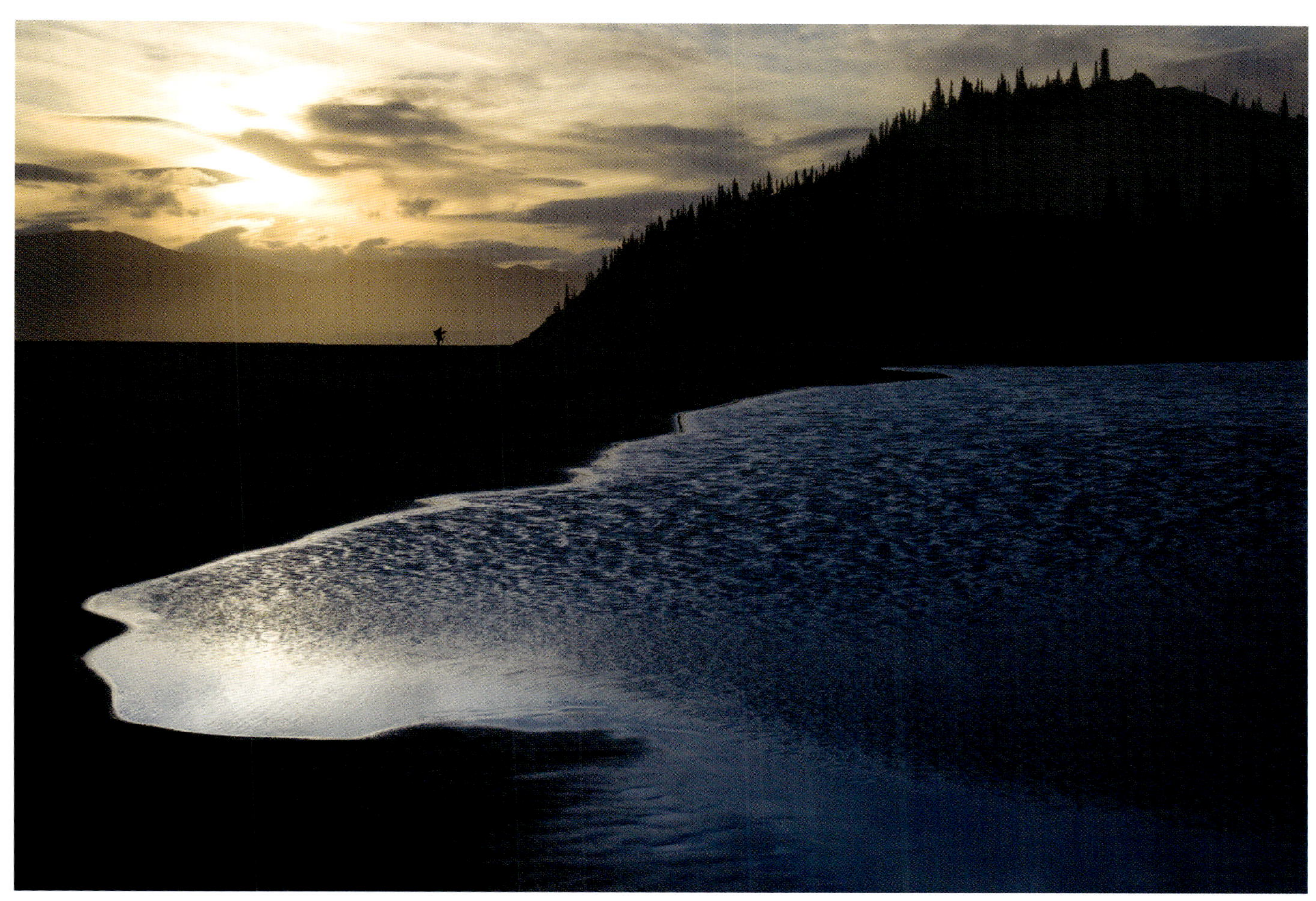

Take Me to Church
Kluane National Park, Yukon

Nunavut

WIDE OPEN SPACES

Many of Canada's regions are defined by their immense size and the wildness of their territory, but almost none compare to Nunavut, Canada's truly Arctic territory. The land – almost two million sparsely populated square kilometres of it – is a defining characteristic of its people. One of the statements you hear most often living in Nunavut is "I'm heading out on the land" or "he or she is currently on the land." The land is life, it's religion, it's everything. Nunavut, in fact, means "our land" in Inuktitut, the language of the Inuit indigenous peoples – inhabitants and guardians of this territory for thousands of years.

To love Nunavut, a photographer has to have an appreciation, if not a love, for wide open spaces. A love for general emptiness. It's one of the most sparsely populated areas in the entire world, and the distances between communities (and sometimes recognizable landmarks) is vast. To head out for exploration means being prepared and having an immense respect for the endless landscape. To photograph Nunavut means looking beyond the emptiness and realizing just how rich and full a subject it is.

Before Nunavut, I had never really considered *wide open* as a source of comfort. I came from a land of trees and buildings and people. A couple years before we lived in Nunavut, we lived in Kaohsiung, Taiwan – a city of almost three million, where humans essentially live on top of one another; where confinement is a natural state of being. When I explored in and around Nunavut, however, I quickly realized the beauty of the great wide open. Watching cloud systems come from kilometres away gave me peace, as did the endless dance of a setting sun.

Then there's the light. Oh, Northern light. Arctic light has characteristics that are hard to explain to someone who hasn't experienced it firsthand. In the winter, when you have an absence of light (in Resolute, it disappears for almost three solid months during "dark season"), you're forced to get creative and find your own light to work with – and you're filled with longing for what you know will eventually come. In the spring months, when light finally returned to the snowy tundra, I found the light would often take on a vivid pastel, dreamlike quality: soft pinks and magentas that would brighten the land long after the sun slowly dipped behind the horizon. In the summer months, when the sun would visit almost the entirety of the day, you'd experience endless magic light in the early mornings and evenings, as this period was essentially one long sunrise/sunset.

Photographically, it's in these two components – light and space – that I find Nunavut inspires me most. Its vastness makes me feel alive. Its lands make me appreciate our natural world, and I'll always look forward to its light in future explorations and visits. Want to find me happy? Find me sitting, somewhere, by Northern light.

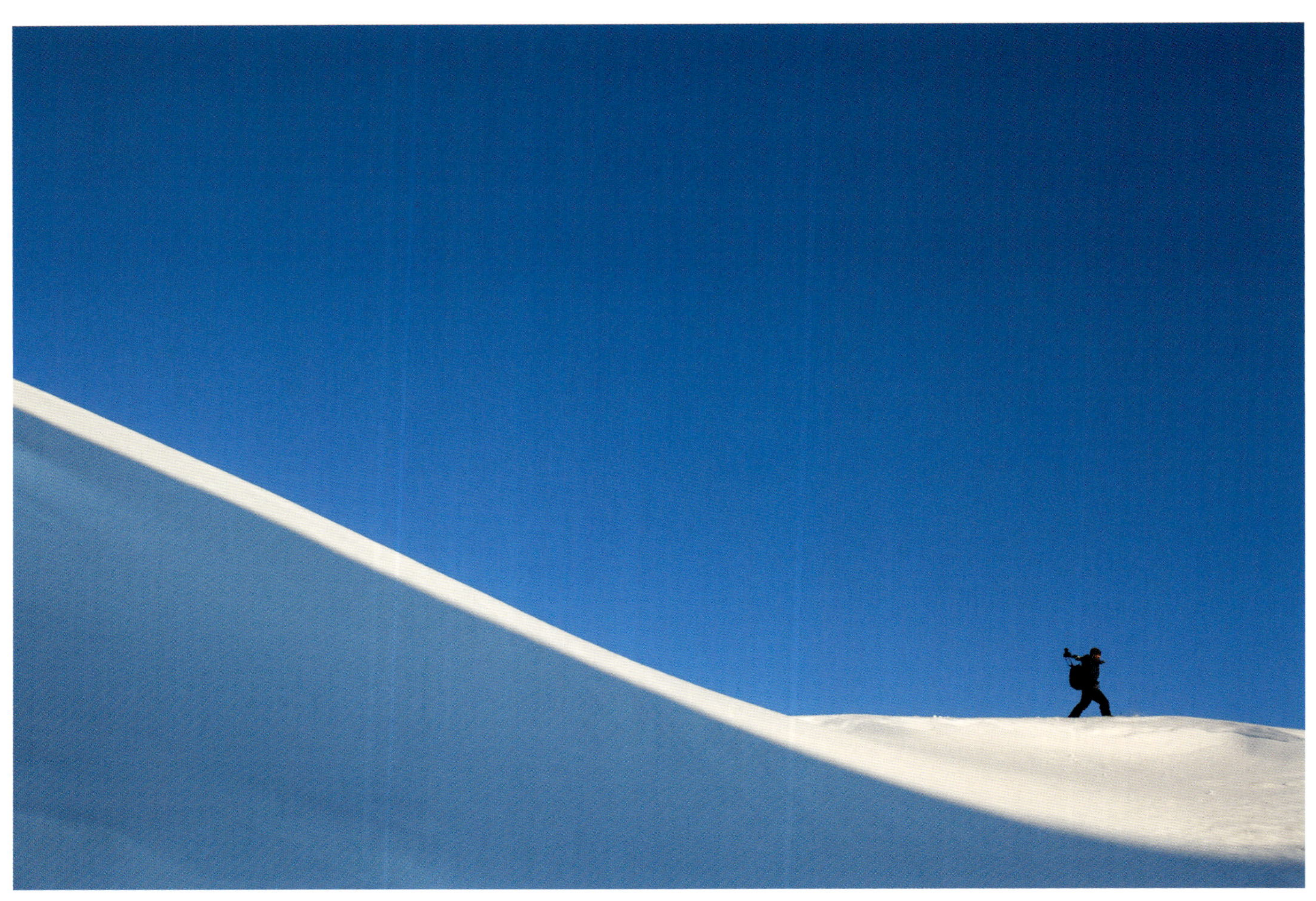

A Spoonful of Magic
Paul Zizka in Arctic Bay, Nunavut

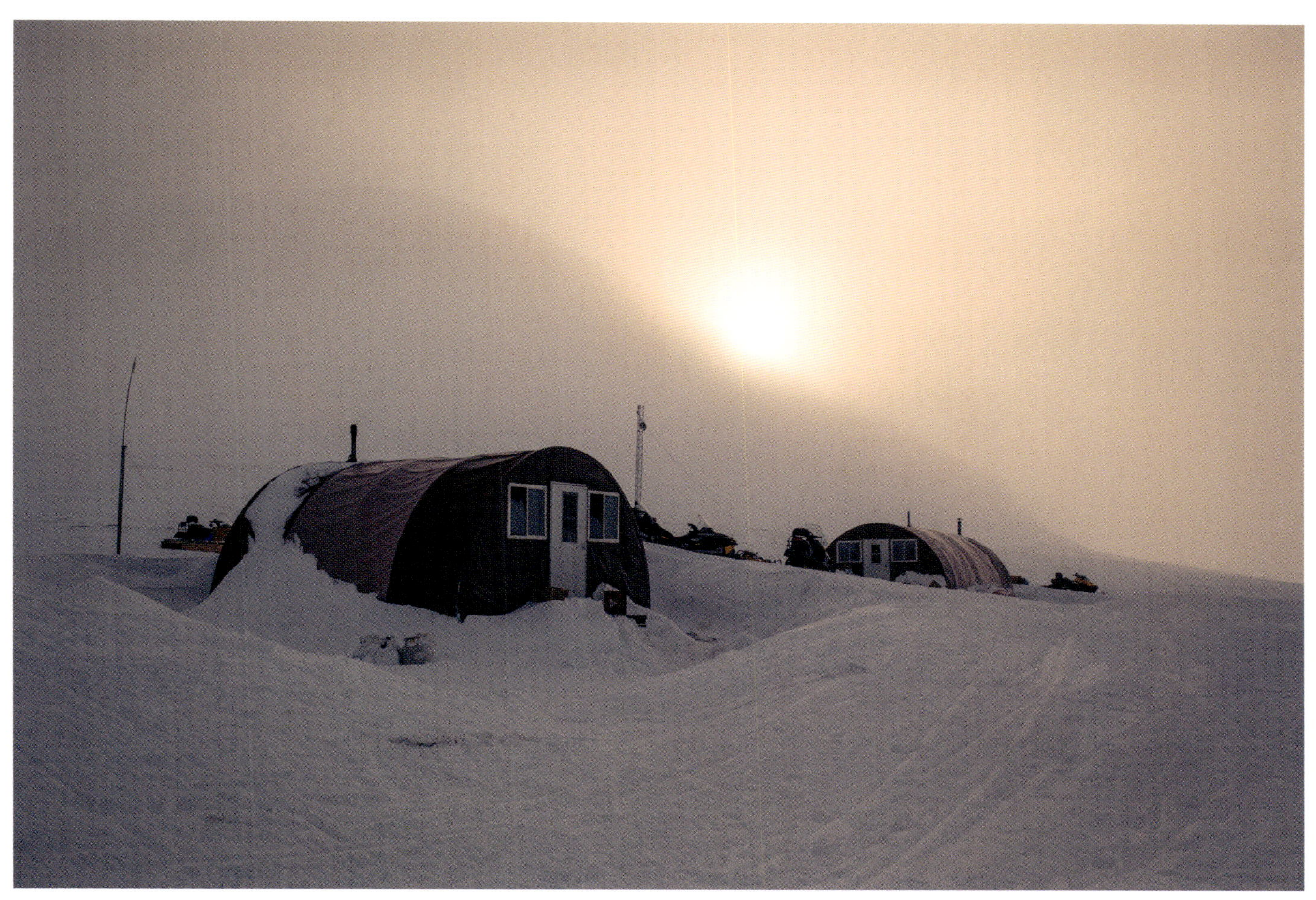

Socked In
Ward Hunt Island, Nunavut

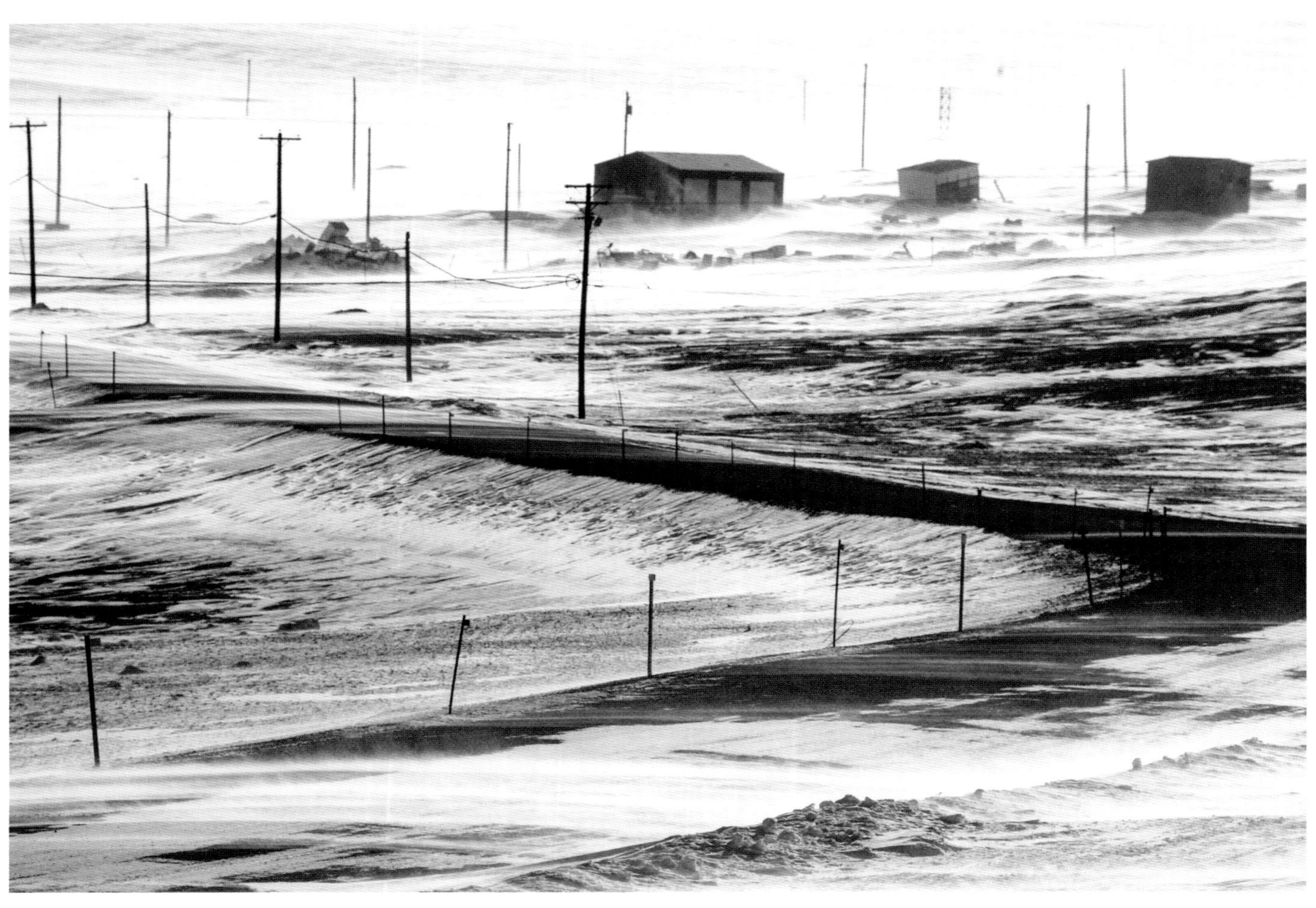

222 *Happy Trails*
Resolute Bay, Nunavut

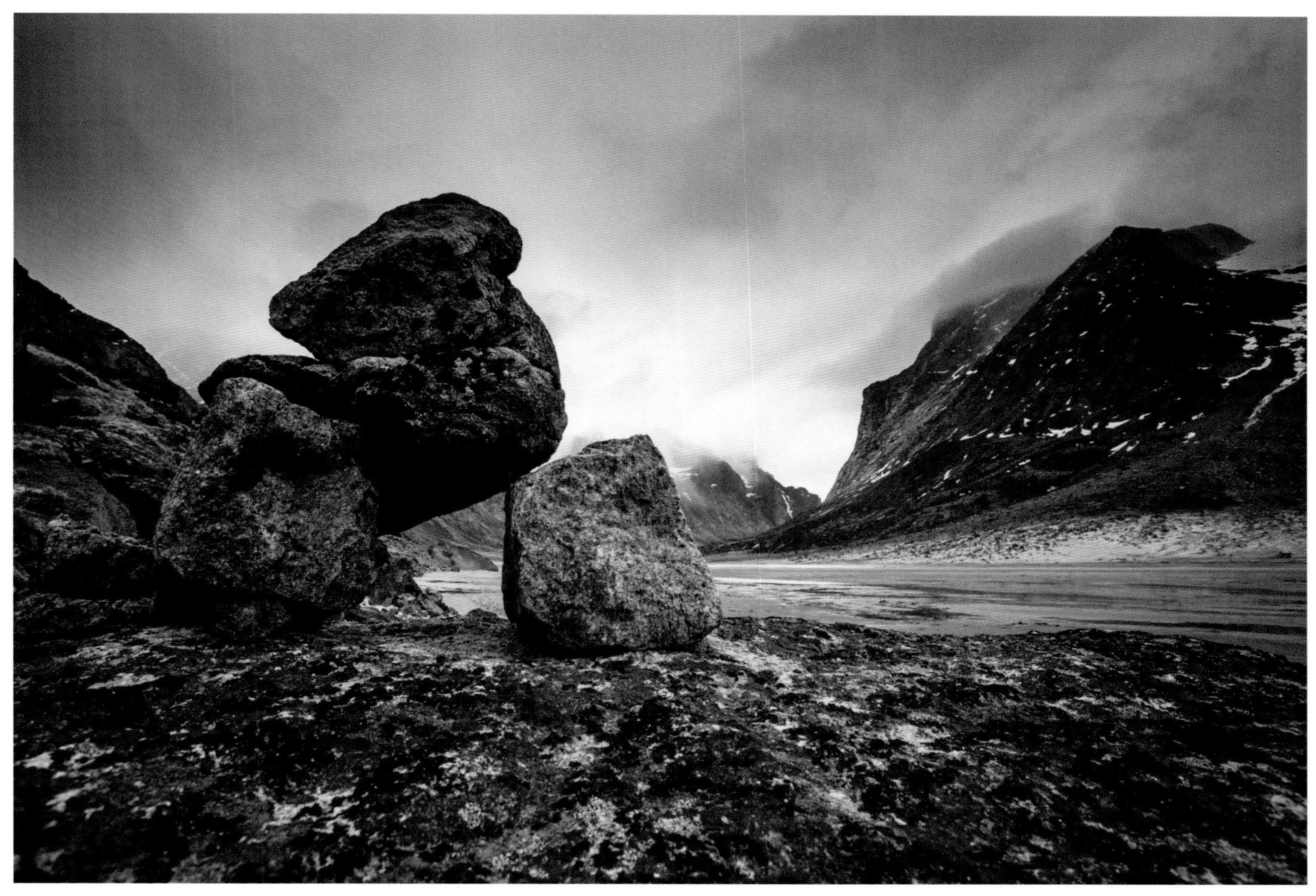

We, The Land

Auyuittuq National Park, Baffin Island, Nunavut

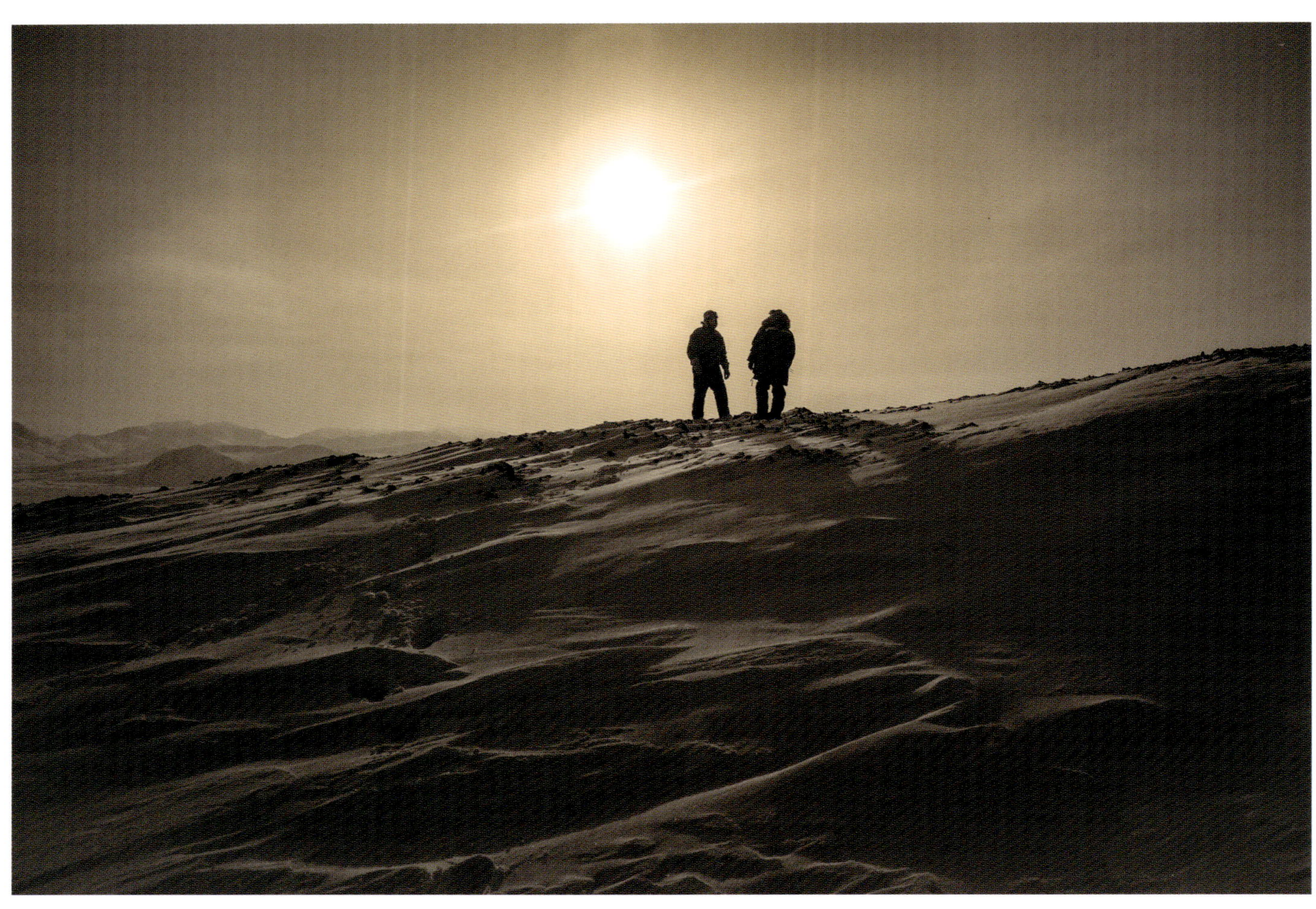

 Which Way to Go
Ward Hunt Island, Nunavut

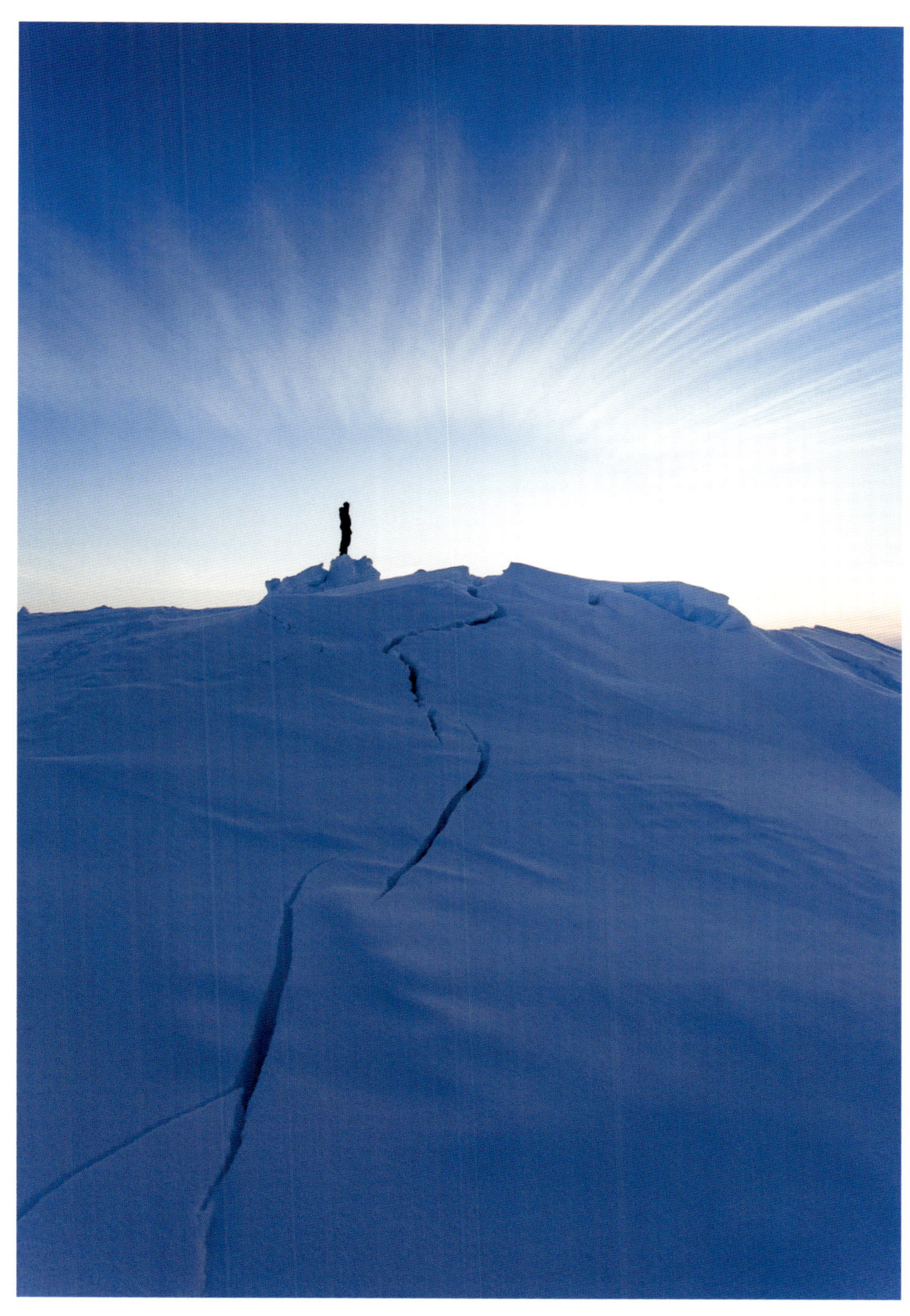

Winter Whispers

Paul Zizka in Arctic Bay, Nunavut

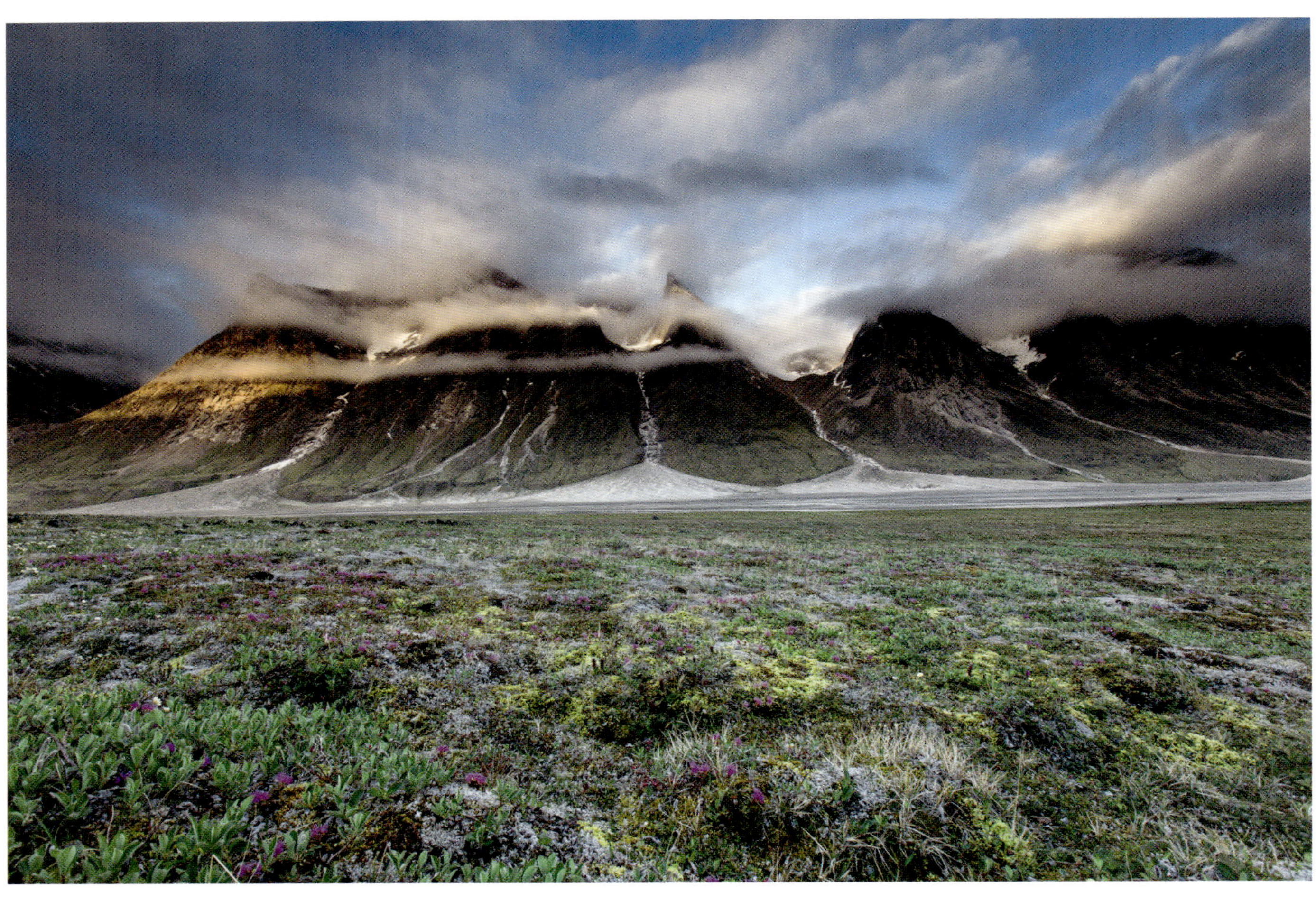

A Breath of Baffin

Auyuittuq National Park, Baffin Island, Nunavut

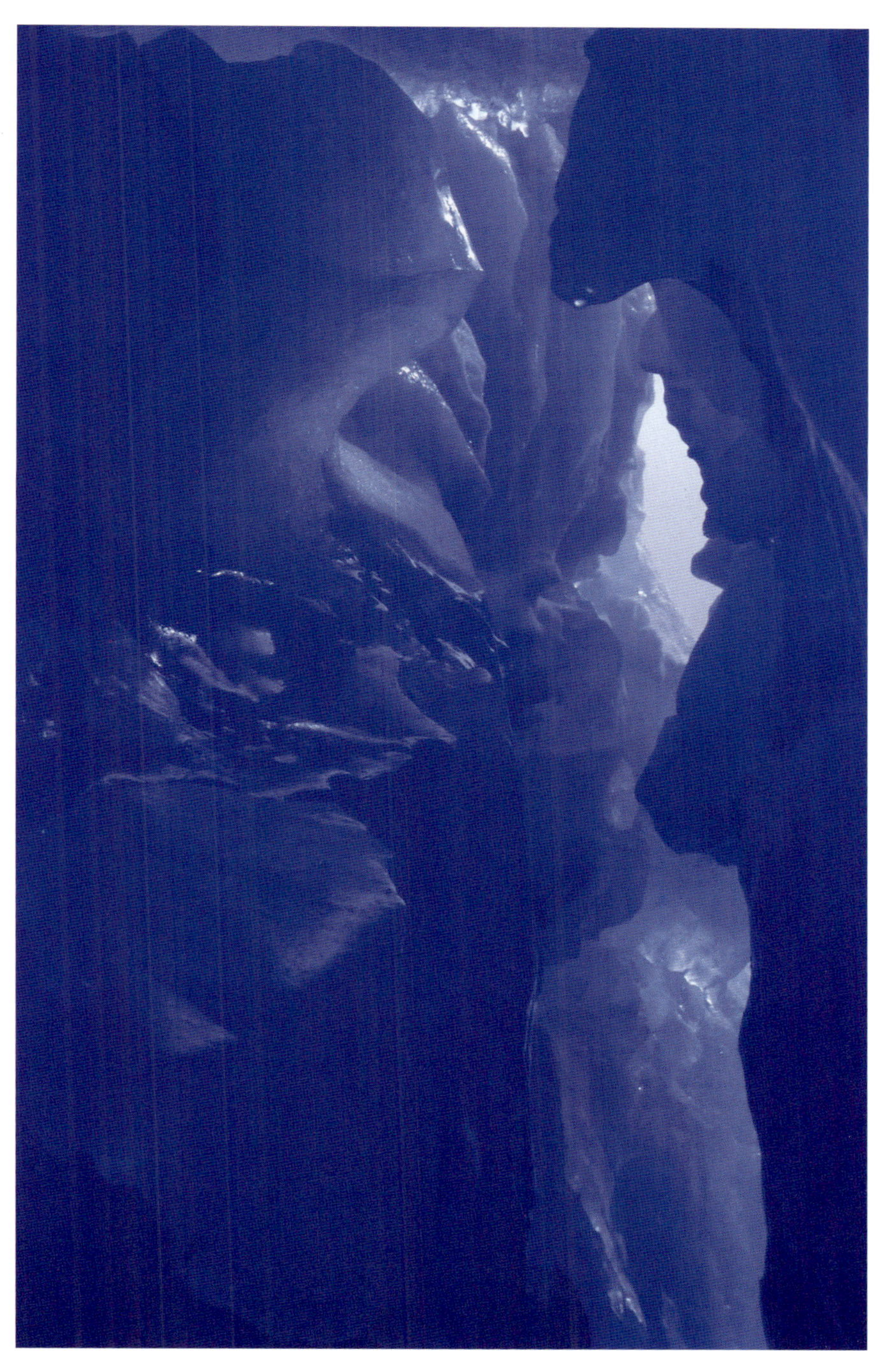

Blue Harmonium
Griffith Island, Nunavut

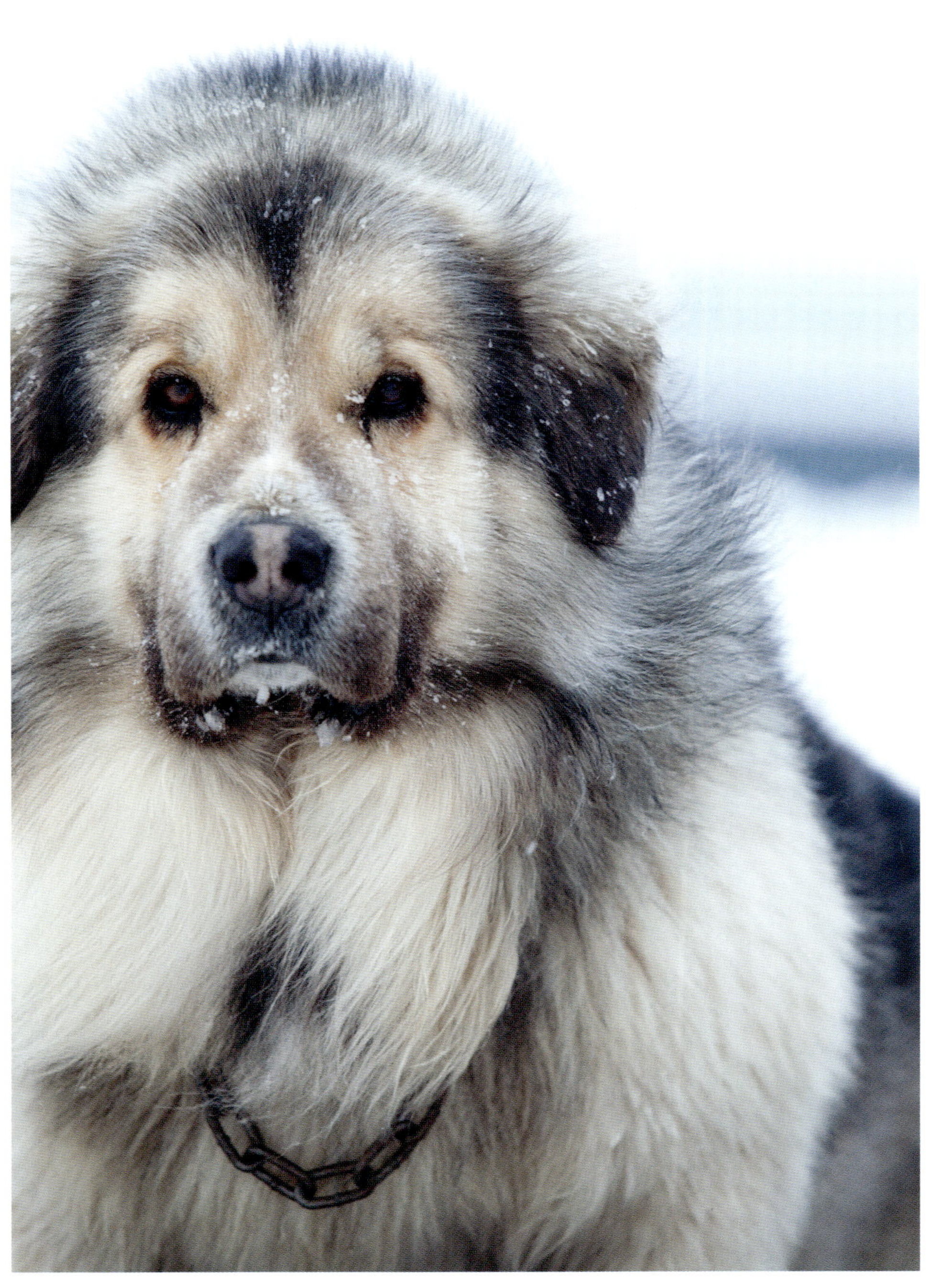

The Weathered
Iqaluit, Nunavut

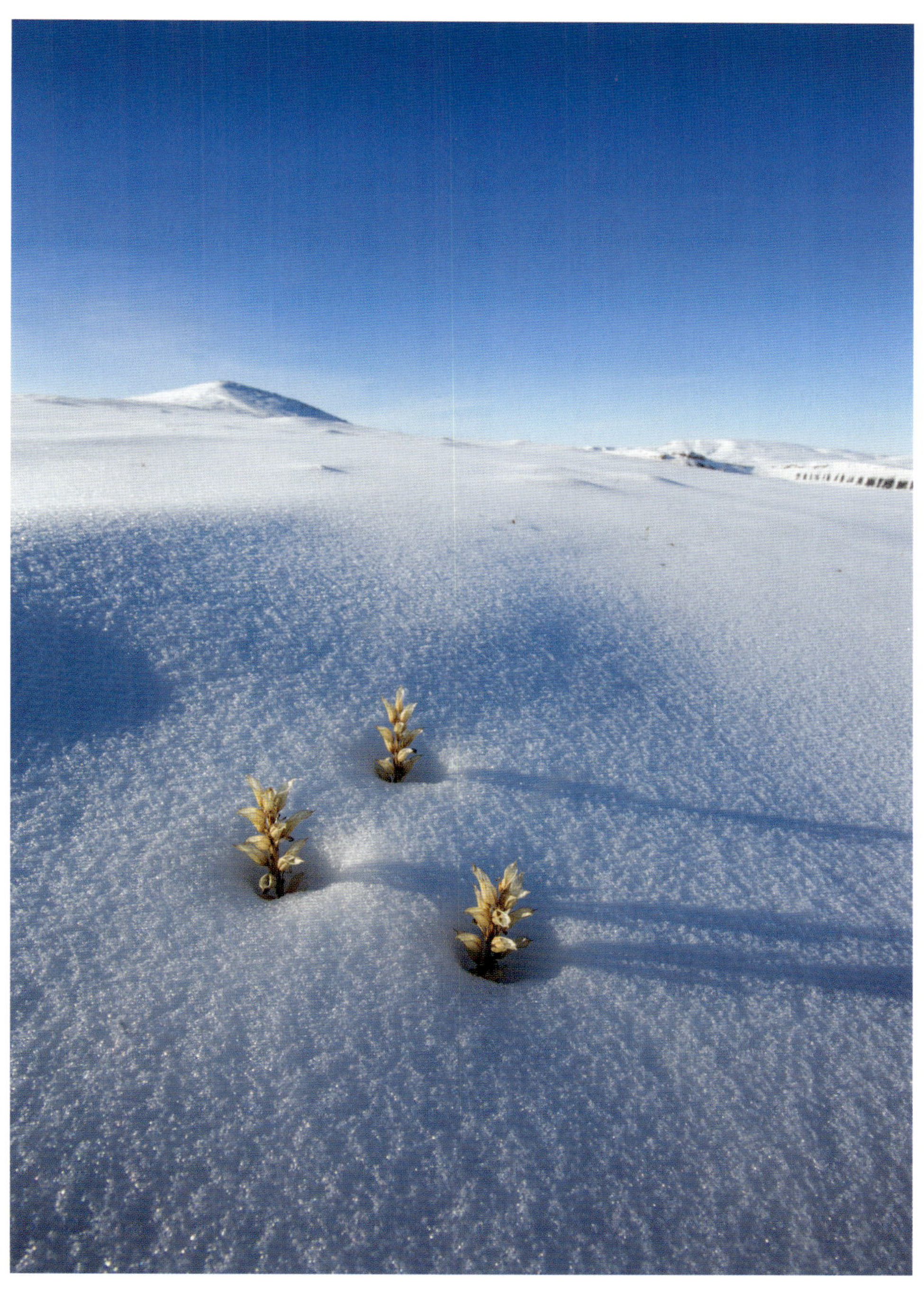

Emergence

Arctic Bay, Nunavut

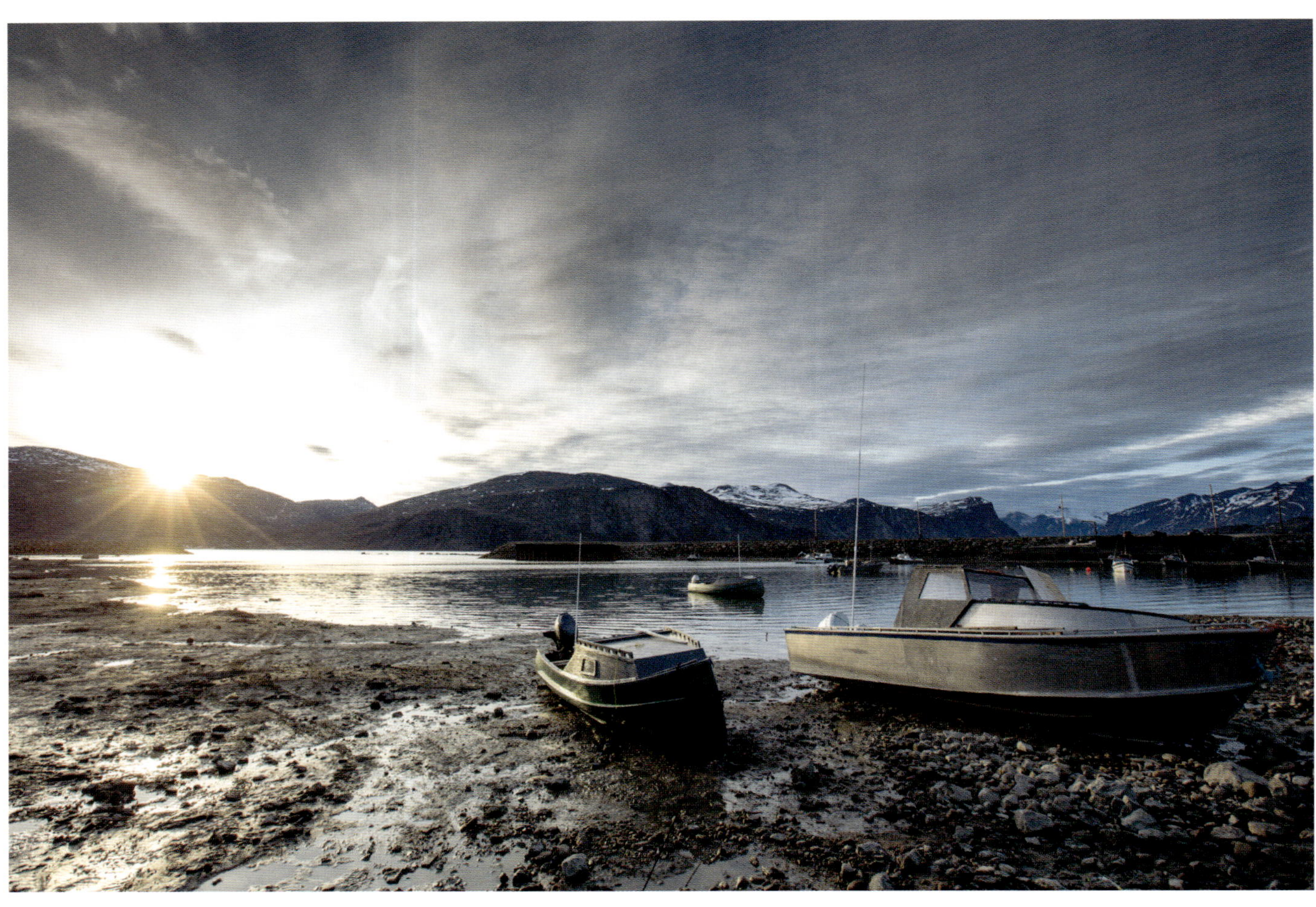

 The Boats of Baffin
Pangnirtung, Nunavut

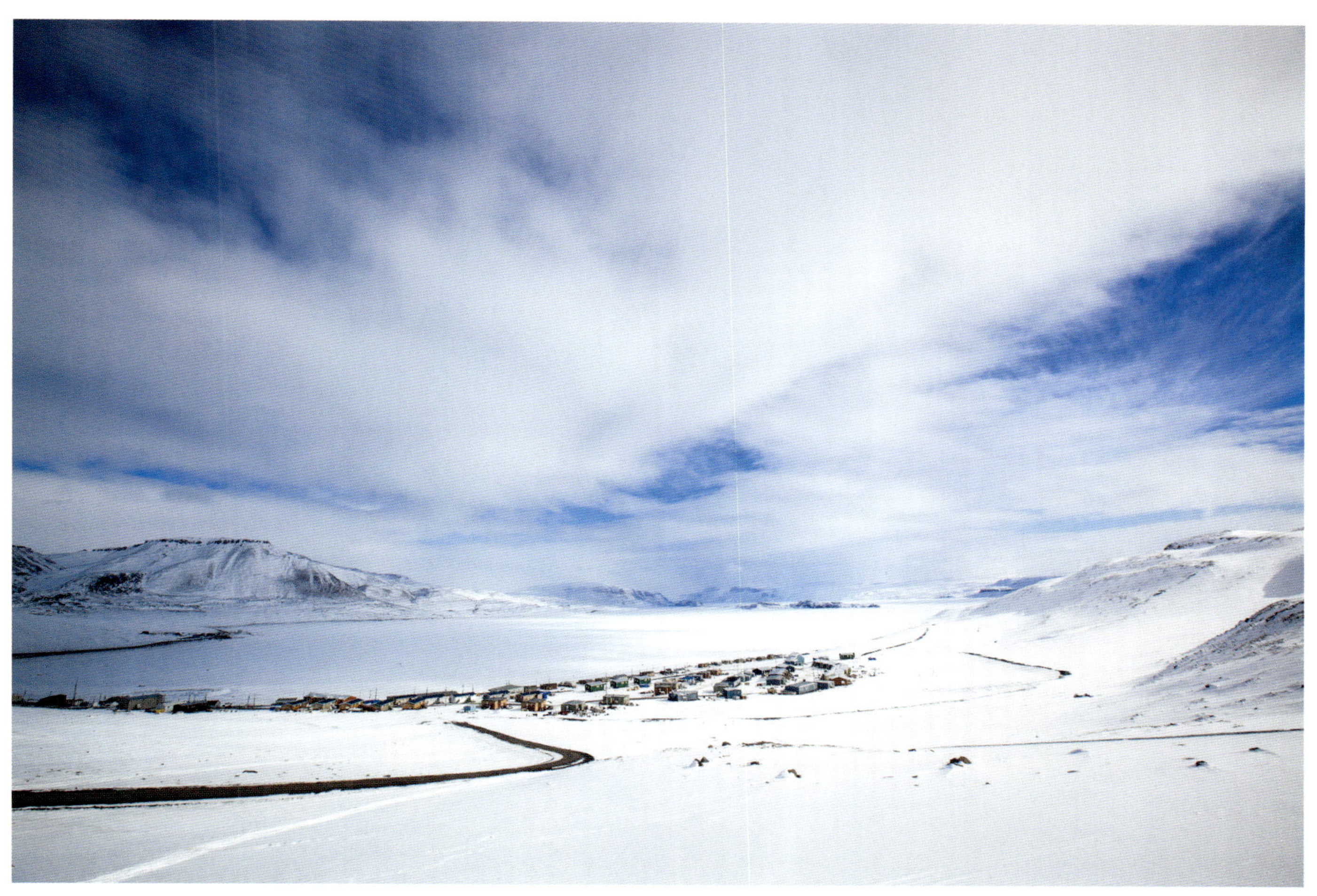

The Arctic Way
Arctic Bay, Nunavut

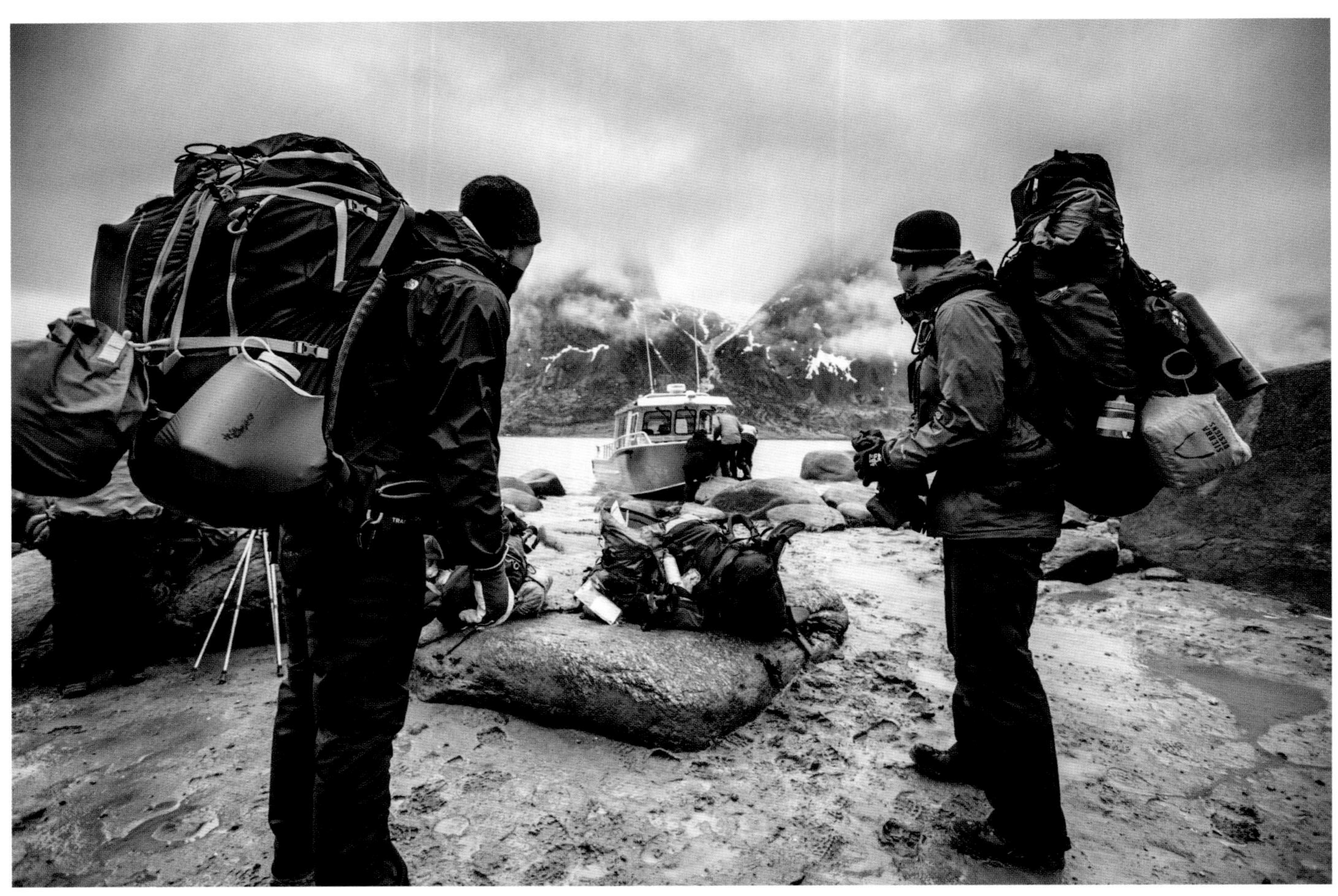

Parting Ways

Auyuittuq National Park, Baffin Island, Nunavut

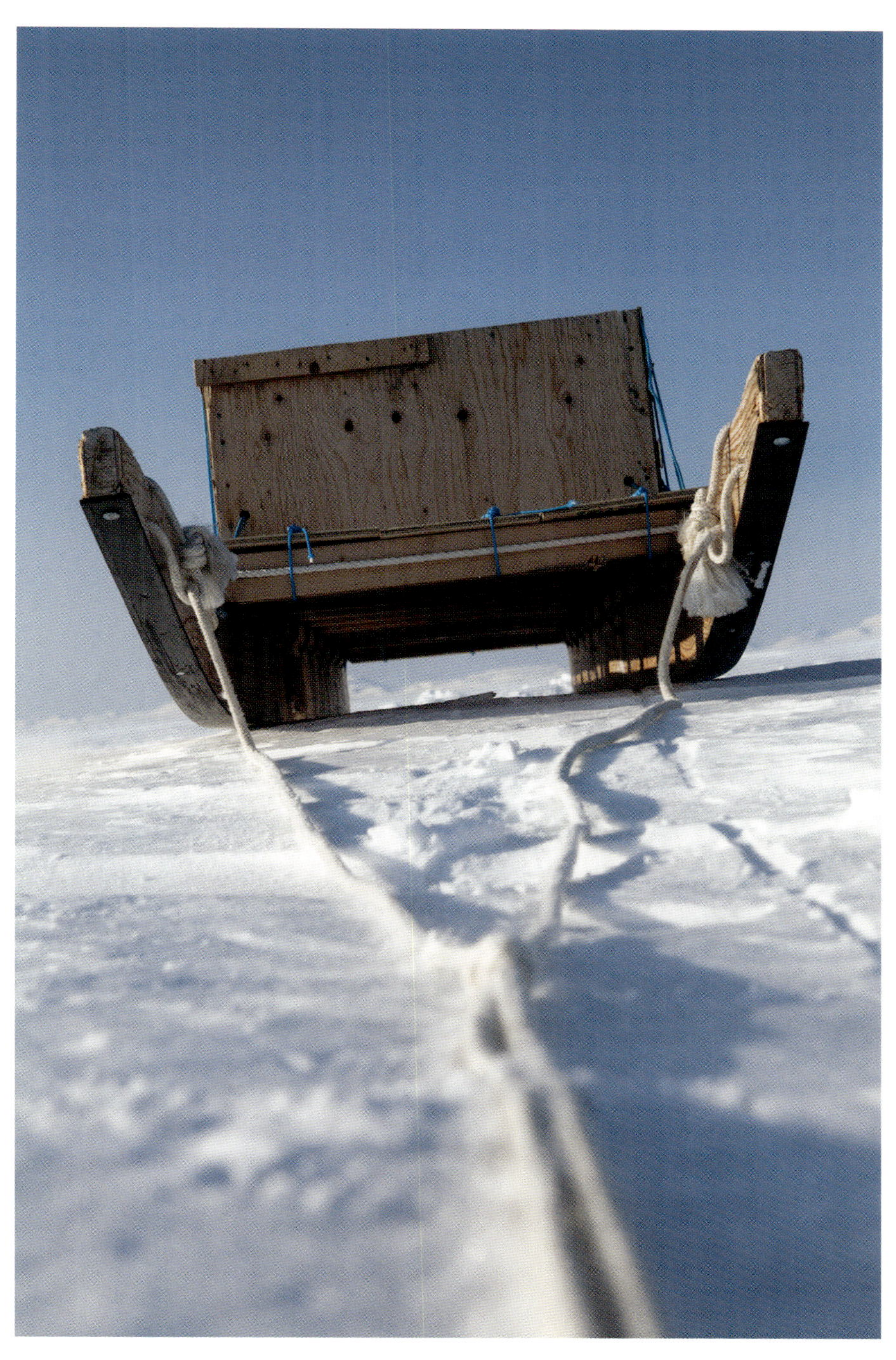

Qamutiik
Alert, Nunavut

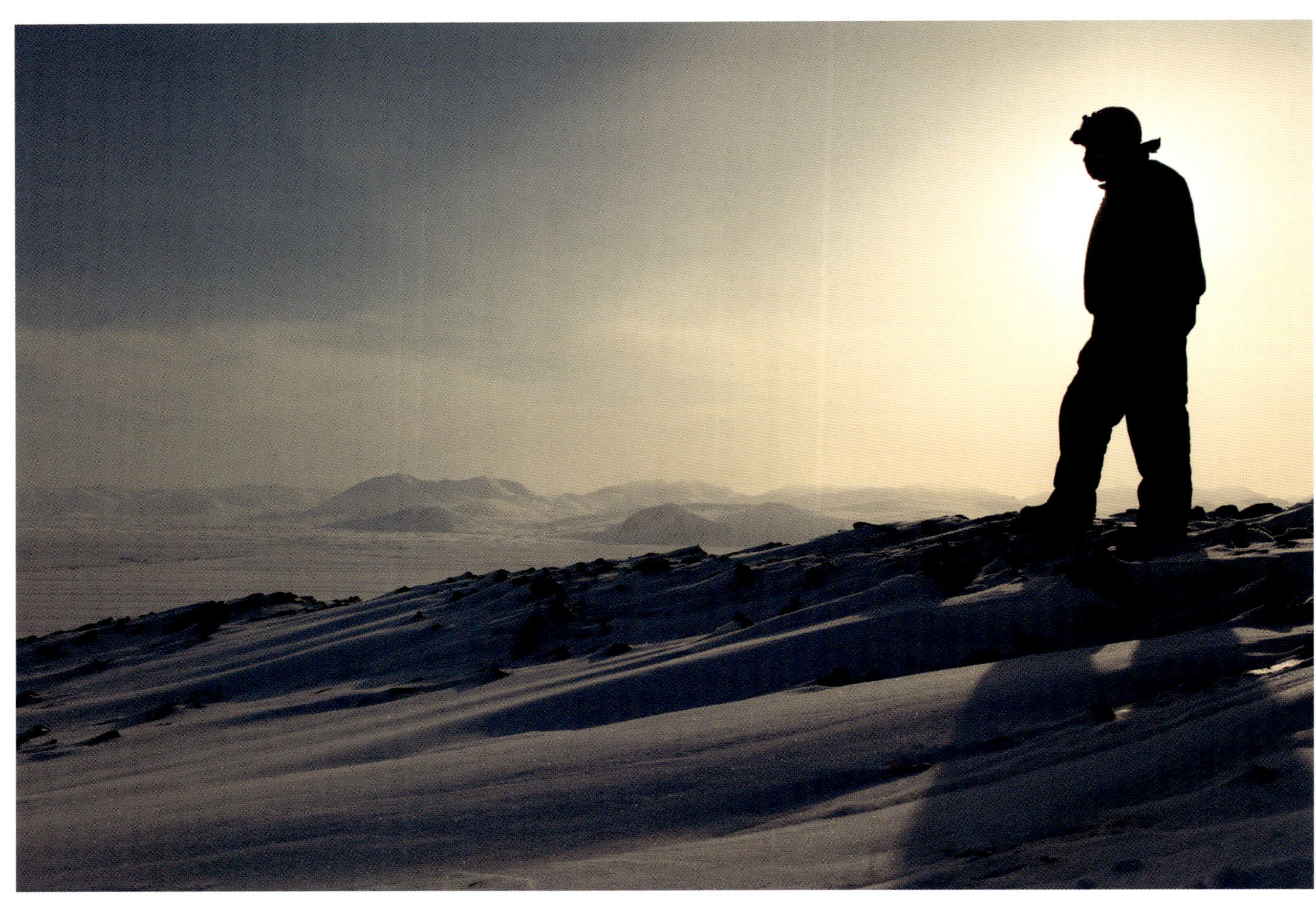

 Top of the World
Ward Hunt Island, Nunavut

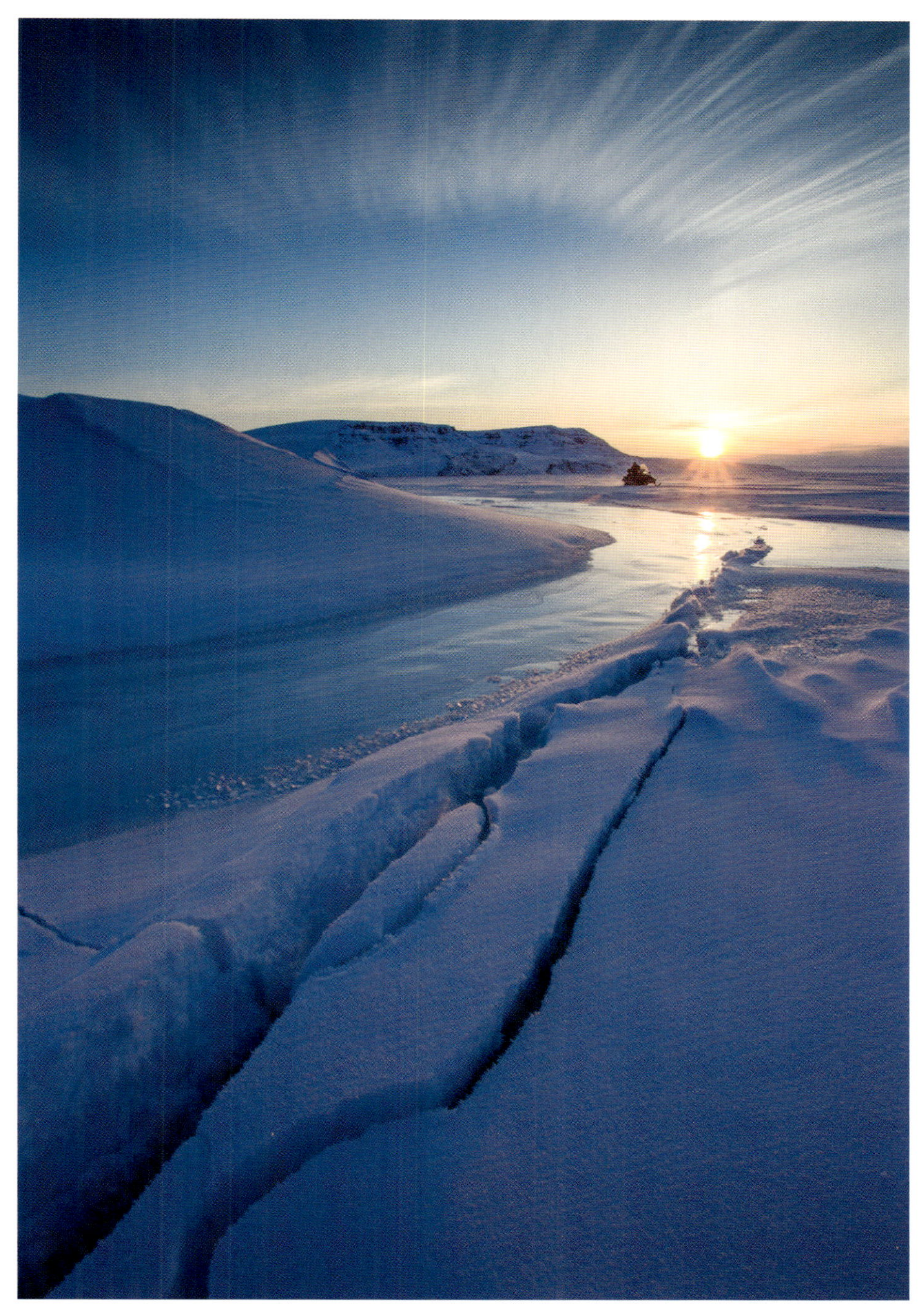

The Long Way Home
Victor Bay, Nunavut

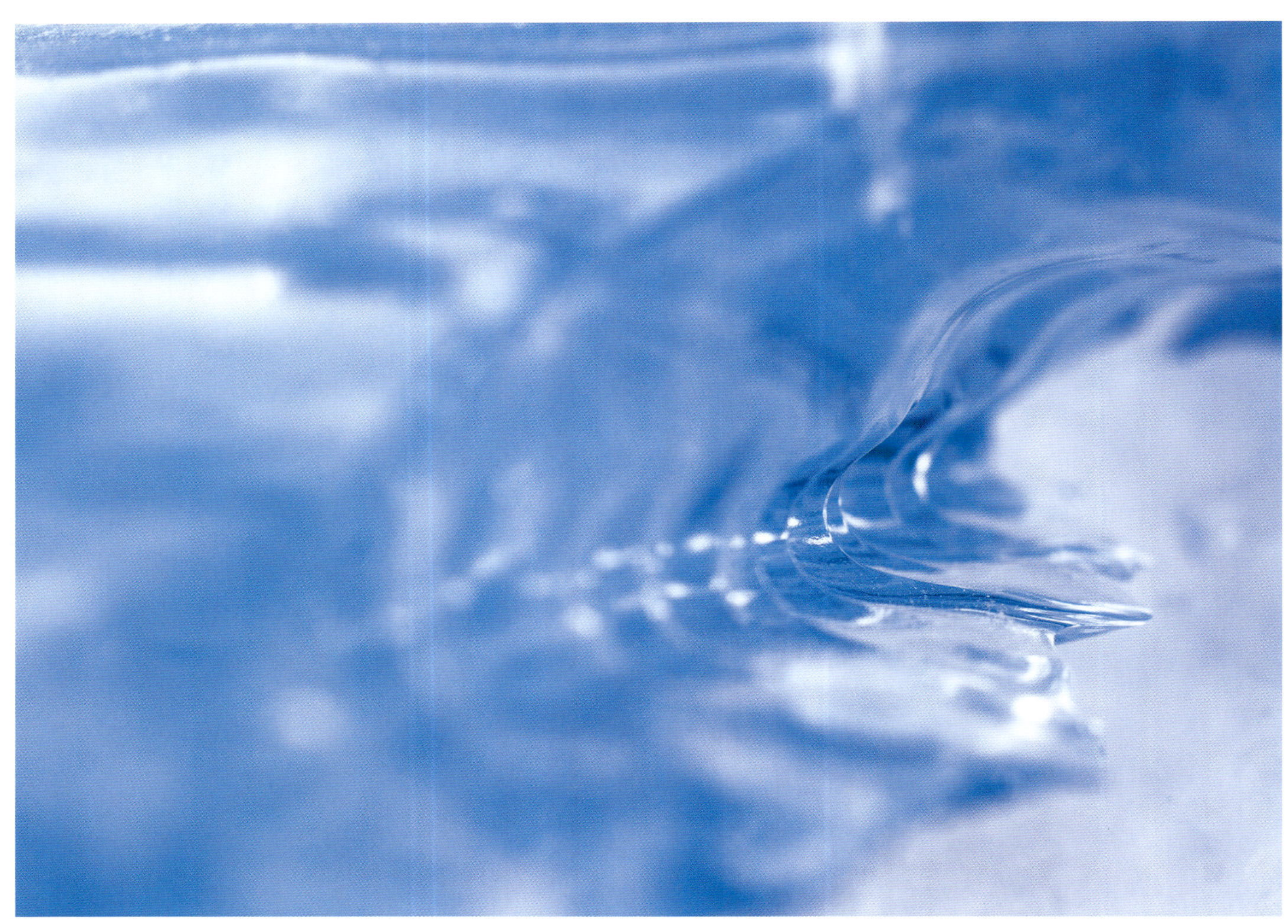

Ice Abstract
Clyde River, Nunavut

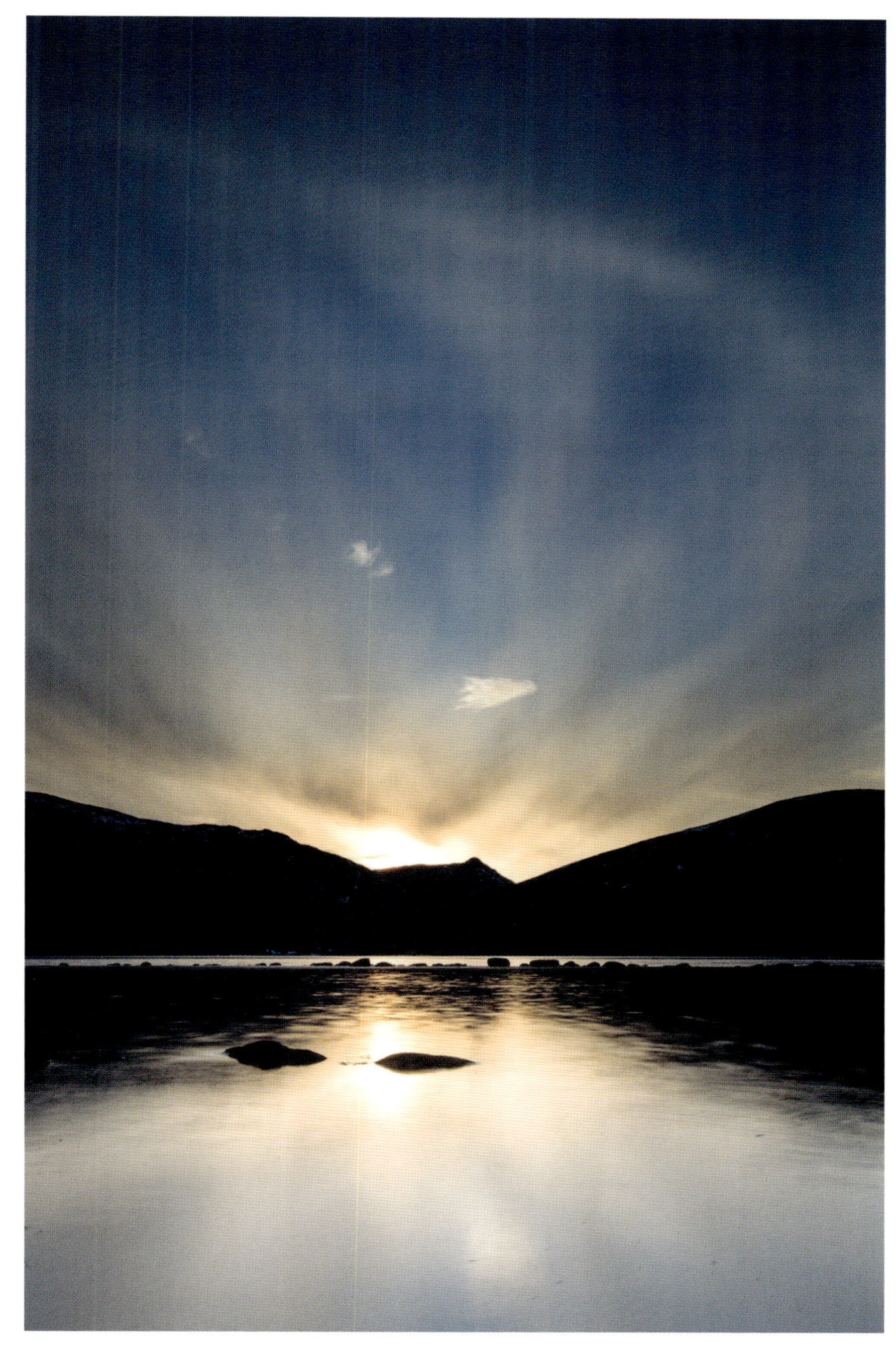

Nightfell
Pangnirtung, Nunavut

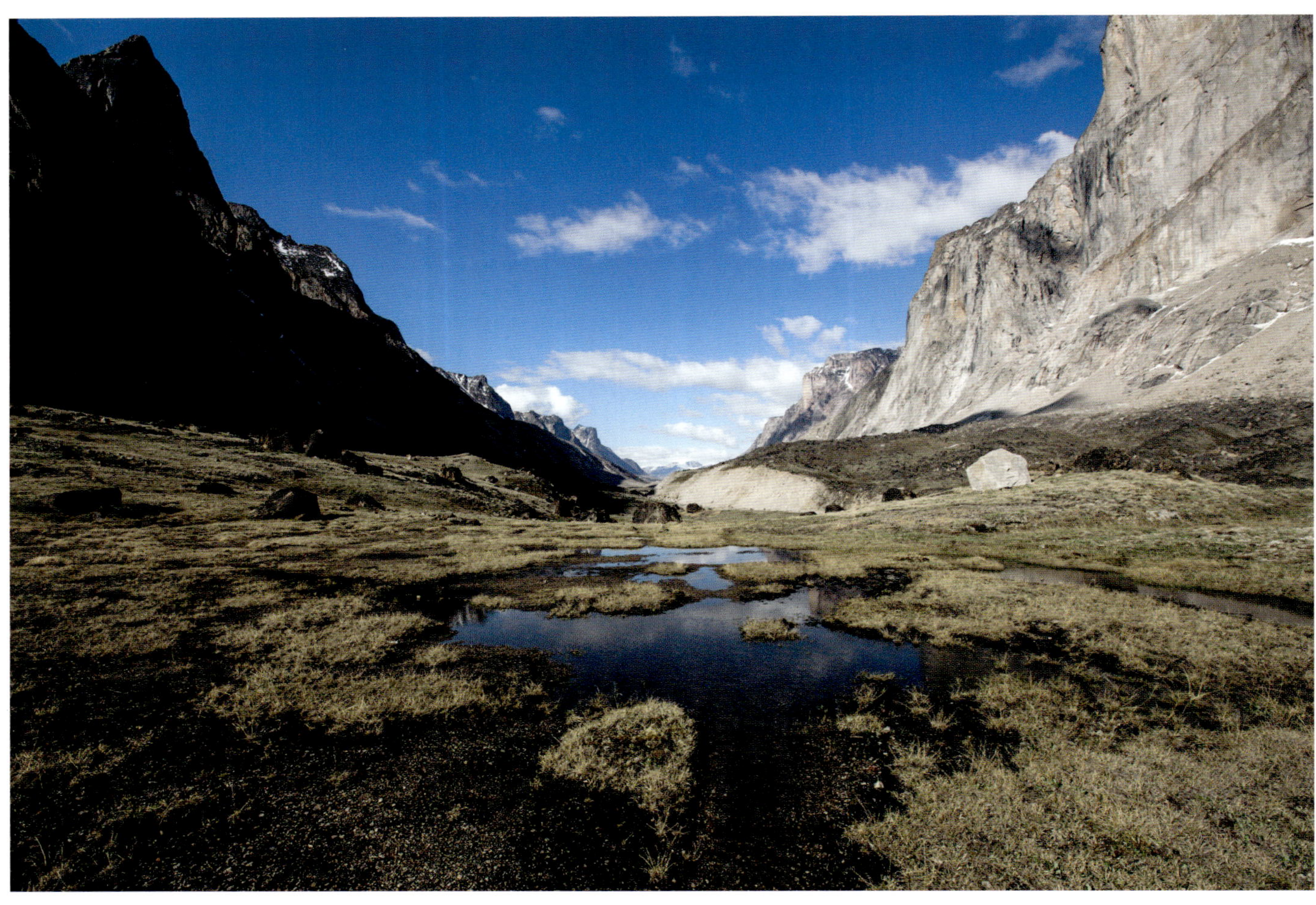

The Barren and the Beautiful

Auyuittuq National Park, Baffin Island, Nunavut

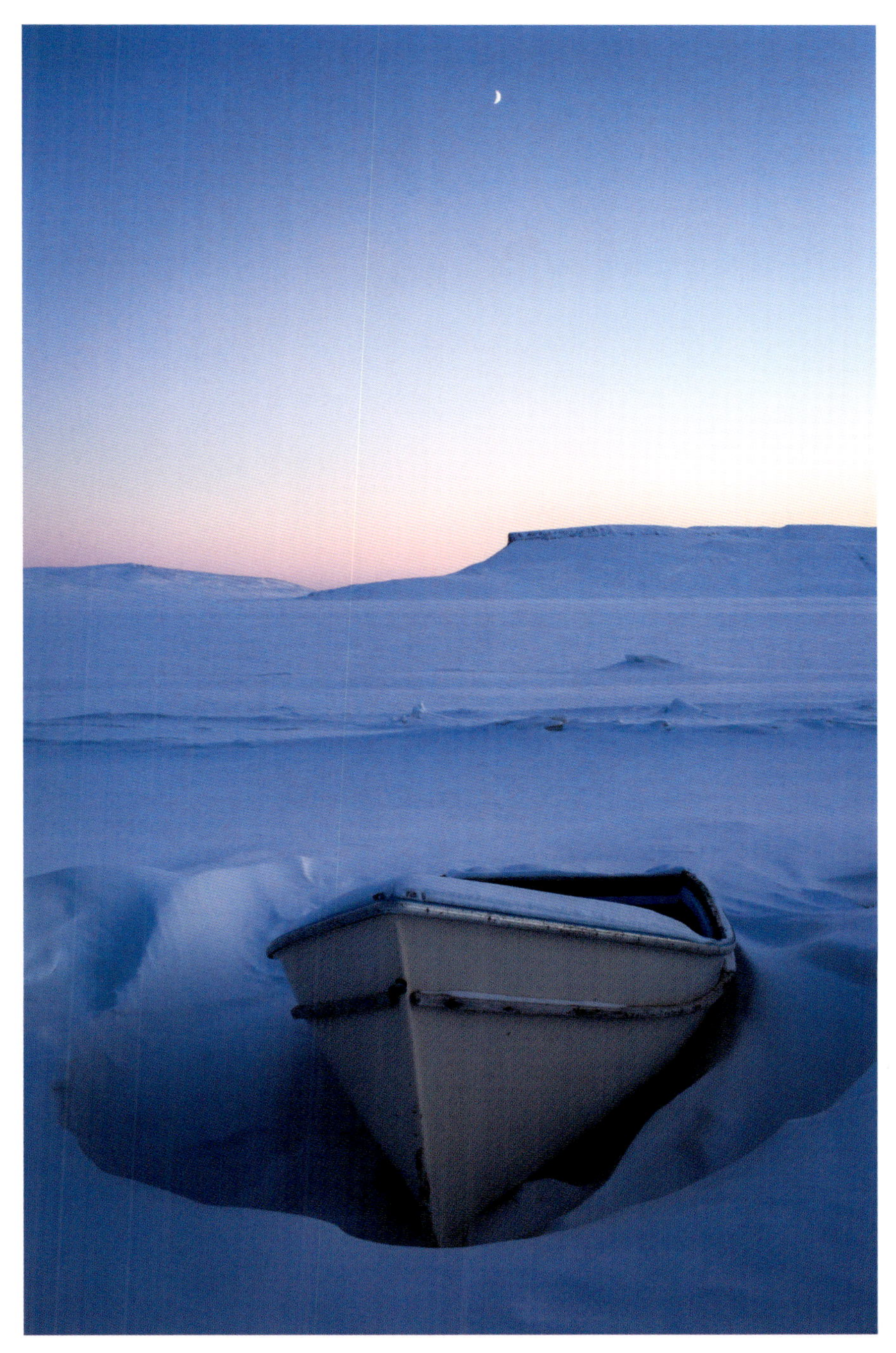

Silent Night
Arctic Bay, Nunavut

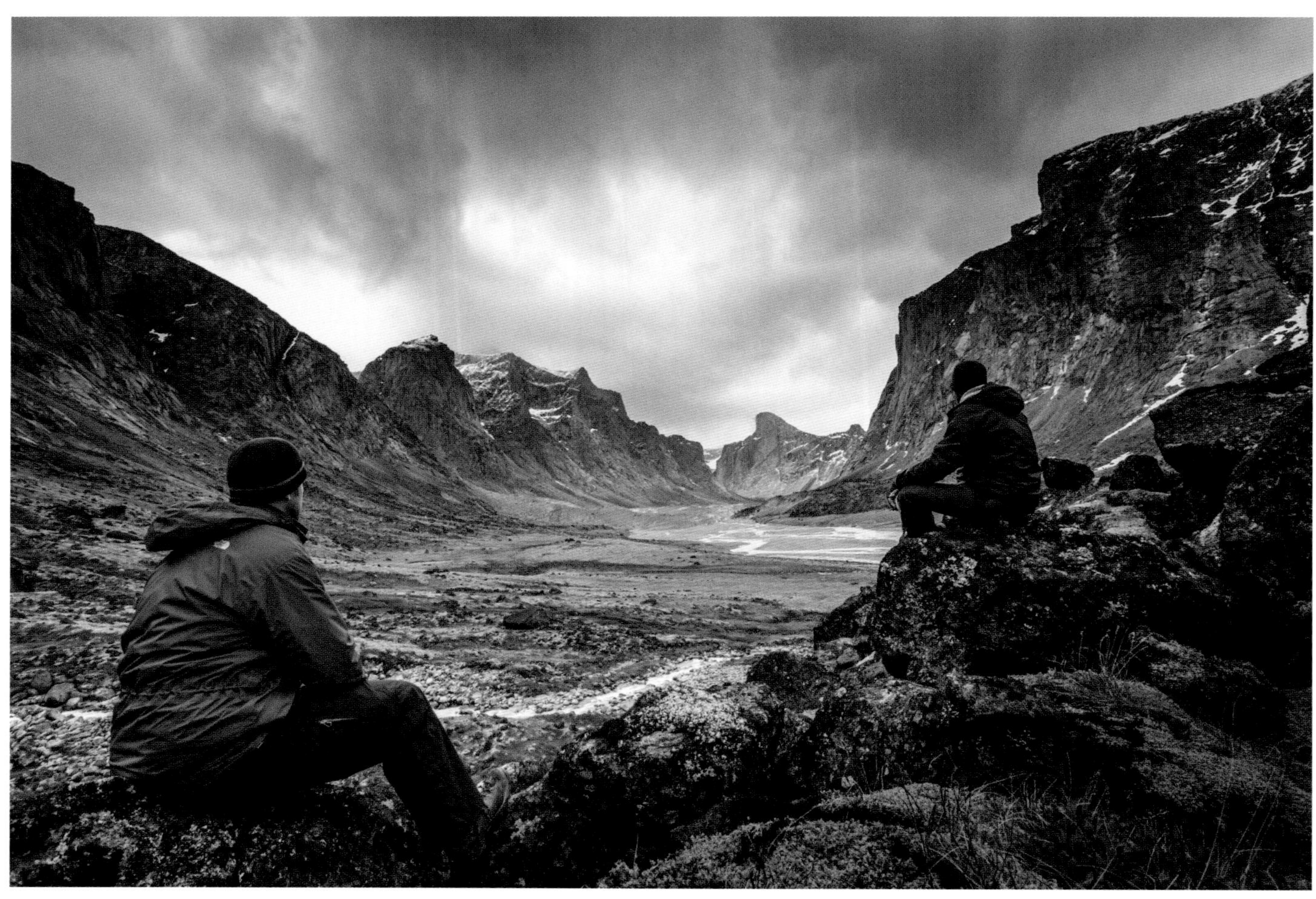

 Thor's Throne

Robbie Craig and Sam Shannon in Auyuittuq National Park, Baffin Island, Nunavut

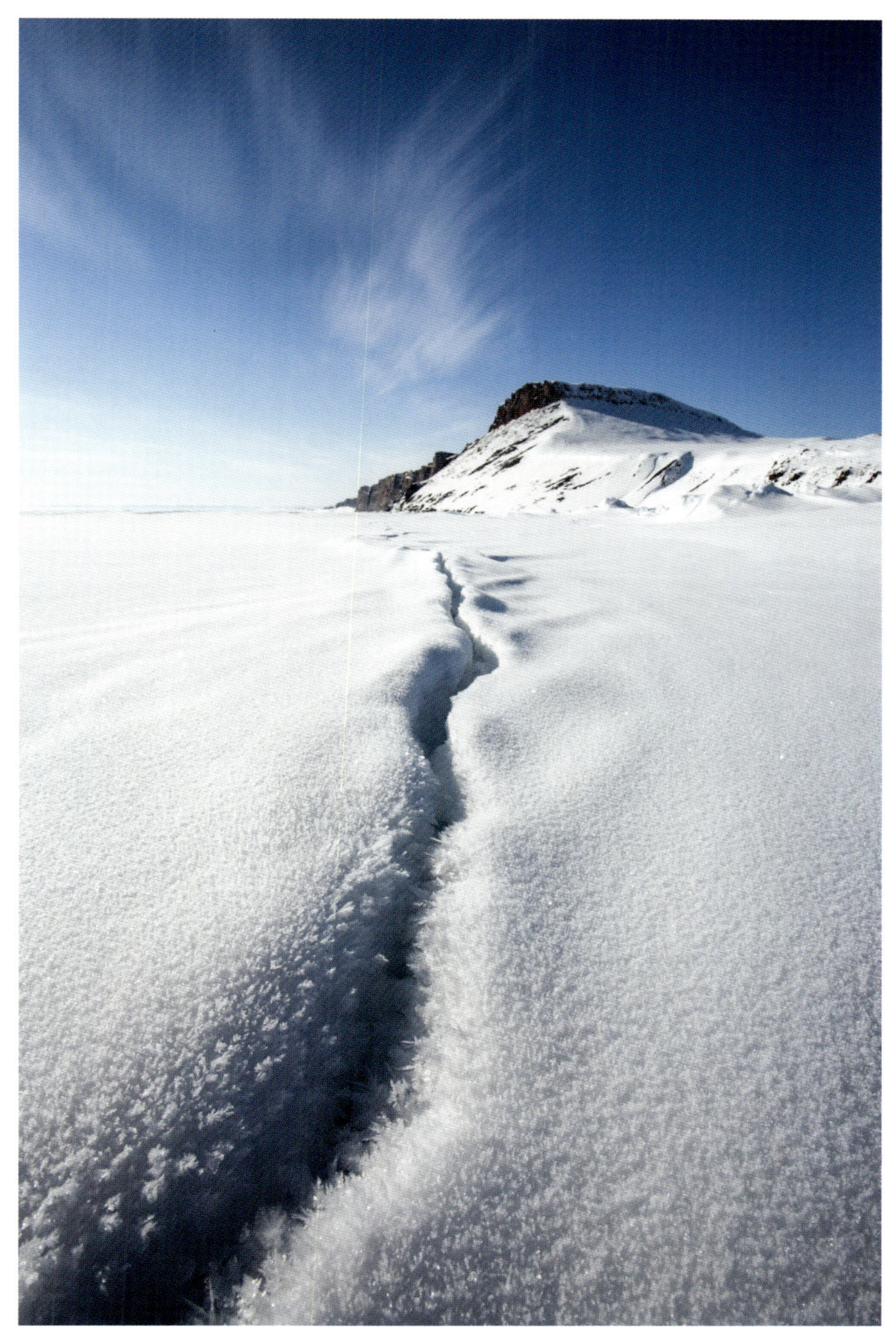

The Great Divide
Arctic Bay, Nunavut

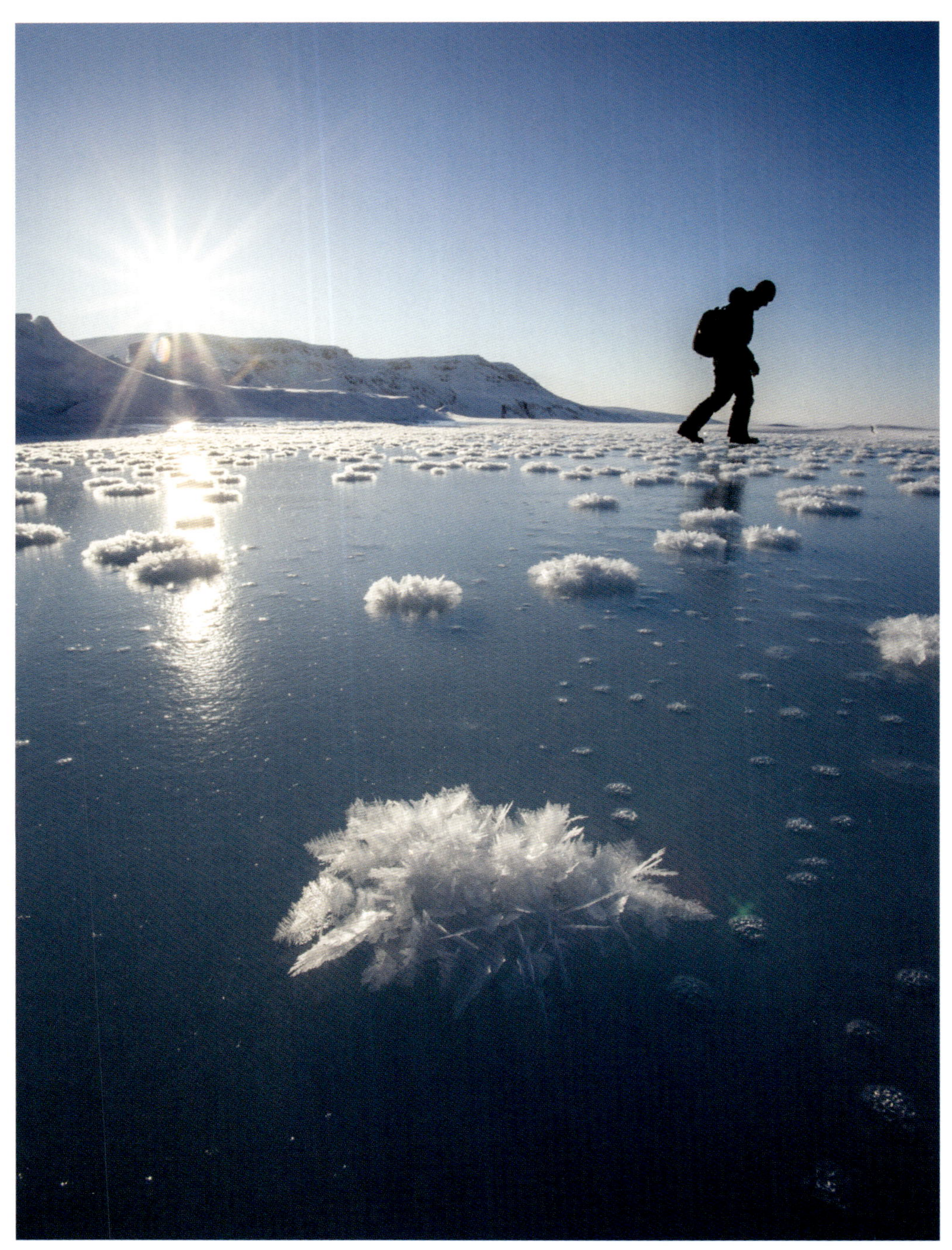

Trinity

Paul Zizka at Victor Bay, Nunavut

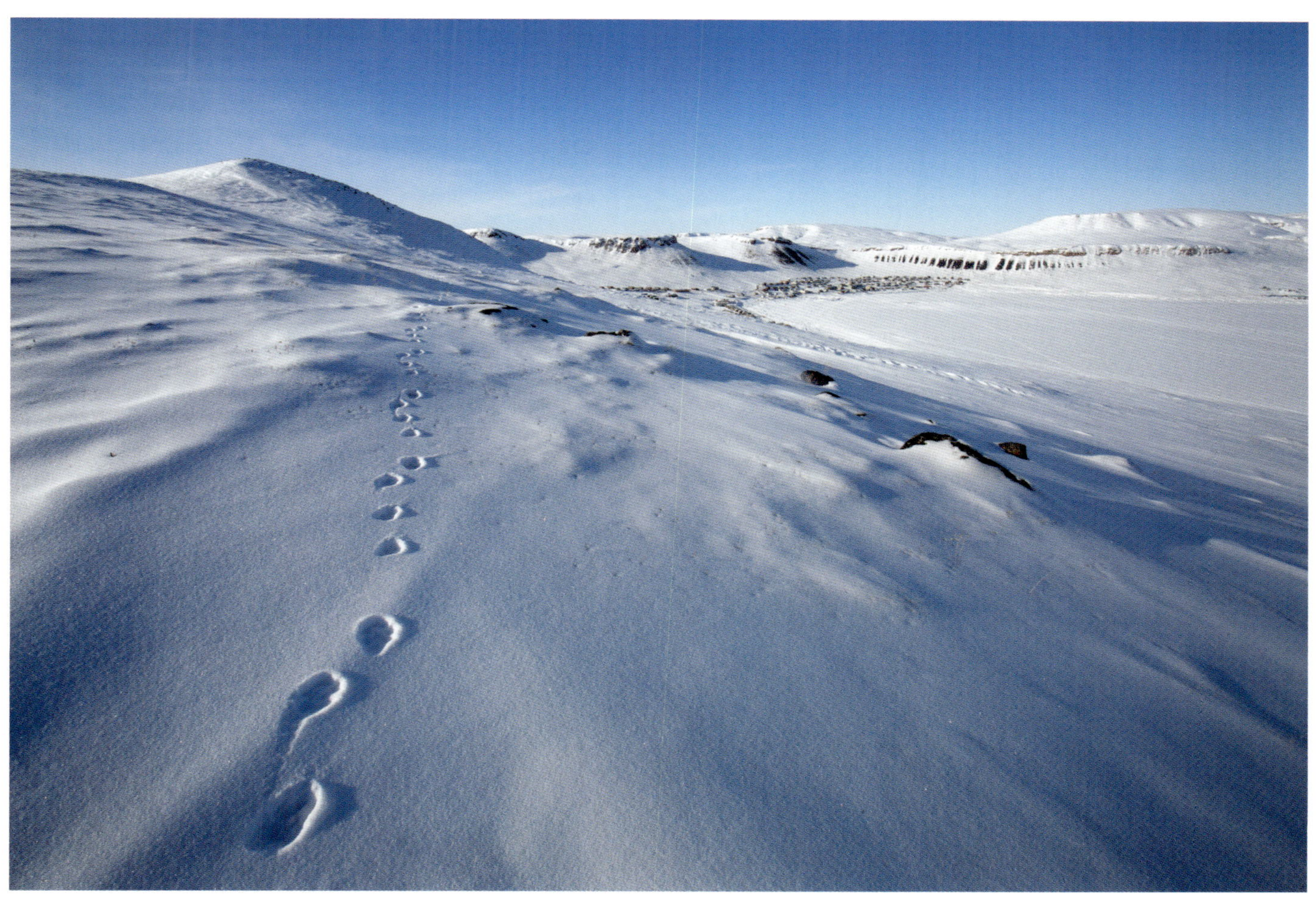

Heading Home
Arctic Bay, Nunavut

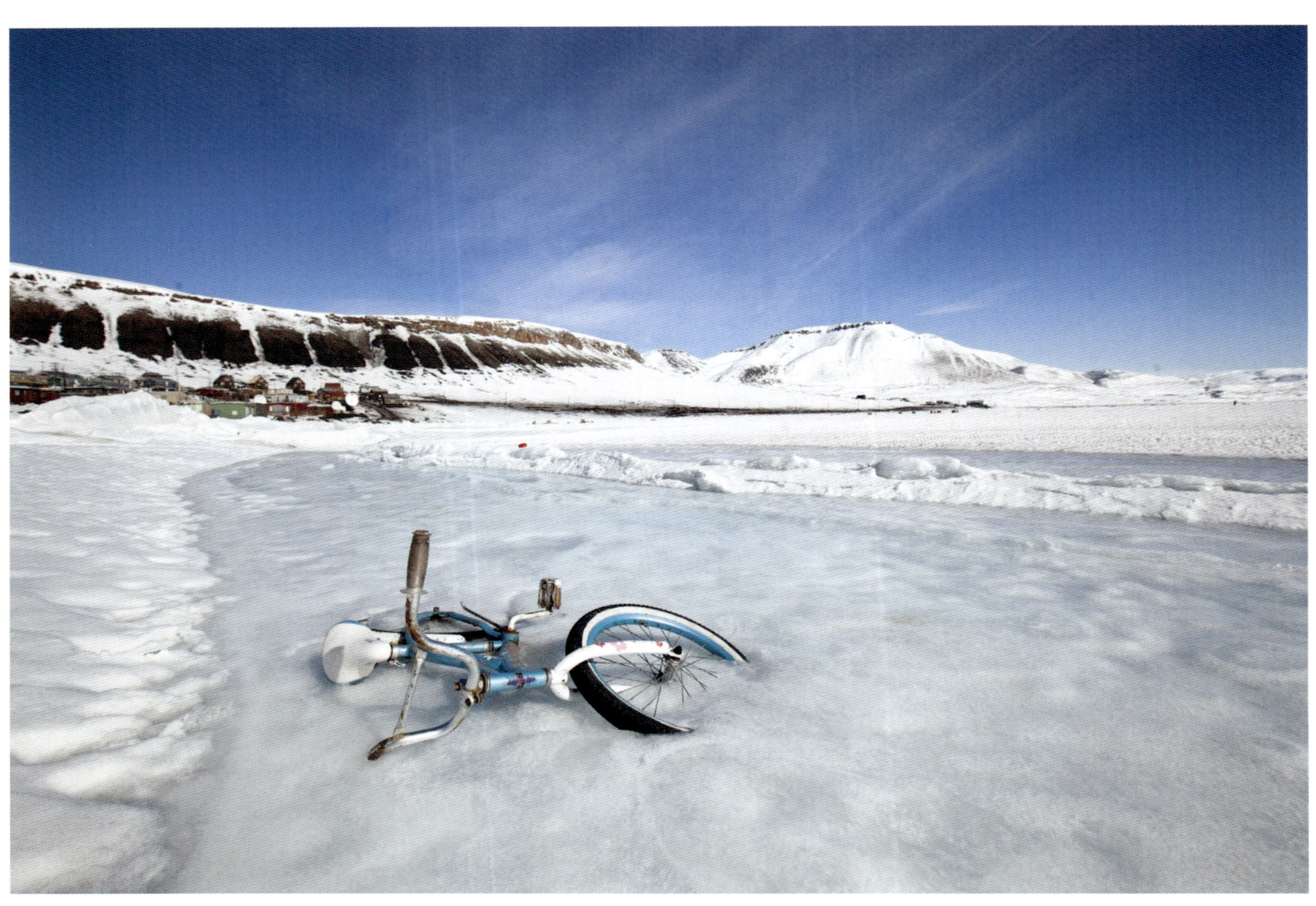

Frozen Dreams
Arctic Bay, Nunavut

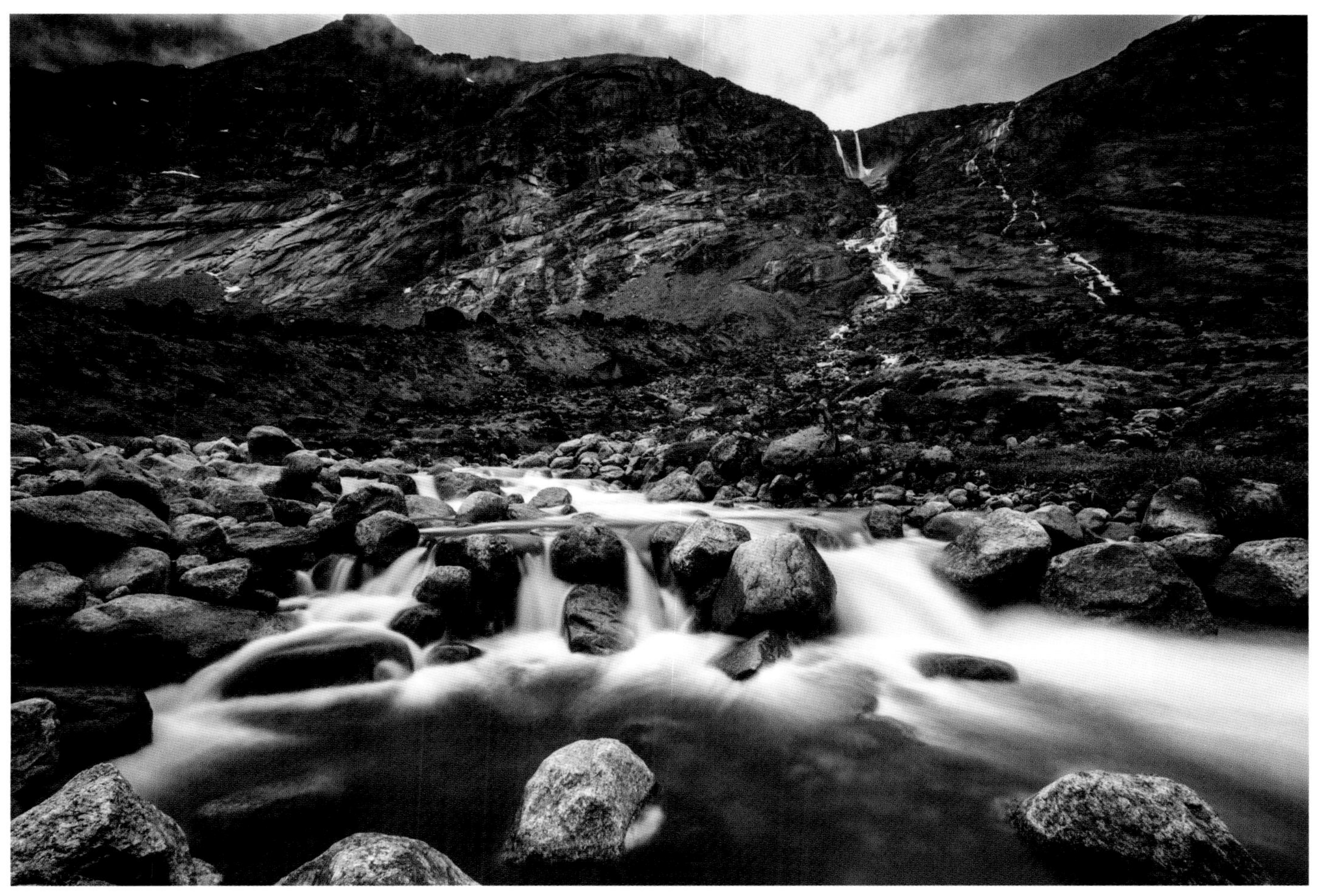

All Fall Down
Auyuittuq National Park, Baffin Island, Nunavut

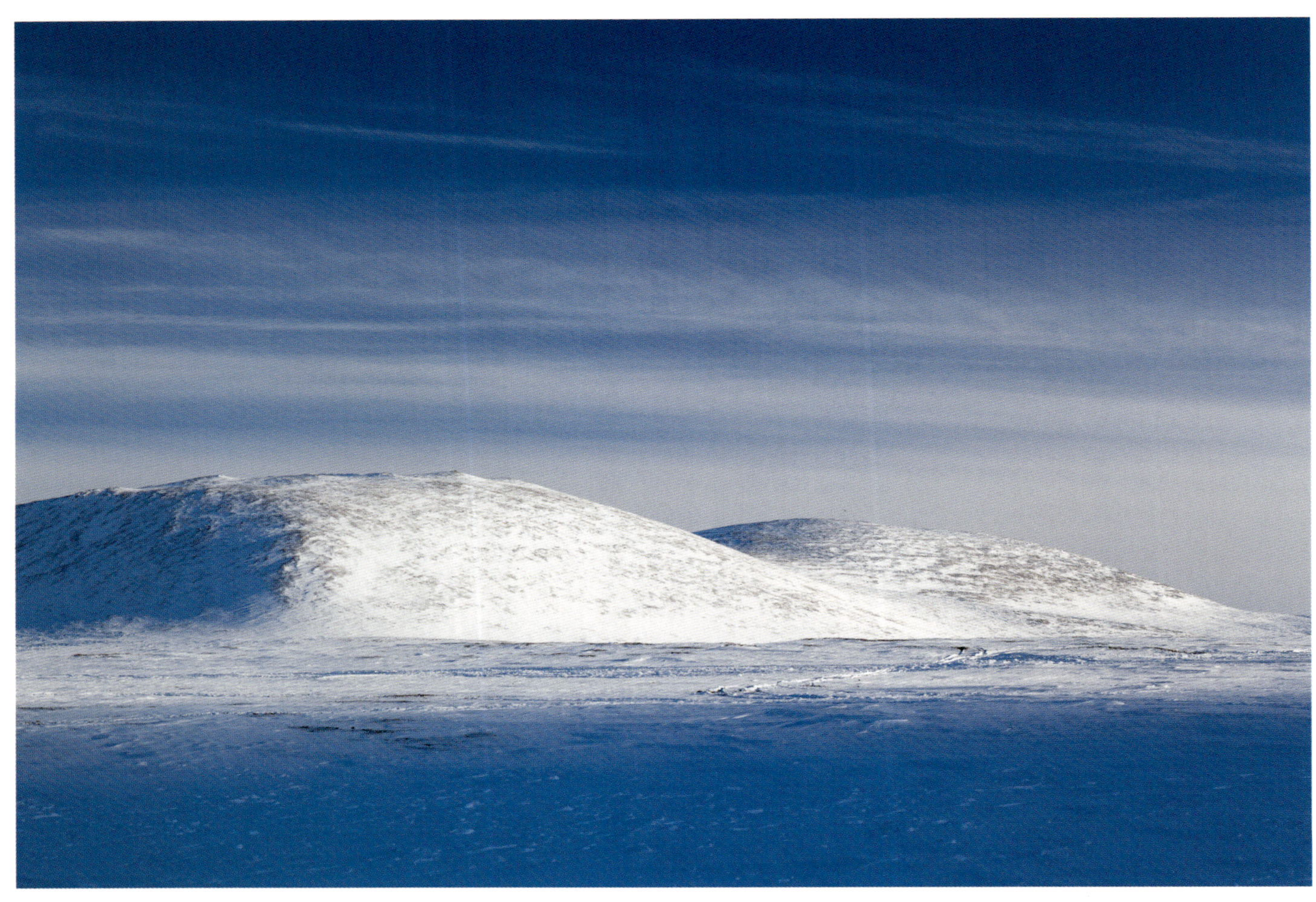

Ellesmere Calm
Ellesmere Island, Nunavut

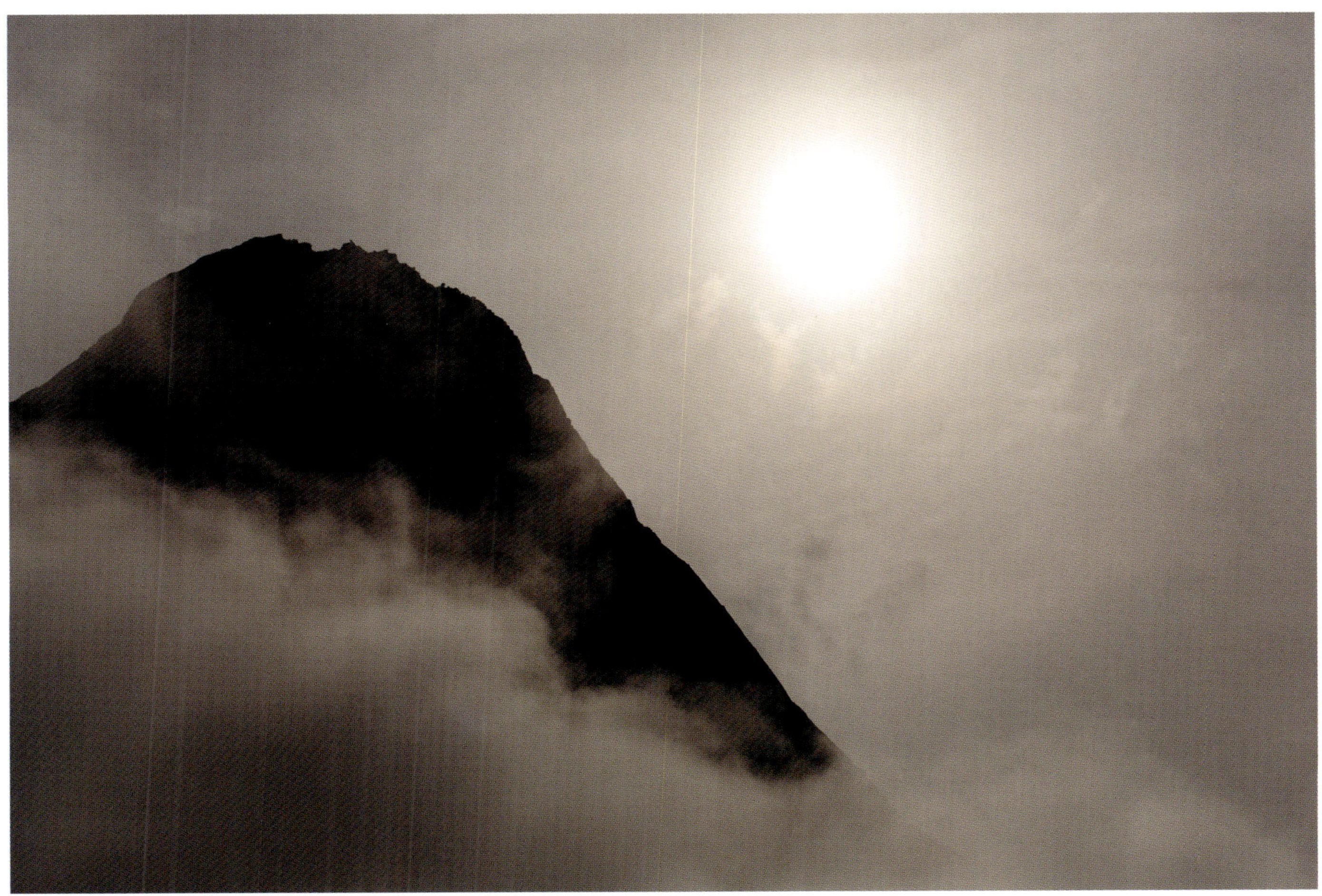

Elemental
Auyuittuq National Park, Baffin Island, Nunavut

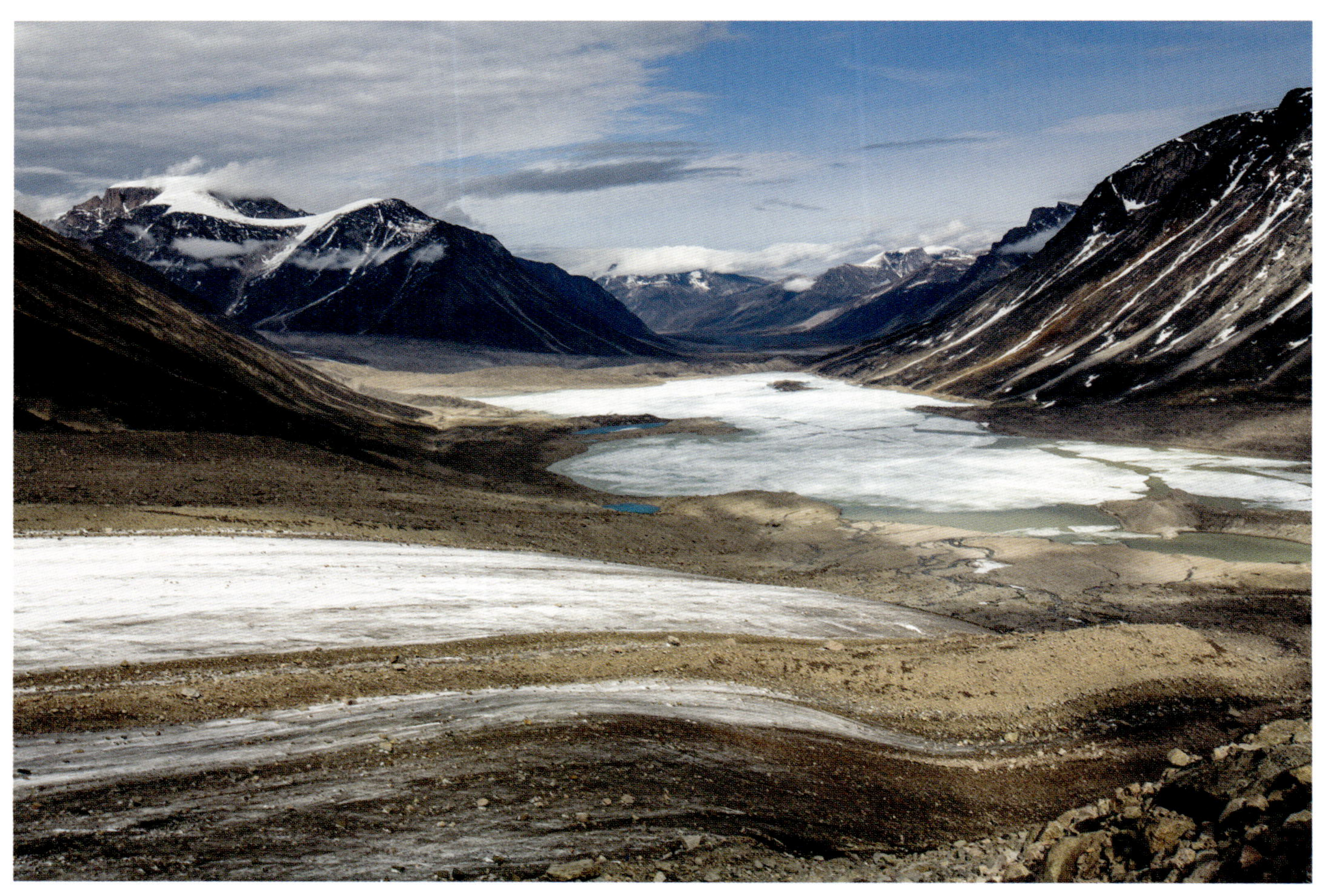

Turner Glacier

Auyuittuq National Park, Baffin Island, Nunavut

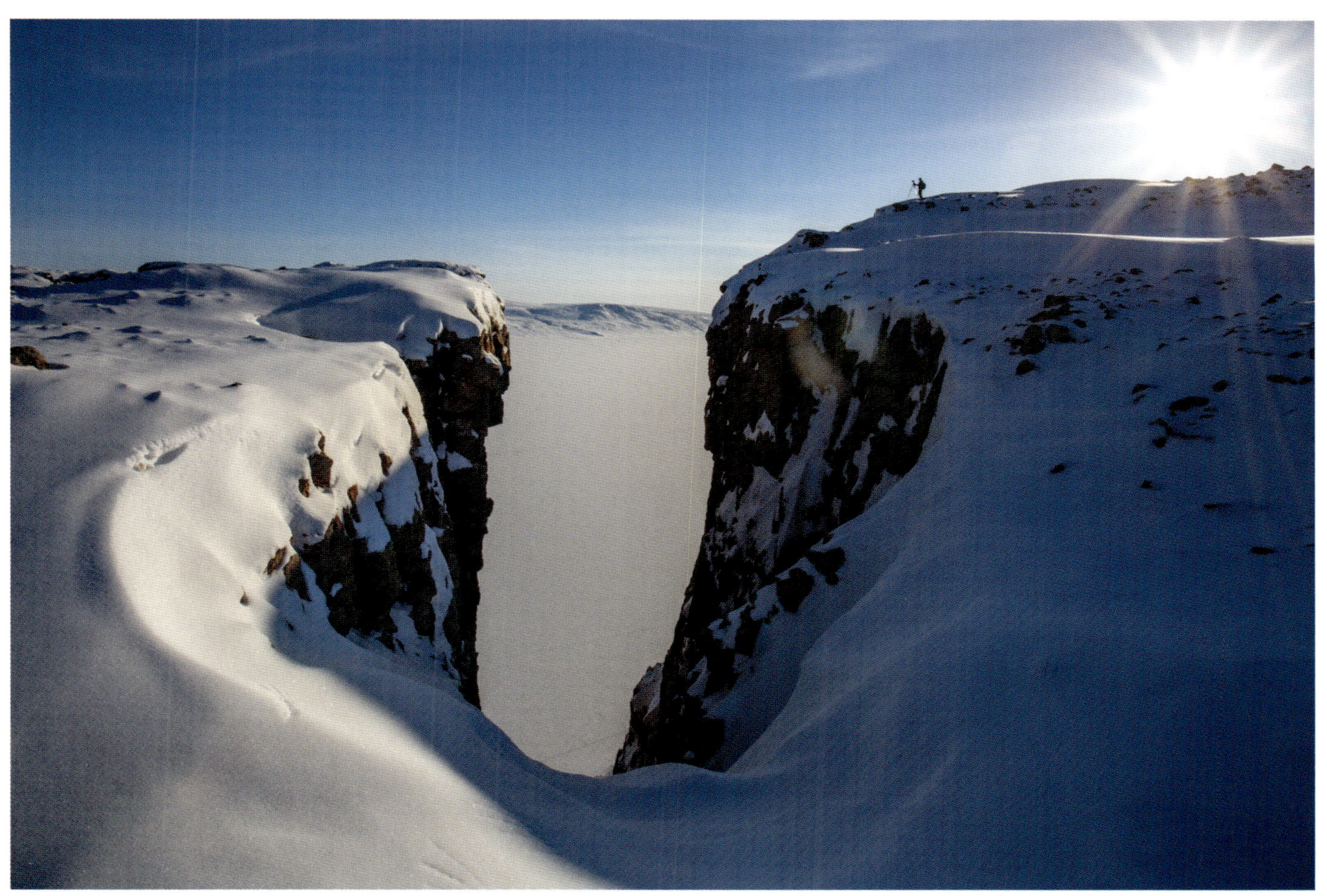

St. Georges Society Cliffs
Arctic Bay, Nunavut

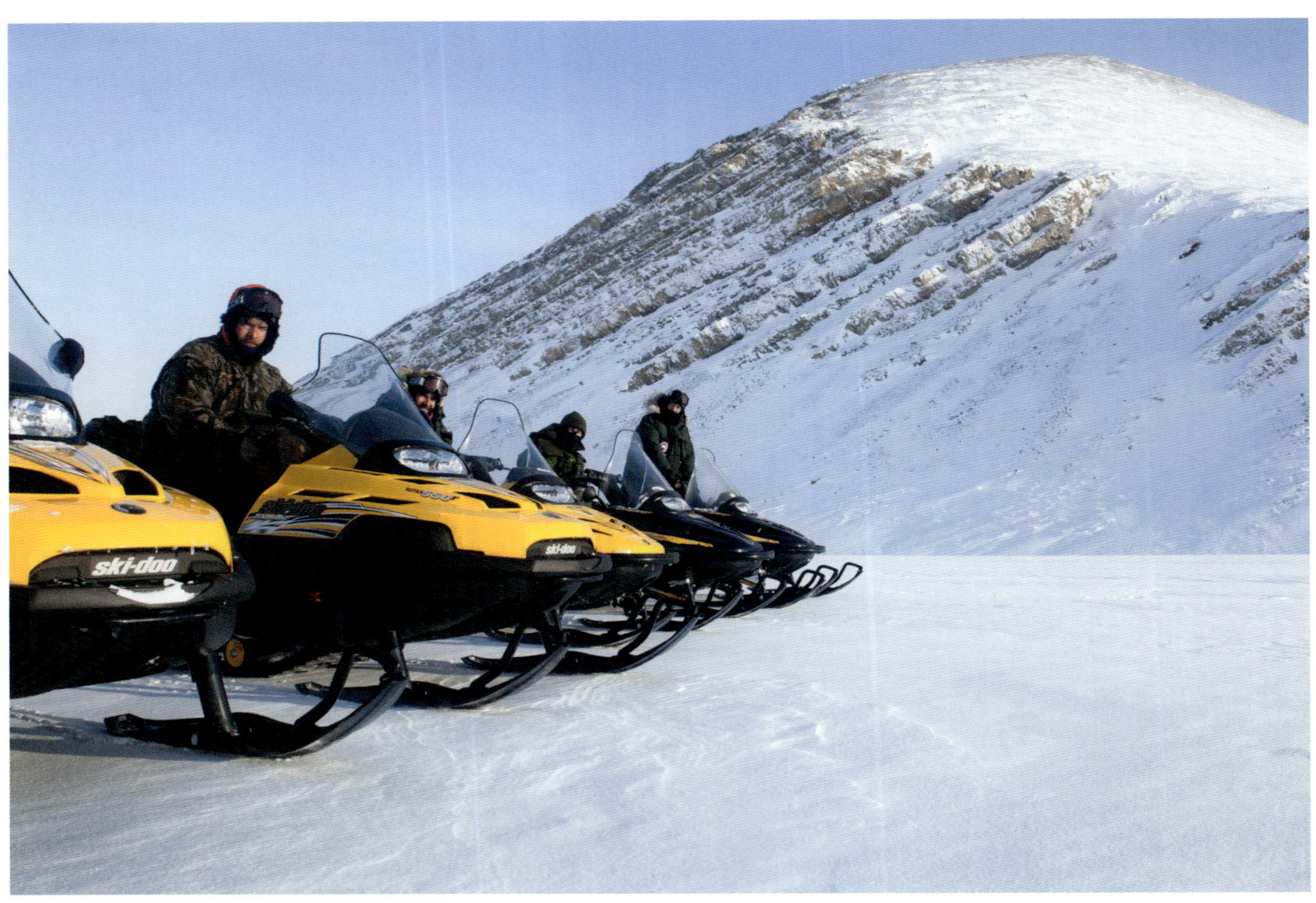

The Parkway
Ward Hunt Island, Nunavut

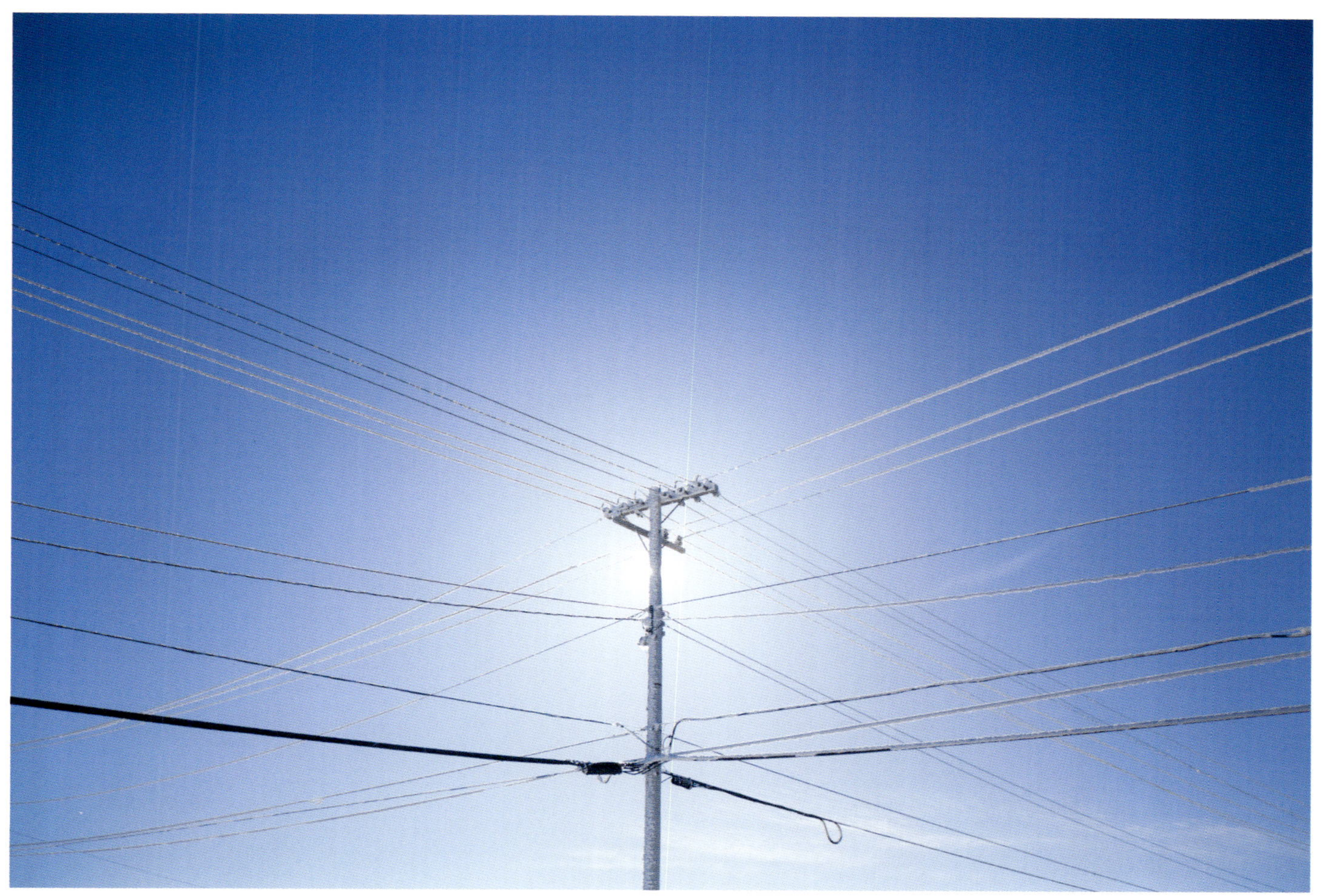

Connected
Rankin Inlet, Nunavut

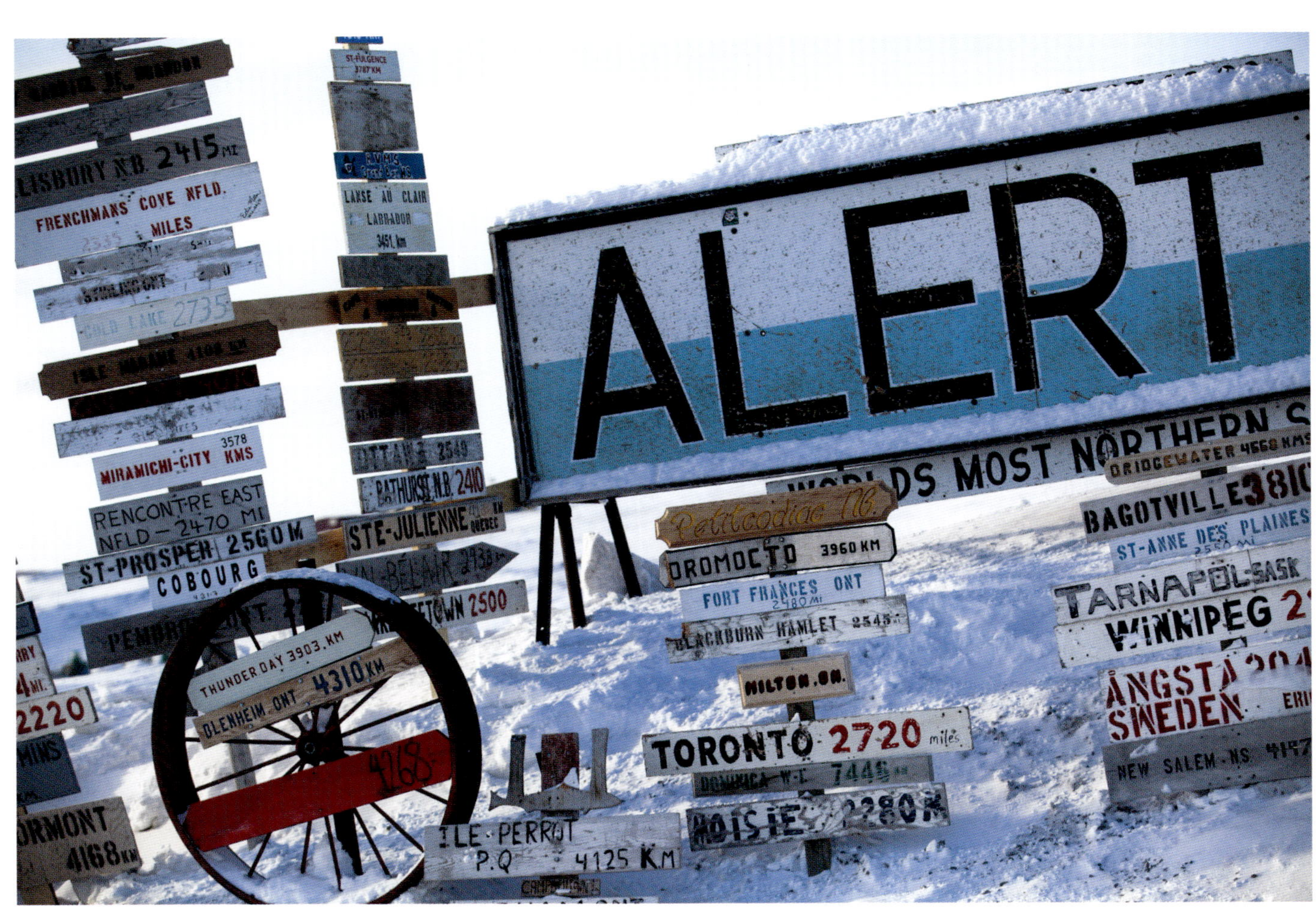

 Alert Welcome

Alert, Nunavut

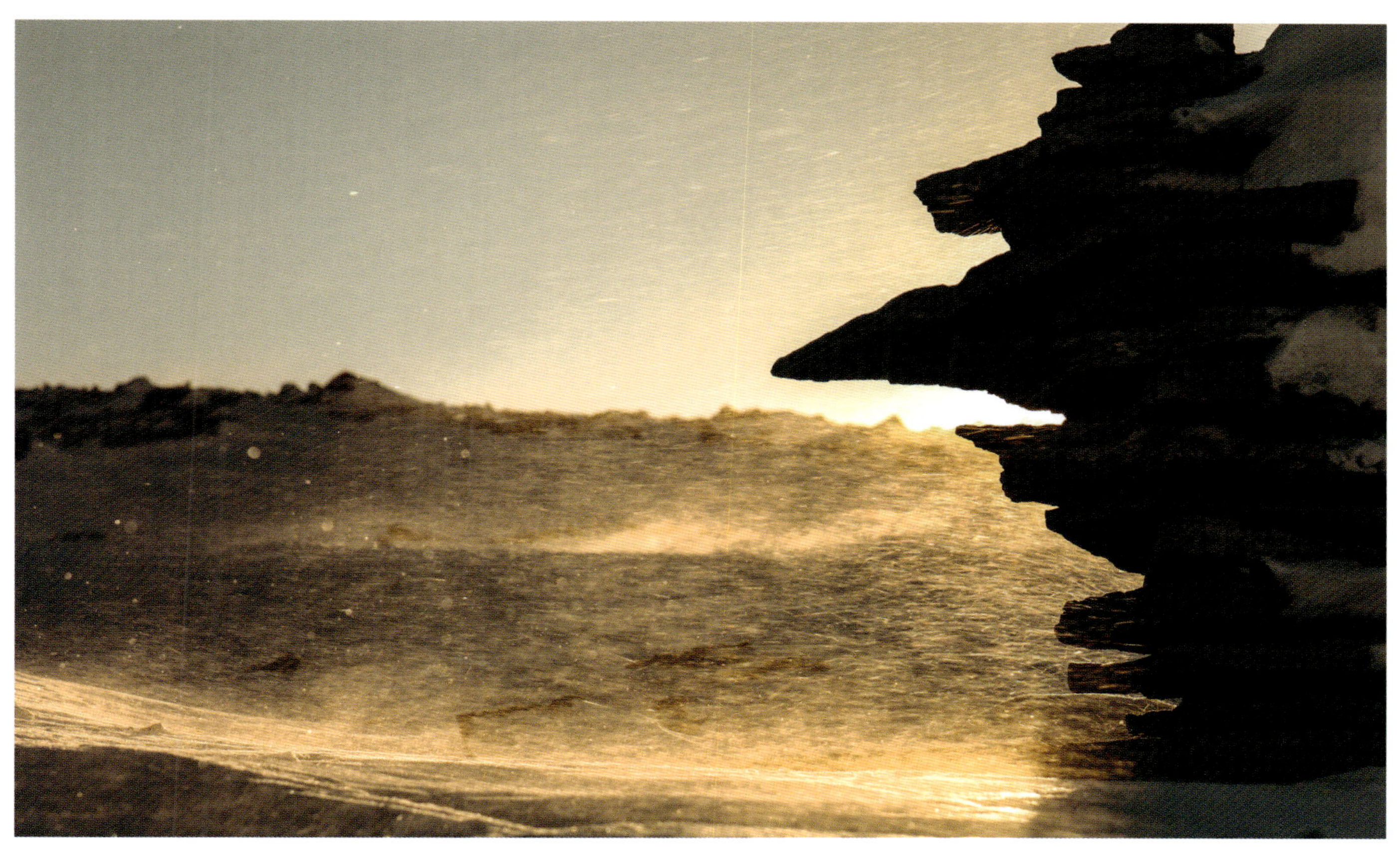

Arctic Winds
Resolute Bay, Nunavut

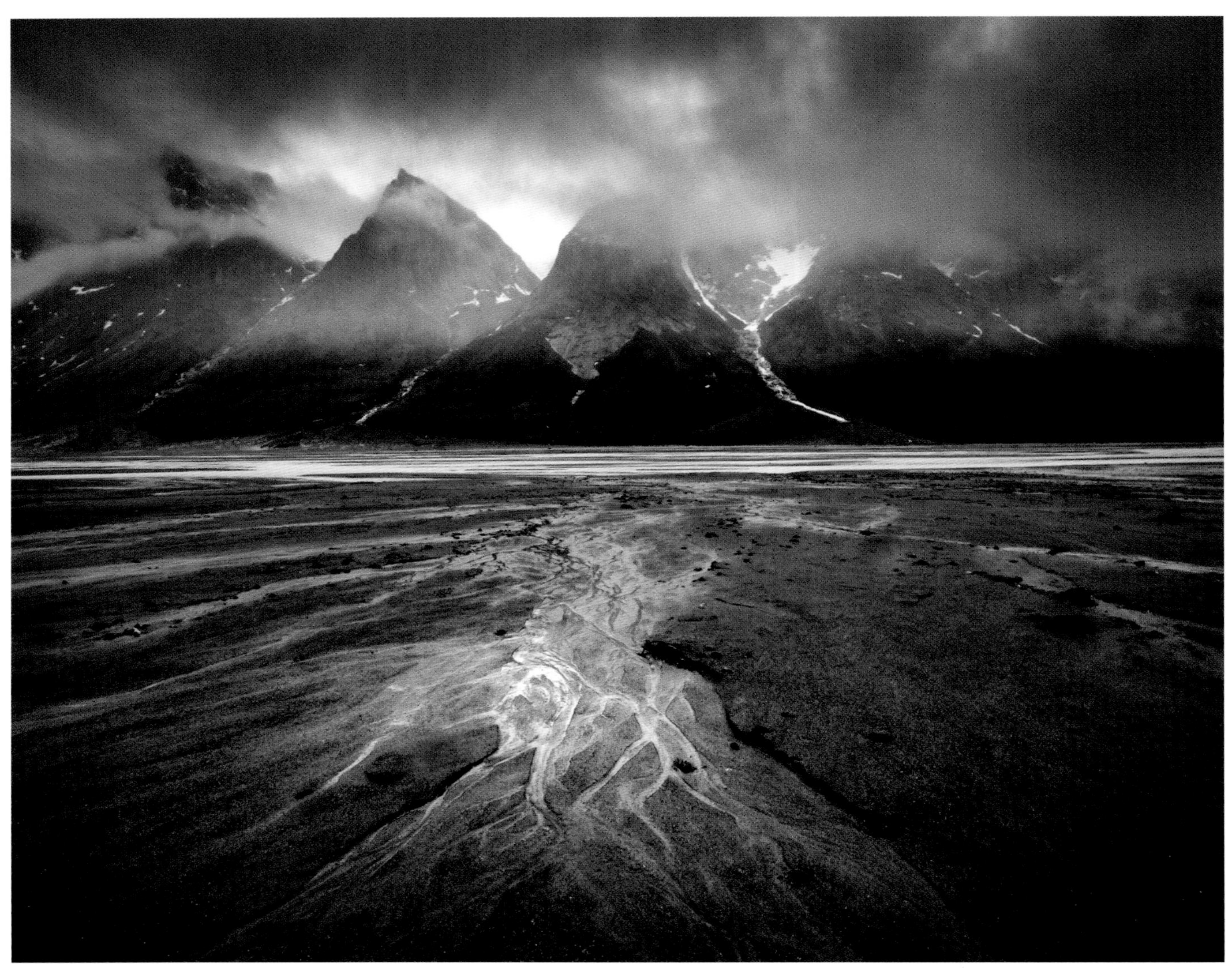

It Was All a Dream

Auyuittuq National Park, Baffin Island, Nunavut

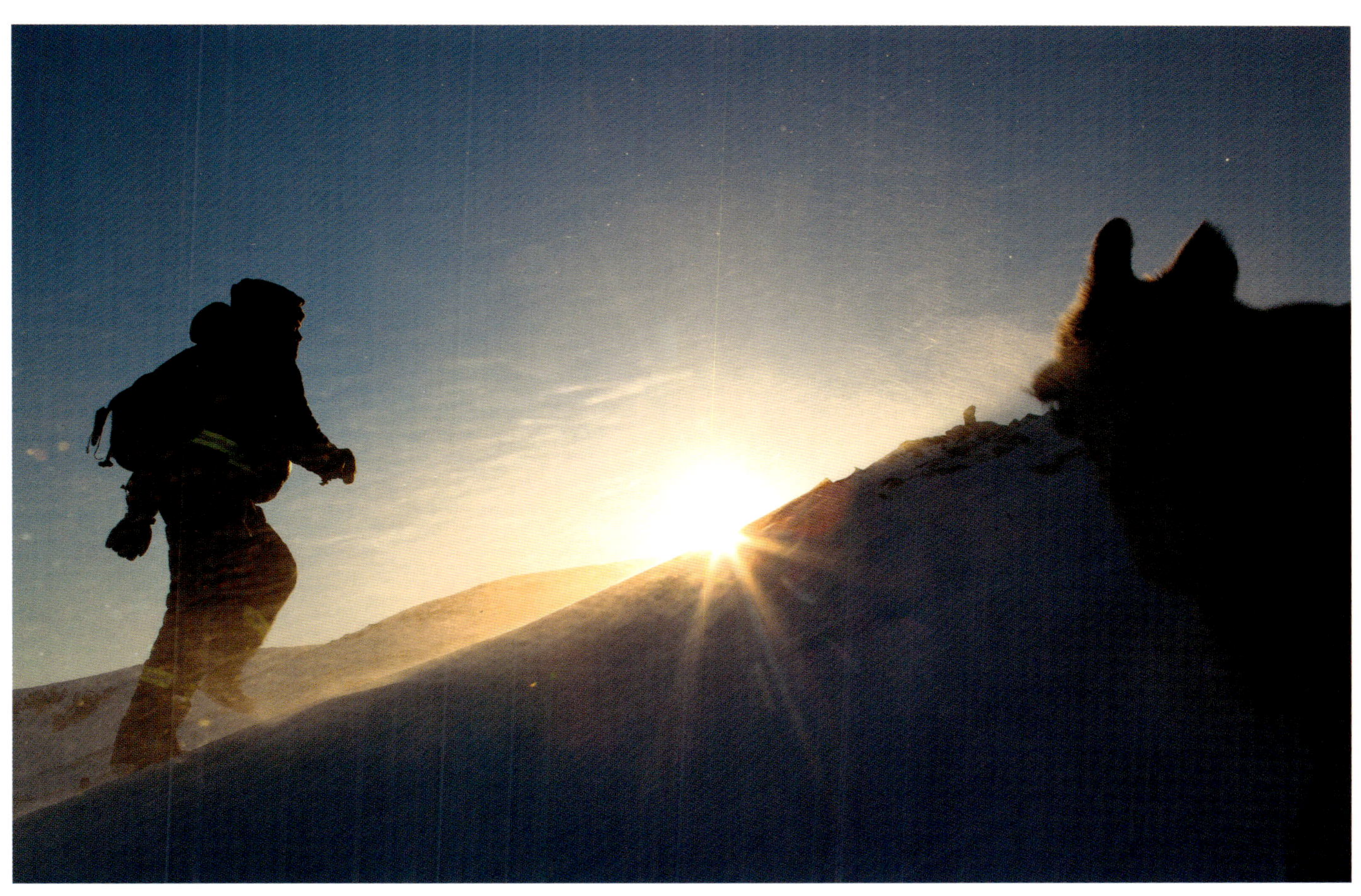

Keep Calm and Carry On

Self-Portrait in Resolute Bay, Nunavut

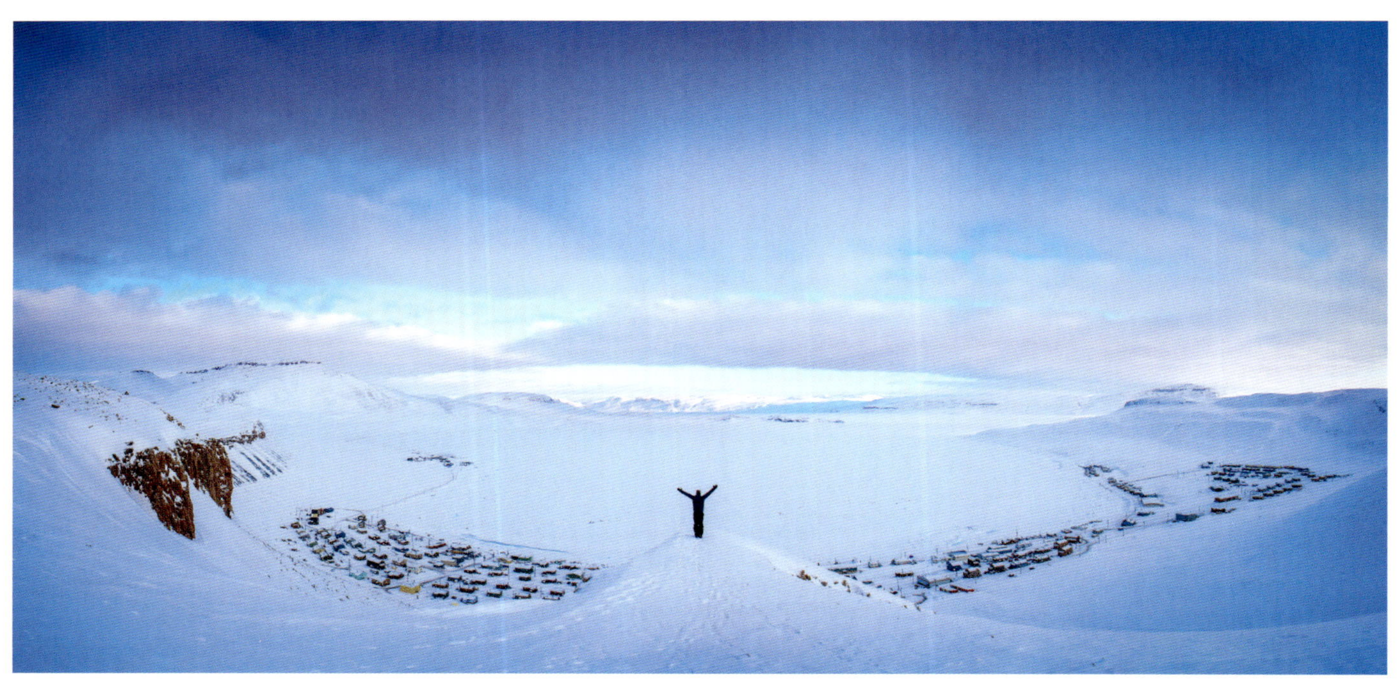

 The Wings That Let You Soar
Paul Zizka at Arctic Bay, Nunavut

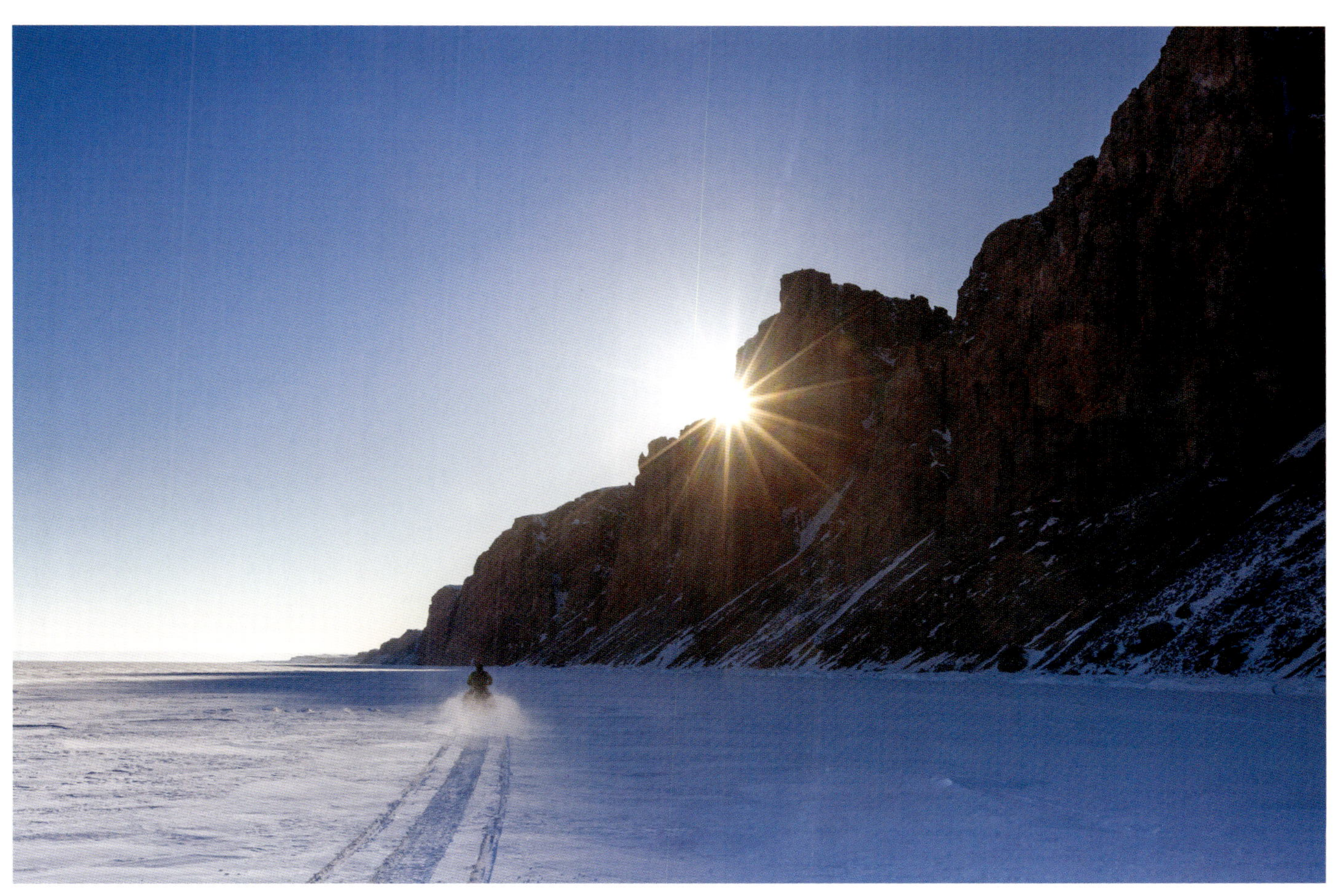

The Cliffs
Arctic Bay, Nunavut

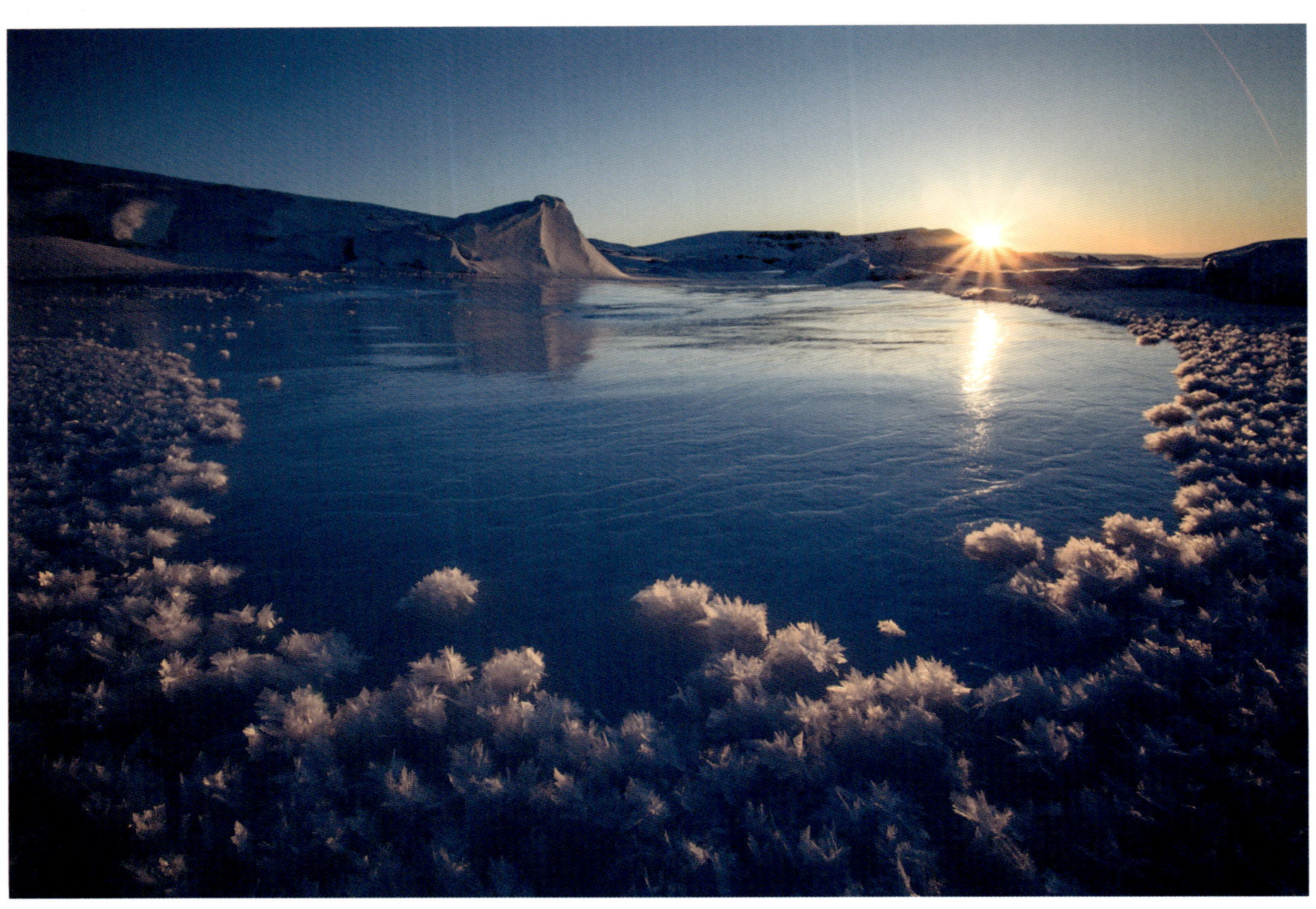

The Frost Flowers of Victor Bay

Victor Bay, Nunavut

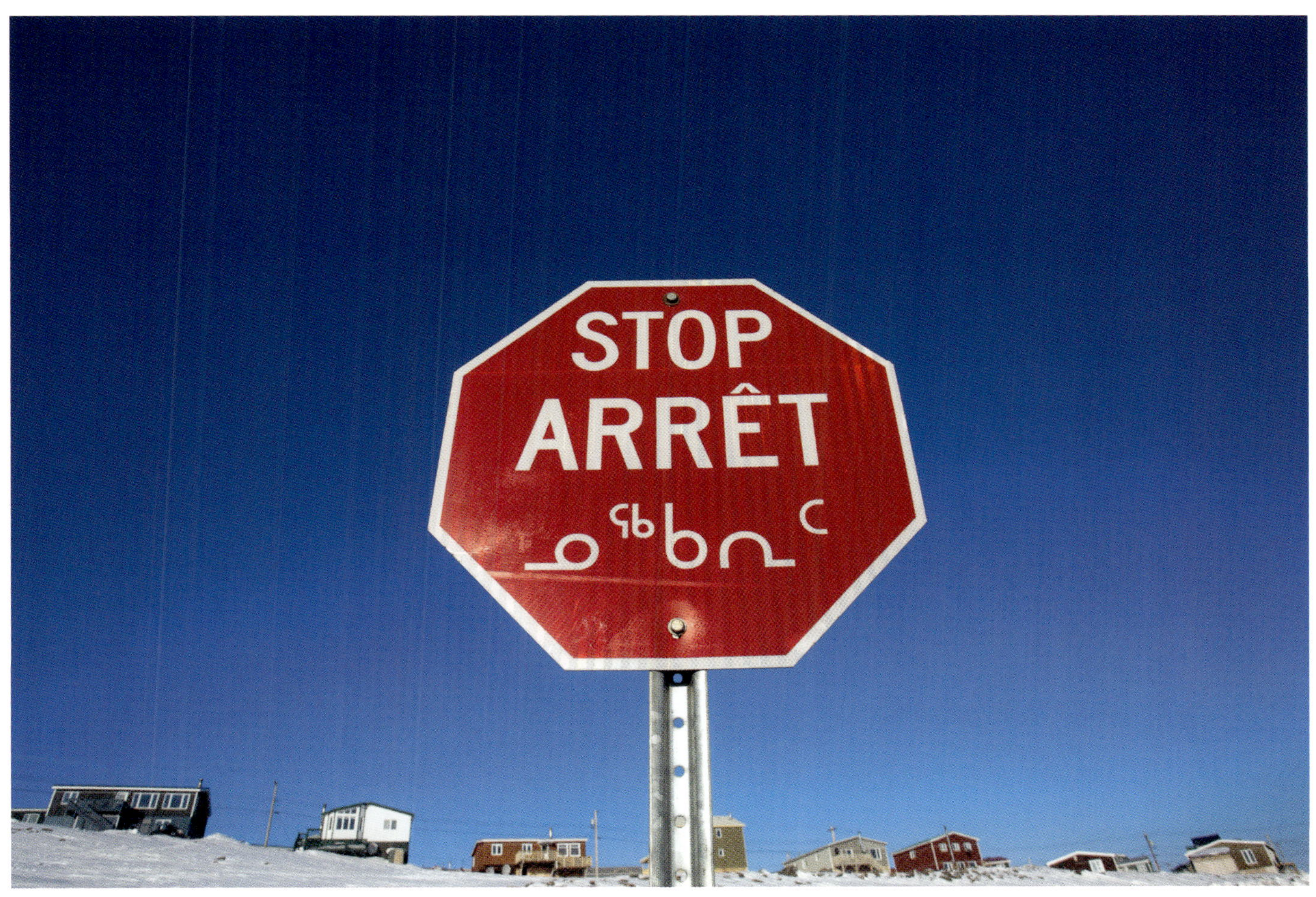

I Saw the Sign
Iqaluit, Nunavut

Behind the Scenes

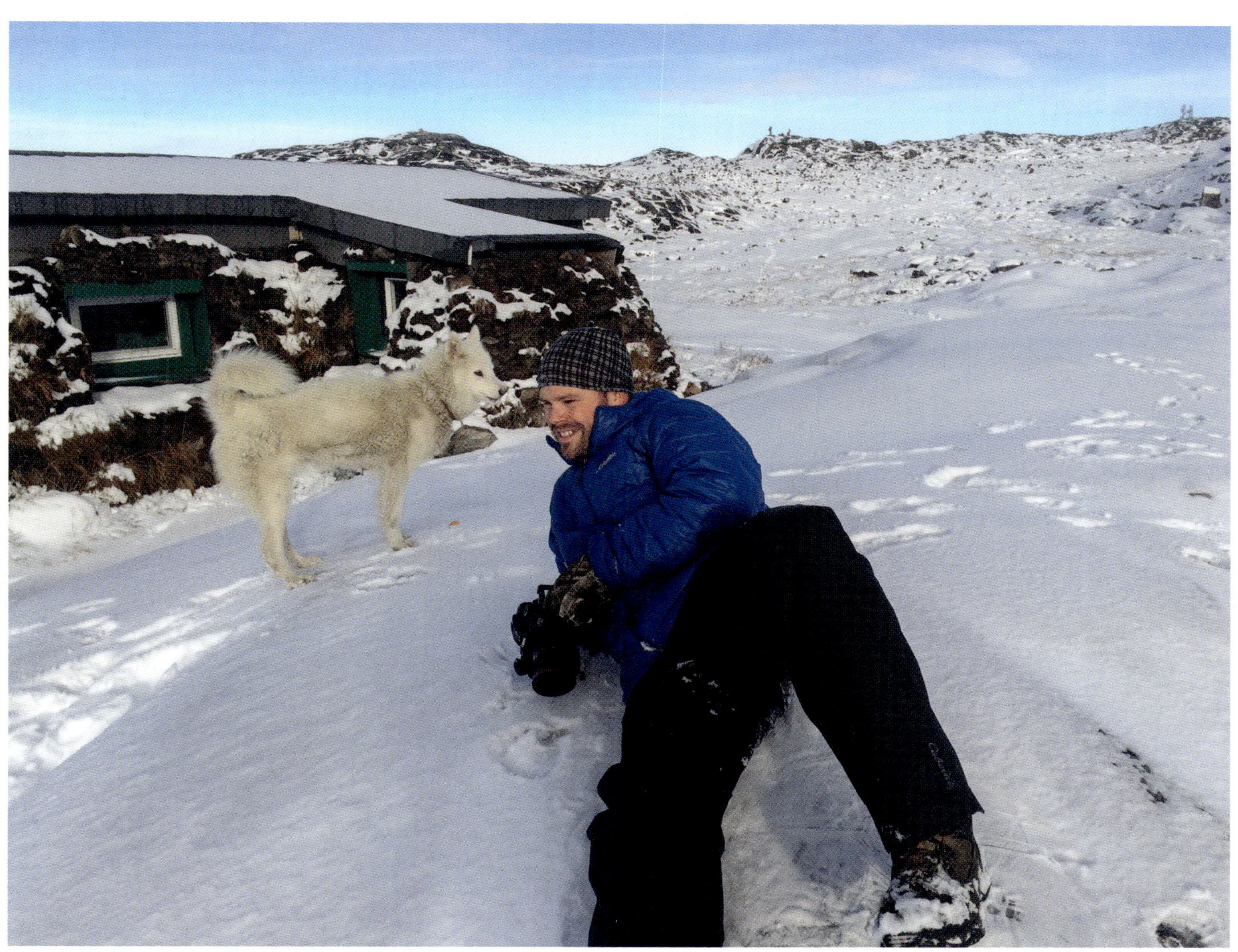

Ilulissat, Greenland
Photograph by: Stephen DesRoches

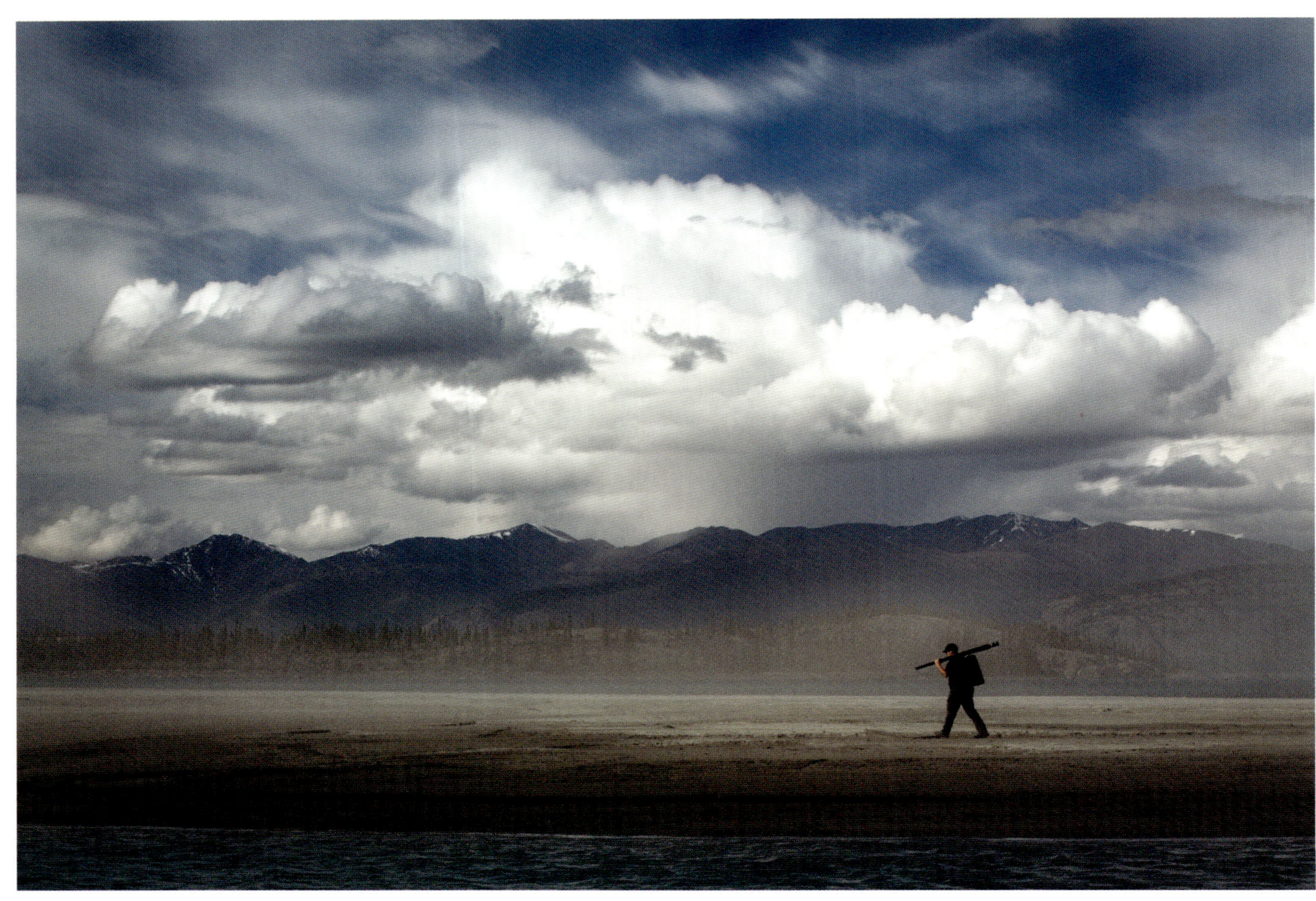

Kluane National Park, Yukon
Photograph by: Paul Zizka

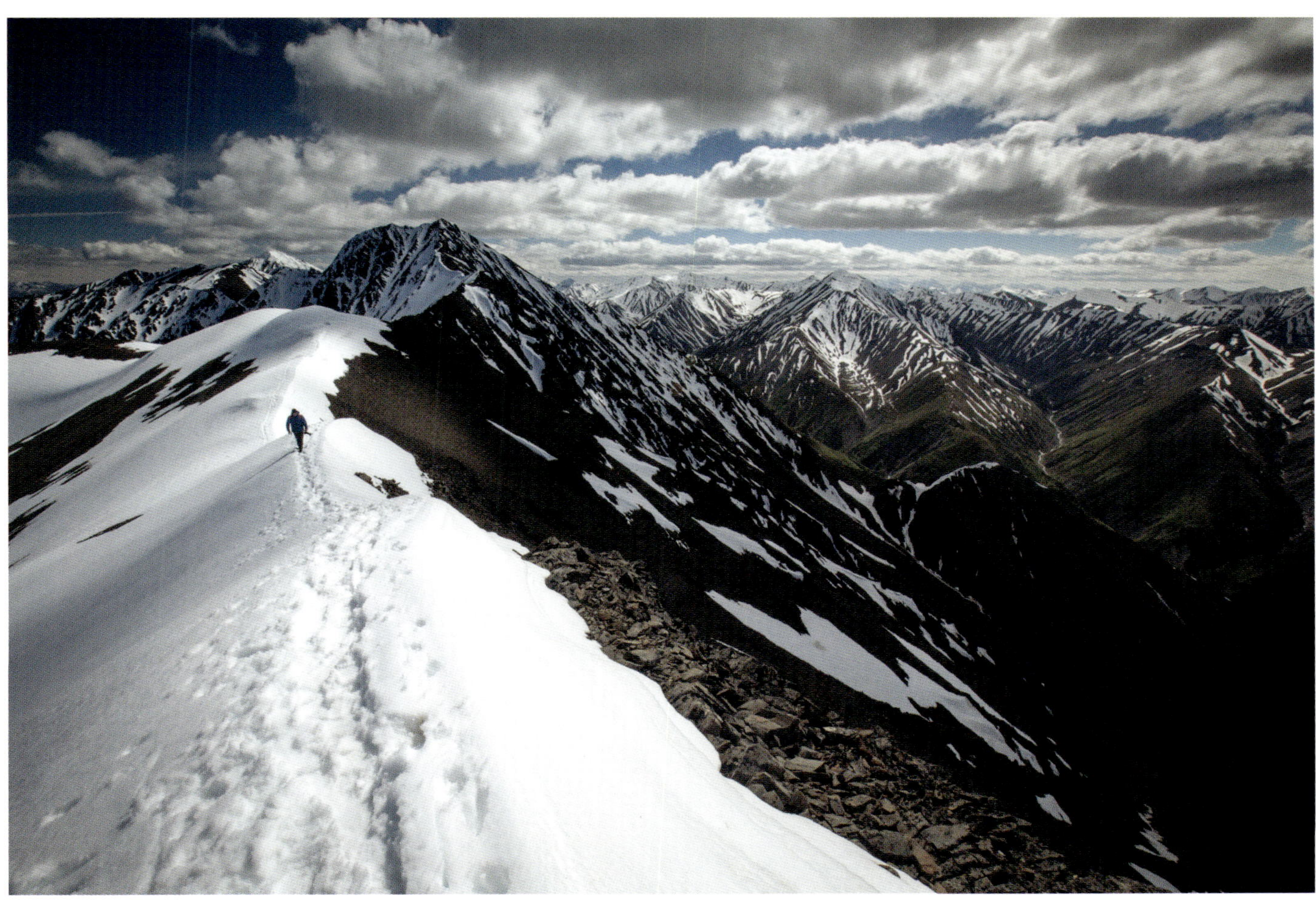

King's Throne, Kluane National Park, Yukon
Photograph by: Paul Zizka

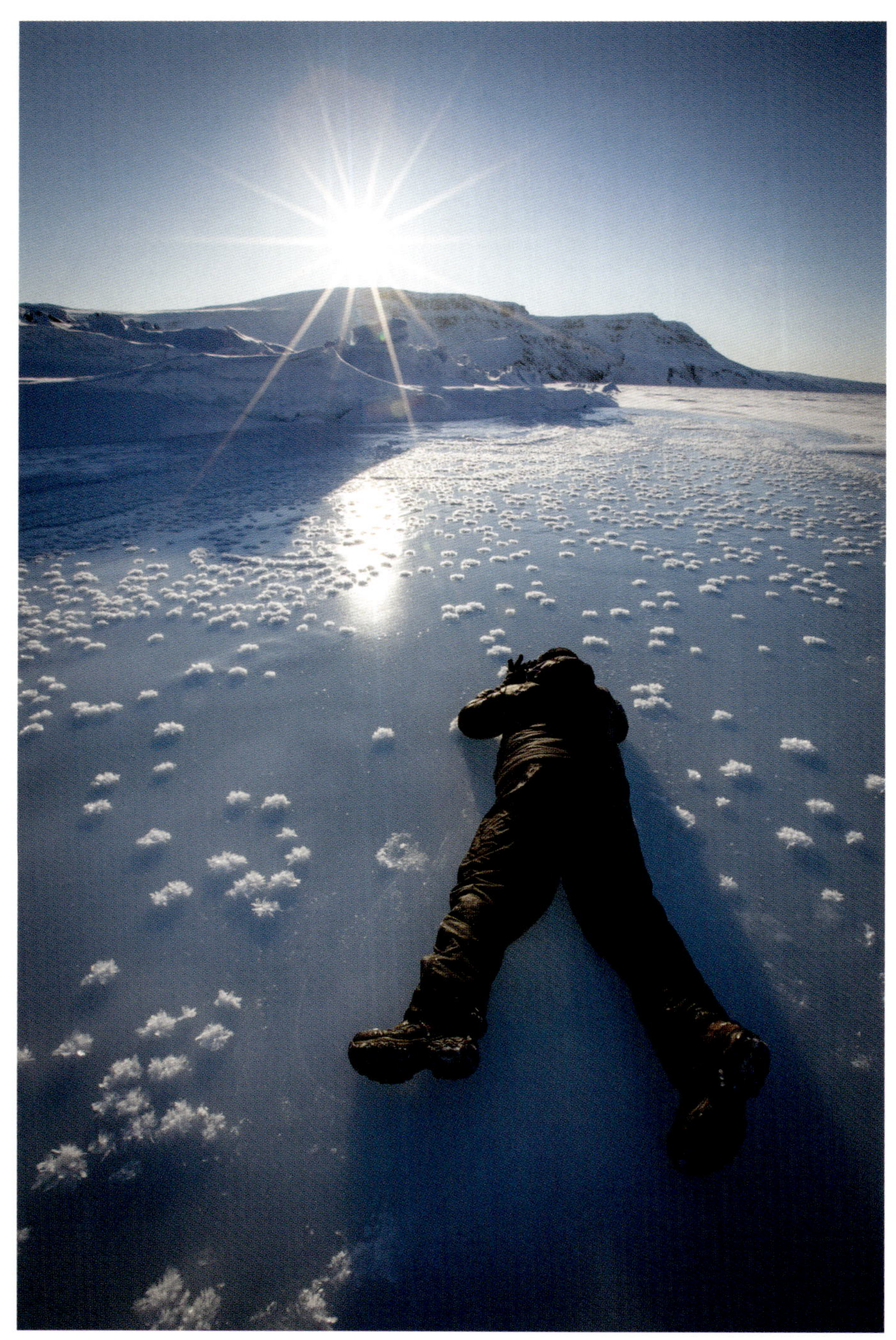

Victor Bay, Nunavut
Photograph by: Paul Zizka

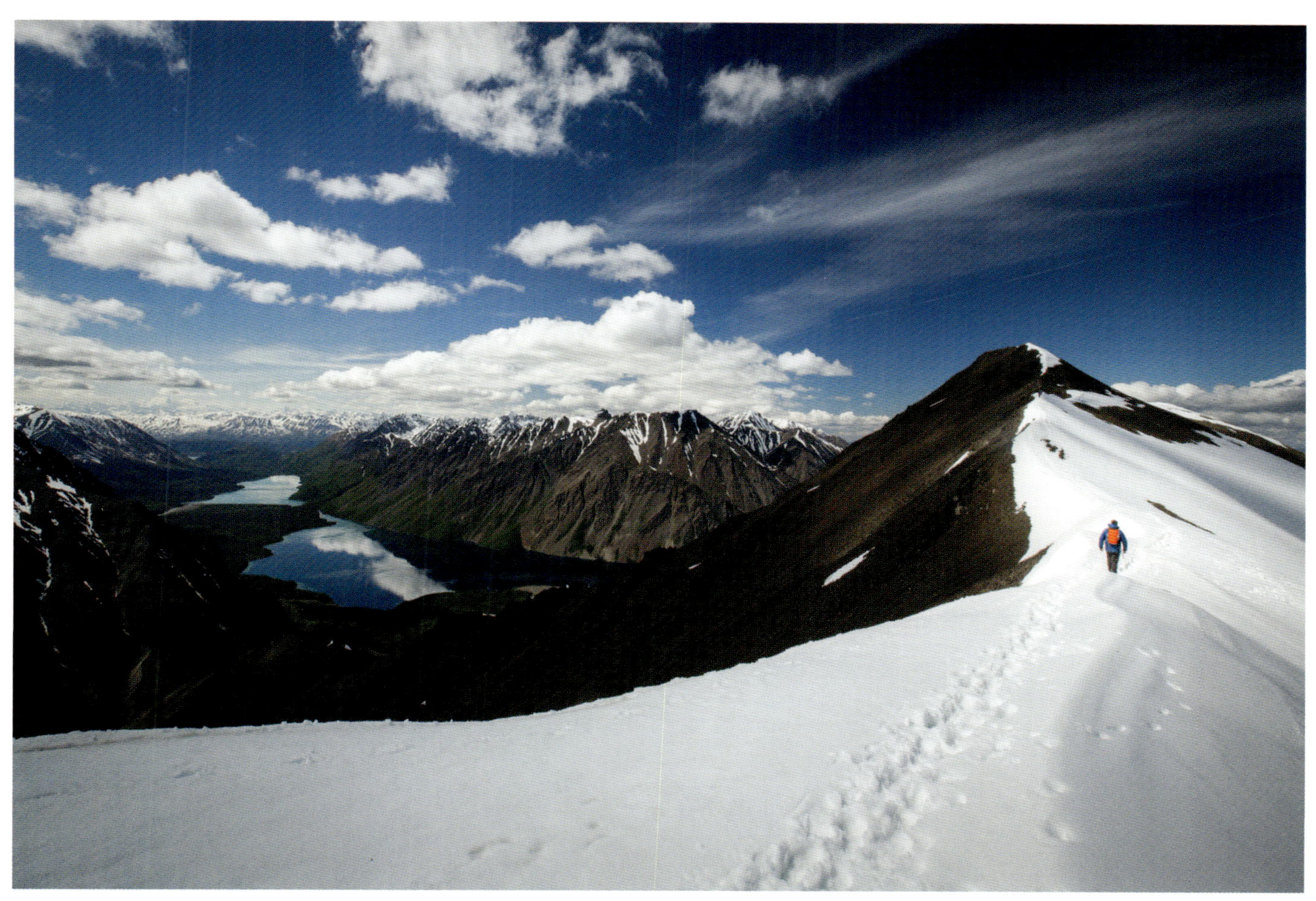

King's Throne, Kluane National Park, Yukon
Photograph by: Paul Zizka

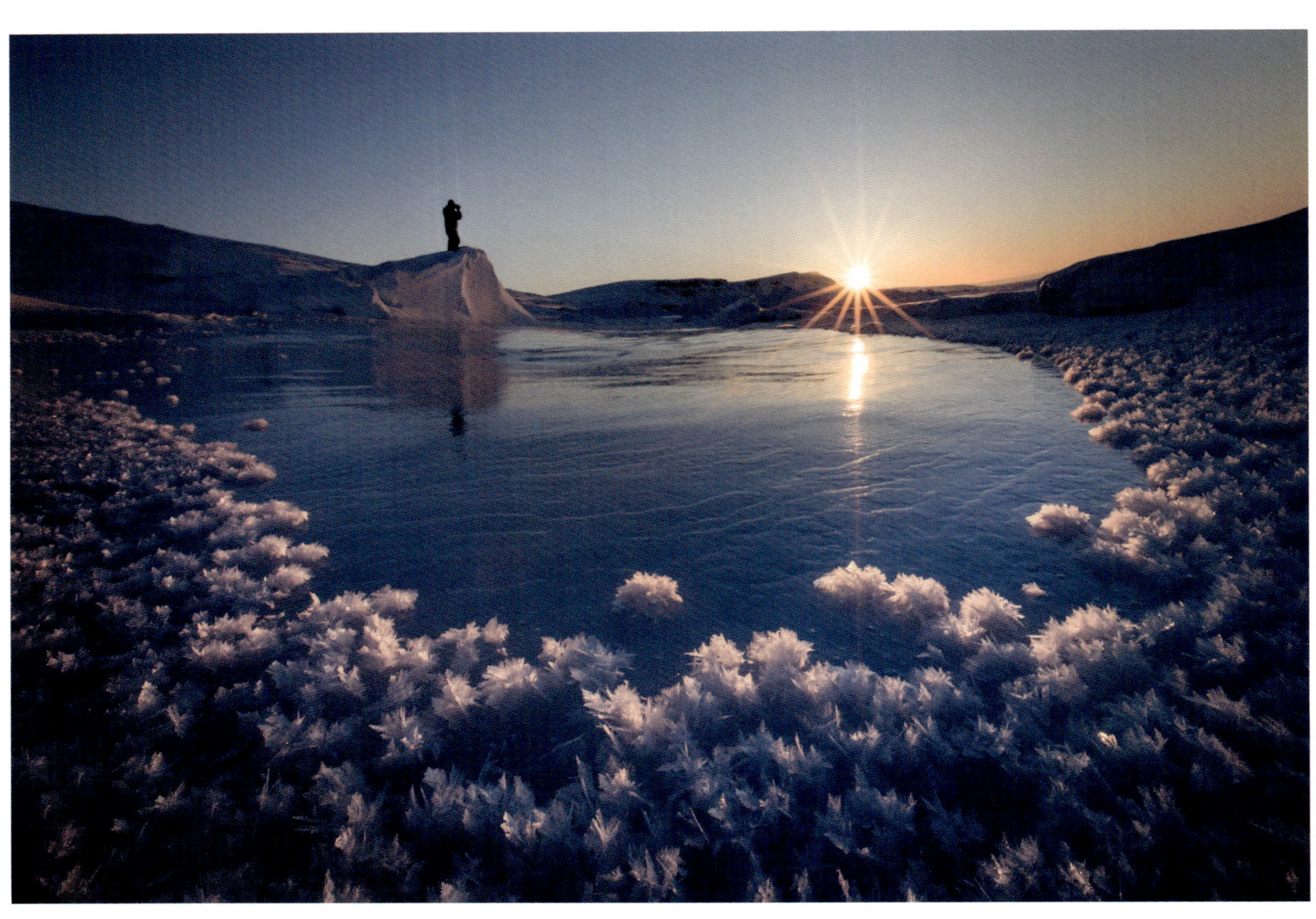

 Victor Bay, Nunavut
Photograph by: Paul Zizka

First Edition

RMB | Rocky Mountain Books Ltd.
rmbooks.com
@rmbooks
facebook.com/rmbooks

Cataloguing data available from Library and Archives Canada
ISBN 9781771602983 (hardcover)

Design by Chyla Cardinal

Printed and bound in China by 1010 Printing International Ltd.

Distributed in Canada by Heritage Group Distribution and in the U.S. by Publishers Group West

For information on purchasing bulk quantities of this book, or to obtain media excerpts or invite the author to speak at an event, please visit rmbooks.com and select the "Contact Us" tab.

RMB | Rocky Mountain Books is dedicated to the environment and committed to reducing the destruction of old-growth forests. Our books are produced with respect for the future and consideration for the past.

We acknowledge the financial support of the Government of Canada through the Canada Book Fund and the Canada Council for the Arts, and of the province of British Columbia through the British Columbia Arts Council and the Book Publishing Tax Credit.

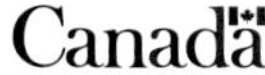

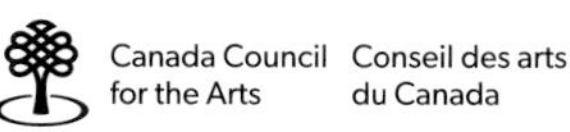

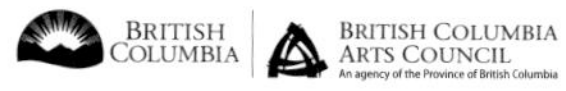